Leibniz on the Trinity and the Incarnation

MARIA ROSA ANTOGNAZZA

TRANSLATED BY GERALD PARKS

Leibniz on the Trinity and the Incarnation

REASON AND REVELATION IN
THE SEVENTEENTH
CENTURY

Yale University Press
New Haven &
London

Published with assistance from the Ernst Cassirer Publications Fund; the
Carnegie Trust; the University of Aberdeen; and the foundation established in
memory of Philip Hamilton McMillan of the Class of 1894, Yale College.

Originally published in Italian as *Trinità e Incarnazione: Il rapporto tra filosofia
e teologia rivelata nel pensiero di Leibniz* (Milan: Vita e Pensiero, 1999).

Set in Sabon by Integrated Book Technology.

Printed in the United States of America by IBT.

Library of Congress Cataloging-in-Publication Data

Antognazza, Maria Rosa.
    Leibniz on the Trinity and the Incarnation : reason and revelation in the
seventeenth century / Maria Rosa Antognazza ; translated by Gerald Parks.
        p. cm.
    Includes bibliographical references and index.
    ISBN 978-0-300-10074-7 (cloth : alk. paper)
1. Leibniz, Gottfried Wilhelm, Freiherr von, 1641–1716.   I. Title.
B2598.A5813 2008
193—dc22   2007011549

A catalogue record for this book is available from the British Library.

To my parents

Contents

Note on the English Edition

This work was first published in 1999 by Vita e Pensiero (Milan) under the title *Trinità e Incarnazione: Il rapporto tra filosofia e teologia rivelata nel pensiero di Leibniz*. It appears here in a revised version translated by Gerald Parks, professor of language and translation at the University of Trieste. Generous grants from the Yale University Cassirer Fund, the Carnegie Trust, and the University of Aberdeen have supported the costs of translation and production. I would also like to express my gratitude to Robert M. Adams for his encouragement and Sarah Broadie for drawing my attention to Gerald Parks as a possible translator. It is very sad that Professor Parks's untimely death deprived him of the satisfaction of seeing his fine work in print. I have reviewed the translation myself, and any mistakes, especially in the translation of Leibniz's original texts, should therefore be ascribed to me.

Acknowledgments

This book owes its origin to Mario Sina, who suggested this topic and guided my research on it from its earliest beginnings as a dissertation written for the attainment of a Research Doctorate in Philosophy at the Università Cattolica of Milan. During the long periods that I spent at the Leibniz-Archiv in Hanover, I came to owe a great deal to the many people whose knowledge and cordiality supported and helped me in this project, in particular, Albert Heinekamp, Herbert Breger, Wilhelm Totok, Heinrich Schepers, the collaborators on the *Akademie Ausgabe* at Hanover and Münster, the staff of the Niedersächsische Landesbibliothek (now Gottfried Wilhelm Leibniz Bibliothek), and the friends and companions who participated in many evening discussions in Hanover.

Two years of research in Wolfenbüttel and Oxford, made possible by a *Vollstipendium* from the Herzog August Bibliothek and by a fellowship for advanced study abroad from the Università Cattolica, allowed me to further the study of Leibniz's sources. Participation in the work of an international research group meeting at the Institute for Advanced Studies of the Hebrew University of Jerusalem was very important in refining some aspects of this research, and for this I am especially grateful to Marcelo Dascal and Massimo Mugnai.

The final part of the work was supported by a Postdoctoral Fellowship from the British Academy and by a Research Fellowship from the University of Aberdeen. I express my gratitude to the colleagues and friends of the Department of Philosophy in Aberdeen and of King's College London, in particular to Eric Matthews and Deborah Rooke. I am very grateful to the Department of Philosophy of the Università Cattolica of Milan for including the Italian version of my work in their publication series. Thank you Dave Luljak for preparing the index for the English edition.

My greatest debt, however, is to my parents, Gianluigi and Giuseppina, and my husband, Howard Hotson. I owe Howard not only for the daily support and encouragement of a husband but also for the irreplaceable help provided by continual, profound discussion with a colleague from whom I have learned much. Our children, John, Sophia, and Francesca, kept me from overindulging in research as only children can do.

Introduction

In the seventeenth and early eighteenth centuries, the dissemination of Socinian theology sparked lively debates across Europe. Rejecting the dogmas of the Trinity and the Incarnation as irrational, the Socinians became the principal target of those who sought to defend these mysteries, central to traditional Christian theology. Although theological in origin, these Trinitarian debates were interwoven with many philosophical problems, such as the relationship between reason and revelation, knowledge and faith; the issue of the limits of human understanding, of the degrees of knowledge, and of the epistemological status of belief; the question of the scope and validity of the principle of noncontradiction; the reflection on the role and meaning of analogy; the inquiry into the concepts of 'nature,' 'substance,' and 'person'; and the theory of relations.

Leibniz participated directly in these disputes, and he can therefore serve as an exceptionally learned and insightful guide for anyone who wishes to observe their philosophical implications. His numerous but hitherto largely neglected writings on the Trinity and the Incarnation constitute, in fact, a paradigmatic case of the reciprocal relationship that existed between theology and philosophy in the seventeenth and eighteenth centuries. Indeed, Leibniz's active participation in theological debates repeatedly compelled him to reflect on problems fundamental to his own philosophy. This book aims to characterize the relationship between philosophy and revealed theology in Leibniz's thought as reflected in his writings on two central mysteries of Christian revelation around which the debate was particularly lively.

The first and most immediately apparent characteristic of Leibniz's writings on revealed theology is that they are very numerous and extremely fragmentary. In itself, this is not unusual: Leibniz scholars have come to realize that the full scope of his thinking on any issue can only be reconstructed by relating his major statements to far larger collections of more fragmentary texts. But the case of revealed theology is nevertheless exceptional. In part this is because a major, mature, and synoptic statement is lacking, around which the minor writings could readily be grouped. While key aspects of Leibniz's natural theology are expounded in the *Theodicy*—one of Leibniz's last and most voluminous polished works—nothing strictly similar pulls together his key reflections on revealed theology. This imbalance alone has doubtless contributed to the preconception in the minds of some students of Leibniz that he is a deist rather than a theist; and in an age of increasing secularization, Leibniz's reputation as a hard rationalist further distracted serious and sustained attention from his scattered reflections on revealed theology. Perhaps in consequence, in the definitive, ongoing edition of his complete works being produced by the Academy of Sciences, which he founded in Berlin, no separate series has been devoted to theological writings, which the diligent student must therefore hunt down and abstract from collections of material on other subjects before even becoming fully aware of their numerical extent, thematic range, technical sophistication, and substantial consistency.

This brings us to a second main characteristic of Leibniz's writings on revealed theology: if their form is remarkably fragmentary, their content is no less remarkably consistent. His theological reflections began early: already in the years between 1663 and 1671 we can recognize the genesis of doctrines that were later to be resumed and developed. It has therefore seemed advisable to devote special attention to his writings during these formative years, prior to his trip to Paris. From these writings it emerges that Leibniz's position regarding the Trinity and the philosophico-theological problems related to it was established early and remained remarkably constant during the ensuing years. Although undergoing occasional corrections and marked by changes in tone and emphasis as his philosophical tools and doctrines matured, these theological doctrines and strategies remained substantially unchanged in their main outlines for the rest of his life. The central challenge in reconstructing Leibniz's approach to the problems of revealed theology is therefore to tease out the substantial continuities and subtle ongoing changes from the disorderly mass of his fragmentary theological writings. The bulk of the body of my book is devoted to this task, beginning with the fragments and plans sketched in his early youth and proceeding to the strands of revealed theology woven into the immense fabric of the *Theodicy* and the *Monadology*. With a view to preparing the reader to follow the various threads of Leibniz's thought in these difficult circumstances, it seems advisable to give a preliminary sketch of the general outlines of his consistently defended and developed position at the outset, not so much as a demonstration but rather as a heuristic aid in following the more detailed and documented discussions that follow.

Reason and Revelation

The first of these threads is the doctrine regarding the relation between reason and revelation, within which can be situated the problems posed by the special epistemological status of those revealed truths that are grouped together under the category of mystery, and of which the Trinity and the Incarnation are the examples par excellence within the Christian tradition. Leibniz's position on this is grounded in his acceptance of the traditional distinction between what is against reason and what is above reason. A truth can never be against reason, that is, it can never imply a contradiction. Indeed, for Leibniz the principle of noncontradiction, as the ultimate criterion for distinguishing truth from falsehood, lies at the foundation of the very possibility of reaching the truth. If it were to fail in the supernatural sphere— if, that is, it had no absolute validity—it would be meaningless to speak of truth and falsehood. The truths revealed in the mysteries, precisely because they are truths, can therefore never be contrary to reason. The mysteries, in other words, must always comply with the principle of noncontradiction. On the other hand, they can be superior to reason, where by reason one means the finite reason of human beings and not reason in an absolute sense: while they are incomprehensible to humankind, they are perfectly understood by the infinite reason of God.

At this point, however, the question arises: How can human reason judge the contradictoriness or noncontradictoriness of what is by definition superior to its capacity of comprehension? If human reason cannot make this judgment, does this not imply that there is no longer even the possibility of distinguishing between "above reason" and "against reason"? Should not one then concede victory to those who, with the true or presumed intention of safeguarding revelation and faith in it, maintain the absolute separation and incommensurability between faith and reason, revelation and rational knowledge, so that the two spheres are regulated by completely different laws? Or might not the Socinians be right in their views? Affirming as Leibniz did the conformity between faith and reason, they proposed to eliminate as contradictory everything that human reason cannot manage to comprehend, thus denying that there is in fact a difference between "against reason" and "above reason." In short, how is it possible to guarantee the noncontradictoriness of the mysteries and at the same time preserve their status as suprarational truths?

Leibniz solves the difficulty by pointing out, first of all, that it is one thing to judge the noncontradictoriness of a given proposition, and quite another to demonstrate the truth of the proposition. The fact that the mysteries are beyond our capacity of comprehension makes it impossible for human reason to arrive at a demonstration of the truth of the mysteries, but not impossible to judge whether the revealed propositions are self-contradictory or not. The judgment on their noncontradictoriness is, however, subject to another limitation. There are some ambiguities in Leibniz's position, due more to terminological fluctuations than to any change in doctrine; but with the passage of time it becomes increasingly clear that, in his view, this judgment is not a positive demonstration of the possibility (that is, the noncontradictoriness) of the mysteries. Indeed, a positive demonstration of their possibility would lead to the very dissolution of the mysteries.

According to the description Leibniz proposes in the *Meditationes de Cognitione, Veritate et Ideis* (Meditations on Cognition, Truth, and Ideas) (1684), there are two ways of knowing the possibility of things: a priori and a posteriori. The manner of knowing is a priori when the notion is reduced to its elements, that is, into other notions whose possibility is known. If this analysis is conducted down to the last terms and no contradiction appears, the notion's possibility is demonstrated without any doubt. The manner of knowing is a posteriori when it is based on the experience that the thing actually exists, because what exists or has actually existed is also certainly possible.[1] Now, the application to the mysteries of an a priori demonstration having the requirements described above would imply the complete elimination of the suprarational sphere, in that it would coincide with adequate knowledge. On the other hand, Leibniz is the first to admit that there is no example in nature that corresponds adequately to what is indicated by the mysteries and can therefore demonstrate their possibility a posteriori. The possibility of the mysteries must therefore be assured in some other way, which turns out to be twofold. On the one side, the possibility of the mysteries is maintained by shifting from a positive argument to a negative argument, that is, from the demonstration of their possibility to the demonstration that their impossibility has not yet been proved. On the other side, the argument proceeds by recourse to reasoning by analogy.

The first part of this twofold strategy involves applying to the revealed truths the notion (derived from jurisprudence, which Leibniz studied as a young man) of a 'presumption of truth' combined with an argumentative procedure well established within the *ars disputandi* (art of debate): the 'strategy of defense.' For a proposition whose truth has not yet been demonstrated, or cannot be demonstrated, one can invoke a presumption of truth, which is valid until a proof of its falsity is given. This is precisely what Leibniz invokes in favor of the mysteries transmitted through the centuries of church tradition. It is therefore the acceptance of the traditional doctrine of what Leibniz calls "the universal church" that provides the starting point. By making appeal to the presumption of truth, *it is admitted from the start* that the mysteries are true (and hence noncontradictory), although superior to our capacities of comprehension. The presumption of truth, however, is valid, as has been said, only until a proof to the contrary has not been given. If the deniers of the mysteries (in this case, the Antitrinitarians) were able to demonstrate that the mysteries presumed to be true in reality imply a contradiction, this demonstration would amount to an incontrovertible proof of their falsity.

At this pont the 'strategy of defense' comes into play. The presumption of truth has the power to shift the *onus probandi* (burden of proof) from the one who defends to the one who attacks a given thesis.[2] Therefore, it is the Antitrinitarians that have to demonstrate positively that the mystery of the Trinity implies a contradiction. It is enough for the defenders to show that such contradictoriness or impossibility has not yet been proved, limiting themselves to rejecting the adversary's arguments, without having to supply positive proof of the possibility or noncontradictoriness of the thesis being defended. So long as they are able to show the lack of conclusiveness of their adversary's arguments, the presumption of truth remains intact; in the specific case of the dogma of the Trinity, it is the presumption of noncontradictoriness of this mystery that remains valid: "Anything is presumed to be possible, until the contrary is proved."[3] We are therefore dealing not with a demonstration of the mystery's possibility but with a demonstration that its impossibility has not been proved and that consequently the mystery is legitimately presumed to be possible (noncontradictory). Having established the general strategy, at this point it is a question of winning the individual battles, by rebutting any accusations of contradiction produced by the enemies of the mysteries. Leibniz does not draw back from the fray: with the Socinians he engages in a refined logical duel aimed at demonstrating the fallaciousness of his enemy's arguments. It is a close confrontation, which starts already in his youth and continues throughout the years that follow. A good deal of the textual analysis and philosophical narration in the body of this book will retrace the course of this debate.

The second, more positive strategy chosen by Leibniz to uphold the possibility of the mysteries is reasoning by analogy. This is a classical procedure in the Christian tradition, of which Augustine's teaching is the most outstanding example so far as the mystery of the Trinity in particular is concerned. Once again its aim is not a positive demonstration of the possibility but something more subtle: namely, the discovery of "a trace," "an image," "a shadow" in the natural sphere, of what is affirmed about the supernatural sphere.[4] Although it is not possible to produce adequate examples of the existence in nature of what is maintained in revelation, one can nevertheless show that relations similar to the one indicated by the mystery in question actually exist in the natural sphere—in the case of the Trinity, Leibniz reproposes the traditional analogy with the mind and in particular with the reflection of the mind on itself; in the case of Incarnation, he points to the (also traditional) analogy with the union in humankind of soul (mind) and body. This actual existence is an indication of the possibility that there may be something similar also in the sphere of the divine. When we recall the two ways of proving the possibility of something that Leibniz proposes in the *Meditationes de Cognitione, Veritate et Ideis,* this procedure can be seen as a 'softer' form of the proof a posteriori—softer because conducted by analogy.

Knowledge and Faith

Although it lacks stringent conclusiveness, analogy with natural examples makes it possible to reach one of the essential conditions of faith in revealed propositions: namely, a certain degree of knowledge, however partial and confused, of their meaning. Leibniz is convinced that faith is a form of knowing endowed with cognitive value. The object of faith is not words but the meaning of these words ("faith is of the meaning, not of the words").[5] To believe is "to hold as true [verum putare],"[6] that is, to hold that the propositions expressing the mysteries correspond to the truth. Now, in order to be able to speak of truth, one must, to some extent, know what the words mean. Here, however, the problem posed by the special epistemological status of the revealed truths arises again. How is it possible to know their meaning if the propositions that express the mysteries are by definition beyond the capacity of human reason to comprehend? The solution proposed by Leibniz retraces the basic distinction of the degrees of knowledge laid out in the *Meditationes de Cognitione, Veritate et Ideis:* although one cannot arrive at an adequate comprehension of the mysteries, in order for these to be justifiably placed in the cognitive sphere it is sufficient to have a confused knowledge of their meaning. Knowledge, in other words, is not limited to what is clear and distinct: it also embraces notions of which we have only a confused understanding. This is the way to resolve another difficulty related to the use of the concepts of 'nature,' 'substance,' and 'person': Is human reason able to possess these concepts, and consequently is the use that is made of them to explain the mystery of the Trinity justified? Leibniz readily acknowledges that we do not have a clear and distinct knowledge of the concepts of 'nature,' 'substance,' and 'person' when they are used with reference to the divine sphere. Yet our use of them, even when it is extended to the explanation of the mystery of the Trinity, is nevertheless justified precisely because knowledge is not limited to what is clear and distinct. However imperfect and inadequate the resulting explanations may be, one should not forgo them.

From such an analysis emerge the three broad categories under which it is possible to gather "motives of credibility" for presentation before the tribunal of reason.[7] Together these "motives of credibility" make it possible for reason to leave room for a faith that is not fideism and a belief that is very different from credulity. If the starting point of faith is the acceptance of the teachings of the revelation contained in the scriptures and handed down by church tradition, the first basic task of reason is to verify, with the tools of philology, textual criticism and history, the genuineness and authenticity of the scriptures and the faithfulness of the tradition. This is a preliminary task, which does not deal directly with the content of revelation. Reason, however, also has a role to play regarding the content of revealed propositions. The second task entrusted to reason is, in fact, the explanation of the mysteries "as far as is necessary to believe them."[8] This produces a knowledge, albeit a confused knowledge, of the meaning of the revealed propositions, which is necessary for these not to be reduced to a mere *flatus vocis* (breath of the voice) that would preclude the very possibility of faith in them. This confused knowledge must, however, be accompanied by an indispensable condition: the absence of a proven contradiction in what one believes. This is the third basic task of reason, which is called upon to guarantee the noncontradictoriness of the mysteries through the 'strategy of defense.'

Theology and Metaphysics

Throughout his career, therefore, Leibniz undertook to reserve room for the mysteries, constantly defended the Trinity in general, and repeatedly stated that the Trinitarian conception of God is the true one. It is clear that in working out a Trinitarian theology and a Christology of his own, which can be reconstructed on the basis of a series of fragmentary writings and of the *Examen Religionis Christianae (Systema Theologicum)* (Examination of the Christian Religion [Theological System]) (1686), he was working within the quite variegated orthodoxy of the three main Christian confessions: Lutheranism (to which he officially belonged), the Reformed Church, and the Roman Catholic Church.

At this point another basic question demands an answer: namely, the question of the relationship between this theological project and Leibniz's basic metaphysical and epistemological views. There are three general possibilities. In the first place, it is possible that these two aspects of Leibniz's thought contradict one another. In this case one would probably be inclined to think that Leibniz's professions of support for the doctrine of the Trinity are insincere attempts to win the favor of his patrons. In the second place, there is the possibility that his theological doctrines and his metaphysical doctrines are entirely independent of one another. In this case it would still be possible for there to be a serious commitment on Leibniz's part to Trinitarian theology, but there would not be much point for the historians of philosophy to deal with the matter. Finally, there is the possibility that Leibniz's views on the Trinitarian nature of God and the metaphysical structure of the universe are neither contradictory nor unconnected but, rather, coexist comfortably in Leibniz's thought, perhaps even reinforcing one another.

Perhaps the most striking evidence in support of the third of these possibilities are the traces in Leibniz's texts of the classic doctrine of the *analogia Trinitatis* (analogy of the Trinity). According to this ancient idea, the Trinitarian nature of the Creator is reflected in that of his creatures, who thus manifest a triadic order similar to that of the three persons of the Trinity. Traces of this notion are to be found scattered throughout Leibniz's writings: even some main aspects of his metaphysics are occasionally presented in the terms of the analogia Trinitatis. Two particularly important examples are found in the *Examen Religionis Christianae* and the *Theodicy,* where the distinction between the essence and existence of things (the basis for Leibniz's solution to the problem of evil) and the traditional doctrine that sees *posse, scire,* and *velle* (power, knowledge, and will) in the Trinity are reinterpreted in terms of one another.[9] A clear application of the analogia Trinitatis also powerfully reappears at the climax of Leibniz's metaphysics, in the *Monadology.*[10]

Somewhat more subtle but perhaps even more profound is the connection of Trinitarian theology with Leibniz's conception of universal harmony. It does not appear that Leibniz ever explicitly connected universal harmony

with the Trinitarian nature of God, as does an author he read with enthusiasm and profit in his youth, Johann Heinrich Bisterfeld.[11] Yet, on several
occasions he identifies God with harmony: "God, or the Mind of the Universe," he writes, "is nothing but the harmony of things,"[12] "the greatest
Harmony of things,"[13] "Universal Harmony."[14] A more complete and explicit clarification of the conception of God used in this equation and its precise relation with the idea of universal harmony is lacking in these passages;
but a comparison between some of the typical definitions Leibniz gives of
harmony and the terminology he uses to express the Trinitarian nature of
God helps to illuminate these identifications of God with the *harmonia rerum* (harmony of things).

Consider first Leibniz's definitions of universal harmony. In the *Elementa
Juris Naturalis* (Elements of Natural Law) (1670–1671), Leibniz writes:
"The harmony is greater when the diversity is greater, and yet it is reduced
to identity."[15] The greatest harmony is therefore to be found where the greatest diversity is reduced to identity. Leibniz develops this idea further in *De
Conatu et Motu, Sensu et Cogitatione* (On Conatus and Motion, Sense and
Cogitation) (1671), defining harmony as *unitas plurimorum* (the unity of
many things) or *diversitas identitate compensata* (diversity compensated by
identity).[16] A letter to Arnauld of November 1671 presents the same formulation,[17] which recurs another time in the *Confessio Philosophi* (The Philosopher's Confession) (1672–1673), where harmony is defined as "similarity
in variety, or diversity compensated by identity."[18] On the basis of such passages as these, it has therefore been maintained that "in his thoughts of 1671,
harmonia means unity of the manifold"[19] and that the many definitions of
harmony offered by Leibniz can be condensed into a single formula: *varietas
identitate compensata* (variety compensated by identity).[20]

Now, both of these formulations can be closely related to Leibniz's conception of the Trinity. In the case of harmony as "unity of the manifold," the
language is very similar. In such writings as *De Scriptura, Ecclesia, Trinitate*
(On the Scripture, Church, Trinity) (1680–1684) and *Sceleton Demonstrationis* (Outline of a Demonstration) (1695), the Trinitarian mystery is characterized precisely as "plurality in unity."[21] And in the case of the second
formulation, it is not difficult to maintain that, if harmony is defined as *diversitas identitate compensata* (diversity compensated by identity), the most
perfect example of harmony is given precisely by the traditional doctrine of
a Trinity of distinct persons in one single essence. In the Trinity, the unity in
plurality is so perfect and the diversity of the persons, while remaining such,
is so perfectly compensated for by the identity of the single, unique essence
that the entity in question surpasses the limits of human comprehension and

is therefore regarded not as a doctrine of philosophy but as a mystery of theology. In other words, to say that the Trinity is the most perfect conceivable realization of this idea of harmony is, in fact, not to say enough: for it is an even more perfect compensation of diversity by identity than the human mind can conceive, and precisely for this reason it qualifies as a mystery.

If one begins from the other side of the equation—with the formulations traditionally employed to express the doctrine of the Trinity—one reaches results that are equally closely connected with Leibniz's conception of harmony. Underlying the philosophical term *immeatio* ("immeation")—a characteristic term of Johann Heinrich Bisterfeld's metaphysics, which Bisterfeld uses to express an idea of universal harmony very close to that of Leibniz's—there is the theological term *emperichōrēsis* or *perichōrēsis,* used by patristic theology to indicate the relation between the persons of the Trinity. In his last years, Leibniz also uses this very term to express his conception of universal harmony. In the *Tractatio de Deo et Homine* (Treatise on God and Man) (composed around 1702), he explains that the harmony and *perichōrēsis* of all things proceed from God.[22] In a letter to Des Bosses of November 1710, this idea is further developed.[23] The "perichōrēsis rerum" of which Leibniz writes in 1710 seems to correspond to his explanation of 1702 regarding "the admirable harmony and *perichōrēsis* of all things . . . which causes all things to be most appropriately connected."[24] For the finite intellect of human beings it is impossible to arrive at an adequate comprehension of even a minimal part of nature, precisely because, in the infinite number of things existing in nature, each one is related to every other. Inversely, this same "perichōrēsis rerum" is also the reason why an adequate comprehension of even a minimal part of nature would correspond to a perfect comprehension of the whole universe, something that only the infinite divine intellect can achieve. It is significant that Leibniz, in seeking to express the reason that prevents the finite mind of human beings from grasping the 'mystery' of the universe in a clear and distinct conception, should choose to use, in place of the normal philosophical term harmonia, the much more unusual term *perichōrēsis.* In section 23 of the "Preliminary Discourse" of the *Theodicy,* universal harmony even takes on explicitly the characteristics of a 'mystery,' in analogy precisely with the mystery of the Trinity.[25]

One last Trinitarian formulation comes (at least originally) from Bisterfeld. Leibniz himself recognizes a description of the Trinity in Bisterfeld's description of an "entity, by which an entity is related to an entity [entitas, quâ entitas est ad entitatem]."[26] What does this formula mean? An "entity, by which an entity is related to an entity" is evidently an essentially relational entity, that is, an entity of which the property of being-in-relation, being *ad aliud* (related to another), is an essential ontological feature. Later on Leibniz reformulates this idea from the point of view of relations, describing the relations between the Father, Son, and Holy Spirit as "essential" or "substantial relations"; each person of the Trinity involves an essential relation to the other persons so that one cannot exist without the others.[27] In other words, the divine persons are constituted "through relations [per relationes]," that is, their distinctiveness is constituted by the ways in which they relate to each other.[28]

Since for the young Leibniz "harmonia" is a structure of relations,[29] the Trinity—a being constituted "through relations"[30]—seems once again to be a perfect realization of Leibniz's idea of harmony. Just as an individual substance that enters into the constitution of a given possible world could not exist without the other individual substances of that given world on account of the universal harmony by which everything is related to everything else, so in the Trinity one person could not exist without the others on account of its essential relation to the other persons. Just as the actually existing world is a concrete, complex system, the strong unity of which is guaranteed by the fact that no component could be removed from it, so the Trinity seems to be conceived by Leibniz as a concrete, complex system of which the three persons are constituents (albeit not "parts"). On the other hand, while taking into account all the caution necessary to avoid Tritheism, as well as the desire not to be seen as opposing scholastic theses, and a certain amount of experimentation with alternative formulations, Leibniz basically seems to hold that the best way to preserve the robust subsistence required by orthodoxy for both the one Godhead and the three divine persons is to speak of three relative substances constituting—"ut sic dicam [so to speak]"—one absolute substance.

In short, Leibniz's metaphysics of the Trinity tries to deal (like any orthodox Trinitarian theology) with the Scylla and Charybdis of Tritheism and modalism. His conception is consistent with his nominalism or conceptualism about essences and relations insofar as it ultimately denies that the persons of the Trinity are relations and prefers to conceive of them as "relative substances." This conception, however, leaves a number of questions open. First of all, there is the concept of "relative substance," that is, of a substance that is essentially related to other substances and therefore could not exist separated from these other substances. It seems that this is the condition of each individual substance of a given possible world. Could this substance be properly regarded as *ens per se subsistens*? Or, in other words, can an entity that cannot exist separated from other entities be properly regarded as a substance? Rather than being a question unique to Trinitarian theology, however, this is a question for Leibniz's metaphysics as such. The same applies, secondly, to the issue of "essential relations," that is, of relations founded in essential properties that are constitutive of the correlated subjects. Given Leibniz's superessentialism and his doctrine of the complete concept, one might well wonder whether his metaphysics has the resources sufficient to ground the distinction between essential and nonessential properties. This leaves his Trinitarian theology open to the objection voiced by the Socinian Christoph Stegmann that then there would be as many persons in God as there are relations; yet once again this is not a problem peculiar to Leibniz's theology but is shared by his philosophical system as regards his defense of contingency. Finally, Leibniz's Trinitarian theology is clearly relevant to the issue (much debated in the context of Leibniz's treatment of corporeal substances) of whether a plurality of substances can constitute a single substance.[31] Although at first it might seem that in his conception of the Trinity Leibniz indulges in a good deal of special pleading, a more attentive consideration reveals that his metaphysics of the Trinity is closely molded on his metaphysics more generally (of course *mutando mutandis*, due to the fact that, as Leibniz acknowledges, we are dealing with a mystery). As a consequence, some of the puzzling points of his conception of the Trinity are in a certain sense exacerbations of problems common to his metaphysical system in general.

At any rate, Leibniz's efforts to defend the Trinity from the logical point of view and his wider justification of the epistemological status of revealed propositions as being above but not contrary to reason seem to be complemented by a tacit assumption of the coherence of a Trinitarian conception of God with his conception of the metaphysical structure of the universe. Without entering into speculations regarding the personal faith and piety of Leibniz, and taking into account the strong pragmatism colouring his theological activities, we find that two conclusions emerge from a survey of Leibniz's writings on the theological mysteries. On the one hand, he was clearly convinced that the doctrine of the Trinity could be cleared of the charge of contradiction, and he repeatedly maintained that, owing to the long ecclesiastical tradition, it should be accepted as a revealed truth. On the other hand, more subtly but perhaps still more significantly, he endeavored to give an explanation of this mystery consistent with the main tenets of his philosophy and an account of his philosophy consistent with this mystery. Observed from an overall standpoint, Leibniz's discussion of the problems posed by revealed truths shows a profound, and in many respects surprising, openness to the sense of mystery, an openness not confined to the supernatural sphere but one that ultimately engulfs the natural world as well. The finitude of the human intellect places a structural limit on its capacity for comprehension. As Leibniz writes on 8 August 1701 in the *Annotatiunculae Subitaneae ad Tolandi Librum De Christianismo Mysteriis Carente* (Hasty Notes on Toland's Book *Christianity Not Mysterious*), it is for this reason that not only the mysteries of faith are ultimately above (human) reason: "To the created intellect the comprehension itself of individual substances is impossible because they involve the infinite. Whence it comes that a perfect explanation of the things of the universe cannot be given [Unde fit ut rerum universi perfecta ratio reddi non possit]."[32] The limited capacities of the finite human intellect entail that not only the mysteries of faith but also all individual substances ultimately surpass human comprehension.

PART I

Early Writings (1663–1671)

Leibniz's Program:
The Plan of Catholic Demonstrations

When he was just twenty-two years old, Leibniz drew up a "plan of catholic demonstrations" (*Demonstrationum Catholicarum Conspectus*) so wide ranging that it included not only the whole of theology but also, as prolegomena, the first principles of metaphysics, logic, mathematics, physics, and politics.[1] This vast project was never completed by the young Leibniz; and even in his later years he did not succeed in composing a systematic work along these lines, including all the *Prolegomena* and the chapters already minutely outlined in the *Conspectus*. Yet the *Conspectus* nevertheless represents a leitmotif in Leibniz's life, a project to which he remained faithful.[2] Although not gathered together into a single work, the individual chapters of the *Conspectus* do gradually take shape, sometimes merely as brief, incomplete texts, at other times assuming a scale and organization sufficient to justify the title (which is not Leibniz's) of *Systema Theologicum* (Theological System).[3] If read in the light of this plan, many of Leibniz's texts, although generally fragmentary and incomplete, can be seen to compose a surprisingly coherent whole.

The idea of organizing many of Leibniz's interests and works around a theological plan such as the one indicated by the *Conspectus* would certainly seem risky if it were not Leibniz himself who suggested the rereading of his youthful researches and studies from this perspective in a letter in the autumn of 1679 to Duke Johann Friedrich of Hanover.[4] This letter provides perhaps the best and most authoritative introduction both to the text of the *Conspectus* as a whole and to the part that deals specifically with the mysteries of the Trinity and the Incarnation. It therefore demands attention at the outset. Leibniz asked for the duke's help in obtaining the approval of Rome concerning some of his positions on religious matters.[5] In dispute were some points of the Council of Trent that Leibniz had already discussed with his patron Baron Johann Christian von Boineburg.[6] The baron's death in December 1672 made it impossible to obtain the hoped-for approval by way of his protector's support. He therefore now turned to the duke,[7] expounding the plan of the catholic proofs he intended to bring to completion once he had received the declarations from Rome:

> Now supposing these declarations of Rome were obtained, I would have formed the plan of a work of the greatest importance that M. de B[oineburg] greatly approved of: the title of which is: *Catholic Demonstrations*. It should contain three sections: The *first section* is to demonstrate the existence of God, the immortality of the soul, and all natural theology; since in effect I have attained surprising demonstrations.[8] The second section should be about the Christian religion, or revealed Theology; in it I would like to demonstrate the possibility of our mysteries of the faith and solve all the difficulties raised by those who claim to show there are absurdities and contradictions in the Trinity, in the Incarnation, in the Eucharist, and in the resurrection of bodies. For the proofs of the Christian religion are only moral, because it is not possible to give others in matters of fact; now all the proofs that carry only a moral certitude can be overturned by stronger contrary proofs, and therefore one must also answer the objections to satisfy oneself entirely, since a single proven impossibility in our mysteries would capsize the whole boat.[9]

With a way of reasoning that, in many respects, anticipates that of section 5 of the "Preliminary Discourse" of the *Theodicy*,[10] Leibniz here regards the mysteries as having an epistemological status similar to that of truths of fact. The common feature that justifies this juxtaposition seems to be the kind of certainty that can be reached by humankind both as regards the mysteries and as regards truths of fact.[11] As in the case of truths of fact the maximum degree of certainty obtainable is moral certainty, based on the choice of the wise, so too in the case of the mysteries the maximum degree of certainty obtainable is not absolute certainty based upon demonstration but moral certainty that rests on the words of the wise (in this case, on revelation). With this extension of the status of truths of fact to the mysteries, Leibniz seems to want to underline the limits of the human intellect. In the case of the mysteries little emphasis is placed on that aspect of truths of fact whereby they are called upon to guarantee the difference between necessity and contingency (and hence human and divine freedom); instead, another aspect clearly appears: that whereby truths of fact mark the limits of human comprehension. As it is only the limitations of our intellect that prevent us from seeing, for every fact, the reason why it is thus and not otherwise, so too it is only the obscurity of the human mind (*caligo mentis humanae*) that prevents us from seeing how God can be both One and Three.[12]

Having concluded the presentation of the plan of the work with a brief exposition of the last part, dedicated to the church,[13] Leibniz underlines the need to add to the *Demonstrationes Catholicae* a series of *Prolegomena*,[14] understood as "foundations of those great demonstrations . . . that help to understand the main work."[15] Being therefore subservient, in the last instance, to Leibniz's great theological project, these *Prolegomena* are nothing less than the "proven elements of true philosophy," including in particular a new part of logic, necessary "to judge of proofs in matters of fact and morals, where there are ordinarily good reasons on one side and on the other, and it is a question of knowing which side to give more weight to"—in other words, a logic that is fit for knowing "the degrees of probability."[16] In recent years attention has been drawn to the importance of this aspect of Leibniz's thought, still little known in many respects.[17] By the explicit declaration of the most authoritative of all witnesses, Leibniz himself, one of the main reasons for the development of this new logic is the special status of revealed truths,[18] truths that—as is the case with what is "about facts and morals"— are not confined to the narrow sphere of demonstration. However, Leibniz does not stop here: in the final culmination of his studies and interests in the great theological plan, he calls upon metaphysics,[19] physics,[20] morals,[21] politics,[22] mathematics,[23] and, last but not least, the long-cherished project of a "universal characteristic."[24]

At this point we may suspect whether Leibniz is being sincere in this letter. Is he not perhaps exaggerating, in order to gain the duke's favor? If, on the one hand, it seems prudent to take Leibniz's clear-cut statements with a grain of salt, recognizing his need to convince his powerful interlocutor, on the other it seems equally unjustified to doubt Leibniz's genuine, strong involvement aimed at the solution of the theological problems indicated in the *Conspectus*. That Leibniz was serious about theology (and, as this book will try to show, the theology of the Trinity in particular) is immediately obvious to anyone who reads Leibniz's work without the distorting lens of modern priorities. A warning against hasty conclusions tending to underestimate the presence of an authentic theological-religious interest in Leibniz[25] comes from the philosopher himself. In a curious letter probably dating from the autumn of 1679, Leibniz speaks of a person he met in Paris; in actuality, this person, who studied and successfully practiced the human, historical, and legal sciences, and went to Paris to improve his knowledge of mathematics, is Leibniz himself. Concluding his self-description, Leibniz writes: "I discovered him one day reading some books of controversies, and I expressed my astonishment, having been led to believe he was a professional mathematician because he had done practically nothing else in Paris. It was then that he told me a big mistake had been made, that he had quite other views, and that his main meditations concerned Theology. He said that he had applied himself to mathematics as if it were Scholastic philosophy, that is, only for the perfection of his spirit and to learn the art of invention and demonstration."[26]

The *Demonstrationum Catholicarum Conspectus,* drawn up at the beginning of Leibniz's early period, thus traces the main lines of a task that Leibniz also considered of primary importance in the ensuing years. His fidelity to this program emerges in more detail through a comparison of that part of the *Conspectus* directly related to the subject of my book[27] with some of Leibniz's later writings, in which the problems that are merely stated in the plan are dealt with. It is therefore worthwhile to concentrate our attention on the third part of Leibniz's plan, entitled "Demonstration of the Possibility of the Mysteries of the Christian Faith."[28]

Next to the title, Leibniz notes: "Regarding the one Philosophical and Theological Truth against the Averroists, Hofmann and Slevogt."[29] The references are, respectively, to Daniel Hofmann and Paul Slevogt,[30] lumped together with the Averroists as supporters of the doctrine of double truth. Starting in 1598, a violent polemic saw Hofmann opposed to some professors in the philosophy faculty at the University of Helmstedt.[31] The origin of the controversy was the work in 101 theses prepared by Hofmann for the doctoral degree of Casparus Pfafradius, in which he highlights the dangers implicit in the use of philosophy in theology.[32] Hofmann, appealing to the authority of Luther, seems to take sides in favor of the doctrine of double truth.[33] The professors of the philosophy faculty rose up against Hofmann's theses, defending the oneness of truth and the usefulness of philosophy in theology. The controversy culminated in 1600 with the publication in Marburg of two works by Hofmann, respectively entitled *Pro duplici veritate Lutheri . . . Disputatio* and *Aurea et Vere Theologica Commentatio Super Quaestione Num Syllogismus rationis locum habeat in regno fidei.* The matter was referred to the authorities, and Hofmann was finally forced to retract. In a *Declaratio* of 1601 he recognizes his error and acknowledges that it is not the use but the abuse of philosophy in theology that is to be condemned.[34] However, the fire was not completely extinguished. In 1623 Paul Slevogt rekindled the controversy with the publication of his *Pervigilium de dissidio theologi et philosophi in utriusque principiis fundato* (Jena: Impressum Gansanii), in which, among other things, he tackles the question of whether God can accidentally be the cause of sin.[35] Slevogt's thesis is that depending on whether one applies to the matter the principles and methods of philosophy or those of theology, one arrives at opposite conclusions. According to Leibniz's interpretation of this thesis in the *Theodicy*,[36] Slevogt's aim was not to maintain the existence of a disagreement between theology and philosophy but rather to show the abuse of philosophical terms by theologians. Thus the blunt condemnation of Hofmann's and Slevogt's doctrines expressed by Leibniz in his early years was later replaced by a more serene judgment.

What is important to note here is that, right from the start, the need to ensure the possibility of the mysteries of the Christian faith is accompanied by the rejection of the existence of two truths (one theological and one philosophical) on the same issue, or, in other words, by the conviction of the "conformity of faith with reason." Leibniz remains convinced of this all his life, and his conviction finds final expression in the fundamental "Preliminary Discourse" of the *Theodicy*. There, besides refuting decisively the doctrine of the Averroists, he discusses, in section 13, the positions of Daniel Hofmann and Paul Slevogt. There is, however, very soon after the *Conspectus*, in the *Refutatio Objectionum Dan. Zwickeri contra Trinitatem et Incarnationem Dei*,[37] a new mention of Hofmann and Slevogt, with regard to the exclusion of double truth made by the Fifth Lateran Council (1512–1517).[38] Many years later, in the *Nouveaux Essais*, Leibniz returns to Hofmann, in a paragraph where, while directly attacking the Averroists, he frames the relations between faith and reason with great clarity, in terms of the conformity that exists between them.[39] Therefore this approach, so typical of Leibniz, in which the exclusion of double truth is indissolubly linked to the need to guarantee the possibility of the mysteries, is undoubtedly already present in his early period.

After having said that he would tackle, in the first four chapters of the third part of his plan, the problems posed by some divine attributes, such as eternity, omniscience, omnipotence, and omnipresence, Leibniz defines the subject of the fifth chapter as the question of the Trinity, formulated in the following terms: "Chap. 5. The possibility, nay the necessity, of the Triunity, by composition from that which understands, that which is understood, and the act of understanding. *Ex henos, pantōn kai panthenōsei. From the coming together of Universals in a third entity*.[40] The possibility of the mystery of the Trinity is therefore viewed by Leibniz as the possibility that there is a "three-in-oneness" ("Trinunitas"). But Leibniz does not stop here: by adding the parenthetical expression "nay the necessity," he seems to want to demonstrate also the necessity of this "Trinunitas." This is not a trivial addition: Leibniz seems to uphold the hypothesis that it is possible to achieve a demonstration of the mystery.

Now, this would be in clear contrast with what he never tired of repeating throughout his life, starting with his presentation of this *Conspectus* to the duke of Hanover: it is necessary to guarantee the possibility of the mysteries, but demonstration of them is ruled out.[41] However, Leibniz's parenthetical expression, if read in the light of the entire statement in which it occurs, does not really seem to contradict this position. With the phrase "the possibility, nay the necessity, of the Triunity, by composition from that which understands, that which is understood, and the act of understanding," Leibniz seems to want to show how to demonstrate the possibility of a "Trinunitas" by use of the analogy of mental operations in which the subject of thought, the object of thought, and the very act of thinking necessarily entail one another: the fact that this necessary entailment exists in the mind shows the possibility, indeed, in this case the necessity, of a "three-in-oneness." The object of the demonstration is not, thus, directly the Trinity ("Trinitas") but the "Trinunitas," and this seems to confirm that Leibniz does not at all intend to undertake the demonstration of the necessity of the Trinity but intends to demonstrate the existence in nature of a case of "three-in-oneness." This same existence proves the noncontradictoriness of a "Trinunitas" relation and thus the possibility that it may occur also in God.[42] The fact that the comparison between the mind and the Trinity remains, even in this case, in the sphere of analogy seems to be supported also by the formulation given in chapter 6, where Leibniz speaks of the "shadowing" of this same type of relation in space and in the body: "The shadowing of the same in Space: from the Point, Line and Surface; in the Body: from matter, shape and motion."[43]

Leibniz began to deal with the themes indicated in these two chapters of the *Conspectus* in 1669, with the *Defensio Trinitatis*,[44] and in 1671, in two short texts respectively entitled *De Conatu et Motu, Sensu et Cogitatione* and *Trinitas. Mens.*[45] In *De Demonstratione Possibilitatis Mysteriorum Eucharistiae*,[46] again in 1671, he tackles the subject of "Trinunitas," taking a very clear position on the limits of the human mind, which is able to defend the possibility, but not to show the necessity, of the "three-in-oneness" in God. In the following years, though not denying a shadowing of the Trinity in bodies, Leibniz concentrates mainly on analyzing the relation of analogy between the mind and the Trinity, recognizing in the thinking mind the example that best enables us to approach the mystery of the Trinity.[47]

Finally, some attention should be paid to the following expression contained in the title of chapter 5: "*Ex henos, pantōn kai panthenōsei.*"[48] It seems this sentence can be understood as meaning "from one, (which is) of all things and (which leads) to the unification of all things": that is, Leibniz seems to want to infer the "possibility of Three-in-Oneness" from the order of things, characterized by the presence of a principle of unity that makes it possible to unify what is manifold, in the image of "plurality in unity" of God, who is both Three and One.[49] Understood in this sense, the sentence would seem to refer back to one of the passages underlined by Leibniz some years earlier, between 1663 and 1666, in *Philosophiae Primae Seminarium,* a work by the obscure German philosopher and theologian Johann Heinrich Bisterfeld:[50] "Every multiplicity both can and must be recalled to unity. Wherefore it is necessary that there be, in turn, a first term, a middle term, and a final term of the universal order. Therefore, unless we wish to do manifest violence to the truth, it must be said that the universal harmony of all things is founded in the holy Trinity, and that this itself is the source, norm and end of every order. When this is acknowledged and affirmed, the whole of nature and Scripture is pure light; when this is ignored, or denied, there is nothing but darkness and horrendous chaos."[51] It is these *Notae ad Joh. Henricum Bisterfeldium*—one of Leibniz's earliest texts—that are the first certain sign of Leibniz's lively interest in the question of the Trinity.[52]

The importance of Bisterfeld's writings in the development of Leibniz's thought and, in particular, in the evolution of the idea of universal harmony has been repeatedly and authoritatively pointed out.[53] In Bisterfeld's works, Leibniz encounters the idea of the most perfect universal harmony, of unity in diversity, of the agreement and difference of every part, from the smallest to the largest.[54] Now, as we can already see from the passage just quoted, according to Bisterfeld the *panharmonia* of all things ("omnium rerum panharmoniam") is grounded in the Trinity, the source, norm, and end of all order. Emblematic of this thesis, the veritable heart of Bisterfeld's metaphysics, is the choice of the unusual term *immeatio* to indicate the idea of harmony. Immeatio, writes Bisterfeld, is the varied concourse, combination, and complication of relations, whose *varietas* (variety) and *societas* (connection) link all things with all things and of which all logic is the mirror. In other words, immeatio is that universal relation and tie of all things to all things that constitutes the very idea of harmony. This concept of immeatio, however, is nothing but the translation into the domain of logic and metaphysics of the theological concept of *emperichōresis* or *circumincessio,*[55] traditionally employed to explain the relation of 'co-inherence' of the three persons of the Trinity in the divine essence and in each other.[56] Nor is it just a matter of applying a theological concept to philosophy. The discovery of immeatio also in nature and in knowledge entails, for Bisterfeld, the recognition of a true and proper *analogia Trinitatis* (analogy of the Trinity). The triune nature of God is reflected in the ontological constitution of the creatures. Therefore, the ultimate roots of the structure of the universe must be sought in the Trinity.[57]

When he expresses great appreciation for Bisterfeld's writings,[58] the young Leibniz is well aware that, in Bisterfeld's thought, the universal harmony is founded on the harmony of the three divine persons. This can be seen from Leibniz's copy of *Philosophiae Primae Seminarium,* where several passages in which Bisterfeld explicitly states that the Trinity is the foundation of his idea of harmony are clearly underlined.[59] Nor is this all; Leibniz shows that he is able to discover and make explicit the analogia Trinitatis informing Bisterfeld's metaphysics even when it is not mentioned by Bisterfeld himself. Three examples from his marginal notes to *Philosophiae Primae Seminarium* are particularly illuminating.[60] In the passage which states that the triadic order is the key of all nature and of the entire encyclopedia of nature, Bisterfeld quotes, to support his thesis, Romans 11:36, where Paul writes of God: "Ex ipso, per ipsum, et in ipsum, sunt omnia [For from him and through him and to him are all things]." Leibniz underlines "ex" (from) and adds "Pater principium" (Father the first principle); he underlines "per" (through) and adds "Filius medium" (Son the mediator); he underlines "in" (to) and adds "Sp[iritus] S[anctus] finis" (Holy Spirit the end).[61] In this way, he shows that he interprets in a trinitarian sense both the passage of scripture and the classification of terms proposed by Bisterfeld at the beginning of the chapter: "Terminus est primus, à quo, medius, per quem, ultimus, ad quem [The first term is that from which, the medium term is that through which, the last term that toward which]."[62]

A second example is Leibniz's comment on the thesis that, as regards the *appetitus operativus primarius* (primary operative appetite), there cannot be an infinite regress. At this point Leibniz notes: "Whence is manifest the Ternary in the Trinity [unde patet Ternarius in Trinitate]."[63] In this case, he seems to read the passage in the light of the doctrine expounded later by Bisterfeld according to which it is the existence in every order of three principles (first, middle, and final), corresponding to the three persons of the Trinity, that prevents infinite regress.[64] The third example is even more complex. In *Philosophiae Primae Seminarium,* Bisterfeld proposes a definition of *habitudo* as an "entity, by which an entity is related to an entity [entitas, quâ entitas est ad entitatem]." While the analogia Trinitatis underlying this definition may not be immediately obvious to modern readers, it evidently was to Leibniz: he underlines the passage twice, writing above it "Trinitas."[65] It stands to reason that the young Leibniz would have been able to uncover the theology underlying the dense metaphysical passages just quoted only if he were already well versed in Trinitarian theology in the mid-1660s; as the years passed, he became actively engaged in the explanation and defense of the mystery of the Trinity.[66] Thus the enthusiastic reaction of the young Leibniz to Bisterfeld's texts is particularly significant, and not only as the first sign of this enduring interest of his. If, as has been acknowledged, Bisterfeld's doctrines left significant traces on Leibniz's general idea of harmony, they also provide an important key to the interpretation of Leibniz's texts, as they make extremely explicit what in Leibniz remains implicit: namely, that this idea of universal harmony coheres with and complements the trinitarian conception of God that is constantly defended by Leibniz.[67]

Indeed, Leibniz committed himself to the task of the "Driving Away of the Darts of the Socinians" against the dogma of the Trinity[68] in chapter 7 of the *Conspectus,* and he undertook the work at once by confuting the antitrinitarian theses of the Socinian Wissowatius in the *Defensio Trinitatis,*[69] as well as with his *Refutatio Objectionum Dan. Zwickeri contra Trinitatem et Incarnationem Dei* of a little later.[70] To carry out successfully this battle against the Socinians, and to be rescued more generally from the impending risk of atheism (in which the Socinians were also involved), Leibniz felt it indispensable to revive Aristotle's philosophy, as he clearly indicates in the famous early letter addressed to his teacher, Jakob Thomasius.[71] On the contrary, in his view, Descartes' philosophy would end up playing into the hands of the atheists, naturalists, and Socinians, as it would make the mysteries of the Christian faith inexplicable.[72]

Leibniz's commitment to combating Socinianism, which began in his early period, never waned. Besides the numerous polemical remarks directed against the theses of the Socinians, ranked among the most dangerous enemies of Christianity, there are extant, among Leibniz's writings, two texts directly attacking the Socinians. The first, composed around 1678, criticizes the positions held by Samuel Przypkowski[73] in a brief work entitled *Simboli Apostoli et Antisymboli eius Articuli XIII inter se collati;*[74] the second, dating from the middle of 1708, is an attack on Christoph Stegmann's manuscript treatise *Metaphysica Repurgata* (1635).[75] Starting in 1693, Leibniz's attention was concentrated on the affairs involving the "Socinians of England," as he calls the exponents of English antitrinitarianism in his letters to Thomas Burnett of Kemney.[76] Besides his correspondence with

Thomas Burnett of Kemney, his letters to the princess electress Sophie,[77] to his nephew Friedrich Simon Löffler,[78] and to Thomas Smith[79] are essential in this connection. Leibniz, in particular, took part in the controversy aroused by the anonymous publication of an antitrinitarian work by William Freke[80] and in the discussions caused by Stephen Nye's book *Considerations on the Explications of the Doctrine of the Trinity, by Dr. Wallis, Dr. Sherlock, Dr. S-th, Dr. Cudworth, and Mr. Hooker,* which was published anonymously in London in 1693.[81] Lastly, mention should be made of Leibniz's exchange of letters with the Socinian Samuel Crell in the years 1707 and 1708, as well as a text in which Leibniz expounds the differences between the theology of Faustus Socinus and that of Samuel Crell.[82]

After the "Driving Away of the Darts of the Socinians," Leibniz aims to tackle, in chapter 8 of the third part of the *Conspectus,* the problem of the procession of the Holy Spirit: "Chap. 8. The procession of the Holy Spirit from the Father and the Son against the Greeks."[83] The young Leibniz thus sides with the Latin theological tradition, according to which the Holy Spirit proceeds from the Father and from the Son (*Filioque*), and not, as the Greek tradition would have it, from the Father through the Son. Later, however, he seems to recognize that the two doctrines, if correctly understood, differ more in formulation than in substance: though he continues to prefer the Latin tradition,[84] he also accepts the Greek doctrine, highlighting the fact that the procession of the Holy Spirit from the Father through the Son ("ex Patre per Filium") in any case comes about "by way of a single principle."[85]

Chapter 9 deals in particular with the second person of the Trinity: "Chap. 9. A harmonious reason is given as to why only the second person of the Deity is incarnated."[86] The fact that the Incarnation is a prerogative only of the second person of the Trinity is upheld by Leibniz in the *Defensio Trinitatis* against the objections advanced by Wissowatius.[87] Having cleared the field of the charge that this doctrine would be contradictory, Leibniz in later years endeavored to show that redemption, which is carried out by the Incarnation of the second person of the Trinity, could not have been accomplished in any better way.[88]

In chapter 10 Leibniz intends to deal with a problem posed by the first person of the Trinity: "Chap. 10. In what way GOD Father is the source of Divinity, and yet co-eternal with the other persons; prior in nature, not in time."[89] The solution is already suggested in the second part of the title: the generation of the Son, like the procession of the Holy Spirit, is an eternal act, outside time. Later, in *De Scriptura, Ecclesia, Trinitate,* Leibniz clarifies his statement with reference to the procession of the Holy Spirit from the Father and from the Son, indicating a logical and not a temporal priority.[90]

However, the problem referred to by this chapter of the *Conspectus* is already tackled by Leibniz in the *Defensio Trinitatis,* in answer to Wissowatius's sixth argument.[91]

Chapter 11 is the last one devoted specifically to the exposition of the doctrine of the Trinity, this time in reference to the dogma of faith whereby the three divine persons operate externally with a single act.[92] Instead, the immanent actions, that is, the divine processions, are separate.[93]

Chapters 26–33 are dedicated to the solution of the problems related to the mystery of the Incarnation.[94] In the first of them, the question of the Incarnation is connected to some remarks in which Leibniz's 'scientific' outlook clearly emerges. In fact, Leibniz rejects those solutions that needlessly rely on supernatural and miraculous causes in the explanation of natural phenomena, when these can be explained by natural causes and the ordinary course of nature: "Chap. 26. That except for one incarnation it is probable that there are not divine miracles (angelic miracles are another matter), but the appearance of them arises perhaps from the ordinary course of nature destined beforehand to this end."[95] These remarks seem to be connected to the inquiry into the boundaries between science and philosophy that occupied Leibniz in those years, as the initial part of the *Confessio Naturae contra Atheistas* shows. Intimately interwoven, here as in the *Confessio Naturae,* with theological problems, these reflections are of great importance as Leibniz's first attempt to identify the distinct spheres and tasks reserved, respectively, to science and philosophy.[96]

Shortly after drawing up the *Conspectus,* Leibniz picked up the theme indicated in chapter 26 in a text expressly dedicated to the solution of the problem of the hypostatic union: *De Incarnatione Dei seu de Unione Hypostatica.*[97] In the following chapter of the *Conspectus* it is the "congruence" of the Incarnation that is faced: "Chap. 27. On the congruence of the incarnation, or: why GOD is man. St. Anselm's book: Why is GOD man?"[98] It does not appear that Leibniz ever returned to the arguments by which Anselm in *Cur Deus Homo* seems to want to prove the absolute necessity of the Incarnation.[99] As for the other mysteries, so too for the Incarnation: Leibniz is content to uphold its possibility, and goes no further. Even when he tries to identify the 'why' of the Incarnation, the reasons given all fall, so to speak, in the sphere of the logic of the 'best of all possible worlds': just like the creation of this world, the Incarnation of the Son of God is a free decree of the divine will:[100] since both correspond to the choice of what is best, just as this is the best of all possible worlds, so too the redemption of humankind could not have come about in a way better than the way in which it actually did, by means of the Incarnation.[101]

In chapters 28–33 Leibniz plans to deal with the 'mode' of the Incarnation, attacking a series of doctrines that incorrectly formulate (or even deny) the relation between human nature and divine nature in Jesus: "Chap. 28. On the mode of the incarnation, against the Arians[102] and Nestorians.[103] Chap. 28 [a]. On the same against the Eutychians.[104] Chap. 29. Against the Lutheran Communication of Properties [Communicatio Idiomatum], of Godhead in humanity, or against Ubiquitism.[105] Chap. 30. About the Tübingen-Giessen *Tapeinosigraphias* controversy.[106] Chap. 31. Against the communication of properties of the Theopaschites, of Humanity in Godhead.[107] Chap. 32. Against the Monothelites.[108] Chap. 33. Against the Aphthartodocetes."[109] Leibniz's doctrine regarding the 'mode' of the Incarnation, in which he remains constantly opposed to the theological currents indicated above, began to take shape already in his early period, in the *Defensio Trinitatis*,[110] in the *Refutatio Objectionum Dan. Zwickeri contra Trinitatem et Incarnationem Dei,* and especially in *De Incarnatione Dei seu de Unione Hypostatica.* In the following years he increasingly clarified its outlines, basing himself on two fundamental pillars: on the one hand, the acceptance and analysis of the tradition that proposes the analogy between the union of soul and body in humankind and the union of the divine and human natures in Christ; and, on the other, the rejection of the communication of properties (*communicatio idiomatum*).[111] Thus it is that Leibniz intends to reply to the objections raised from the most disparate quarters against the dogma of the Incarnation. In the same period in which he was composing the *Conspectus,* Leibniz found a particularly significant discussion of the possible difficulties presented by the acceptance of this mystery, as well as of the other doctrines taught by the Christian religion, in the *Colloquium Heptaplomeres de Rerum Sublimium Arcanis Abditis* by Jean Bodin.[112] In the third part of Leibniz's plan for the *Demonstrationes Catholicae* many of the topics discussed by the seven participants in the *Colloquium* reappear; so it may be thought that the reading of Bodin's work played a significant role in Leibniz's identification of the main themes of this part of the *Conspectus.* In the notes taken in 1668 and 1669 from a manuscript copy of the *Colloquium,*[113] Leibniz's aim does not seem to be to reply immediately to the objections raised against the Christian revelation. He seems, rather, to wish to take advantage of the great erudition displayed in Bodin's book to gather a large range of arguments used on various sides for and against the mysteries of Christianity: in most cases, Leibniz merely summarizes the theses held by the seven participants in the discussion, although the way in which the different arguments are reported often veils an interpretation, occasionally made explicit by a brief comment. In this period Leibniz's overall judgment on Bodin's book was very severe, and he even hoped that the *Colloquium* would never be published.[114] Instead, at the end of his life, in 1716, he came out in favor of a well-annotated edition.[115] However that may be, suffice it to note here that of the many theological positions mentioned in the *Conspectus* and in the notes from Bodin's *Colloquium,* the polemical target against which Leibniz, in the course of his entire life, directed his major effort was composed of those who, by resuscitating Arius's heresy, seemed in those years to represent one of the greatest dangers for Christianity: the Socinians.

The Early Polemic against the Socinians

The "Depulsio Telorum Socinianorum" ("Driving Away of the Darts of the Socinians"), to which Leibniz committed himself in the *Conspectus,* concentrates in this youthful period above all on the defense of the Trinity and the Incarnation against the objections of two important exponents of Socinianism: Andreas Wissowatius and Daniel Zwicker. Although both Antitrinitarians, Wissowatius and Zwicker were very different from one another: the former, the nephew on his mother's side of Faustus Socinus, was a recognized representative of the Socinian church;[1] the latter, though linked to the Socinians, declared that he considered himself merely a Christian and hoped for a general union of all the churches.[2] Against them the young Leibniz wrote, respectively, the *Defensio Trinitatis per nova Reperta Logica contra adjunctam hic Epistolam Ariani non incelebris, ad Illustrissimum Baronem Boineburgium* of 1669[3] and the *Refutatio Objectionum Dan. Zwickeri contra Trinitatem et Incarnationem Dei* of 1670.[4] In both cases Leibniz uses the 'strategy of defense,' as he himself points out in the *Defensio Trinitatis.*[5] It is not his task, he insists, to prove anything positively. Rather, that is his adversary's task. In order for Leibniz to reach his aim (that is, to uphold the possibility of the mystery of the Trinity) it is sufficient merely to reply to the objections, since "anything is presumed to be possible, until the contrary is proved."[6] This procedure is a well-honed argumentative technique foreseen in the *ars disputandi* (art of debate), and its system of codified rules was well known to both Leibniz and his adversaries.[7]

A reconstruction of the method of dispute in use in the modern era, which seems to sum up very well also the procedure used by Leibniz, especially in the *Defensio Trinitatis,* is given by Ignacio Angelelli.[8] According to this method, the *respondens* (respondent) or *defendens* (defendent) (in this case, Leibniz) begins by affirming a thesis A. The *opponens* (opponent) must then produce an argument whose conclusion is the negation of A.[9] When the *opponens* has formulated his argument, the *respondens* must above all repeat the argument.[10] After the *repetitio* (repetition), the *respondens* must limit himself to "distinguishing," "conceding," or "denying,"[11] referring exclusively to what is maintained in the premises or inferences by his adversary, without having to bring any positive proof of the thesis that he intends to defend, which is presumed to be true until the contrary is proved.[12] This is exactly what Leibniz claims for the mystery of the Trinity when, after having rejected Wissowatius's first argument against the Trinity, he concludes: "For, until the contrary is better proved, we remain of this opinion, that the Son and the Holy Spirit are he who is the one most high GOD; and yet they are not the father, from whom all things, including both the son and the holy spirit as well, arise."[13] Here, as in all of the *Defensio Trinitatis,* the concept of 'presumption' or 'presumptive knowledge' is operative; Ezequiel de Olaso ascribes great importance to this concept in Leibniz's ars disputandi.[14] It is particularly useful in the case of truths that cannot be positively demonstrated, such as the mysteries.[15] For truths that have not been, or cannot be, proved, one can appeal to a "presumption of truth" that remains valid until the contrary has been demonstrated: that is to say, one can legitimately hold something to be true until its opposite has been proved.[16]

According to a description given by the young Leibniz in a rough draft of the *Elementa Juris Naturalis,*[17] the distinction between "presumption" and "probability" is similar to that between demonstration and induction: "The difference between presumption and probability is that between demonstration and induction *(a)* science and experience. *(b)* For in presumption, from the nature of the thing we show that it is easier and hence to be presumed more frequent. . . . On the contrary, we know by induction that what is probable is more frequent and therefore we presume it to be easier. *To presume* is *(a)* to hold something uncertain as being certain in practice *(b)* to take something as certain until the opposite is proved."[18] In the case of the mysteries, this distinction between "presumption" and "probability" seems to fit perfectly. We have seen that, in the presentation to the duke of

Hanover of the *Demonstrationum Catholicarum Conspectus*, Leibniz emphasizes the need for a new form of logic to deal with "facts and morals," including revealed truths. Now, although this logic takes, in his letter to the duke, the general outlines of an "art of weighing probabilities," in opposition to the stringent procedures of demonstration,[19] the logic required by the mysteries cannot be, strictly speaking, identified with a logic of probability. The mysteries, as Leibniz writes in the *Commentatiuncula de Judice Controversiarum*,[20] are *improbable* from a rational point of view.[21] This improbability, however, does not in any way entail impossibility.[22] One can therefore legitimately "hold as true" ("verum putare"),[23] or, to use the words of the *Elementa Juris Naturalis*, "to hold as certain" ("pro certo habere") what has been transmitted by revelation, until the opposite has been proved ("donec oppositum probetur").[24]

The epistemological status of presumptive knowledge is further specified in the *Nouveaux Essais* and in the *Theodicy*. In the *Nouveaux Essais*, Philalethe affirms that one presumes something "when one holds it as true before having proof."[25] Theophile, in his reply, states: "As for *presumption*, which is a term of the Jurists, good usage among them distinguishes it from *conjecture*. It is something more which must pass provisionally for truth, until the contrary is proved. . . . *To presume* is not therefore meant in the sense of *taking before* the proof, which is not permitted, but *taking in advance*, albeit with reason, while waiting for a contrary proof."[26] In paragraph 33 of the "Preliminary Discourse" of the *Theodicy*, Leibniz reiterates: "The Jurists call *presumption*, what has to pass for provisional truth, if the contrary is not proven, and it says more than *conjecture*."[27]

This description of presumptive knowledge seems once again to fit the case of the mysteries very well. One of the problems posed by the mysteries is the following. How can reason recognize as true that which exceeds its limits of comprehension? By means of the concept of 'presumption,' Leibniz in the *Defensio Trinitatis* seems to offer the following solution: *we assume from the start* that the mysteries are true, and hold fast to that assumption until it is proved that they are impossible. At this point another characteristic of presumptive knowledge comes to the fore. The 'presumption of truth' admits the possibility that the contrary may be demonstrated: that is to say, it admits the possibility that the thesis presumed to be true may be shown to be false. When, in the *Commentatiuncula*, Leibniz writes that faith "stands in fear of its opposite" ("fidem cum formidine oppositi consistere"),[28] he seems to mean this: since "on account of the obscurity of the human mind"[29] the truth of revealed propositions cannot be demonstrated, we must admit the hypothesis that the contrary of these propositions may be demonstrated. At this point, the task of the defender of the mysteries will be exactly that of driving away "the fear of the opposite," rebutting all attempts to prove the contrary of the thesis that is being defended. The 'wager' is that such a proof does not actually exist.

In conclusion, the 'strategy of defense' Leibniz adopts, by which, thanks to the presumption of the possibility that the mysteries may be true, the burden of proof (*onus probandi*) falls on the attacker of a thesis and not on its defender,[30] harmonizes perfectly with the distinction between 'against reason' and 'above reason'; in other words, it makes it possible to maintain a balance in the mysteries between the element of intelligibility and the element of unintelligibility. These two elements are both necessary if there is to be a sphere of truth with a 'mysterious' character (guaranteed by the element of unintelligibility), which also has, thanks to the element of intelligibility, a real cognitive (and not merely emotive or ethical) value.[31] The 'strategy of defense,' by which Leibniz rejects the charge that the mysteries are against reason, rescues their truth value, without having to provide positive proof of the truths being defended. In any case, such a proof could not be given, since the mysteries by definition are truths that surpass human comprehension.

What we have said so far naturally goes together with the exclusion of double truth. This conviction, as we have seen, was already operative in the *Conspectus*[32] but is reiterated forcefully in the *Refutatio Objectionum Dan. Zwickeri*.[33] It is worth repeating that the doctrine of faith conforming with reason was already fixed in Leibniz's earliest writings. At this juncture we should, however, point out that also for the Socinians there must be agreement between faith and reason. For them as for Leibniz, an authentic revelation must be in conformity with reason: any dogmas that were to be recognized as self-contradictory, far from being a divine revelation, would instead be the senseless inventions of theologians.[34] The target of Leibniz's attack on the doctrine of double truth is thus not the Socinians but those who, in upholding this doctrine, admit that mysteries such as the Trinity and the Incarnation are self-contradictory, and thus surrender to the Antitrinitarians.[35]

The difference between Leibniz's position and that of the Socinians lies farther back, in the *way* in which one determines what is or is not an authentic revelation. For the Socinians, in this decision reason is given primacy: human reason is the judge of the rationality or irrationality of the content of revelation and thus rejects as irrational all those dogmas that it cannot comprehend. For Leibniz, instead, the matter is posed differently, thanks to the role of tradition in determining what is or is not authentic revelation:[36] the dogmas accepted and handed down through the centuries by the church can legitimately be held to be true (even if they surpass the limits of human reason) until it has been proved incontrovertibly that they are self-contradictory. And it is here that the basic role assumed by reason lies: in the defense of such dogmas from the charge of being contradictory, so that one is justified in maintaining their possibility until the contrary is demonstrated.[37] In other words, the impossibility of the dogmas handed down by tradition and accepted by the church must be positively demonstrated,[38] since it is not sufficient to reject them on the basis that they are incomprehensible to man's limited understanding. Until such a demonstration is forthcoming, they can legitimately be accepted as truths superior to (human) reason.[39] Not even the observation that nature holds no examples that adequately instantiate what is expressed in the dogmas is sufficient to reject them as impossible.[40] This lack of examples does not prevent reason, on the other hand, from giving an explanation of such dogmas,[41] since it can still appeal to analogy with what occurs in nature.

Notes on the Origin and History of the Defensio Trinitatis *(Defense of the Trinity)*

Of all Leibniz's writings dealing with the mystery of the Trinity, the *Defensio Trinitatis* is certainly the most famous. The events that led up to its composition take us back to the strong tie between the young Leibniz and Baron Johann Christian von Boineburg, probably dating from the end of 1667. It was, in fact, on behalf of Boineburg that Leibniz decided to reply to the objections against the Trinity brought by Andreas Wissowatius in a letter written at Mannheim in October 1665 and addressed to Boineburg himself.[42] It came in the wake of a previous exchange of letters between the two, concerning in particular the question of the divinity of Jesus and the adoration due to him.[43] The reason why Boineburg did not reply personally this time is unknown; perhaps the complexity of the arguments presented by Wissowatius[44] led him to entrust the reply, following the advice of the Socinian himself,[45] to the young protégé whom he highly esteemed. The *Defensio Trinitatis* is not the only work that Boineburg commissioned Leibniz to write in this period. In the spring of 1669 the baron was getting ready to leave for Warsaw, intending to support the claim of Philipp Wilhelm von Neuburg (1615–1690) to the Polish throne. To this end, on Boineburg's request Leibniz, under the pseudonym Georgius Ulicovius Lithuanus, wrote the *Specimen Demonstrationum Politicarum pro Eligendo Rege Polonorum Novo Scribendi Genere Exactum.*[46] The baron probably intended to take along also the reply to Wissowatius's objections on his trip to Poland;[47] but there is no further mention of the events connected with the composition of the *Defensio Trinitatis* in the correspondence between Leibniz and Boineburg.

It was first published a year after Leibniz's death, in [Leyser], *Apparatus Literarius Singularia Nova Anecdota.*[48] But it had already been mentioned in 1716 by Fontenelle in his eulogy of Leibniz delivered at the Academy of Sciences in Paris.[49] Wolff speaks of it in the *Elogium Godofredi Guilielmi Leibnitii,* published in the "Acta Eruditorum" in July 1717,[50] and Louis de Jaucourt devotes some passages of his *Vie de Mr. De Leibniz* to the *Defensio Trinitatis.*[51] Leyser, moreover, accompanies his edition of the *Defensio Trinitatis* with a commentary, in which he appears anything but favorable toward Leibniz's efforts to defend the Trinity. He is convinced that the mystery of the Trinity is contrary to reason, which, according to him, is not entitled to judge of divine matters, as its competence is limited to the sphere of what is finite.[52] Jakob Carpov is of the diametrically opposite opinion.[53] Carpov reprinted the text published by Leyser in 1717, adding his own series of replies to each group of replies given by Leibniz to Wissowatius's arguments.[54] In 1768, Dutens reprinted the text of the *Defensio Trinitatis* given by Leyser in 1717, but omitting Wissowatius's letter.[55]

Lessing's edition of 1773 deserves special attention. Under the title *Des Andreas Wissowatius Einwürfe wider die Dreieinigkeit,* he published the *Defensio Trinitatis* accompanied by his own commentary.[56] Lessing's opinion seems to be that Leibniz's defense of the mystery of the Trinity from the charge of being in contradiction with undeniable truths of reason is merely to raise up the shield of the incomprehensibility of the mysteries. As supernatural truths revealed by God, they lie outside the sphere of judgment of man's natural reason, which can make no objection so long as one admits that they are mysteries; precisely because they are such, reason cannot understand them. And Lessing's pungent comment is that, to carry on such a defense with success, there was no need of an intellect such as that of Leibniz.[57] Nor, continues Lessing, can one accuse Leibniz of not believing in what he defended. On the contrary, he did *believe* in these mysteries as the object of revelation and he did not claim to prove them by the use of reason, as do certain theologians. They, Lessing ironically writes, have "so many compelling reasons for belief, and so many irrevocable proofs for the truth of the Christian religion are in hand, that I cannot wonder enough, how people can be so short-sighted as to take the belief in these truths for a supernatural effect of grace."[58] After Lessing's edition, two other important ones should be mentioned. In 1880, C. I. Gerhardt, basing himself directly on the manuscripts conserved in Hanover, published the *Defensio Trinitatis* in the fourth volume of the *Philosophische Schriften.*[59] The last, and definitive, edition is that published in 1930 by the Berlin Academy of Sciences.[60]

In Catholic circles Leibniz's replies to Wissowatius's arguments were favorably received, as is shown by their inclusion in *Theologiae Cursus Completus* by Migne.[61] Leibniz's defense of the Trinity was instead liquidated as "nichtssagend" (literally, "saying nothing") by Ferdinand Christian Baur, professor of evangelical theology at the University of Tübingen.[62] According to Baur, it is merely a repetition of the dogma of the church, which does not demonstrate whether this dogma is or is not self-contradictory.[63] This is an opinion that seems not to do justice to Leibniz's attempt, as a close examination of Leibniz's arguments will show.[64]

Wissowatius's Arguments and Leibniz's Answers

According to Leibniz, the heart of the matter, thanks to which it is possible to solve all the difficulties proposed by Wissowatius, however intricate they may seem, lies in the nature of the copula used in syllogistic propositions.[65] In fact, in concluding the *Defensio Trinitatis* he states: "I do not deny that you have brought up some knotty problems, and indeed the most difficult that any of your fellows could raise. Once having found the beginning of the thread, that is, the nature of the copula of a proposition in a syllogism, we will be seen to have solved them perfectly."[66] The "Nova Reperta Logica [New Logical Discoveries]" to which Leibniz refers in the title of his work against Wissowatius[67] would seem to be precisely the clarification of this matter, with all the consequences that stem from it. It is indeed on the clarification of the nature of the copula in syllogistic propositions that Leibniz hinges his defense of the mystery of the Trinity, starting right from the reply to Wissowatius's first argument, which is formulated as follows: "The one most high GOD is that Father from whom all things come. The son of GOD JESUS CHRIST is not that father from whom all things come. Therefore the Son of GOD JESUS CHRIST is not the one most high GOD."[68] Leibniz begins with a premise, valid also for the following arguments, regarding the correct way of interpreting the copula in the premises of the syllogism: "To argument I, I premise in general, that also in the following it should be observed that copulas in the premises of syllogisms are commonly not rightly conceived. Moreover, one should distinguish between propositions regarding the thing itself and others regarding accidents of the thing, for example, we say rightly and simply: Every man is rational, but we are not right in saying that every man is white, even if it be true, because whiteness is not an immediate attribute of a human being; but one should say, everyone who is a man, is white.

Likewise, one should not say: every Musician is white, but: everyone who is a Musician is white. Which also Ioh. Raue of Berlin partly noted in his most original speculations on the copula."[69] Leibniz therefore distinguishes between propositions in which the predicate belongs essentially to the concept of the subject (*propositiones per se*) and propositions in which the predicate does not belong essentially to the concept of the subject (*propositiones per accidens*): thus, while reason belongs to the nature of man, whiteness does not belong to the concept of man qua man or to the concept of musician qua musician. In the case of propositions *per accidens,* they must be reformulated in the way shown by Johannes Raue in his studies on the copula.[70]

We must turn to Raue's work in order to understand the context in which Leibniz's remarks are made. Raue states that in ordinary language, in propositions of the type *Homo est animal* (Man is an animal), the true and legitimate copula is omitted. The *est* that appears in the proposition is, in reality, an essential part of the predicate.[71] In the proposition *Homo est animal,* the subject is therefore "Homo" (Man) and the predicate is "est animal" (is an animal), while the copula—formed of "est" (is), a demonstrative pronoun ("ille," "is," "id," . . . [he, the one . . .]) and a relative pronoun ("qui," "quod," . . . [who, which])—is omitted.[72] As an example Raue presents a series of propositions in which the place of the omitted copula is marked by two *lineolae* (slashes): "Christ // is God. Piety // is useful for all things. Faith // justifies. The impenitent // are necessarily damned [.] Christ // is our only mediator."[73] Putting in the copula, these propositions are expanded as follows: "Christ / is he who / is God. Piety / is that which / is useful for all things. Faith / is that which / justifies. The impenitent / are those who / are necessarily damned. Christ / is he who / is our only mediator."[74] In *Prior Fundamentalis Controversia pro Logica Novissima*, Raue again tackles the problem of the copula and discusses it at length, summing up his conception in the last part of the work (significantly bearing the title of "Filum Ariadnaeum" (Ariadne's Thread).[75] He distinguishes the material parts of the proposition from the formal parts: the material parts are composed of the subject and the predicate, with their respective "auxiliary copulas" ("est S"; "est P"); the formal parts are composed of the true copula, responsible for joining subject and predicate, and of the occurrences of the demonstrative and relative pronouns; for clarity's sake, the formal parts and the material parts are separated by the use of a single lineola.[76] The function of the pronouns is to refer to a *commune tertium* (a common third thing or term), of which both the subject and the predicate are predicated.[77] It is therefore the pronouns that, by referring to this 'single substratum,' constitute the 'hooks' that the copula needs in order to join subject and predicate.[78] According to Raue, the pronouns must be placed "either before the Subject, or 2. before the Predicate, only; or 3. simultaneously before both the Subject and the Predicate[.]"[79] Thus we shall have: "He who / redeems us // is our Messiah. 2. Christ / is he who / redeems us. 3. He who / is Christ / is he who / is our Messiah."[80] In Raue's opinion, "That form of the utterance is indeed most perfect which has these Pronouns both before the Subject and before the Predicate."[81]

One more thing should be said[82] in order to understand better the way in which Leibniz reformulates Wissowatius's syllogisms. This regards the terms "Every, Any, A certain, Not any, etc.," called "Quantitative signs":[83] they include the demonstrative pronouns *this, that, the one,* and so on, and can replace them in the proposition. Thus, whereas "It is commonly said: *Every / man // is an animal.* The most regular form is, *Everyone who / is a man / is the one who / is an animal.*"[84] "Is a man" and "is an animal" are the material parts of the proposition (respectively, subject and predicate), "everyone who" and "is the one who" are the formal parts of the proposition, responsible for joining the subject and predicate thanks to the true copula and to the reference to the commune tertium made by the pronouns.

Returning to Leibniz's remarks, we may first of all observe that in the propositions per se there is no need of the 'mediation' of the copula to join subject and predicate, since the predicate is essentially (and hence "immediately," that is, without mediation) part of the concept of the subject (*immediatè cohaeret*).[85] On the contrary, in the propositions per accidens, it is necessary to highlight the commune tertium that, as a 'single substratum,' makes possible the joining of subject and predicate. This is what Leibniz does, putting the terms "everyone" and "who" before the subject.[86] With the help of the lineolae, Leibniz's reformulation of the proposition "every man is white" becomes "everyone who / is a man // is white." As can be seen, the 'true copula' is omitted. Perhaps hearkening to the criticisms of Johannes Scharff, who claimed that Raue's multiplication of copulas, far from simplifying understanding, made it more difficult,[87] Leibniz seems to feel that the crucial point in Raue's doctrine is the introduction of the pronouns, with their function of referring to a commune tertium. As we shall soon see, an 'abbreviated form' of Raue's analysis also appears in the reformulation of Wissowatius's syllogisms.

Leibniz follows Raue also in his analysis of singular propositions as universal ones. In fact, in the *Dissertatio de Arte Combinatoria* (1666) he writes:

> 'Socrates is the son of Sophroniscus,' if it is resolved following nearly the mode of Joh. Raue, will be like this: Whoever is Socrates is the son of Sophroniscus. Nor will it be badly said: Every Socrates is the son of Sophroniscus, even if he be only one. (For we are not talking about the name, but about the

man.) Likewise also if I should say: I bequeath to Titius all the clothes that I have, who will doubt it even if I have only one to be given over to him? Nay, according to the Jurists, universality subsists in the single one at some time or other. . . . For the word "Every" does not imply a multitude, but the inclusion of single things. Indeed, supposing that Socrates did not have a brother, even so I say rightly: Every son of Sophroniscus is Socrates. . . . Therefore in general we dare to say: in a syllogism, in respect of its mode, every singular Proposition is to be taken as Universal.[88]

The fact that in the syllogism every singular proposition is to be considered universal is reiterated in the *Defensio Trinitatis,* where Leibniz, in his reply to Wissowatius's first argument, refers precisely to the passage from the *Ars Combinatoria* quoted above: "On the same basis it must then be noted[89] that all singular propositions are, by virtue of a latent sign,[90] universal, as has been noted also by the author of the treatise on the Combinatory Art, for example, if the signs and copula are rightly placed, this proposition, Peter the Apostle was the first Roman Bishop, is formulated thus: Everyone who is Peter the Apostle was [the first] Roman Bishop."[91] At this point, having concluded the premise, Leibniz applies this way of formulating propositions to Wissowatius's syllogism: "Accordingly we shall therefore form the first argument: Everyone who is the one most high GOD is that Father (est Pater ille) from whom all things come. The son of GOD JESUS CHRIST is not that father (non est Pater ille) from whom all things come. Therefore, the Son of GOD JESUS CHRIST is not the one who is (non est is qui est) the one most high GOD."[92] As was mentioned above, Leibniz prefers an abbreviated form of the analysis, given in this case by the specification of the universal nature of the major premise (through the introduction of the "universal sign" *everyone*), by the insertion of the pronouns before the subject (*that,* implied in *every,* and *who*) with their function of referring to the commune tertium, and, lastly, by making explicit the 'true copula' only in the conclusion of the syllogism. Using the lineolae (slashes), the reformulation appears as follows: "Everyone who / is the one most high GOD // is that Father from whom all things come. The Son of GOD JESUS CHRIST // is not that father from whom all things come. Therefore the Son of GOD JESUS CHRIST / is not that who / is the one most high GOD."

Once he has reformulated the syllogism in this way, Leibniz begins his reply by defining what is meant by "omnia [all things]."[93] If by "omnia" we mean only the creatures, then Leibniz concedes the major premise, but he denies the minor premise because, as the Socinians themselves admit, all creatures are created through the Son.[94] In this case, the line of defense adopted by Leibniz seems to agree with the dogma that the three divine persons operate together externally (*ad extra*): with respect to the world, God is a single principle of operation, a single creator.[95] We may therefore affirm that "everyone who is the one most high GOD" is the one from whom all things, that is, all creatures, come, while it must be denied that the Son of God Jesus Christ is not this creator [*pater*] of all things. If, instead, by "omnia" one means also the Son, then the minor premise is conceded and the major premise is denied,[96] that is, "It is denied that the major premise is universal. For it is not true: Whoever is the one most high GOD is that father from whom all things come. Now in truth even a singular proposition is universal, as, for example, every Peter the Apostle is the first Roman Bishop."[97] Leibniz's ultimate aim seems to be the denial of the major premise.[98] The commune tertium to which the terms "everyone" and "who" refer is (as Leibniz was to say later) *God taken absolutely or essentially,* namely, God considered according to the divine essence, numerically one, of which the three persons partake.[99] The key point is the denial that "whoever is" *God taken absolutely or essentially,* that is, the only *One Most High God,* is *Father.* In fact, in a much later text Leibniz writes: "For in the Trinity there is a difference between these two: *to be God the father,* and *to be he who is God the father.* For God the son is not God the father, and yet he is the same one who is God the father, that is, the one most high God."[100]

By denying, respectively, the major or the minor premise, Leibniz feels that he has confuted Wissowatius's syllogism and, thanks to the presumption of truth whereby a thesis can rightfully be considered true until its falsity has been proved, he can therefore conclude: "For, until the contrary is better proved, we remain of this opinion, that the Son and the Holy Spirit are he who is the one most high GOD[.]"[101] Continuing, Leibniz justifies the statement "until the contrary is better proved" by showing that, to prove the truth of the premises, it is not enough to quote the sentence of Paul in which Wissowatius claims that both the major and the minor premise are contained.[102] According to Wissowatius, Cor. 8:6 ("Yet for us there is one God, the Father, from whom are all things and for whom we exist, and one Lord, Jesus Christ, through whom are all things and through whom we exist") states the superiority of the Father with respect to the Son.[103] On the contrary, Leibniz maintains: "For the *Father from whom* all things [are], and *the Lord through whom* all things [are], it is possible to understand one and the same Being, namely the most high GOD. For in general, by natural law, whoever is a father is the same Lord of his children. And the prepositions 'from' and 'through' are not so different that we cannot thus say: from whom all things are, through him also all things are. For also Paul elsewhere simultaneously utters these two particles regarding one and the same most high

GOD, together with a third, 'to,' when he says: For from him and through him and to him are all things [Rom. 11:36]. This phrase has deservedly been seen by certain authors as a foreshadowing [adumbratio] of the Trinity."[104] After having proposed this biblical reference, Leibniz intentionally does not proceed further in the argument in support of his thesis. Later on he states clearly: "In truth it is not now up to me to present arguments, but to reply,"[105] thus confirming the adoption of the 'strategy of defense.' As regards the verse of Acts 2:36 "Let all the house of Israel therefore know assuredly that God has made him both Lord and Christ, this Jesus whom you crucified," used by Wissowatius as further scriptural proof of the subordination of the Son to the Father, Leibniz affirms: "It is not necessary that Paul's I. Cor. VIII. 6. and Peter's Act. II. 36. employ the word Lord in relation to Christ in the same respect; the former can speak of Christ as [quatenus] God, and the latter as [quatenus] a man."[106] Already here we can see a procedure that Leibniz will frequently resort to: namely, distinguishing between the different meanings taken on by the same term in different propositions,[107] by using the reduplicative operator *quatenus* (= insofar as). This procedure was later to become fundamental for Leibniz's defense of the mystery of the Trinity from the accusation of being in contradiction of the logical principle that things that are equal to a third thing are equal to each other.[108]

Again from the standpoint of the rules of the ars disputandi (art of debate), whereby the defender of a thesis has only to reply to positively formulated objections, Leibniz neither discusses the merits of the other scriptural passages listed by Wissowatius nor indicates what difficulties they would present with respect to the dogma of the Trinity.[109] He merely comments: "Now there is no time to roll out all the passages quoted, and justify the arguments by means of them; if any difficulty is concealed in them, it should be [explicitly] shown."[110]

The "method of the copula" is also applied in Leibniz's replies to the arguments that follow. I shall limit myself to illustrating a few points. Wissowatius's second argument refers to the passages of the Gospels where Jesus declares that only the Father knows the day of judgment.[111] Now, Wissowatius reasons, it would be contradictory to maintain that one who does not possess the divine attribute of omniscience is nonetheless God. Leibniz, after having reformulated Wissowatius's syllogism by the 'method of the copula,'[112] denies the major premise: "Whoever did not know the day of judgment, is not he who is the most high GOD."[113] In fact, according to the hypothesis of the Trinity, he who does not know the day of judgment, that is, a man, can at the same time be he who is God.[114] Now, until the falsity of the hypothesis that "the same person can be simultaneously GOD and man" is demonstrated,[115] to maintain its impossibility is to beg the question, since "anything is presumed to be possible, until the contrary is proved."[116]

The reply to Wissowatius's third argument[117] too hinges on the 'method of the copula' and on the related principle that "in a syllogism, in respect of its mode, every singular Proposition is to be taken as Universal."[118] However, it is worthwhile making some further remarks on the problem raised by Wissowatius at the end of the argument. The Socinian points out that, if one accepted the Trinitarian conception of God, "the most high GOD was one not absolutely and simply by the strictest unity, but one in some manner."[119] Wissowatius's objection, basically, is that the Trinitarian conception introduces a multiplicity into the Godhead, where multiplicity is understood as imperfection. This is clearly a fundamental ontological problem, above all in the context of the monadological conception of substance developed by Leibniz later on.[120] Leibniz begins his reply by admitting, "Thus in the strictest sense it cannot be said that GOD is one, so that in him in reality or before the operation of the mind distinct entities [distincta] do not exist. For if a mind exists, it must be that there are in it: the one who thinks, the one thought of, and the act of thinking [intelligens, intellectum, et intellectio], and those things that coincide with these: power, knowledge, and will. In truth, it would be a contradiction if there were not a real difference [reale discrimen] among these. To be sure, since they are formally different, this will be a difference by reason of analysis [differentia rationis ratiocinatae]; on the other hand, this difference has its foundation in the thing itself [habet fundamentum in re]; there will therefore be in GOD three really distinct foundations [tria fundamenta *realiter distincta*]."[121] There is, therefore, in some way a plurality in God.[122] The existence of these *distincta*, corresponding to the persons of the Trinity, does not, however, imply imperfection: "But this does not imply an imperfection in GOD, since a multitude and composition is not, in itself, imperfect, except as it contains separability, and thus the corruptibility of the whole. But separability is not implied by this. Rather, see above letter u,[123] it is demonstrated that it is impossible, and implies contradiction, that one person of the Deity can exist without the other."[124]

At this point, it is natural to ask what relation there is between these early statements and the monadological ontology of Leibniz's maturity. The fact that the monad is a "simple substance, . . . that is, without parts,"[125] does not mean that in it there is not a plurality: "It is necessary that in a simple substance there is a plurality of affections and relations although there are no parts."[126] We must therefore recognize "a multitude in unity or in the simple,"[127] and "we ourselves experience a multitude in the simple substance, when we find that the least thought of which we are aware contains a variety in the object.

So all those who recognize that the Soul is a simple substance have to recognize this multitude in the Monad."[128] Therefore, what makes the simplicity and unity of a substance is not the absence in it of a multitude or plurality but its not having separable parts. It is precisely this separability that makes the difference between the "multitude in unity" characterizing the monad and the multitude characterizing compound substances, indicated in the *Principes de la Nature et de la Grace* by the term "Multitudes" in opposition to "Simple substances."[129] Thus, multitude as such is not an imperfection, only that multitude which entails separability and, consequently, corruptibility.[130]

This is what the young Leibniz had already said in an extremely lucid way when, in accordance with the ontology of his maturity, he wrote in the *Defensio Trinitatis:* "Multitude and composition is not, in itself, imperfect, except as it contains separability, and thus the corruptibility of the whole."[131] If separability is excluded, *multitudo* and *compositio* are, indeed, a source of greater perfection. This is what the young Leibniz implies when he writes in the *Elementa Juris Naturalis:* "There is the greater harmony when there is the greater diversity, and yet it [such diversity] is reduced to identity."[132] This explains the peremptory tone used by Leibniz in absolutely excluding the notion that the persons of the Trinity can exist one without the other, that is, that there is a 'separability' in God: the Trinity does not destroy the unity of God if and only if this is a plurality in unity wherein the persons are not mutually separable parts.[133] This exclusion is so important for Leibniz that he even abandons his usual caution when speaking of the mysteries as being truths above reason, for which we do not have proof; here he does not hesitate to use expressions of the greatest demonstrative force, such as "to be impossible" and "imply contradiction."[134]

On the other hand, this does not seem to be an oversight by Leibniz, who, driven by the need to exclude absolutely any separability in God, would not have realized the contrast with his usual doctrine regarding the mysteries. Once again,[135] it seems that Leibniz's statements should be placed in the context of an argument based on analogy. If here—unlike his approach in other cases[136]—Leibniz does not explicitly state that the juxtaposition of mind and Trinity is an analogy; this fact would in any case seem to emerge from the last part of his reply. In it he proposes an analogia Trinitatis that embraces both minds and bodies: "Nor should GOD be multiplied. Indeed, just as size, shape, and motion are really distinct in the body, yet it does not follow from this that there are three bodies, one for size, one for shape, and one for motion. The same goes for a stone: it may be long, round, and heavy. And so too even if judgment, idea, and intellection really differ in the mind, it does not follow that there are three minds. For there is only one mind that, when it reflects on itself (NB), is that which thinks, that which is thought, and that by which it thinks and is thought."[137] For the first time Leibniz specifies the analogy of mind and Trinity as an analogy with the mind that thinks itself. It is precisely this case, here simply set beside the others, that gradually comes to be, in his later writings, the example that best enables human beings to approach the mystery of the Trinity. In particular, between 1684 and 1686, in the fragment entitled *De Mundo Praesenti,* Leibniz again forcefully advances the analogy between the mind and the Trinity, identifying it in the *compositio rei indivisibilis* [composition of an indivisible thing]: "As God is Mind and thinks and loves himself, hence arises a certain admirable diversity of himself from himself, or the composition of an indivisible thing, as we acknowledge in the persons of the Holy Trinity; and of which we have a certain trace in our mind thinking itself."[138]

To return to Leibniz's replies in the *Defensio Trinitatis,* in his answers to the fourth, fifth,[139] sixth, and seventh arguments by Wissowatius,[140] it is once again the implicit application of the 'method of the copula' that enables him to solve the difficulties. Leibniz thus feels at the end of his letter that he has been fully victorious in meeting the challenge launched by the Socinian: "If someone finds a good solution of these difficulties for me, then at last I will confess that this opinion [the dogma of the Trinity] is not absurd."[141]

The Refutation of Daniel Zwicker's Objections against the Trinity and the Incarnation of God

The *Refutatio Objectionum Dan. Zwickeri contra Trinitatem et Incarnationem Dei*[142] can perhaps be linked to a letter by Johannes Fabricius (1644–1729), written from Hamburg in August 1670 and addressed to Boineburg. This letter, of which Leibniz made a copy, contains some information on Zwicker's activities, which aim at spreading the Socinian doctrine.[143] Leibniz, who is usually moderate in his tone and always ready to acknowledge the merits of his adversaries, is this time very severe toward the Antitrinitarian Zwicker, whom he defines uncompromisingly as an "an arrogant, inept man, childish and redundant, whom any school boy can easily refute."[144] The biting sarcasm that runs through the *Refutatio* reaches its high point in the concluding poem, in which Zwicker is mercilessly mocked. Unlike in the case of Wissowatius, an adversary whom Leibniz respects, recognizing the acuteness of his arguments, here Leibniz considers the difficulties Zwicker raises about the dogma of the Trinity to be absolutely insubstantial, and he even affirms: "I have never before seen a Socinian who is so barbarously stupid, so childishly ferocious."[145]

The origin of this violent reaction is the work by Zwicker mentioned by Leibniz in the first sentence: "Dan. Zwickeri Tractatus Tractatuum de Contradictione, qva sola cognita Ecclesiae collapsae, Romana, Graeca, Lutherana et Calviniana instaurari, et ad pacem mutuam adduci possint."[146] This is a brief text (eight pages in all) printed in 1666 without indication of the place and year of publication. Zwicker's thesis is that the church (whether Catholic or Protestant) upholds doctrines that contradict reason and lead to idolatry, namely, dogmas such as the Trinity and the Incarnation. Since, as even the Catholic and Protestant theologians admit, what is self-contradictory cannot be true and the mysteries of the Trinity and the Incarnation are problematic from a philosophical point of view, they must be rejected as false. The churches that uphold them, by making themselves guilty of contradiction and idolatry, are condemned to eternal damnation if they do not acknowledge their error and embrace the true faith.[147] Zwicker's argument to prove the contradictory nature of the dogma of the Trinity hinges on the concept of essence: "1. *In this, in turn, all Theologians should agree, that God is some nature or essence, and this is intelligent in the highest degree. . . . 2. The divine person, whatever it may be said to be, as it is intelligent, necessarily is an essence. . . . 3. That which is indivisible in itself and its essence, and* [is] *separated from anything else, is necessarily one.*"[148] Now, argues Zwicker, to say that in God there are three persons but only one essence means to say that the persons of the Trinity do not have an essence of their own. However, this would go against what is stated in point 2 regarding the divine persons, and consequently each person of the Trinity "will at the same time be and not be a person: which is contradictory."[149] In the same way, "if a singular essence, one in number, is said to be common to three persons, then it will both be and not be singular or one in number: which again is a manifest contradiction."[150]

Leibniz solves the problem at the root by replying dryly: "The essence of GOD cannot be called intelligent, but that by which God understands [id quo Deus intelligit]. Therefore a Person will also not be an essence, although it is intelligent. Action does not belong to the essence or nature, but to the suppositum or person."[151] The definitions of *Substantia, Suppositum,* and *Persona* given in a text that probably dates from 1668 (*De Transsubstantiatione*)[152] help to clarify Leibniz's answer. Leibniz writes: "I call Substance a Being subsisting through itself [*Ens per se subsistens*]. All the Scholastic philosophers agree that a Being subsisting per se is the same thing as a Suppositum. For Suppositum is a Substantial individual [*individuum Substantiale*] (just as a Person is a rational substantial individual) or some Substance in the individual. Moreover, the School commonly laid down that it is proper to the Suppositum that it is denominated by action; hence the Rule:

actions are proper to Supposita [*actiones sunt Suppositorum*]. From which it is clear that the Suppositum, Substance, and the Being subsisting per se, which are the same, are also rightly defined by the Scholastics: that which has the principle of action in itself, for otherwise it will not act but will be the instrument of an agent."[153] Therefore, substance is a being subsisting per se, coinciding, when considered in the individual, with the suppositum (= some substance in the individual). The suppositum, in its turn, is to be understood as the subject of actions (actions are proper to supposita, "actiones sunt suppositorum"). Now, Suppositum (or Substance or Being subsisting per se) is defined as "that which has the principle of action in itself." But what is the principle of action? Leibniz replies: substantial form or nature. In fact, he later writes: "From this furthermore it follows: Substantial Form is itself the principle of action. . . . The same sense of substantial form comes also from another principle of Aristotle and the Scholastics, so that the harmony may appear all the greater. For Substantial Form is nature, as Aristotle himself sufficiently hinted, and very noble Followers of his."[154]

Summing up, we can say that substance (or, considered in the individual, the suppositum) is a being subsisting through itself because it has in itself its own substantial form (= principle of action), unlike the case with accidents.[155]

Coming back to Leibniz's reply to Zwicker, it seems that in it Leibniz uses the term "essence" (or "nature") in the sense given above of "principle of action": it is said, in fact, that the "Essence of God" is "that by which God understands [id quo Deus intelligit]."[156] In turn, "person" coincides with "suppositum."[157] As such, although person is the subject of action, and though it has in itself the principle of action (= "essence" = "that by which it understands"), it is distinguished from the principle of action: "Therefore a Person will not be an essence although it is intelligent."[158] Once again the 'strategy of defense' is operative; according to it, the defender has only to 'distinguish,' 'concede,' or 'deny' with reference to the inferences of the adversary. In this case the contradiction is removed by the distinction between essence or nature understood as the principle of action (= "that by which God understands") and person or suppositum understood as the subject of action (= that which is intelligent). In this way the two starting premises of Zwicker's reasoning are denied: the first ("that God is some intelligent nature or essence")[159] because it is shown that the essence cannot be called "intelligent" (since it is not the subject of action but the principle of action), the second ("the divine person . . . is an essence")[160] because it is shown that person and essence do not coincide.

Having thus confuted the argument whereby Zwicker asserts several times that "the sentence regarding the Trinity . . . entails a contradiction in every

Philosophy,"[161] Leibniz contests also the interpretation given by his adversary to some passages taken from the works of Roberto Bellarmino (a Catholic) and Balthasar Meisner (a Lutheran). In these passages, according to Zwicker, the two theologians maintained that the Trinity and the Incarnation "are perplexing [*implicare*]" in philosophy,[162] which Zwicker takes as an admission of the contradictory nature of the dogmas in question. In Leibniz's opinion, this interpretation is erroneous, since both these authors are convinced that no article of faith can entail contradiction.[163] "Implicare in Philosophia" should therefore be understood as being problematic with respect to the ordinary laws of nature: "Just as it is perplexing in Philosophy for a heavy stone to hang in the air without any support: that is, it is problematic that this be done by the forces of nature . . . to be sure, when it is commonly said that something is false Philosophically, it is not said to be simply false, but it is said that it is false that it can be produced naturally."[164] Here already we find sketched out the argument in defense of the noncontradictory nature of the mysteries based on the distinction between the laws of nature and the eternal truths: the former, which depend on God's will, can be suspended by God when superior reasons overcome the general considerations of goodness and order that led to their choice; the latter are absolutely necessary, and no exceptions are possible. Therefore, the fact that in the case of the mysteries (as in the case of miracles) the laws of nature are suspended does not imply any contradiction of the eternal truths.[165]

3

The Inquiry into the Mind

"I therefore intend to compose the Elements of Mind [Elementa de Mente], just as Euclid did with regard to Magnitude and Shape, and Hobbes with regard to the Body or Motion."[1] So writes Leibniz in a brief "Discourse" entitled *De Usu et Necessitate Demonstrationum Immortalitatis Animae* (On the Use and Need of the Proofs of the Immortality of the Soul), sent to Duke Johann Friedrich together with his letter of 21 May 1671.[2] The promised *Elementa de Mente* (Elements of Mind), Leibniz goes on, "will be small in size, but great in worth."[3] In fact, besides containing the first principles of such sciences as ethics, jurisprudence, and natural theology, they will also have to serve to defend the mysteries of revealed theology against the charge of being contradictory.[4] The reason for this is that "they provide the hypothesis whereby all these phenomena or mysteries of faith can be salvaged, since it is not their truth that can be demonstrated, but their possibility (for, as the truth of the phenomena of nature depends on the senses, so the truth of these depends on revelation: and indeed, the task of justifying Revelation pertains to a separate doctrine to be evinced from the light of the Histories, regarding the Truth of the Christian Religion)."[5] The *Elementa de Mente* will therefore have to provide the basis for proving not the truth of the mysteries, which depends on revelation, but their possibility.[6] The importance of an investigation into the mind in connection with theology and, in particular, with the defense of revealed truths is repeatedly confirmed. Already in the *Demonstrationum Catholicarum Conspectus*, in fact, the idea of a work devoted to the mind appears among the *Prolegomena* of the *Demonstrationes Catholicae*.[7] The *Elementa philosophica de mente* are, moreover, included "in defense of true Theology" in the encyclopedic plan conceived by Leibniz between the fall of 1669 and the beginning of 1671 as a completion of the *Encyclopaedia* by Johann Heinrich Alsted.[8] In the first letter to Antoine Arnauld, dating from the beginning of November 1671, Leibniz again reiterates his intention to write the *Elementa de Mente*, which, among other things, ought to help in defending the mysteries, such as the Trinity and the Incarnation.[9]

Just how, in Leibniz's opinion, this investigation into the mind is connected with the mysteries becomes clear from a passage of *De Uso et Necessitate Demonstrationum Immortalitatis Animae*, in which the problem of the Trinity and the Incarnation is posed as follows: "In what way two minds can be compounded in one person, or, of the incarnation; in what way several persons can be compounded in one mind, or, of the Trinity."[10] As regards the Trinity, the connection stemming from the traditional recognition of the analogy between the mind and the Trinity is strengthened by the substitution, within the canonical formulation of the dogma of the Trinity, of the concept of mind for that of nature (or essence). The mystery of the Incarnation is, in its turn, connected with the investigation into the mind, on the basis of a reinterpretation of the traditional parallel between the union in Christ of the divine and human natures and the union in man of soul and body, in terms of the union in Christ of a perfect mind (the mind of God) with an imperfect mind (the human mind) paralleled by the union in man of mind and body.[11]

On the Incarnation of God or On the Hypostatic Union

The *Elementa de Mente* remained unfinished. Therefore, the doctrine regarding the mind developed during Leibniz's early period must be reconstructed on the basis of some fragmentary writings. One of these is a short text, probably composed between 1669 and 1670, to which Leibniz at first gave the title "De Incarnatione Filii DEI seu incarnatione Hypostatica [On the Incarnation of the Son of GOD or the Hypostatic incarnation]."[12] The investigation into the problem of the hypostatic union carried out in it, starting from the need to explain the mystery of the Incarnation, at the same time gives Leibniz an occasion for dealing more generally with the problem of the relation between mind and body. The text's contents thus go beyond the sphere of theological reflection on the mystery of the Incarnation, so much so that Leibniz later cancelled the original title.[13] The problem of the relation between mind and body is here solved in terms of a hypostatic union. This is a provisional solution, as is the explanation given of the mystery of the Incarnation: although it is not explicitly rejected, it does not appear to have been picked up later. If, therefore, *De Incarnatione Dei seu de Unione Hypostatica* is a passing phase in Leibniz's thought, it yet seems likely that in his mature thought there are still traces of this youthful conception. This hypothesis appears to be justified on the basis of the following considerations. Leibniz constantly repeats that Christ is not an "Ens per aggregationem [Being by aggregation]"[14] but enjoys a true unity, the unity of the person.[15] At the same time, also the reference to the analogy between the union in Christ of divine nature and human nature and the union in man of soul and body is kept constant.[16] Now, if this latter problem is solved by the doctrine of preestablished harmony, a similar doctrine should be able to be applied also to the case of the Incarnation. But wouldn't this bring us perilously close to the Nestorian heresy,[17] which Leibniz decidedly rejected?[18] In other words, would the unity of the person really be saved? Leibniz must have felt how problematical a solution of this kind was: it seems that there are no texts in which the doctrine of preestablished harmony is explicitly extended also to the case of the Incarnation.

On the other hand, in the last decade of his life, Leibniz himself, although continuing to defend his system of preestablished harmony as a means for explaining naturally what the followers of Descartes (that is, the occasionalists) explained by continual miracles, admitted that it does not exhaustively account for the union of body and soul. This occurs in his reply to some remarks by Father R. J. Tournemine published in the *Mémoires de Trévoux* in March 1704.[19] Leibniz writes: "I have only tried to account for the Phenomena, that is to say, the relationship one perceives between the Soul and the Body. But as the Metaphysical union added to it is not a Phenomenon, and has not even been given an intelligible notion, I have not taken it upon myself to find a reason for it. However, I do not deny that there is something of this nature."[20] The doctrine of preestablished harmony therefore explains only "the phenomena," not the metaphysical union that is added and that is not a phenomenon. The problem of what kind of unity is the unity of a human being, composed of soul and body, thus remains open, and the discussion regarding the "substantial bond," or *vinculum substantiale,* that developed in these same years between Leibniz and the Jesuit Bartholomew Des Bosses (1668–1735) is also an attempt at least to come closer to explaining the "Metaphysical Union" between soul and body.[21] In this correspondence with Des Bosses there is a significant passage concerning the Incarnation. Leibniz writes on 10 October 1712: "I am afraid that we cannot explain the mystery of the Incarnation and other things unless real bonds or unions are added."[22] Thus, in order that, in the case of Christ, as in the case of man, we may have a true unity and not a mere "aggregation," Leibniz feels the need for a *vinculum substantiale* (substantial bond) or *vincula realia* (real bonds). At this point one may ask whether the notion of vinculum substantiale does not contain within itself some trace of that concept of hypostatic union wherein the young Leibniz, reflecting on the Incarnation, glimpsed also a possible solution to the problem of the union between mind and body. It seems, in short, that we can find an attempt to account for the "Metaphysical Union" existing between soul and body in the early doctrine of the hypostatic union. This "Metaphysical Union" is not sufficiently explained by the system of preestablished harmony, and Leibniz continues to feel the need for it[23] even though, having come to the end of his life, he makes it plain that it is, in the final analysis, a mystery.[24]

The first scholar to draw attention to the *De Incarnatione Dei seu de Unione Hypostatica* was Willy Kabitz. He published Leibniz's fragment as an appendix to *Die Philosophie des jungen Leibniz*,[25] seeing it as one of the "pieces" to be used to reconstruct the uncompleted *Elementa de Mente*.[26] In discussing this short work by Leibniz, Kabitz takes into consideration the aspect concerning the mind-body relation, leaving in the background the problem of the Incarnation, the solution of which is the primary aim of the text. Here, instead, we shall turn our attention to this primary aspect of the work.

Leibniz defines the hypostatic union as "the action of a thing having in itself the principle of action immediately through another thing."[27] According to what is stated in *De Transsubstantiatione*,[28] a thing having the principle of action in itself coincides with a thing subsisting through itself (*res per se subsistens*), that is, a substance. Leibniz further states that there is a hypostatic union "in those things of which one perpetually acts on another in virtue of a peculiar action, or of which one is the immediate instrument of action of the other."[29] The subjects between which there can be hypostastic union are: "1) God and Mind, 2) Mind and Body, 3) Body and Body through a shared mind."[30] In fact, these three cases meet the conditions required for hypostatic union, which are listed later: "1.) The thing subsisting through itself or having in itself the principle of action, to which [something] is united. 2.) The other thing, whatever it is, that is united. 3.) The action of the subsisting [thing], through the united [thing], on a third thing, that is, the united [thing] must be an instrument of the subsisting [thing]. 4.)The immediacy of its action, that is, it must not act through another thing to which the same thing acted upon, and which was called the united to the first thing, is not united. For the united of the united is the united of the first thing."[31] Instead, the possibility of a hypostatic union between body and body is ruled out because the body is not a substance (= "res per se subsistens") and therefore the first of the conditions listed above is not met.[32]

Before going further, we should take a close look at the statement that the body is not a substance (expressed here in the words "No body subsists through itself"). This is, in fact, a considerable departure from the Cartesian doctrine of the *res extensa* as a corporeal substance distinct from the *res cogitans* (thinking substance). Once again, we have to turn to *De Transsubstantiatione*. From the definition of substance as "ens per se subsistens [being subsisting through itself]," or "that which has the principle of action in itself,"[33] Leibniz deduces that, if the body is a substance, then it must have in itself the principle of action, coinciding, in this case, with motion. The demonstration that motion is the proper action of the body is based on the identification of the body's essence with "esse in spatio [being in space]"[34]—a conception that is still very close to Descartes' notion, although Leibniz does not draw from this doctrine (which he later modified) the same conclusions as Descartes.[35] The text goes on to deny that the body by itself contains in itself the principle of motion: "No body, without mind concurring, has the principle of motion in itself. This is demonstrated in the first part of the Catholic Demonstrations, where the existence of God is demonstrated."[36] In reality, the demonstration Leibniz refers to here is only stated in the *Demonstrationum Catholicarum Conspectus*.[37] The proof is, instead, contained in one of the works that can be considered the fulfillment of part of the *Conspectus*: the abovementioned *Confessio Naturae contra Atheistas*. Leibniz identifies three main qualities in body: size, shape, and motion.[38] Now, if these qualities cannot be deduced from the definition of body, they cannot exist in bodies left to themselves; that is to say, bodies are not self-sufficient. Since every affection must have a reason, if this reason cannot be deduced from the thing itself, it will have to be deduced from something external.[39]

What, therefore, is the definition of body? Leibniz replies that it is "spatio inexistere [to exist in space]."[40] However, from the two terms constituting the definition (*spatium* and *inexistentia*) one of the three main qualities of the body, namely, motion, cannot be deduced or, to put it more precisely, in bodies "sibi relicta [left to themselves]" the *ratio* (the principle) of motion cannot be found.[41] It must therefore be sought in something other than the body, and this "other than the body" can, by definition, only be an incorporeal principle. This incorporeal principle, Leibniz explains in his letter to Jakob Thomasius of 20/30 April 1669, is *Mens* (Mind).[42]

Coming back to the reasoning of *De Transsubstantiatione*, from the demonstration that the body does not have the principle of motion in itself Leibniz can conclude that the body is not a substance but an accident.[43] Thus, starting from a definition of body that is close to that of Descartes, Leibniz does not conclude, like Descartes, that the res extensa is a corporeal substance distinct from a thinking substance: two substances that, albeit united in a human being, always remain two *res*. His solution is much closer to that of Aristotle, in which the soul (*mens*) is the form of the body. The body cannot exist by itself, just as an accident cannot exist by itself without a substance in which it inheres.[44] The body acquires the status of substance only if considered in its union with mind: the mind is, in fact, the principle of motion, and the body comes to have in itself the principle of its action only if it is joined to the mind. This seems to be the sense of the statements with which the text of *De Transsubstantiatione* continues: "8.) Whatever is taken with a concurring mind is Substance, without mind it is accident. Substance is union with the mind. Thus the Substance of the human body is union with the human mind. . . . 9.) Therefore the Substance of a body is union with a sustaining mind."[45] Besides excluding a hypostatic union between body and body, because the body is not a substance, in *De Incarnatione Dei* Leibniz also excludes as impossible a hypostatic union between two imperfect minds. Indeed, in this case another of the conditions required for hypostatic union would not be met: the immediacy of the action of the *unitum* (united).[46] The unitum (coinciding in this case with an "imperfect mind") could not be an immediate instrument of the "thing subsisting through itself" (coinciding again with an "imperfect mind") in that "an imperfect mind does not act outside itself except through the Body."[47]

This, however, is not true in the case of a perfect mind, which therefore may form a hypostatic union with an imperfect mind.[48] This clarification is very important: if such a union were not possible, also the Incarnation of the Son of God would not be possible. In this connection, we must first ask: Can there be a hypostatic union between God and bodies?[49] Leibniz replies in the negative.[50] The reason is that "God does not act on bodies, except by creating":[51] apart from destruction and creation, God does not act on bodies except by giving them motion, and, for Leibniz, this coincides with continuous creation.[52] Since therefore "there is no hypostatic union except through the action of one thing through another"[53] and the body cannot be an instrument of God's action because in creation the only one who acts is the one who creates,[54] it follows that there can be no hypostatic union between God and a body. The mind can instead be an instrument of God's action: through the mind that is united with him, God acts in bodies in a way different from the way he acts when he creates. When this happens, there is a hypostatic union between God and mind.[55] In this way it is possible to solve the problem of the Incarnation: if the body of Christ cannot be joined to God directly (since, as we have seen, a hypostatic union between God and bodies is impossible), it can nonetheless be joined to God through the mind. A trace of this conception seems to be found years later in *De Persona Christi*, where Leibniz distinguishes three natures in Christ: "In the incarnation there are three natures (Godhead, soul, flesh [deitas, anima, caro]) with one person."[56]

At this point, the objection arises that between the body of Christ and the divine nature there is thus no hypostatic union, since one of the conditions for it is the immediacy of the relation between the "uniens" (that is, the "thing subsisting through itself") and the "unitum." Leibniz replies: God and mind, joined hypostatically, form a single A; this single A, precisely because it includes also the mind, which functions as an "intermediate thing subsisting through itself," can act immediately on the body (B) and therefore be joined hypostatically to B;[57] in fact, "unitum uniti est unitum primi [the united of the united is the united of the first thing]."[58] The presupposition of this conclusion is one of the first statements of *De Incarnatione*: the statement, that is, that between mind and body there can be a hypostatic union. It is, in fact, only thanks to the hypostatic union of the body with the mind, which in its turn is, in the case of Christ, hypostatically joined to God, that the Incarnation can be explained.[59]

Leibniz, convinced that, after many vain efforts, he has finally solved the problem of the hypostatic union,[60] ends his work by polemically turning against the most dangerous adversaries of the dogma of the Incarnation, the Socinians: "It should be noted that the doctrine of the Socinians is far more dangerous than that of the Catholics. For the Catholic Church worships only one God, nor him for any other reason than that He is the Most High. Even though it recognizes in him a triple way of subsisting, it does not in this way either divide up or multiply God. On the contrary, the Socinians worship one they hold to be a creature, whom they do not consider to be the most high God, and whom they think is distinct in his essence from the most high God; therefore they have two Gods. They worship a mere man, we God inhabiting a man."[61] Secure of the position he has just gained, thanks to which he feels he has overcome the Socinian objection regarding the impossibility of the Incarnation, Leibniz seems not to want to lose the chance to revert to his adversaries the charge of idolatry that they normally bring against those who believe in the Trinity. Here we can perceive the echo of the contemporary controversies with Andreas Wissowatius and Daniel Zwicker. In particular, we have seen that Zwicker, in his *Tractatus Tractatuum de Contradictione*, accuses the churches that worship the Trinity of the sin of idolatry, which leads to perdition. Leibniz now replies that the Socinian doctrine is instead much more dangerous, in that Jesus Christ, who is considered a mere creature, is nonetheless accorded divine honors. It is therefore not the worshipers of a God who is One and Three that have more than one god but the Socinians, who worship a mere man.

The Comparison between the Trinity and the Mind

Among the preparatory writings for the *Elementa de Mente* are two fragments, datable to between the spring and autumn of 1671, in which the Trinity-Mind parallel is discussed.[62] Both presuppose the new doctrine of motion that Leibniz formulated in 1670 and 1671.[63] This doctrine marks a turning point also in the conception of body and mind, thanks to the introduction of the concept of *conatus*.[64] In his letter to Arnauld of early November 1671, Leibniz presents the following order of sciences: "I saw that Geometry, or the philosophy of place [philosophia de loco], built the steps to the philosophy of motion or body, and the philosophy of motion led to the science of mind."[65] As Leibniz affirms in *De Usu et Necessitate Demonstrationum Immortalitatis Animae,* the geometrical doctrines on the point and angle and the doctrine of motion will therefore be the key to explaining the nature of thought with the same clarity and distinctiveness as in geometrical proofs.[66] In fact, Leibniz says in the letter to the duke of Hanover to which this writing is attached: "My Demonstrations are based on the difficult Doctrine of point, instant, indivisibles and *conatus;* then just as the Actions of the Body consist in motion, so the Actions of the mind consist in *conatus,* or the very smallest point, as I may say, of motion[.]"[67] First of all, therefore, we must dwell on these doctrines in order to understand the theory regarding the mind developed by Leibniz in these years, and consequently be in a position to grasp the meaning of the Mind-Trinity analogy he puts forward.

Leibniz derives the concept of conatus from Hobbes, who writes in *De Corpore:* "Let us define *conatus as motion through less space and time than what is given, that is, determined, or, if you wish, assigned whether by exposition or by number, that is, through a point.*"[68] This definition corresponds to Leibniz's conception of conatus as "motion in the very smallest or in the point."[69] In one of the *fundamenta praedemonstrabilia* (predemonstrable foundations) of the *Theoria Motus Abstracti* (Theory of Abstract Motion), he states: "*Conatus* is to motion, as the point is to space, or one to the infinite, for it is the beginning and end of motion."[70] Conatus is, in the instant, what constitutes the beginning of motion in time. No conatus without motion lasts more than an instant, except in minds. This last clarification, again contained in the *Theoria Motus Abstracti,* is of fundamental importance. Here, says

Leibniz, the way is opened for reaching the true distinction between mind and body,[71] and he rightly points out the substantial novelty of this distinction, especially with respect to Descartes' doctrine. This new conception of mind and body is, in fact, no longer marked by the dualism of res extensa and res cogitans, since even the body can be understood as "momentary mind, that is, lacking *memory*."[72] What does Leibniz mean by this? The difference between mind and body lies in the capacity to *remember*, that is, the capacity to conserve all the conatus, comparing and mutually harmonizing them: "The retention of all the *conatus*, indeed of the comparisons in them, that is, of all states of it. This makes the mind."[73] Thanks to this faculty (possessed by the mind and not by the body) of conserving, comparing, and harmonizing all the conatus, these last beyond the instant, but without there being motion: "In the mind all *conatus* last. . . . *Anything which at some time or another has conatus without motion, is mind.*"[74] Thought is nothing but "the sense of comparison, or more briefly, the sense of many things at the same time or one in many [sensus plurium simul aut unum in multis],"[75] and this "unity of the manifold" corresponds to *Harmonia*. While, in fact, motion is the composition of conatus, but only of the last ones, Harmonia (made possible by the mind) is the composition of all the previous conatus; it is precisely the fact that in the mind all the conatus, not just the most recent ones, are taken into consideration that makes the difference between the actions of the body and those of the mind.[76] In order for there to be sensation, pleasure, and pain, it is necessary for there to be the conservation (= *retentio, memoria*) of opposing conatus, and their comparison and composition in Harmonia. Since the body lacks this capacity to "hold in the memory," to remember, it also lacks the sensation of its actions and passions, and thus lacks thought.[77] This is the meaning of its being "momentary mind, that is, lacking memory," a statement Leibniz reiterates at the beginning of November 1671 in his letter to Arnauld.[78]

At this point we find another important stance that differentiates his conception of the body from that of Descartes. After having enunciated the concept of body as *mens momentanea* (momentary mind), Leibniz certainly could no longer accept the identification of the body with esse in spatio (being in space)[79] (although, as we have seen, he did not draw from it the dualistic consequences of Descartes): the essence of the body, he now says, is not extension but motion. He arrives at this conclusion by admitting the existence of the void, from which it is deduced that the essence of bodies does not consist in extension, since empty space, although extended, is necessarily different from bodies. The essence of the body consists, rather, in motion, since there is no body without motion ("there is no body at rest"), and motion cannot be deduced from the notion of space, as the latter is reduced to mere extension.[80]

Even after developing the concept of conatus, Leibniz still maintains the idea that bodies *taken in themselves* (or, to use the words of the *Confessio Naturae,* "sibi relicta [left to themselves]")[81] are not sufficient unto themselves. In fact, the principle of motion is the conatus, which constitutes the action proper to the mens.[82] Bodies can indeed be considered "mind," but only a "momentary," "instantaneous" mind, which has its continuity only in the real mind. Therefore, the new advances in physics do not change, but rather confirm, the metaphysical intuition underlying the *Conspectus,*[83] the *Confessio Naturae, De Transsubstantiatione,* and *De Incarnatione Dei:* the principle of bodies is an incorporeal principle, because bodies are not sufficient unto themselves.

In this context, also the preparatory fragments for the *Elementa de Mente* in which the parallel between the Trinity and the mind is indicated become clearer. In *Trinitas. Mens,* the two are unequivocally linked even in the title. Although extremely short, this note by Leibniz condenses several interesting points in a few lines. In the first part of the fragment three triads are presented: the first referring to "body" and "world," the second and third to "Mind" and "God":[84]

Trinity. Mind

BODY. WORLD.	MIND. GOD	
Space	Intellect	Being [Esse]
Shape	Imagination	Knowing [Scire]
Motion	Will, Power	Doing [Agere] or Endeavoring [Conari]

A *vestigium* of the Trinity (to use an expression of Saint Augustine's) can be recognized also in bodies or in the "world," in line with what has already been said both in the *Demonstrationum Catholicarum Conspectus* and in the *Defensio Trinitatis.*[85] The first element of the triad identified by Leibniz as the indication of a "shadowing" (*adumbratio*)[86] of the Trinity in bodies nevertheless undergoes some variations. In the *Defensio Trinitatis* we find size—shape—motion.[87] These are the three "prime qualities" of bodies spoken of in the *Confessio Naturae.*[88] They reappear as characterizing bodies in the letter to Thomasius of 20/30 April 1669[89] and in *De Rationibus Motus* (probably composed between August and September 1669).[90] In the *Conspectus,* Leibniz instead advances the triad matter—shape—motion,[91] which would seem to be the equivalent of the triad space—shape—motion, reread in the light of a fragment entitled *De Materia Prima.*[92] Prime matter, which in itself has neither motion nor form, receives motion from a mind and through motion takes on a form."[93] It is identified with space: "Prime matter and space are the same thing."[94] If space or prime matter can and must be conceptually distinct from the body in that they are only "the possibility of bodies"[95] and not yet body (lacking in themselves motion and shape), in reality, as pure *spatium* or *materia prima* "left to themselves" they do not exist.[96] Therefore, space, although in a certain way distinct from shape and motion, cannot exist without them. In bodies, space—shape—motion, while different from one another, cannot exist one without the other, and in this unity in diversity that characterizes the whole bodily world Leibniz sees an "adumbratio" of the Trinity.

As regards the two triads relating to the mind and to God, Leibniz seems to indicate with the first triad the three faculties of the mind, while the second recalls more directly the triad *esse—nosse—velle* with which Saint Augustine identifies the *imago Trinitatis* (image of the Trinity) in the human soul.[97] In each of the three triads, the third element refers to action.

In the second part of the fragment Leibniz develops the meaning of the analogia Trinitatis represented by the mind, indicating a series of aspects that the mind and God have in common. The first of these is indestructibility, on which Leibniz bases immortality: "Just as, when the creatures are destroyed, God remains, so when the body is destroyed the Mind remains."[98] Yet, even in their similarity, there is an important difference between the created mind and God. The indestructibility of the mind is not absolute: even if minds cannot perish naturally, as happens with bodies, one cannot exclude the possibility that they, like all creatures, may be annihilated by God.

The fragment goes on: "And as God thinks those things that are not perceived by any sense, for they follow from his nature, so also does the Mind."[99] "Those things that are not perceived by any sense" would seem to be the eternal verities: necessary and immutable truths, because grounded in the divine nature itself, they are grasped a priori, that is, independently of the senses and experience, also by the human mind.[100] The parallel between the mind and God is later brought forward again, this time in reference to "things existing in act": "As the thinking Mind has intellect and will or Love of things existing in act, so God [has] word [verbum] and love."[101] The reference to the mystery of the Trinity is clear: just as in the *Defensio Trinitatis* Leibniz proposes the analogy between the mind and the Trinity by recalling the diversity in unity of "the thinking being, the thing thought, and the act of thinking [intelligens, intellectum, et intellectio], and what coincide with these: power, knowledge, and will [posse, scire, velle],"[102] here God and mind, thinking what exists in act, recall the first person of the Trinity (*intelligens*); "intellectus" and "word" refer to the second person;

and "will or Love" refers to the third. God and mind, moreover, share the need to think themselves as existing in act: "If, indeed, God did not think himself existing in act, he would certainly think, but he would not perceive [nec perciperet], nor would he be happy. Just as it cannot be but that God thinks himself being in act; so it cannot be but that the mind thinks itself being in act."[103] Here we are very close to Descartes' *cogito ergo sum:* in the awareness of thinking is implicit the awareness of being. But the influence of Saint Augustine and his cogito is even clearer.[104] Throughout the fragment, moreover, one notes a heavy debt to the Augustinian tradition that identifies, in the mind, an image of the Trinity, since the mind *is, knows* itself, and *loves* itself.[105] In the concluding part of *Trinitas. Mens,* Leibniz sums up in a few words both the greatness and the limits of the analogy between the mind and God. The great simile that makes the mind the most perfect image of God to be found in all creation stops only when faced with the insuperable difference between a creature (characterized, qua creature, by finitude) and the Creator: "Mind and God differ only in that one is finite and the other is infinite."[106]

As I indicated earlier, a meaningful assertion of the analogy between the mind and the Trinity is found also in *De Conatu et Motu, Sensu et Cogitatione.*[107] In the last part of the text, Leibniz advances his explanation of circular motion:

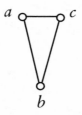

> I therefore say that if a body *a* has a tendency to move [conatur] at the same time in three straight lines *ab, cb, ac,* two of which are concurrent in a point *b,* namely *ab, cb,* and they also make a smaller angle than toward a third line *ac,* then body *a* will be moved in a circular motion.[108]

If, instead, the triangle *efg* is an equilateral triangle, the motion is not circular, as the sufficient reason for *e, f,* or *g* to be taken as the center of motion is lacking.[109] Leibniz asks what happens at this point. Even if there is no circular motion, there must be some effect and action ("effectus atque actio quaedam").[110] While the case of triangle *abc* corresponds to the behavior of bodies, the case of triangle *efg* corresponds to the mind, about which Leibniz writes in *De Conatu et Motu:* "Anything which at same time or another has conatus without motion, is mind[.]"[111] He then explains what "some action" consists of: "*E* and *f* will have a tendency to move [*conabuntur*] around a center *g*, *e* and *g* around *f*, *f* and *g* around *e*. Therefore, there will be that which, on account of harmony resulting from resistance, would be in a sense a conatus around the center of the Triangle. From that moment the composition of the conatus in a single motion will cease, and the composition of harmonies will follow."[112] This is the action proper to the mind: the composition in harmony of contrary conatus. The example of triangle *efg* too is illustrated by a figure. It is here that Leibniz explicitly mentions the analogy between the mind and the Trinity, indicating the *Mens* as *symbolum Trinitatis:*[113]

Mind symbol of the Trinity

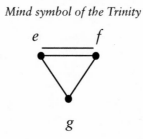

In what sense is the mind a symbol of the Trinity? It is easy to see, behind this affirmation, a reference to the Augustinian tradition, which takes on new resonance thanks to the specific doctrine of the mind elaborated by Leibniz in this period. In a specifically Leibnizian sense, the mind is a symbol of the Trinity because of a peculiar characteristic it possesses: the recomposition of unity in diversity. As we have seen, in one of the fragments that make up *De Conatu et Motu, Sensu et Cogitatione*, Leibniz defines thought as the perception of many things together, or the unity of the manifold: "Thinking is nothing but the sense of comparison, or more succinctly, the sense of many things simultaneously or one in many."[114] Immediately below, it is the mind itself that Leibniz qualifies as unity of the manifold, where the unity of the manifold or diversity compensated by identity is equivalent to Harmonia and appears to be founded directly in God.[115] Later on Leibniz explains more clearly how the unity of the manifold is realized in thought: "When I think immediately I think myself and something else. That is: when I think immediately I perceive [*sentio*]. Indeed, when I think immediately I think many things, and one in many. Whatever it is that I think, that is what I perceive: certainly I perceive myself and something else [*me sentire et aliud*], or diversity."[116] At this point, however, the objection arises that the mind that thinks grasps the object as other (*aliud*). How, then, can one speak of the Trinity, where the "thing thought" is a divine person and not something "other" than God? In developing this investigation into the act of thinking in later years, Leibniz advances, as the example that most closely approaches the unity in diversity of God, who is One and Three, the mind that thinks itself: in the case of self-awareness, the subject and object of thought, the thinker and the thing thought, coincide.[117]

4

The Relation between
Revelation and Knowledge

In the mysteries, "we also try to *elevate* what we understand of the ordinary development of Creatures to something more sublime that can correspond to them in relation to the Divine Nature and Power, without being able to conceive in them anything sufficiently distinct and sufficiently appropriate to form an entirely intelligible Definition. It is also for the same reason that, down here, one cannot perfectly account for these Mysteries, nor understand them entirely. There is [in them] something more than mere Words, but nevertheless one cannot obtain an exact explanation of the Terms."[1] So Leibniz writes in 1708 in replying to Father Tournemine.[2] These few lines seem to sum up very well Leibniz's position concerning the limits and the tasks of reason as regards the mysteries of faith. In the case of the mysteries, the finite intellect of human beings cannot reach a "completely intelligible definition," coinciding with adequate knowledge. On the other hand, even if there is no exact explanation of the terms and consequently humans cannot "comprehend" the mysteries, there must be a certain degree of intelligibility if statements regarding the mysteries are not to be mere noises. In short, the element of unintelligibility present in the mysteries must be joined with an element of intelligibility. Only in this way can they be considered truths above reason, that is, truths that surpass the limits of human reason but are nonetheless grasped by reason as *truths* and hence part of the cognitive sphere.

This conception of the relation between faith and reason, revelation and knowledge that Leibniz left at the end of his life started to take shape already in his early years. In particular, it is to be found in the two texts examined in this chapter: the *Commentatiuncula de Judice Controversiarum*[3] (Little Commentaries on the Judge of Controversies) and *De Demonstratione Possibilitatis Mysteriorum Eucharistiae* (On the Demonstration of the Possibility of the Mysteries of the Eucharist).[4]

Marcelo Dascal, in commenting on these writings,[5] identifies in them two different solutions to the problem of the mysteries, understood as attempts to rescue both the element of intelligibility and the element of unintelligibility of mysteries. In the *Commentatiuncula,* however, Leibniz seems to concede too much to unintelligibility. The mysteries, in fact, would end up being assimilated to what Leibniz was later to call "confused knowledge":[6] a degree of knowledge that does not sufficiently guarantee the possibility of its object, that is, a confused understanding of some complex term or expression that could hide a contradiction, in which case the alleged knowledge would turn out to be no knowledge at all (as happens, for example, in the case of the expression "square circle").[7] By contrast, *De Demonstratione Possibilitatis Mysteriorum Eucharistiae* seems to concede too much to intelligibility, consequently leading to complete comprehensibility. In fact, in Dascal's view, in order to avoid the abovementioned danger proper to confused knowledge, Leibniz tries to give a proof of the possibility of the mysteries that would be like an a priori proof: to see whether a given combination of concepts is possible, it would be necessary to provide an analysis of the object in question that leads to a distinct knowledge of all its components.[8] According to Dascal, Leibniz reached an equilibrium between the two aspects at the end of his life, in the "Preliminary Discourse" to the *Theodicy.*[9] Here the novelty lies in the fact that the guarantee of noncontradiction of the content of the mysteries stems not from the proof of their possibility but from the possibility of defending them against objections. Concerning this penetrating analysis by Dascal, it should be pointed out that the solution advanced, which is capable of guaranteeing, thanks to the adoption of the 'strategy of defense,' both the element of intelligibility and the element of unintelligibility present in the mysteries, was not reached by Leibniz only at the end of his life, in the *Theodicy.* On the contrary, it is clearly present in his early period, above all in the argumentative procedure adopted in the *Defensio Trinitatis,*[10] during the same years in which Leibniz wrote the *Commentatiuncula de Judice Controversiarum* and *De Demonstratione Possibilitatis Mysteriorum Eucharistiae.* Nor is this all: even in the *Commentatiuncula* there is a 'corrective' aimed at avoiding the dangers of confused knowledge—a corrective that, as we shall see, implicitly entails the 'strategy of defense.'

The Balance of Reason and the Norm of the Text:
The Debate Concerning the Judge in Controversial Matters

The *Commentatiuncula de Judice Controversiarum, seu Trutinâ Rationis et Normâ Textus* were probably written in the years 1669 to 1671. Although finished, the essay was not published during Leibniz's life. It deals with a problem that was the subject of lively debate at the time: the problem relating to the determination of the last judge of appeal in controversies. Who is the last judge, legitimately delegated to put an end to a controversial question? In this work, Leibniz tackles the problem in reference both to questions regarding religious controversies and to worldly questions. However, the second part of the title ("seu Trutinâ Rationis et Normâ Textus [or of the Balance of Reason and the Norm of the Text]") already indicates that the original interest was in religious controversies, which hinged on the question of whether final judgment should lie with reason or with the text of the holy scriptures. Most of the work is indeed dedicated to the solution of this problem.

As I mentioned above, Leibniz's essay on the judge of controversies is part of a more general debate going on in his times.[11] In particular, it should be related to the discussion aroused by the anonymous publication in Amsterdam of two controversial works: *Philosophia S. Scripturae Interpres* (Philosophy the Interpreter of the Holy Scripture) (1666) by Lodewijk Meyer[12] and the *Tractatus Theologico-Politicus* (1670) by Spinoza.[13] The former work, erroneously attributed to Spinoza, was reissued in 1673 together with the *Tractatus Theologico-Politicus* under the general title *Danielis Heinsii P. P. Operum Historicorum Collectio Prima. Editio Secunda, priori editione multo emendatior et auctior accedunt quaedam hactenus inedita* (Leiden).[14] Although there is certainly a connection between the two works,[15] the theses upheld, respectively, by Spinoza and by Meyer are very different. For Spinoza, revelation is on a plane different from that of rational knowledge: faith and philosophy, having different foundations and aims, are completely independent of one another, and consequently scripture should be interpreted only by reference to the scriptures themselves.[16] Instead, Meyer tackles the question of the interpretation of scripture, taking a position decidedly in favor of philosophy (or reason).[17] Scripture is obscure and ambiguous;[18] the balance of truth,[19] the norm of interpretation, must be reason, since it is "the true, certain, and indubitable understanding of things."[20] Reason therefore has the last word on controversial doctrinal points,[21] contrary to what is maintained by the Roman Church, which considers itself the judge and norm of interpretation, and the position held by Protestants, who make scripture itself the only infallible norm of interpretation.[22] Meyer, however, is careful to differentiate his position from that of the Socinians and Arminians (or Remonstrants), who in his opinion are still too moderate as regards the use of reason in the interpretation of Holy Writ.[23] Referring explicitly to the Cartesian method of clarity and distinction,[24] he insists on the function of absolute judge assumed by reason as the "touchstone" by which both the clear and the obscure passages of scripture should be examined.[25]

Such a precise stance did not fail to inflame passions, setting off a hot debate that pitted "Rational" theologians against "Antirational" ones, as Pierre Bayle called them in his lively and ironical presentation of the affair in chapter CXXX of his *Réponse aux Questions d'un Provincial* (Rotterdam 1704–1707). In particular, Ludwig van Wolzogen[26] attacked Meyer in his *De scripturarum interprete adversus exercitatorem paradoxum libri duo* (Utrecht 1668)—a work destined in its turn to give rise to controversy,[27] inasmuch as in it Wolzogen (according to his attackers) shares the basic rationalism of *Philosophia S. Scripturae Interpres,* despite his apparent confutation of the interpretative rules proposed by Meyer.[28]

Leibniz's essay is directly related not only to the works of Meyer and Wolzogen (explicitly mentioned in the *Commentatiuncula de Judice Controversiarum*),[29] and the reading of Spinoza's *Tractatus Theologico-Politicus,* but also to the writings of two authoritative representatives of the Catholic camp in the seventeenth century: the brothers Adrian and Peter van Walenburch.[30] They were the authors of numerous polemical works against the Protestants; their treatises were collected by Peter in two volumes, published in Cologne in 1670 under the respective titles *Tractatus Generales de Controversiis Fidei* and *Tractatus Speciales, de Controversiis Fidei.*[31] The first of these treatises (*Examen Principiorum Fidei*) considers, respectively, the position of the Protestants and that of the Catholics on some questions regarding Holy Writ, summarized as follows: "The Protestants hold by way of principle that: 1. *Scripture alone is sufficient to prove the articles of faith. 2. There is a true interpretation of Scripture that proves faith. . . .* Catholics hold that there is only one principle of faith: *the Word of God as taught by the Church. . . .* The common principle is: *The doctrine of the Christians of the early centuries, as it is found in the books of the Holy Fathers and the ancient Councils, is uncorrupted, at least as regards the necessary articles.*"[32]

The van Walenburchs object that scripture alone does not suffice to determine which are the articles of faith needed for salvation, as is proved by the fact that the Protestants themselves do not agree on them.[33] On the contrary, it is necessary to have a last judge, namely, the Catholic Church, to guarantee the correct determination of the articles needed for salvation, a judge authorized to take a final decision in controversial cases.[34] According to the two theologians, the Protestants "think that one and the same thing is judge, norm, rule, and measure. . . . We do not deny that Scripture is the norm and rule for deciding controversies of faith. But [we object] because the Protestants want the scripture *alone* to be the norm and rule of faith."[35] Even more clearly, in the *Compendium Controversiarum Particularium,* the van Walenburchs reiterate: "Everyone knows that the rule is one thing, and the laborer or artisan is another: the law is one thing, the judge another. Those who say that *Scripture alone is the judge of Controversies* confuse the law with the judge."[36] The Catholic principle of "the Word of God as taught by the Church,"[37] on the other hand, does not mean that human beings act as the judges of the Word of God; also for Catholics the true meaning of God's Word is revealed by the Holy Spirit, who is present in the church.[38]

These very same problems are faced by Leibniz in the first part of the *Commentatiuncula de Judice Controversiarum,* where first of all he underlines the urgency of the matter of the judge of controversies at that particular moment in history, lacerated by religious divisions and quarrels.[39] Leibniz traces a basic, broad distinction between the position of the Catholic Church and that of the Protestants, who in this case are united more by their separation from Rome than by a common doctrine regarding the interpretation of the scriptures and the judge of controversies: "(§ 3.) To be sure, the *Roman Church* maintains that there is need of some visible, infallible judge, so that controversies can be brought to an end, and there may be once and for all an end to disputes; and this pertains to God's providence, that he would not seem utterly to have abandoned the cause of his people, that is, the Church. (§ 4.) Regarding the Protestants, that is, those who seceded from the Roman Church, some are *textual,* some *mixed,* others *rational.*"[40]

Leibniz's attention is turned to the definition of these three different Protestant positions, starting from that of the Textuals (*Textuales*), which he undoubtedly views sympathetically: "*Textuals* are those who establish that the judge of controversies is the text itself of the Holy Scripture; even if others admirably criticize this position, yet it seems to me that they are wrong in doing so. For they maintain that the text of the Holy Scripture should not be made the interpreter of itself, nor can it be said to be a judge of religious controversies any more than the writing of laws is sufficient in a Republic, unless interpreters or judges are established who apply them to individual cases."[41] In the position of those who oppose the Textuals, it is easy to recognize the objection of the van Walenburch brothers: whoever makes the scriptures the sole judge of controversies confuses the law with the judge, who is someone who has to interpret the rule and apply it to concrete cases. Leibniz's reply is very decisive and is based on the conviction that the fundamental articles of faith, necessary to salvation, are contained in the text *in terminis,* that is, in a clear and evident way: "(§. 6.) So they argue, but captiously. For I confess that the text itself is not sufficient for deciding exactly the questions regarding its meaning, unless other subsidiary things are brought forward. And yet I say that the text itself is sufficient for all questions of religion pertaining to faith. But is this not a contradiction? Not at all. For the questions that are of faith, or pertain to the foundation of salvation, must not be derived from the text as a result, but must be contained in it *in terminis.*"[42]

The rule that follows seems to indicate Leibniz's adherence to the doctrine that sees in the distinction between fundamental and nonfundamental articles of faith the way to overcome religious altercations: "(§. 7.) If this rule is held to: *nothing is to be admitted as being known to be necessary to salvation, except what is contained in terminis in the Holy Scripture,* then all questions regarding the saving faith will be made easier, and consequently scripture will be the judge of all controversies necessary to salvation."[43] Precisely because the fundamental articles of faith, needed for salvation, are contained unequivocally in the scriptures, it suffices to refer to them. The van Walenburchs' objection, which distinguishes between the law (coinciding with the scriptures) and the interpreter, only holds good for those questions not already decided in terminis in the law itself. But, repeats Leibniz, this is not the case of the fundamental articles.[44] The adversaries point out, however, that even in the religious field there are questions left undecided by the scriptures, such as, for example, those regarding marriage and divorce.[45] Behind Leibniz's answer we can once again see the doctrine of the distinction between fundamental and nonfundamental articles of faith: "I reply that these questions do not concern faith, but customs; they are not theoretical, but practical; we are not told to believe them, but to carry them out."[46] In such practical matters, continues Leibniz, registering on this point his disagreement with the Textuals, it is not scripture that is the judge of controversies.[47]

The real problem, however, arises with regard to other questions that are not of a practical nature: the Trinity, the nature and person of Christ, the Eucharist, and predestination.[48] Leibniz reiterates that "in these things no proposition is to be admitted as being of faith unless it is contained *in terminis* in the Holy Scripture translated verbatim from the sources[.]"[49] But the difficulty lies precisely in deciding whether these articles of faith are, or are not, contained in the scriptures and whether or not they are necessary for salvation. This is where the conflict arises: between Trinitarians and Anti-trinitarians regarding the translation and interpretation of the passages of scripture in which the Trinity and the divine nature of Christ are said to be asserted; and between Catholics and Protestants regarding the meaning to be given to the passages in which the Eucharist is established and those said to uphold the doctrine of predestination. In particular, the Trinity and the Incarnation are dogmas of central importance in the faith of the church, and yet, according to their deniers, there is insufficient evidence of them in the scriptures. The adversaries of the Textuals point out that the rigorous application of the rule (reproposed also by Leibniz) that "nothing is to be admitted as being known to be necessary to salvation, except what is contained *in terminis* in the Holy Scripture,"[50] may lead to an arbitrary reduction of the fundamental articles of faith needed for salvation. Indeed, they say that this is exactly what happened, opening the way to Antitrinitarianism.

Leibniz, convinced that "the Holy Scripture much more favors the Trinity and is sometimes violently twisted by the Anti-Trinitarians,"[51] first tackles the problem from a philological point of view.[52] A preliminary question discussed is, in fact, that of the authenticity of the scriptures, and the discussions of the Trinity are an eloquent example of how this is one of the decisive issues; one of the main arguments of the Antitrinitarians, in fact, is their rejection of the authenticity of the scriptural passages in which the Trinity is most clearly asserted. It is therefore a question, first of all, of arriving at a philologically correct version of the biblical text, starting from some fixed points on which all versions agree,[53] and gradually reaching agreement on doubtful passages. In this context section 16 of the *Commentatiuncula* is particularly interesting, since it indicates a first important task of reason.[54] The starting point is the admission that the scriptures cannot be the arbiter of their own authenticity: although the Bible claims to be the Word of God, the veracity of this assertion must be proved from other sources. In fact, if a self-testimony of authenticity contained in the text were sufficient, there would be no way of distinguishing the divinely inspired Word of God from the numerous pseudo-revelations. It is at this point that reason intervenes: through historical research and philological analysis, it has the task of judging not the content of the revelation but the authenticity of the text.

The question, however, is not limited to a correct historical-philological reconstruction. Providing the correct form of the text has been determined, there remains the problem of its interpretation, that is, the problem of the meaning to be assigned to the propositions contained in the text.[55] While any judgment on the authenticity of the scriptures does not directly involve the content of revelation, there is also a second important task of reason, which does involve the content of revelation. Reason has a role to play also in the sphere of faith, because faith is not a mechanical repetition of empty sounds, of meaningless formulas that one does not understand at all, but a form of knowing endowed with a cognitive value. The object of faith is not the words but the meaning of the words ("fides est sensûs, non vocum"). In order to be able to believe, one must therefore, to some extent, know what is being said, that is, one must to some degree understand the meaning of the words uttered. "For indeed we do not know what he said if we keep only to the words, ignoring their force and power." The justification of such assertions is based on a conception of truth as the conformity of a proposition to reality (or, in Thomas Aquinas's terms, as *adaequatio rei et intellectus*) in which understanding to some extent what the words mean is an indispensable preliminary condition for one to be able to speak of truth. Now, writes Leibniz, "Faith is believing. Believing is to hold as true. Truth is not of words but of things [Fides est credere. Credere est verum putare. Veritas est non verborum sed rerum]; for whoever holds something to be true, thinks he grasps the thing according to what the words signify, but no one can do this, unless he knows what the words mean or at least thinks about their meaning."[56] That is to say, to hold as true, according to the abovementioned conception of truth, means to hold that things are as the propositions say they are, and no one can do this without knowing what the words mean or without thinking at least about what they mean. In short, there must be a certain degree of intelligibility of the revealed propositions in order for them to qualify as *truth*.

At this point, however, the problem of faith in all its ramifications is posed, for faith is certainly a form of knowing, but a form of knowing *sui generis*, inasmuch as it surpasses the limits of human reason. This is, substantially, the problem of the mysteries: if, in order to believe, it is necessary to understand the meaning of what is said, how is it possible to have faith in propositions that express the mysteries if they are by definition beyond the capacity of comprehension of finite human reason? Although aware of the difficulty of this passage, Leibniz believes, nonetheless, that there is a solution. In fact, in sections 21 and 22 he writes:

> (§ 21.) This is a very hard problem, but not an insoluble one. For I answer that it is not always necessary for faith to know what sense of the words is true as long as we understand it, nor do we positively reject it, but rather leave it in doubt even though we might be inclined toward some other [sense]. Indeed, it suffices that we believe in the first place that whatever is contained in the meanings, is true, and this first and foremost in the mysteries in which

the practice does not change, whatever the meaning may finally be. (§ 22.) Nonetheless, it is necessary that the intellect should not fall nakedly over the words, like a parrot,[57] but that some sense should appear before it, albeit a general and confused one, and almost disjunctive, as the country fellow, or other common man, has of nearly all theoretical things.[58]

The solution, therefore, is based on the fact that it is not necessary to have a clear and distinct (or even adequate) knowledge of the meaning of the mysteries.[59] For one to be able to believe legitimately in them, Leibniz seems to indicate two conditions: 1) one must have at least a confused knowledge of the meaning of the mysteries, like the knowledge that the man in the street has of theoretical matters; 2) the mysteries must not be positively rejected, so that the presumption of truth can be saved. This latter condition seems to represent the necessary 'corrective,' aimed at avoiding the risks inherent in any legitimization of faith in the mysteries based only on a confused knowledge, which, as we have seen, would not sufficiently guarantee the possibility of its object, that is, its noncontradictory nature.[60] By laying it down that the content of the mysteries, besides having to present a certain degree of intelligibility,[61] must not be positively rejected,[62] Leibniz seems to resort to the 'strategy of defense.' In so doing he opens the way to the third basic task of reason in the sphere of faith: to ensure that the propositions that are the object of faith are not self-contradictory. In other words, reason, by defending them from objections, is called upon to guarantee that the mysteries do not contain any proven contradiction.[63]

At this point, however, Leibniz takes a further step forward. Not only does the man in the street have only a confused knowledge of the terms that appear in theoretical propositions, but philosophers too (here represented by the Scholastics and Aristotle) make ample use of the term *cause,* for example, without being more able to give, in this broad sense, a definition of it in which even more obscure terms do not appear.[64] From this, Leibniz draws his consequences as regards the mysteries: if even in philosophy one uses notions of which one does not have a distinct knowledge and of which one is unable to give a definition without this involving a delegitimization of philosophical discourse, then there is all the more reason to admit, in the sphere of faith, notions of which one has only a confused knowledge.[65] Indeed, Leibniz lets it be understood, in concluding the part devoted to the Textuals, that a clear and distinct knowledge of the meaning of the mysteries would lead to the actual proof of the truth of the mysteries, and such a proof would take away faith as such, that is, as "holding something as true": the "truth" would no longer be *believed* but *proved.* Thus the fact that faith admits "a more and a less" would no longer have any justification. Whoever, out of fear that the consequence of this doctrine would be a weakening of faith, denies that faith is an "opin-ion" (that is, "holding something as true"), does not realize that in his doing so faith, far from being strengthened, is simply swept away.[66] On the other hand, the opinion that Leibniz speaks of can certainly not be understood as an arbitrary and unmotivated belief. On the contrary, there must be "motives of credibility," corresponding to the three tasks assigned to reason in the *Commentatiuncula*. In particular, the first of them—which, as I mentioned above, does not yet directly involve the content of revelation—emerges in this context as an indispensable preliminary condition for being able to proceed further: if we consider that faith is based on the witness of Christ,[67] it then becomes fundamental to establish first of all the veracity of the witness.[68]

In section 33, Leibniz goes on to discuss the position of the Rationals (*Rationales*), subdivided into radical rationalism and moderate rationalism.[69] So long as we are dealing with something that can be demonstrated by reason or else is contained in terminis in the scriptures, there is no problem: both the *Rationales meri* (pure Rationals) and the *Rationales mixti* (mixed Rationals) acknowledge it as true.[70] Controversy arises when the sense of the text is in doubt, or when reason cannot determine anything for certain. In cases such as that of the real presence of the body of Christ in the Eucharist or of the Trinity in God, a conflict between the text and reason arises. However, Leibniz at once points out that it is not an absolute conflict, that is, an ir-reconcilability based on the impossibility that what seems to be asserted by the text can actually occur, but a "conflict of probability": that is, both the real presence in the Eucharist and the Trinity in God are probable according to the text, but improbable according to reason. The question arises whether the final word should be given to reason or to the words of the text.[71] Before tackling this question, Leibniz takes pains to point out the reasons why it is illegitimate to pass from improbability to impossibility, as the Socinians do with regard to the mystery of the Trinity, and as the Reformed Church does regarding the real presence of the body of Christ: "Merely the improbability of a thing is proved by induction from other examples, as when the Socinians say that in all of nature there is to be found no Being that is one in number which has three Subsistences;[72] from this impossibility is not inferred, only improbability. Induction infers improbability, Demonstration impossibil-ity."[73] The assertion that induction proves only the improbability of a thing and not its impossibility is based, in the last analysis, on the conviction of the quantitative and qualitative infinity of the universe, a conviction that was already present in Leibniz's early work.[74] It is this infinity that prevents the finite and limited human mind from knowing everything that exists, has existed, or will exist, and thus from concluding that whatever has not been observed is impossible. The only way to prove the impossibility of the mysteries is therefore to demonstrate their self-contradictoriness.[75]

In section 34 Leibniz comes out into the open, expressing his opinion.[76] Priority should be given to the text, but with the addition of an important proviso: one must give credit to what is said in it, provided this does not involve any proven contradiction ("dummodo possibilis"). Here the role of vigilance on the possibility of the mysteries assigned to reason reappears. In the background, however, one can recognize also the other task of reason, that of a historical-philological analysis: if the credit given to the words of the text, despite their improbability according to reason, rests on the peculiar characteristics of "the One who has promised," then it is essential to verify the authenticity of the revelation. If it is God speaking, then, on the one hand, his wisdom prevents the scriptures from misleading us, and on the other his power ensures that he can accomplish what he promises. Leibniz proposes the example of two men—Titius, rich and just, and Caius, poor and a born liar—who both promise a large sum of money. Although it is inherently improbable that anyone would give such a large sum of money to another person, Titius's words (uttered, moreover, under oath) are worthy of trust, considering his reputation as a just man and the fact that he is both able and willing to keep his promise. On the contrary, it is not only improbable but actually impossible that Caius should keep his promise (supposing that he does not have, and in the future will not have, so much money). One should therefore not trust in his words, unless one takes them metaphorically.[77] Leibniz concludes:

> Let us transfer this to God. God is obviously this Titius. Indeed, he is also very rich or rather very powerful, and very wise as well, so that his words outweigh all the words sworn by others. This God promises that our bodies will be resurrected, just as numerous as we now bear. Considering this in itself, without the promise it is indeed not impossible, as all admit, but yet it is improbable ever to be, that the parts of a thing, scattered in thousands and thousands of places, should be gathered together again. Hence the Socinian concludes that it is improbable even if it is taken with the promise, and the words of the promise must be interpreted otherwise, indeed forcibly, metaphorically, figuratively; on the contrary, the Catholic concludes that, taken with the words of the promise, and adding the circumstances of the person speaking, it is probable and to be kept in practice, that God wants his words both to be understood in the proper sense and thus put into execution; and as he can he will do.[78]

The concluding words "it is probable and to be kept in practice" on the one hand show the strong pragmatic component in Leibniz's theological thought, and on the other make it clear that we are in the sphere of *verum putare* (holding something as true), based on reasons for credibility, and not in the sphere of demonstration. In any case, one thing is clear: even when an article of faith is not contained in *terminis* in the scriptures, what is probable according to the text is to be "held true," provided there is no proven contradiction. The dogma of the Trinity, although it is only "probable" according to the text,[79] should also therefore be "held true." Nonetheless, the question remains: Is the Trinity one of the fundamental articles of faith, that is, those necessary and sufficient for salvation? Granted, on the one hand, that the dogma of the Trinity is not contained in *terminis* in the scriptures, and given, on the other, that according to the rule of the Textuals "nothing is to be admitted as being known to be necessary to salvation, except what is contained in *terminis* in the Holy Scripture,"[80] one should infer that the mystery of the Trinity is not one of the fundamental articles of faith. It does not seem, however, that Leibniz draws this conclusion: even if he undoubtedly shows strong sympathy for the Textuals, one cannot say that his position is rigorously 'textualist.' In fact, even at this early date his recognition of a principle of authority identified with the tradition of the "universal church" is certainly operative.[81] Indeed, even in the *Commentatiuncula,* before passing from religious controversies to secular ones,[82] Leibniz limits the possible solutions to the problem of the infallibility of the judge required by religious controversies pertaining to fundamental articles of faith to only two: the Roman Catholic position, and that of the Textuals, with the exclusion of the Rationals.[83] Leibniz's specific position can be found in the synthesis of these two positions. This synthesis was later to become more explicit, but already the title of the fourth part of the *Conspectus* ("Demonstration of the Authority of the Catholic Church. Demonstration of the Authority of Scripture")[84] is both the emblem and the program of it.[85]

On the Demonstration of the Possibility of the Mysteries of the Eucharist

De Demonstratione Possibilitatis Mysteriorum Eucharistiae probably dates from the autumn of 1671.[86] The fragment is divided into two parts: in the first part there are some general observations regarding the demonstration of the possibility of the mysteries; in the second, the specific problem of the Eucharist is dealt with.[87] Here we are directly concerned with the first part. Leibniz indicates right after the title what he means by "demonstrating the possibility of something":

To *demonstrate* the *possibility* of something is to explain some *Hypothesis* or possible way [modum possibilem] (*possible*, i.e. clearly and distinctly intelligible), supposing which, it follows that the thing is produced: or to show in which manner [ostendere qua ratione] a given problem could be construed, at least by God. So to show that an Ellipse is equal to a circle, the problem is one that can be construed and solved by Geometry; but to move the Earth out of its place, to reduce a given body to nothing, to transubstantiate bodies while maintaining their species—these are problems that can be posed only to God. Therefore, although we cannot solve [them] by the work itself, yet we can do so by contemplation, i.e. we can demonstrate a possible way clearly and distinctly, which it is now our intention to exhibit in the Mysteries of the Eucharist.[88]

A demonstration of this kind applied to the mysteries (or, at least, to the mystery of the Eucharist) undoubtedly entails problematical consequences. In fact, it falls into that type of demonstration of possibility later called a priori demonstration by Leibniz in the *Meditationes de Cognitione, Veritate et Ideis:* "Moreover, we know the *possibility* of a thing either a priori or a posteriori. And we know it a priori, when we reduce the notion into its requisite elements, or into other notions known to be possible, and we know that there is nothing incompatible in them; and this is done, among other things, when we know the way in which the thing can be produced."[89] If one had a demonstration of this kind, the mysteries would be completely intelligible, and would thus lose their character as truths superior to reason, in contrast with what Leibniz normally maintains. He must have noticed this incongruity, since in the *Theodicy* he explicitly declares: "The Mysteries can be *explained* insofar as is necessary for belief; but one cannot *comprehend* them, nor make it understood how they happen."[90] He therefore openly abandons his youthful attempt to prove the possibility of the mysteries by indicating the manner in which the thing could be done, if not by us, then at least by God. It should immediately be added, however, that (at least as regards the mysteries of the Trinity and the Incarnation) the way that Leibniz then actually took for the demonstration of their possibility is not, as it appears, the one indicated here. On the one hand, it goes in the direction of an a posteriori argument conducted by analogy, and on the other, it goes in the direction of a defense of their possibility against objections (and thus not a positive demonstration of their possibility).

Leibniz goes on to point out what he means by mysteries of faith:

The *Mysteries of Faith* are astonishing or paradoxical revealed propositions, such as: God is Three in One, God became a man. When I say *revealed,* I consequently confess that they are not known by demonstration, either on account of the obscurity of the human mind [ob caliginem mentis humanae], as in the case of the *Triunity*, for otherwise, if a vision of the Divine Essence were given, a Demonstration of the Triunity will be given, i.e. it will be clearly and distinctly evident from the Divine Essence itself that Triunity necessarily follows; or because they are facts, such as the *Incarnation*, which, because it depends on the will of God, in any case cannot be known except by God's Revelation. When I say they are astonishing or paradoxical, I mean they seem impossible at first sight [prima fronte impossibiles videri].[91]

Indeed, the mysteries of the Trinity and the Incarnation are particularly significant examples of those "astonishing or paradoxical revealed propositions" that seem to be apparently impossible. This is a statement that, in another form, we have already come across, and it will also return in the following years until it is clearly fixed in the *Theodicy:* that is, the statement that "the mysteries are contrary to appearances, and do not at all seem likely when one regards them only from the standpoint of reason."[92] Now, the truths expressed in these "astonishing or paradoxical propositions" can be known by human beings only by means of divine revelation. Such revelation is necessary for two different reasons, illustrated, respectively, by the case of the Trinity and that of the Incarnation. The mystery of the Trinity cannot be known by demonstration only because of the limits of the human mind ("ob caliginem mentis humanae"): far from its entailing something irrational, if we had the vision of the divine essence, that is, if we had an adequate knowledge of the divine essence, we would also have the demonstration of the Three-in-Oneness of God, because we would see clearly and distinctly that being One and Three necessarily follows from the divine nature. The doctrine of the Trinity, in short, seems to enjoy the same characteristics as the eternal and necessary truths, of the type "the concept of triangle necessarily entails having three angles." However, on account of the obscurity (caligo) of the human mind, we are not able to see clearly and distinctly that the divine essence necessarily implies three-in-oneness.[93] On the contrary, like the other "astonishing or paradoxical revealed propositions," the doctrine of the Trinity seems, at first glance, to be impossible.[94]

Revelation is necessary also for knowledge of the mystery of the Incarnation. It cannot be known through demonstration, because it is a truth of fact and as such depends on God's will. At this point, however, the objection arises that all truths of fact inherently depend on God's will, but Leibniz does not, just because of this, maintain that they can be known only by means of revelation. What, then, does Leibniz mean in saying this?

His statement seems, first of all, related to the observation that introduces the examination of the cases of the Trinity and the Incarnation: namely, the observation that the mysteries are "astonishing or paradoxical" propositions. As such, they go against appearances and the normal course of events regulated by the laws of nature and known by reason. In matters of fact, however, as Leibniz writes in the *Commentatiuncula,* reason cannot determine anything for certain:[95] that is, it cannot legitimately pass from improbability (which means to go against the likelihood established by reason spoken of in the *Theodicy* or against what seems impossible at first sight as mentioned in *De Demonstratione Possibilitatis Mysteriorum Eucharistiae*) to impossibility. By induction from other examples, one can, in fact, only infer improbability, as it is necessary to prove self-contradiction in order to assert that a given proposition is impossible.[96] In the case of the Incarnation, God's will would have changed the normal course of events, giving rise to a fact that clashes with the likelihood acknowledged by reason, provided this fact is not self-contradictory. Precisely because this fact is an exception to the natural laws that normally rule the course of events, it cannot be foreseen by reason and therefore requires a revelation to be known.

Having justified (by means of the typical examples of the Trinity and the Incarnation) the need for revelation, Leibniz concludes: "Just as it is proper of *faith* to admit the truth on account of revelation, so it is proper of *reason* to recognize possibility on account of demonstration."[97] This is tantamount to saying: revealed truths are the objects of faith because, as they cannot be proved by reason, we come to know and believe them on the basis of revelation, on which they depend; reason, however, has a fundamental task, that is, the task of recognizing the possibility of revealed truths (namely, their noncontradictory nature), thus guaranteeing their credibility.[98]

De Demonstratione Possibilitatis Mysteriorum Eucharistiae continues with a comment on the usefulness of a demonstration of possibility: while faith is required for everyone, the demonstration of the possibility of revealed truths is useful only for learned men, who are either driven by the thirst for knowledge or are called upon to defend these truths against atheists, infidels, and heretics. To defeat the charges of impossibility and contradiction brought by such attackers, there is nothing better than the demonstration of possibility.[99] Leibniz thus concludes: "For just as a clear definition is a compendium of a thousand distinctions, so a single clear demonstration is a compendium of a thousand responses."[100] This conclusion brings with it all the difficulties mentioned above with regard to the a priori demonstration of possibility proposed by Leibniz at the beginning of the text, to which he seems to refer here. Such a demonstration would certainly eliminate all objections, but at the same time it would also eliminate the mysteries as such, that is, as truths superior to reason. Leibniz, called "to vindicate truth against the insults of the Atheists, the infidels and the heretics,"[101] was actually forced to follow the longer route that here he would like to avoid: the route of the "thousand distinctions" and the patient reply to every objection.

PART II

Fragments of a System (1672–1692)

5

The Conformity of Faith with Reason

The twenty years that follow Leibniz's first writings contain the scattered pieces of a puzzle called the *Demonstrationes Catholicae*. With the general outline of the *Conspectus* fresh in his mind, Leibniz develops the individual components of his theological system in notes or brief epistolary reflections. In 1686 many, though certainly not all, of the ideas thus elaborated are collected in the *Examen Religionis Christianae* (Examination of the Christian Religion). Although only a partial realization of Leibniz's catholic plan, the scope and organization of this work were sufficiently comprehensive and coherent for it to become known as Leibniz's *Systema Theologicum* (Theological System).[1]

A first group of pieces in this jigsaw puzzle develop the idea noted by Leibniz next to the title of the section of the *Conspectus* devoted to revealed theology:[2] "Regarding a Single Philosophical and Theological Truth against Averroists, Hofmann and Slevogt."[3] Although Leibniz does not mention Hofmann explicitly, the doctrines debated in the polemic surrounding him are central to a text composed in the second half of 1678 and the first half of 1679. In the *Dialogus inter Theologum et Misosophum* (Dialogue between a Theologian and Misosophus),[4] Misosophus echoes (in less confrontational fashion) the anathema launched by the bellicose Hofmann against the use of reason (or philosophy) in matters of faith: "In divine matters," Misosophus claims, "all reasoning must be suspect,"[5] and therefore "it is safer to ban all reasoning from Theology."[6] Three reasons are adduced in the course of the *Dialogus* to support these convictions, in order of increasing argumentative force: 1) it is useless to try to reach by reason what can better be reached through faith;[7] 2) to admit the discriminating power of reason into the sphere of faith is tantamount to dissolving the supernatural element, reducing faith to a purely human religion;[8] 3) human reason in the divine sphere is more a cause of error than knowledge, since its logical and metaphysical principles, surpassed by the omnipotence of God, have no validity in the divine sphere.[9] Leibniz has Theologus say that, in God's eyes, only the proud human knowledge that claims to understand the mysteries is foolish, not (following up on Paul's suggestion) the use of reason in order to glimpse God "as in a mirror" or in defense of the faith.[10] In other words, it is not the use but the abuse of reason that is to be condemned.[11] If it is true that the inner illumination of the Spirit is enough for the faith and salvation of many people, reason nevertheless has a fundamental role in the theological sphere.[12] This is true, it should be noted, even if one should want to eliminate natural theology entirely, reserving even the proof of God's existence to revealed theology.[13]

The specific tasks undertaken by reason in relation to revelation are introduced in the *Dialogus* through the consideration of miracles. According to Misosophus, these are what leads people to believe in revelation. But, replies Theologus, besides the fact that many arguments are needed to prove the truthfulness of miracles that one has not directly been a witness of, the sign of a miracle is not in itself a proof of authentic divine revelation, as the case of false prophets shows. Miracles themselves should rather be examined in the light of the doctrine they are intended to support. Therefore, to avoid the vicious circle formed by the verification of the divine origin of revelation by means of the miracles that accompany it and the verification of the divine origin of miracles through the revelation that they accompany, it is necessary to introduce an independent criterion of verification, consisting in rational analysis.[14] It does not have the task of proving the revelation, but rather has the task of showing the reasons for the revelation's credibility.[15] Leibniz is explicit on this point in a text of 1680 to 1684, specifically devoted to the mystery of the Trinity: "We do not demonstrate this Mystery of faith by reason, we only illustrate it and defend it against objections."[16] Speaking of motives of credibility, it is clear that he is referring to revealed theology or, more precisely, the specific Christian revelation, in favor of which he claims there are 'reasons' that make it more credible than other religions that also consider themselves revealed truths, such as Islam.[17] It would be meaningless to speak of motives of credibility in relation to natural theology, since the latter, being subject to strict procedures of demonstration, reaches truths that have no need of being 'believed,' any more than it is necessary to believe that the sum of the inner angles of a triangle is 180 degrees. Revealed theology, on the contrary, though needing the aid of rational instruments, far from reducing divine faith to human faith, conserves intact the element of 'indemonstrability' and hence of 'superrationality.'[18] There are three basic functions of reason (already identified in the *Commentatiuncula*), through the exercise of which the motives of credibility of the Christian revelation are identified: 1) the historical and philological verification of the authenticity of the revelation or, as the *Examen Religionis Christianae* specifies, of the authoritativeness of the witnesses;[19] 2) the interpretation of the scriptures' meaning, as regards in particular obscure passages; 3) the defense of revealed truths.[20]

Having overcome the first two objections regarding, respectively, the uselessness of reason and the danger of a complete dissolution of the supernatural character of revelation, Theologus still has to face the most intricate problem: that of the validity of human logical and metaphysical principles in the divine sphere. The line of reasoning followed by Theologus takes its basic conception of the *analogia entis* (analogy of being) from the Thomist school. The metaphysical and logical principles (and in particular the principle of noncontradiction) are common to both the human and the divine spheres, since they are the principles of being in general (*ens in genere*), which is common both to God and to his creatures.[21] Although God does not need the syllogistic arguments typical of discursive reasoning, this takes nothing away from their general validity, which in the final analysis derives from the principle of noncontradiction.[22] To maintain the nonvalidity of this principle in the divine sphere would mean the destruction of the distinction between true and false with respect to God: that is, "we could simultaneously admit and reject the Deity or the Trinity; we could simultaneously in the same respect be pious and Atheists, Catholics and Arians."[23] The case of the laws of nature is different. They are valid only in the natural world and can be changed by divine omnipotence.[24] But, at this point, can one really speak of divine omnipotence if what is contradictory is impossible also for God?[25] By way of reply, Theologus gets his interlocutor to admit that for God to do what is contradictory would amount to a diminution of his perfection or, in other words, it would mean admitting that God could be non-God. Therefore, far from being a limitation on divine perfection as regards omnipotence, the validity of the principle of noncontradiction also in the divine sphere is, so to speak, the 'seal' of divine perfection.[26] Having gradually lost ground, Misosophus clutches onto his last argument: "Let me admit (since thus you urge) this principle of contradiction also in divine matters; but let me not

admit that we can judge well in divine matters which one may be contradictory."[27] Theologus brushes away the objection, stating that "if we have eyes
and memory we can also judge of contradiction" and that "in more difficult
matters" (as in the divine sphere) "there is only need of more attention."[28]
The implicit basis for this reply is once again the analogia entis: if one admits
(as even Misosophus does in the end) that the basic logical and metaphysical principles of being in general (ens in genere) are valid both for the divine
sphere and for the human sphere, there is no reason to deny that human
reason, regulated by such principles (first of all by that of noncontradiction),
is able to judge noncontradictoriness in the divine sphere as well.

Therefore the principle of noncontradiction has absolute validity; there
are no truths against reason, nor is there a double philosophical and theological truth. Leibniz never tires of repeating this.[29] In particular, in a text
composed probably between February and October 1685, the principle of
noncontradiction is defended as the ultimate criterion for distinguishing between truth and falsehood both in the natural world and in the supernatural
sphere,[30] and consequently as the foundation of the distinction between what
is above reason and what is against reason.[31] And Leibniz insists that this is
true without exceptions, also in the case of the most problematic mystery of
all, the mystery of the Trinity. That is, defending the mystery of the Trinity
by admitting an exception to the basic logical principle (directly based on the
principle of noncontradiction) that *things that are identical to a third thing
are identical to one another* (*quae eadem sunt eidem tertio sunt eadem inter
se*) ends up leading to consequences contrary to what one desires: namely,
to the confirmation of the Socinian thesis that this mystery is irrational and
therefore is to be rejected as false.[32]

At this point, the key move is to show that this logical principle is not denied in the dogma of the Trinity. Leibniz, therefore, in a series of texts composed between 1678 and 1688, gave shape to his line of defense against the
accusation of contradiction.[33] The 'formula' of the Trinity can be expressed
in the following terms: the Father (B) is God (A), the Son (C) is God (A),
the Holy Spirit (D) is God (A); B, C, and D are different from one another;
nonetheless, A is only one.[34] Now, to affirm at the same time the oneness of
A and the diversity of B, C, and D would seem to involve a clear contradiction.[35] According to the principle that *things that are identical to a third
thing are identical to one another,* given the oneness of A, one should necessarily conclude that B, C, and D are identical to one another; in the terms
of the Trinity, there would be no distinction between Father, Son, and Holy
Spirit. The only way to save this distinction, without falling into contradiction, would be to admit the plurality of A; that is, one would have to affirm

Tritheism.[36] At stake here is the very concept of number, originated by the definition of unity and plurality, which in its turn presupposes the definition of identical and different.[37] Leibniz would seem to be in a blind alley. But he writes in *Circa Geometrica Generalia* that "the contradiction is removed by a distinction."[38] The solution is given to him by a distinction widely used in the Protestant theology of his time: the distinction between *essentialiter* (essentially) or *ousiōdōs* and *personaliter* (as a person) or *hypostatikōs*, that is, between two opposite ways of predicating the names of God.[39] Thus, God taken absolutely or essentially (*Deus absolute seu essentialiter sumtus*) indicates God considered from the standpoint of the divine essence, numerically one, in which the three persons participate; God taken relatively or as a person (*Deus relative seu personaliter sumtus*) indicates one of the persons of the Trinity, equally participating in the single divine essence. Thus, in the propositions "The Father is God," "The Son is God," and "The Holy Spirit is God," the term "God" means something different from the term "God" that appears in the proposition "God is One [Unus est Deus]": in this last case God considered absolutely or essentially is meant, whereas in the previous propositions the meaning is God considered relatively or as a person. That is, Leibniz calls attention to the fact that the propositions "The Father is God" and "God is One" are to be considered reduplicative propositions.[40] The proposition 1) "The Father is God" is to be specified in the following proposition: 1.i) "God, insofar as he is considered relatively or as a person [*quatenus relative seu personaliter sumtus*], is the Father," or equivalently, 1.ii) "God, insofar as he is one or another person of the divinity [*quatenus una aliqua persona divinitatis*], is the Father"; the proposition 2) "God is One" is to be specified in the following proposition: 2.i) "God, insofar as he is considered absolutely or essentially [*quatenus absolute seu essentialiter sumtus*], is One," or equivalently, 2.ii) "God, insofar as he contains all persons or insofar as he is threefold in persons [*quatenus omnes personas continens seu trinus in personis*], is One."[41] Now, although God taken relatively and God taken absolutely are really the same thing (just as "Peter" and "The Apostle who denied Christ" are the same thing), in propositions 1.i) and 2.i) God (taken relatively) and God (taken absolutely) cannot be substituted one for the other, since these propositions fall into the class of cases in which "we are not dealing with the thing but with the way of conceiving it [non de re sed modo concipiendi agitur]."[42] Coming back to the example of Peter, although "Peter" and "the Apostle who denied Christ" are the same and can therefore normally be substituted for one another, this is not true when we are considering not the 'thing' (*res*) but the way of conceiving it (*modus concipiendi*). Thus, in the proposition "Peter insofar as he was the Apostle who denied

Christ, just so far he sinned," "the Apostle who denied Christ" cannot be replaced by "Peter": that is, one cannot say that "Peter insofar as he was Peter sinned."[43] Or again, although "a trilateral figure and a triangle are the same thing," when we say "a triangle considered as such has 180 degrees," the term "triangle" (*triangulus*) cannot be replaced by that of "trilateral figure" (*trilaterus*), since a given property (having 180 degrees) is predicated of a subject on the basis of a particular way of considering the subject (precisely as a triangle and not as a trilateral figure).[44] In the same way, in the propositions "God is the Father" and "God is One" the two predicates "Father" and "One" are attributed to the subject (God) on the basis of different ways of considering the subject: in the first case "as taken relatively or personally" (or "as one of the persons of the Godhead"); in the second case "as taken absolutely or essentially" (or "as containing all persons or threefold in persons"). The subject of the first proposition can therefore not be substituted for the subject of the second (and vice versa), since these are propositions in which "we are dealing not with the thing but with the way of conceiving it"; the two subjects, although they are really the same thing, are considered according to different aspects, and it is precisely this difference in the way of considering them (the *modus considerandi*) that justifies the predications, respectively, of "Father" and "One."

Leibniz sums it up in *De Trinitate*:

> That principle that things that are the same to a third thing are the same to each other, if identity is taken with the greatest rigor, has a place in divine matters no less than in natural affairs. When we say "the father is God" and "the son is God," and "God is One [Unus est Deus]," both father and son, surely the father and the son are the same, unless "God" in the first two propositions is understood as a person of the Godhead and in the last one as the divine nature or the absolute singular substance that we call God. Hence we say that the three persons of the Godhead are yet not three Gods, and in this sense we make some distinction between the person of the Godhead and God, for if between two words there is a difference in the plural usage, so that one cannot replace the other, there will also be between the same some difference in the singular, since the plural form is a repetition of the singular.[45]

The idea of identity in diversity between "God taken absolutely" and "God taken relatively" is expressed by Leibniz in a formulation he had already used in the *Defensio Trinitatis* in the wake of the logical doctrine of Johannes Raue:[46] "Although the father is not the son, yet the father is he who is [est is qui est] the son, namely, the one God in number."[47] Leibniz adds in *De Lingua Philosophica* (On Philosophical Language): "For in the Trinity these two things are different: 'to be God the father,' and 'to be he who is [illum qui est] God the father.' For God the son is not God the father, and yet he is the very one who is [est ille ipse qui est] God the father, namely the one most high God."[48] The same idea is expressed in *De Trinitate* (On the Trinity): "When it is said that 'the same one who is [idem ille qui est] the father is also the son,' the meaning is that in the same absolute substance of God there are two relative substances differing in number from one another. . . . Is it possible to say: 'the father is that only one God [unicus ille Deus]'? I think not, but the father as partaking of the divine nature which is one in number."[49] That is, when one says that the Father, Son, and Holy Spirit are the same God, one means that they partake of the same divine essence, which is one in number.

Nonetheless, it is still clear that we are far away from an exhaustive explanation of the mystery of the Trinity. The divine essence, which is numerically one, is in fact entire in each of the three divine persons:[50] the persons of the Trinity are not the parts of a whole, nor is the divine essence a universal of which the persons are the single individuals.[51] Moreover, although "triangle" and "trilateral" are two different ways of considering the same thing, the persons of the Trinity cannot simply be reduced to three ways of considering the same God, without falling into modalism. Once again we are faced with the 'strategy of defense': Leibniz's argument, that is, limits itself to rejecting the charge of contradiction inherent in a precise formulation. Proving that this specific formulation involves no contradiction is different from a definitive proof of the noncontradictory nature of the dogma of the Trinity.

Leibniz's conclusion is that both the expressions "Pater est Deus"[52] and "Unus est Deus," once they are correctly explained so as to imply no contradiction, are legitimate, although there are no statements in the human sphere that perfectly reproduce the characteristics of these two propositions.[53] The mysteries of faith can be accepted as truths superior to reason without this involving a renunciation of reason in an admission of contradictoriness. Fideism, far from leading to true piety, is often nothing but a hypocritical mask behind which atheism conceals itself. Leibniz points to the cases of Pietro Pomponazzi and Giulio Cesare Vanini: after having raised serious objections to religion, both declared that, despite everything, they yielded to the authority of the church, dissimulating behind this screen their true opinion and actively working for the destruction of the Christian religion.[54] In fact, there is nothing more damaging to religion and piety than to maintain the opposition between faith and reason.[55] On the contrary, the agreement between philosophy and religion is a sign of how one God is the author both of the nature of things and of the salvation received by grace through Christ.[56]

6

Sola Scriptura? *The Interpretation of the Scriptures and the Authority of Tradition*

Already in the early *Commentatiuncula de Judice Controversiarum* Leibniz's position regarding the relationship between scripture and tradition could not be defined as rigorously 'textualist'; yet in the following years his position shifts in a direction that is clearly different from the Protestant principle of *sola scriptura* (scripture alone). Mainstream Protestants typically regarded scripture as the primary, absolute, and sufficient rule of doctrine, and they granted only a secondary role to tradition as a useful but not decisive guide.[1] Leibniz by contrast seems to come closer to the position defined by the treatises of the van Walenburch brothers, who wrote that "Catholics hold that there is only one principle of faith: *the Word of God proposed by the Church.*"[2] Moreover, he also keeps his distance from the Protestant doctrine regarding the fundamental and nonfundamental articles of faith, which is founded on the notion that all fundamental articles necessary and sufficient for salvation are clearly revealed in the scriptures. This is a significant difference of opinion, if we consider that the distinction between fundamental and nonfundamental articles was suggested by many as the way to achieve the reunification of the churches, a cause constantly supported by Leibniz. Certainly he worked on the formulation of a 'theological system' that could be accepted both by Catholics and by Protestants; but to achieve this aim he decided not to follow what was considered by Catholics a misleading shortcut, resulting in the arbitrary reduction of the articles of faith. A letter of August 1692 from Jacques-Bénigne Bossuet to Leibniz does not leave any doubt regarding this matter, indicating how the doctrine of the fundamental and nonfundamental articles of faith could indeed be transformed from a means of reconciliation to another apple of discord.[3]

Leibniz seems to maintain that a rigorously textualist position is not satisfactory, for the following reason: the correct interpretation of the scriptures requires the mediation of the ecclesiastical tradition, not only regarding subjects of secondary importance not defined in terminis in the Bible but also for articles of faith that can threaten salvation and are therefore fundamental. In other words, not all the fundamental articles of faith can be clearly deduced from scripture without resorting to the judgment of tradition. The mystery of the Trinity presents itself once again as the prime example, even perhaps as the main problem that leads Leibniz in this direction. First of all, it is observed that the dogma of the Trinity is not defined in a clear and indubitable way by the scriptures, even if the Bible is certainly more favorable to the Trinitarian hypothesis than to the Antitrinitarian one.[4] According to the doctrine of the fundamental and nonfundamental articles of faith, one should therefore conclude that the Trinity is not a fundamental article of faith and that one may believe or not believe in the Trinitarian nature of God without any threat to salvation. It is at this point that Leibniz's disaccord becomes manifest: in his view, one cannot regard the questions of the nature of God and the divinity of Christ as subjects of secondary importance, to be left as adiaphora or 'matters indifferent' that one can choose whether to believe or not.[5] On the contrary, if the dogma of the Trinity were false it would threaten the salvation of all those souls that, by embracing the dogma, would have fallen into the worst of all mistakes: polytheism.[6] We are therefore confronted with a fundamental question, a question relevant to salvation—a question not answered in terminis in the scriptures, but one about which the Bible contains many hints that cannot simply be ignored. The only way to get out of this impasse is to admit the judgment of the ecclesiastical tradition as decisive and normative.[7] Leibniz buttresses this solution with what we could call 'the argument of providence.' The guarantee that the church cannot fail in matters concerning salvation is given by God himself and by the presence of his Spirit.[8] Divine providence cannot permit the infiltration into the church of such errors as could compromise the salvation of those same human beings for whose redemption God chose to suffer and die on the cross.[9] Scripture and tradition here appear as two inseparable principles, which should be used to judge the correctness of the explanations suggested for the Trinity and the Incarnation and, in general, the articles of faith necessary for salvation.[10]

Leibniz, then, repeatedly stresses the authority of the church as the interpreter of the scriptures.[11] Another reason why the interpretation of the Bible cannot be left to 'the common people' is that it is necessary to have sophisticated philological, linguistic, and historical knowledge in order to make a correct exegesis.[12] This is not, one should note, merely a 'technical' problem, otherwise one should talk not of the normative nature of the ecclesiastical interpretation but of the need for hermeneutic skills required to comprehend the text. Instead, Leibniz clearly maintains that the Christian faith is not a subject of private reasoning or immediate revelation from God to individual people. God makes use of the church for revelation, and therefore one cannot attribute infallibility of judgment to individuals.[13] Leibniz's refusal to adhere to the Roman Church therefore does not seem to result from any dispute regarding the principle of church authority, even when it is defined as papal authority.[14] On the contrary, Leibniz seems to accept the interpretation whereby Antitrinitarianism and atheism would be the extreme consequence of the denial of the authority of the universal church inaugurated by the Reformation. Socinus, on this view, did nothing but apply to the dogmas of the Trinity and the Incarnation the method used, respectively, by the Lutheran and Reformed Churches regarding transubstantiation and the real presence: Luther denied transubstantiation (despite the verdict of church tradition) because he did not find a sufficiently explicit revelation regarding this doctrine in scripture, while Calvin denied the real presence (admitted by the Lutherans) on supposedly rational grounds.

In short, once the tradition of the universal church as the normative criterion in controversial matters has been abolished, there would be no way to stop the gradual slide from the first denials of doctrines accepted by the tradition to the denial of the Trinity, to the consequent reduction of Christ to an ordinary man, to the reduction of religion to the natural religion of deism, and finally to the dissolution of the concept of God himself into the atheism typical of Vanini and Spinoza. Even if the zeal with which the Protestants fight Antitrinitarianism and the various sects arrayed against the Christian religion is to be admired, one cannot hide the responsibility of the Reformation in having opened the door to these sects by claiming 'liberty' from church authority.[15] Ironically, the lack of foundation for such a claim is shown even by Protestant theologians, who, when confronted with dissidents, are forced in practice to deny that same liberty with which they justified in theory their detachment from Rome. If this were not the case, Leibniz concludes, one could only arrive at two opposite excesses: on the one side, the fideism of Anabaptists and Quakers, according to whom "whatever comes to mind" is the authentic revelation of the Spirit; on the other, Antitrinitarian rationalism, with its almost total destruction of the mysteries of the Christian faith.[16]

7

On the Triune God *and* On the Person of Christ

The recognition of the authority of tradition takes concrete shape in the formulation of a theology of the Trinity and a Christology steeped in the teachings of the church fathers and the Scholastics. It is by no means coincidental that Leibniz's most complete sketch of a "theological system"—the *Examen Religionis Christianae* (Examination of the Christian Religion)—is strewn with references to Christian antiquity and the universal church.[1] This does not mean, however, that Leibniz does not make his choices among the many voices of a tradition reinterpreted variously by Lutheran, Reformed, and Catholic 'orthodoxies.' Without abandoning his adherence to the Confession of Augsburg, for example, he unequivocally rejects the doctrine of *communicatio idiomatum* (communication of properties), which was widely (though not unanimously) accepted by Lutheran Christology. He therefore rejects the aprioristic acceptance of the dictates of any one confession, and reserves for himself the right to evaluate the proposals of the various orthodoxies one by one and to adopt those he deems most correct. Yet, at the same time, his indubitable ecumenism cannot be confused with a form of religious relativism. On the contrary, Leibniz's "theological system" is characterized by a quite precise dogmatics. The general result is a peculiar polyphony, in which the voices of the different Scholastics resound with typically Leibnizian accents.

On the Triune God

The doctrine of the Trinity is introduced in the *Examen Religionis Christianae* by a brief, dense paragraph in which the actual formulation of the dogma of the Trinity is encased between the following statements: 1) monotheism, being rationally demonstrable, is a subject of natural theology; the dogma of the Trinity, which instead is superior to human reason, requires revelation; 2) the teaching about the triune nature of God, its superrationality notwithstanding, was transmitted by the early Christians in the way most appropriate to the capacity of human understanding: "Moreover, the Sacred Monuments of the Christians teach that the highest God (which reason itself holds to be only one in number) is none the less three in persons, and that therefore three persons of the divinity exist in a single God (which surpasses all reason), and that they can best be called for human understanding the Father, Son or Word, and Holy Spirit; and that the Son was born of the Father; that the Holy Spirit proceeds from both, as the Latins say, or, as the Greeks say, from the Father through the Son (and that by way of only one principle)."[2]

After having warned against the danger of Tritheist interpretations and having rejected the charge of contradiction launched by the Antitrinitarians, Leibniz dwells on the concept of person in the divine sphere.[3] The starting point is the definition of person in general: "Furthermore, a person in general is a substance, single in number, and incommunicable."[4] This extremely laconic definition can be usefully supplemented with what the young Leibniz stated, around 1668, in *De Transsubstantiatione* (On Transubstantiation): "I call Substance a Being subsisting through itself [Ens per se subsistens]. All the Scholastic philosophers agree that a Being subsisting through itself is the same thing as a Suppositum. For Suppositum is a Substantial individual [individuum Substantiale] (just as a Person is a rational substantial individual) or some Substance in the individual [Substantia aliqua in individuo]."[5] If we reread the definition given in *Examen Religionis Christianae* with these words in mind, we can see more clearly the meaning of the three features of person indicated there: substantiality, that is, the character of person as ens per se subsistens in opposition to what is accidental; individuality, by which the person is indeed substance, but *in individuo sumta* (taken in the individual) (coinciding with the suppositum or *substantia aliqua in individuo*); incommunicability, namely, the possession of a set of distinctive traits or properties that cannot be 'transferred' to others. The characteristic of rationality is not expressed in the *Examen Religionis Christianae*, but it is certainly not suppressed either, as it is essential to a definition of person derived from Boethius, like the one put forward by Leibniz.[6] In the rest of the definition in *Examen Religionis Christianae* Leibniz tries to remove any possible misunderstanding of a Tritheistic type stemming from the admission of three substances or supposita in God. If the abovementioned characteristics of person in general can be extended to the divine persons as well, in this latter case there must also be a special condition: an essential property of each divine person is its being in relation to the other divine persons, so as to constitute a single absolute substance and to imply that no person could exist on its own.[7] "They are therefore," concludes Leibniz, "three related singular substances, one absolute [substance] which contains them [all] and the same individual nature of which is communicated to the singular substances."[8] The identical individual nature (or *essentia* [essence])[9] of the one absolute substance (corresponding to "God taken absolutely") is therefore communicated to three essentially related singular substances (corresponding to "God taken relatively").

Despite Leibniz's efforts to remove possible Tritheist interpretations, in the formulation proposed there is still some ambiguity due to the use of the term *substance* (albeit qualified as "absolute" and "relative") both for God and for the divine persons. Later on, Leibniz was moved to clarify his position: in his correspondence with his nephew Friedrich Simon Löffler in early 1695, he even replaces the expression previously used for the divine persons ("Moreover, they are essentially relative intelligent singular substances") with the more cautious wording "Moreover, they are understood through incommunicable relative modes of subsisting (per modos subsistendi relativos incommunicabiles)";[10] and in commenting on the *Metaphysica Repurgata* of the Socinian writer Christoph Stegmann around 1708, he specifies that only the *subsistens absolutum* (absolute subsistent) can properly be called substance.[11] On the other hand, in the years prior to the *Examen Religionis Christianae* Leibniz shows some interest in a solution contrary to the one adopted in the *Examen;* between 1677 and 1680 he annotates the thesis of Lorenzo Valla according to which the divine persons are "qualities, not substances."[12] One further sign of this difficult search for a balance between the two opposite extremes of Tritheism and modalism is found in some brief notes he made while reading the *Theologica Dogmata* (Lutetiae Parisiorum, 1644–1650) by Denis Petau.[13] Leibniz writes: "A person is not always a *concretum*, because it is not absolute. . . . the person in God is not an *abstractum philosophicum*, but neither is it a *concretum*, but there is between the divine persons the same kind of diversity as that found among the foundations of truths [fundamenta veritatum]."[14] 'Person' in the case of the Trinity is thus not a concretum in the full sense of the term (that is, a concrete independent individual existing for itself), in that the divine persons are not absolute beings but beings essentially related to one another.[15] On the other hand, they are also not *abstracta philosophica*, that is to say, ideal or mental entities which designate the properties of concrete individuals (for example, the property of 'humanity' inhering in a concrete man). Moreover, the diversity among the divine persons is similar to that among the *fundamenta veritatum* (foundations of truths): namely, the properties or features of a thing that constitute the foundation of the truth of a proposition about that thing. In Leibniz's theology of the Trinity, this *fundamentum veritatis* seems to correspond to the *fundamentum relationis* (foundation of the relation) that constitutes (as we shall soon see) the diversity among the persons of the Trinity, in agreement with Leibniz's general theory of relations, according to which relations as such (that is, considered in the abstract) "are not Things, but truths."[16]

The *Examen Religionis Christianae* goes on to indicate the analogy between the mind's reflection on itself and the Trinity: "Of which we grasp a certain likeness in our mind thinking and loving itself."[17] This statement is once again very succinct, but it is developed in a series of fragments dating from the same years in which the *Examen Religionis Christianae* was taking shape.[18] In *De Deo Trino* Leibniz writes: "Now, the way in which different persons can be observed in a thing one in number is nowhere better illustrated, as far as I know, than by the Mind understanding itself. It is in fact clear that there is a certain distinction between that which understands and that which is understood, one of which has the power of perceiving, the other the power of manifesting. Either of the two is the same mind one in number; and nevertheless it cannot wholly and in every respect be said that one is the other, since they are correlated entities [cum sint correlata]."[19] The reflection of the mind on itself is the example that most closely approaches the "plurality in unity" of the Trinity,[20] since, although the mind is a single individual, there is a difference between "that which understands" and "that which is understood" or, in the words of *De Scriptura, Ecclesia, Trinitate* (On the Scripture, the Church, and the Trinity), "between the person perceiving and the person perceived."[21] As Leibniz comments further in *Origo Animarum et Mentium* (Origin of Souls and Minds): "The person who understands and the person who is understood are, in a certain way, certainly two; although in a certain other way they are one and the same. They are in fact one and the same by hypothesis. It is in fact supposed that the mind understands itself. They are nevertheless two for the very fact that the two between which there is a certain relation are in a certain manner different."[22] What Leibniz seems to mean is that every relation must be founded on an intrinsic property of the objects correlated or, in other words, on a real intrinsic difference between the objects: this intrinsic property inherent in the subject of a given relation is said to be the *fundamentum relationis*.[23] In the case of the reflection of the mind on itself, the fundamentum relationis of the relation that has as its subject "that which understands" and as its object "that which is understood" corresponds to the presence in "that which understands" (or "person who understands") of the "power of perceiving [vis percipiendi]"; the fundamentum relationis of the relation that has as its subject "that which is understood" and as its object "that which understands" corresponds to the presence in "that which is understood" (or "person who is understood") of the "power of manifesting [vis exhibendi]." The very fact that "that which understands" and "that which is understood" are related therefore indicates the existence of a real intrinsic difference between the entities correlated:[24] that is to say, the two opposing properties (respectively, the "vis percipiendi" and the "vis exhibendi") inherent in the two correlated entities. On the other hand, if the very existence of a relation is proof of the intrinsic difference between the two correlated entities, in the case of the mind that reflects on itself we are dealing with a diversity in identity or, as Leibniz himself says, the "composition of an indivisible thing."[25]

The balance between identity and diversity is clearly underlined in the application to the Trinity of what was said above about the reflection of the mind. Leibniz writes in *De Mundo Praesenti* (On the Present World): "Every substance has a certain operation in itself, and this is either of the same in itself, which is called Reflection or Cogitation, and such a substance is spiritual, or *Mind*, or it is of different parts, and such a *Substance* is called *Corporeal*. As God is Mind and thinks and loves Himself, from this hence arises a certain astonishing diversity of the same from itself, or the composition of an indivisible thing [diversitas ejusdem a se ipso, sive compositio rei indivisibilis], which we acknowledge in *the persons of the Holy Trinity*; and of which we have some indication in our mind thinking itself." First of all it should be pointed out that the force of the analogy between the two cases is based on the ontological similarity between the human mind and God: both are "spiritual substance," which in its turn coincides with mind. The explanation of how this "diversity of the same from itself" found in the human mind can arise in God is supported in *De Deo Trino* by the doctrine, which originated with Augustine, according to which the persons of the Trinity can be indicated by analogy with the three main faculties of the mind (soul): *posse, scire, velle* (power, knowledge, will):[26] "Truly, the Holy Fathers elegantly expressed the three persons of the divinity through the three primary perfections of the Mind: power, knowledge, will. Whence the father is the origin of all, the son is called Logos or the Word of the Mind, or the Wisdom of the father; the Holy Spirit is called love or will."[27]

From the one God reflected in himself, that is, from God who thinks and loves himself, come the persons of the Trinity. The source of this activity is the Father, from whom the Son is generated; from the Father and the Son the Holy Spirit then proceeds. This order is justified by Leibniz on the basis that the *intellectus* (corresponding to the Son) presupposes the *potentia agendi* (power of acting) (belonging to the Father), just as the *voluntas* (corresponding to the Holy Spirit) presupposes both the power of acting and the power of understanding (*potentia intelligendi*) (this latter belonging to the Son). This distinction, however, does not mean that "to understand and to be understood, to love and to be loved" are not indeed shared by all three persons of the Trinity, just as in the mind that thinks itself, beyond the distinction originated by the reflection itself, everything is shared by both the thinker (*intelligens*) and the thought-of (*intellectus*) (since there is only one mind), so that the person thought of (*persona intellecta*) expresses (albeit derivatively) the thinking (*intellectio*) of the person thinking (*persona intelligens*).[28]

Now, Leibniz points out, departing on this point from the classical Augustinian position, while in the human mind we are in some way justified in speaking of a Binity (constituted by the persona intelligens [person thinking] and the persona intellecta [person thought]), only in God is there a true Trinity, in that also the intellectio (the act of understanding) is "something perpetual and subsisting."[29] Thus the Son or Logos (coinciding with "id quod intelligitur [what is thought]" or "persona intellecta [person thought]") is the image of the Father, since the Father that perceives the Logos perceives what he himself is, that is, that same Mind that thinks itself. The perceptio or intellectio (perception or intellection) (coinciding with love, since for God to perceive himself is the same as loving himself) is the Holy Spirit.[30] It should be pointed out here that if that to which Leibniz attributes autonomous subsistence (thus making it a res [thing] that really exists, as opposed to a merely ideal or mental entity) were the relation of love between Father and Son conceived in the abstract, without considering the two extremes of the relation, we would be faced with a clear divergence from Leibniz's general theory of relations, according to which a relation so conceived, outside the subjects, is a purely ideal entity.[31] On the other hand, Leibniz himself expressly denies that the persons of the Trinity are "relations" as such.[32] Therefore, it seems that we should understand as being "something perpetual and subsisting"[33] not the love relation shared by Father and Son but rather the act of love or perception considered in itself. In this sense the Holy Spirit proceeds from the Father and the Son (or, as the Greek tradition maintains, from the Father through the Son) as the act of love between the lover and the beloved, considered in itself.[34] Thus, what Leibniz says about the persons of the Trinity in general is true also for the Spirit: they are not in themselves relations but are constituted "per relationes [by or through relations]."[35] That is, the Spirit is not the relation between Father and Son considered in the abstract but is constituted ('proceeds' as the act of love considered in itself) through the relation between Father and Son—which in its turn is a double relation founded on, respectively, the properties of Father and Son (the 'being-a-lover' of the former, the 'being-loved' of the latter)[36] and 'results' from the realization of the Father's *vis amandi* (power of loving), thus in the final analysis justifying the Father's being the origin (*principium*) of the Trinity.[37] The last part of *De Deo Trino* is dedicated to a defense of the Holy Spirit as a substantial being or ens per se subsistens (being subsisting through itself), as opposed to what is accidental: basing himself on the scriptures, Leibniz decisively rejects the Antitrinitarian theses according to which the Spirit is to be understood only as an attribute of God or as the choirs of angels.[38]

Having proposed the analogy with the mind that thinks itself, Leibniz hastens to point out that it is only an analogy. "On the other hand, what happens in the created Mind in some way," he writes in *De Deo Trino,* "occurs in God in the most perfect manner [perfectissima ratione],"[39] thus protecting himself from any suspicion of modalism. The same is true also in general for the terms 'person' and 'nature,' whose meaning we do not clearly grasp in the divine sphere, and which can consequently be applied to God only by analogy.[40] However, as these terms are in harmony with the sense of the scriptures and are approved by a long tradition, they remain, according to Leibniz, the most appropriate ones.[41] One should therefore refrain from abandoning them to invent new expressions not authorized by the scriptures and by the universal church.[42] And how justified were Leibniz's fears regarding a deviation from the canonic formulas of the doctrine of the Trinity, through the introduction of a new terminology, was to become clear a few years later with the violent polemic caused by the theories of William Sherlock.[43]

On the Person of Christ

Once again it is the *Examen Religionis Christianae* that is the point of arrival (albeit provisional) of a series of reflections on the doctrine of the Incarnation that came to maturity in the twenty years that separate this text from the early work *Demonstrationum Catholicarum Conspectus*. As I anticipated in commenting on the *Conspectus,* the viewpoint from which Leibniz interprets the mystery of the Incarnation is that of the "best of all possible worlds": following in the footsteps of the tradition that considers the fall of Adam as a *felix culpa* (fortunate fault) because it led to the Incarnation of the Son of God,[44] Leibniz points out that the redemption of the human race could not have taken place in a better way. Realizing the eternal, mysterious design of God's will, the second person of the Trinity took on human nature. With the Incarnation of the only begotten Son of the Father or Word of the divine mind, in whom the ideas or natures of all creatures are eminently *(eminenter)* contained, God's work was fulfilled, reaching the greatest possible nearness of creature to Creator through an expiation of the sins of humanity, carried out in the worthiest way possible. Thus man, already the borderline joining the superior and inferior natures, was raised to the highest degree of dignity, while God, by virtue of his unbounded benevolence, chose to abase himself and to communicate with man in order to establish a "City of God" or "Republic of minds" fit for the capacities of the minds he created.[45]

Following the dictates of orthodoxy established by the Council of Chalcedon (451), Leibniz recognizes in Christ only one person in two natures, divine and human. Christ is therefore true God and true man. In order to guarantee the oneness of the person, it is, however, necessary to point out (as both Lutheran and Reformed Protestant Scholastics taught, on the model of the late church fathers and the medieval tradition) that the human nature taken on by the second person of the Trinity has the features of impersonality: that is, it is not self-subsistent but is assumed into the unity of the person (or subsistence) of the Word by virtue of the Incarnation.[46] The canonical example, reproposed as we have seen by Leibniz, is that of the union of body and soul. Also in this case there are two natures (spiritual and corporeal) in a single person, and also in this case it is perhaps possible to maintain, Leibniz prudently goes on to say, that the body is sustained by the subsistence of the soul or that matter is sustained by the subsistence of the form, so that there is only one subsistence, that of the form.[47] Therefore, just as the person considered as a man (soul and body) is the same as when considered only as a soul, since the 'personality' or subsistence belongs to the soul, so too (Leibniz gives us to understand) the person of Christ is the same whether considered as the eternal, only begotten Son of God or as the Word incarnate, since the personality or subsistence is that of the divine person, in which the human nature is assumed.[48]

The analogy with the union of soul and body serves not only to let us glimpse something of the way in which two different natures are united but also, more modestly, to indicate the actual possibility of such a union, leaving aside man's capability (or rather, incapability) of establishing how this union is possible. This of course leaves open the enormously complex problem of how Leibniz himself conceives of the soul and body and the relation between them. He seems, however, to suggest that it is not necessary to discuss the matter here. The argument based on the actual union of soul and body remains valid no matter how this union is explained. To Spinoza's objection that to maintain that God takes on human nature would be just as contradictory as to attribute the nature of a square to a circle,[49] Leibniz replies: "Those who teach the incarnation explain its meaning by the simile of the Rational Soul united to the body. Therefore they want God to have assumed the nature of a man in no other way than that in which the mind assumed [assumsit] the nature of the body, that is, in the same way in which this is manifested [constat] in experience: no matter what the modes of explication may be. What therefore is said about the circle taking on the nature of the square cannot more forcefully be objected to the incarnation than to the union of the body with the soul."[50] An actual fact—the union of soul and body in human beings—indicates the possibility (and therefore noncontradictoriness) of the union of two different natures in one and the same person, however difficult or even inconceivable for limited human reason the explanation of the "mode" of the union may be. Leibniz is well aware of this difficulty,[51] even admitting at the end of his life—as we have seen—that an exhaustive explanation not only (as we might well expect) of the mystery of the Incarnation but also of the union of soul and body is beyond humankind's reach.[52] However, incomprehensibility does not in any way imply impossibility.

The features of Christology expounded up to here are, largely, those widely accepted by the Lutheran and Reformed schools. Leibniz, however, takes a step forward, remodeling the traditional analogy between the union of divine and human natures in Christ and the union of soul and body in man, and giving it a form that seems to him to present in the most elegant way the "congruence" and the "beauty" of the mystery of the Incarnation, by underlining its "harmony" with the mystery of the Trinity.[53] Driven by his concern to ensure the true humanity of Christ alongside his true divinity, he first of all denounces as erroneous the position according to which the divine nature occupies the place of the soul in Jesus Christ.[54] No, Leibniz insists, the second person of the Godhead took on human nature in its entirety, consisting of body and soul.[55] Therefore, on close inspection, we see that there are three natures in the one person of Christ: divine nature, finite spiritual nature, and corporeal nature. The mystery of the Incarnation therefore harmonizes beautifully with that of the Trinity: "As in the Trinity there are three persons, [but] one nature [una natura], so in the incarnation there are three natures (godhead, soul, flesh) within one person [tres sunt naturae (deitas, anima, caro) cum una persona]."[56]

However that may be, the union of human nature and divine nature in the person of Christ (traditionally referred to by the expression *unio personalis* [personal union]) is the closest and most perfect union possible between Creator and creature; it is not only a moral union, as the Nestorians held, but "a real influence, presence and intimate operation."[57] However, Leibniz warns, no one can claim to know exactly how this union comes to be. It is thus necessary to proceed with extreme caution, keeping to the teachings of the scriptures and tradition.[58] Tradition, in fact, condemns as erroneous two opposite ways of conceiving of this union: Nestorianism, which with its excessive distinction of the two natures ends up by turning Christ into two persons, and Eutychianism, which in order to ensure the unity of the person ends up by confounding the two natures, making Christ's humanity divine and admitting, in the final analysis, only divine nature in the incarnate Word.[59] If it does not reach the excesses of Eutychianism, the interpretation of the consequences of the personal union proposed in the doctrine of the communicatio idiomatum (communication of properties) at least tends, in Leibniz's opinion, in that direction. And, what is more, it is to be irrevocably rejected because it involves a contradiction. This seems to be the real reason, in accordance with his continually repeated statement that what is contradictory cannot but be false, that leads Leibniz to separate himself from the majority of Lutherans and come closer to the solution proposed by the Reformed Church. As we read in *De Persona Christi,* "*the attributes and operations of one Nature are not to be attributed to the other nature . . .* and certainly it seems contradictory to attribute the things that are proper to one nature to the other."[60] The contradiction Leibniz refers to corresponds to the logical error the Reformed thinkers accused the Lutherans of: that is, the teaching of a *communicatio idiomatum in abstracto,* that is, a communication or attribution of the properties of one nature considered in the abstract (respectively as 'divinity' and 'humanity') to the other nature, also considered in the abstract. Thus one reaches the contradictory statements that divinity as such has died (as Theopaschitism maintains) or that humanity as such enjoys ubiquity (as ubiquitism—admitted by Lutherans as a necessary condition for the real presence of the body and blood of Christ in the Eucharist—holds).[61] Leibniz adds to these two errors Monothelitism, that is, the admission in Christ of a single will, considering also this to be an undue confusion between the attributes and the operations of the two natures.[62] The only admissible form of attribution to Christ both of the divine properties and of human ones is attribution in the concrete: the attributes of, respectively, the divine nature and human nature are thus predicated of the concrete person of Christ, in his indissoluble unity of the two natures. Only in this sense is it possible to say that God (and, to be sure, not the divinity considered in the abstract as divinity) has died, or that man (and not humanity considered in the abstract as such) enjoys ubiquity.[63] In other words, "it can be said that a man is omnipresent in the same way as it can be said that a poet treats diseases, if the same man is also a doctor. Let it be understood in a sound way, that is, that he who is [eum qui est] a man, though not qua man, but qua God, is omnipresent, and that he who is [eum qui est] God was born of a virgin, but not inasmuch as he is God [non qua est Deus]. For we speak of the Divine or human nature in Christ according as Divine or human attributes are ascribed to the Christ."[64] Leibniz's solution therefore seems to lead in the direction of the *praedicatio verbalis* (verbal predication) admitted by Reformed thinkers: there is no real communication of properties from one nature to the other but a merely verbal predication of the attributes of both natures to the sole person of Jesus Christ. This praedicatio verbalis is, however, further to be qualified as *praedicatio vera* (true predication), since, for example, the predication of the omniscience or omnipotence of man occurs by synecdoche: a rhetorical figure in which, as is known, the whole is referred to by one of its parts.[65] The union of the two natures, Leibniz goes on, therefore occurs by virtue of the assumption of human nature in the single subsistence (or person) of the divine Word; this does not involve a communication of the divine properties, shared by the three persons of the Trinity, to human nature.[66] If, in fact, the hypostatic union consisted in the communication of properties, objects Leibniz, then the Father would be hypostatically united to the Son, to whom his divine attributes are communicated.[67] The analogy with the union of soul and body is once again useful for illustrating this point: in this case too the union does not involve any communication by the soul of its faculties of will and intellect to the body, just as, reciprocally, the body does not communicate to the soul the attribute of extension in space, and all this is true even though some operations can be understood only in the context of the union of the two.[68] Still, Leibniz is well aware of the distance between the two cases: unlike what happens in the Incarnation, the human soul, by virtue of the union, to some extent does share the body's imperfection.[69] In conclusion, it is enough to believe that, through the Incarnation, all the perfections that created nature is capable of are communicated to humanity, with the exclusion of what in human nature would contravene Christ's task of redemption, and barring any communication of the imperfection of human nature to the divine nature.[70] As for the question, widely debated at the time with reference to the communicatio idiomatum, regarding the state of spoliation and humiliation of Christ,[71] Leibniz considers it sufficient to speak of a state of concealment of the divine nature behind the veil of human nature, without having to admit any communicatio idiomatum. He thus distances himself also in this case from Lutheran Scholastics, favoring instead the Reformed doctrine of *occultatio* (occultation).[72] His solution to the related problem of the knowledge possessed by Christ also goes along these lines. It is not necessary to hold that Christ renounced the attribute of omniscience; it is sufficient, in this case as well, to admit a sort of concealment.[73] Moreover, it is not even necessary that there was always in Christ a *scientia actualis* (actual knowledge); it is sufficient (as Bonaventura and Gabriel Biel hold) to recognize a *scientia habitualis* (habitual knowledge), that is, the presence of the knowledge of everything not actually but only as a capacity or disposition.[74]

In Leibniz's eyes, the communicatio idiomatum, with its confusion of the attributes proper to each nature, presents another danger: that of the adoration of the human nature in Christ. It is, instead, only the person of Christ as God that should properly be worshiped, and both Catholics and Protestants should be reminded of this.[75] Otherwise one would end up by encouraging the charges of anthropolatry brought by Judaism and Islam or the error committed by the followers of Socinus, who, while admitting only the human nature in Christ, nonetheless continue to worship him.[76] Leibniz is very severe on this point, repeating the same idea with monotonous obstinacy. On the one hand, he loses no occasion to affirm the incomparably greater appropriateness of the doctrine of the universal church, according to which Christ deserves to be worshiped only because of his divine nature; on the other, he repeats several times that the Socinian cult is ruinous for salvation, on account of its idolatrous nature—in fact, besides the adoration due to the one God, the Socinians agree to worship also one whom they believe to be a mere man. Certainly the refusal to worship Jesus Christ expressed against Faustus Socinus himself by the Antitrinitarian Ferenc David is more coherent from this point of view; but what difference, wonders Leibniz, is there between this position and that of Islam?[77] Thus once again the Socinians emerge as a main target of Leibniz's theological polemics. And it is to the Socinians, this time those "of England," that he turns his attention in the years that follow.

PART III

English Trinitarian Polemics (1693–1705)

8

Between Tritheism and Modalism

From the early 1690s onward, Leibniz's attention was repeatedly drawn to debates surrounding the "Sociniens d'Angleterre."[1] This growing interest in the Trinitarian polemics that agitated England in the seventeenth and eighteenth centuries is not surprising. The caliber of the persons involved in them was impressive: the combatants range from John Locke, to Ralph Cudworth and John Toland, to the renowned mathematician John Wallis. No less impressive was the importance of the topics discussed: these included the controversy surrounding the concepts of substance, essence, and person unleashed by the theories of William Sherlock; the question of the use of the mathematical method in theology; and the debate on the epistemological doctrine contained in Locke's *Essay* and in Toland's *Christianity not Mysterious*.

A more specific early focus of this attention was a major publication by one of the most important English Antitrinitarians, Stephen Nye's *Considerations on the Explications of the Doctrine of the Trinity, by Dr. Wallis, Dr. Sherlock, Dr. S[ou]th, Dr. Cudworth, and Mr. Hooker*. After obtaining a copy of this work shortly after it appeared anonymously in London in 1693,[2] Leibniz drew an *Extrait*, which he followed up with an ample series of *Remarques*.[3] These are two fundamental texts for Leibniz's reflections on the Trinity: the *Extrait* offers a picture of the Trinitarian doctrines discussed with greatest animation in England at the end of the seventeenth century; and the *Remarques* concisely tackle the major theologico-philosophical problems involved in the defense of this mystery.

Stephen Nye's Considerations *and Leibniz's* Abstract

Leibniz learned of the Trinitarian doctrines of John Wallis, William Sherlock, Robert South, Ralph Cudworth, and Richard Hooker through the filter of the often distorting critical interpretation of them proposed by the Antitrinitarian Nye. Leibniz is well aware of the importance of direct contact with the sources: as he himself points out at the beginning of the *Remarques,* not having at his disposal the texts criticized by Nye, he prefers not to express any judgment on the authors in question.[4] On the other hand, although the theories reported by Nye should be taken with a grain of salt, Leibniz takes advantage of the unique opportunity offered by the little book to gain a panorama of the main English Trinitarian debates at the end of the seventeenth century.[5] The path laid out by Nye and, in his turn, by Leibniz is thus a useful guide for anyone who wishes to venture into the dense forest of polemical writings on the subject of the Trinity that appeared in England toward the end of the seventeenth century.[6]

Stephen Nye is certainly one of the most authoritative sources for information regarding the historical and doctrinal justification given by the English Antitrinitarians to their movement. A contemporary of Leibniz,[7] he wrote the anonymous work in which the term *Unitarians*—which was to become the distinctive name of Socinianism in England[8]—appeared on the title page of an English book for the first time: *A Brief History of the Unitarians, called also Socinians. In Four Letters, Written to a Friend* (London, 1687).[9] His *Considerations* of 1693 summarily review the doctrines he expounded in detail in the *Brief History.* The first of them was the thesis that "'tis the principal Design of both Testaments, by Confession of all Parties, to establish the Worship and Belief of *one only God.*"[10] Now, Nye adds, the problem is that most "modern" Christians believe in a single God only in words, while in reality they affirm that there are three gods.[11] When it is a question of interpreting what is meant by "There is one God," for inexplicable reasons "the plain, obvious and indubitable meaning of these words" proposed by the Unitarians is rejected, and the introduction of a mysterious Trinity is claimed to be justified.[12] Of all Nye's ironical comments made against the arguments put forward by Cardinal Bellarmino, Leibniz takes only the statement that Bellarmino himself "avows that the Trinity, if it had been proposed to the Hebrews, who were coming out of Egypt and imbued with polytheism or a multitude of Gods, would have caused them to fall back into it, and believe in three gods."[13]

In Leibniz's *Extrait* we find an early indication of the line of defense that will be adopted in the *Remarques* as well: one of the basic equivocations of the Unitarians is to understand the doctrine of the Trinity exclusively in the light of our natural experience.[14] "However," Leibniz continues in his summary, "the Trinity having gained the upper hand at the first Council of Nicaea, the Trinitarians were embarrassed to seek for explanations that could reconcile their opinions with this great commandment. Here are some of them[.]"[15] And thus the battle was waged not only between the supporters of the dogma and the Antitrinitarians: equally violent attacks were engaged within the Trinitarian camp as well. In his presentation of the different explanations given of the mystery of the Trinity, Nye starts with the one that seems to him to be most favorable to the Unitarians: the position of John Wallis.[16]

Nye focuses directly on eight letters and three sermons composed by Wallis in 1690 and 1691.[17] In fact, the *Considerations* contain only the last of a series of attacks that Nye made against the Trinitarian doctrine of Wallis[18] in a polemic that started softly but gradually became more heated, reaching its apex in 1693. Among the various objections put forward, the main one—and the one most specifically directed against Wallis's proposed solution—is the following; Wallis really teaches a new kind of modalism, thus reviving the ancient Sabellian heresy.[19] Concerned to ensure the unity of the Godhead, he reduces the divine persons to three relations of God with his creatures: the one God, depending on the 'mode' or 'aspect' by which he is considered in relation to his creatures, presents himself alternatively as creator, redeemer, or sanctifier.[20]

The concept of person presented by Wallis is rightly identified as "the hinge of the Controversie."[21] Wallis affirms that the meaning given by current usage to the term "person" is wrong. In his opinion, the Socinian objection is based on this improper use, according to which, just as in the human sphere by three persons we mean three human beings, thus in the divine sphere three persons that are said to be God are the same as three gods.[22] In fact, the term "person" is often substituted for the words "man" and "woman" when we want to refer to a human being regardless of sex. This usage, however, derives only from the lack, in the English language, of a specific term that indicates in general an individual belonging to the human species, as the Latin term *homo* does. Now it is just this lack that gives rise to the misunderstanding by which one commonly holds that 'another person' must always mean 'another man' (or 'another woman'). To understand what the church fathers meant by the term "person" (*persona*), it is therefore necessary to go back to the original Latin sense. "In approved *Latin* Authours," writes Wallis, "the word *Persona* . . . did signifie *the State, Quality, or Condition of a Man, as he stands Related to other Men.* . . . And so, as the *Condition* varied, the *Person* varied also, though the same *Man* remained. . . . So that there is nothing of *Contradiction*, nothing of *Inconsistence*, nothing *Absurd* or *Strange* in it, for the *same Man* to sustain *divers Persons*, (either successively, or at the same Time;) or *divers Persons* to meet in *the same Man*."[23] In particular, Wallis refers to a passage by Cicero taken from the *De Oratore* (II, 102): "Thus *Tully*, (who well unterstood the Propriety of *Latin* words) *Sustineo Unus tres Personas; meam, Adversarii, Judicis*, (I being One and the same Man, sustain Three Persons; That of my Own, that of my Adversary, and that of the Judge.)[24] And *David* was, at the same time, *Son* of *Jesse, Father* of *Solomon*, and *King* of *Israel*. And this takes away the very Foundation of their Objection; Which proceeds upon this Mistake, as if *Three Persons* (in a proper sense) must needs imply *Three Men*."[25] Wallis's conclusion is therefore that, just as in the human sphere three distinct persons can be a single man, so too in the divine sphere three distinct persons can be a single God.[26] However, he does not tire of repeating that the term "person" can be applied to God only by analogy.[27]

What is more, in Wallis's view, the real heart of the matter is not the notion of "person" but the notion of these three "somewhats" that the church fathers meant to indicate by the term "person." Even if the basic inadequacy of the term were to be established, one could abandon it without compromising the notion that one wants to indicate: that is, that in God there are three "somewhats" whose distinction one from the other is greater than that existing among the divine attributes, but not so great as to represent three gods.[28] It seems to have escaped Wallis's notice, however, that the problem Nye puts his finger on is precisely the *notion* of these three "somewhats" and not simply the *name* used to refer to them. Whether or not one calls them by the term "person," the Antitrinitarian remarks, these three "somewhats" are only "External Denominations" or "Accidental Predications," and certainly not the "three real subsisting Persons" that the church believes in.[29] If the entire doctrine of the Trinity is reduced to the distinction among three "somewhats" or, better still (Nye ironically adds), three "nothings,"[30] then even the Unitarians are ready to subscribe to it.[31]

Whereas Wallis's "Ciceronian Trinity" (as Nye calls it with biting irony)[32] is only a new form of modalism, at the other extreme lies the even more serious error taught by William Sherlock:[33] Tritheism. There had been a lively debate around the ideas of Sherlock, ever since, in 1690, he published in London a

Vindication of the Doctrine of the Holy and ever Blessed Trinity,[34] in which he attacks two classic texts of the Unitarian movement: the abovementioned *Brief History of the Unitarians* (written, as we have seen, by Nye) and *Brief Notes on the Creed of St. Athanasius,*[35] in which, paragraph by paragraph, the text of the creed of St. Athanasius is reported and sharply criticized, with passages of fierce sarcasm.[36] It is mainly the theses expounded by Sherlock in the fourth section of the *Vindication*[37] that aroused considerable criticism both among the Antitrinitarians and among the supporters of the dogma. Sherlock starts from the observation that "the difficulty is, how Three distinct substantial Persons can subsist in One numerical Essence . . . let us then enquire, what it is, that makes any substance numerically One[.]"[38] In the material sphere, the unity of the body is assured by the union of the various parts. However, this cannot hold true in the spiritual sphere, where there are neither extension nor parts.[39] In the case of spirits, the principle of unity is identified by Sherlock in self-consciousness: "This Self-unity of the Spirit, which has no Parts to be united, can be nothing else but Self-consciousness: That it is conscious to its own Thoughts, Reasonings, Passions, which no other finite Spirit is conscious to but itself: This makes a finite Spirit numerically One, and separates it from all other Spirits."[40] If, on the one hand, the consciousness of its own thoughts and passions makes a spirit (or mind) numerically one, on the other this same consciousness is also the principle of distinction from all other spirits or minds. This is true particularly for the unity (and at the same time the distinction) of the person, where by "person" is meant "intelligent Being."[41] Now, just as for finite spirits "the self-consciousness of every Person to itself makes them distinct Persons,"[42] so too in the divine sphere what distinguishes the Father, Son, and Spirit is their distinct self-consciousness.[43] Since we are dealing with God, these three distinct minds must be three infinite minds.[44] Once Sherlock has explained the distinction between the divine persons by the concept of self-consciousness, he still has the problem of showing how these three persons can be one single God. According to Sherlock, the unity of God is guaranteed by the fact that, alongside a distinct self-consciousness, there is also at the same time a perfect mutual consciousness among the divine persons.[45] Self-consciousness and mutual consciousness are thus the key that makes it possible to account perfectly for the two conditions of orthodoxy enunciated in the creed of St. Athanasius: "Neither to confound the Person, nor to divide the Substance, that is, to acknowledge Three distinct Persons, and yet but One God."[46]

The Unitarians' response to Sherlock's *Vindication* was not long in coming; as Nye himself in his *Considerations* informs us, "In about *four* or *five*

Weeks time, out came their *Observations* on the *Vindication* of Dr. *Sher-lock; which in some Editions of them are prefaced, with* the Acts or Gest of *Athanasius.*"[47] According to the anonymous author of the *Observations,* the affirmation of "Three distinct and infinite Minds"[48] would inevitably be tan-tamount to the notion of three gods.[49] The charge of Tritheism returns force-fully also in the *Considerations* of Stephen Nye. As before in the *Observations,* it is particularly the concept of mutual consciousness that is targeted. Nye denies that this mutual consciousness, which is supposed to guarantee the unity of the Godhead, can be a sufficient foundation for numerical unity among the three divine persons, conceived of as three perfectly distinct in-finite minds.[50] The source of this doctrine of the Trinity is to be found, Nye acutely observes, in Descartes' "cogito ergo sum" ("I think therefore I am"), on the basis of which Descartes comes to identify the nature of the mind and spirit with being "a *thinking Being.*" Now, argues Nye, it is just this identi-fication of the essence of the mind and spirit with thinking that opened the doors to Sherlock's claim that an internal and perfect consciousness of the thoughts in one another's mind is the foundation of an essential unity.[51] If Wallis's doctrine is a "Ciceronian Trinity," Sherlock's can therefore be called a "Cartesian Trinity."[52]

It was not only the Unitarians who accused Sherlock of Tritheism. The pages written by the theologian of the Church of England Robert South (1634–1716) are so cutting that they moved even Stephen Nye to come to Sherlock's defense.[53] According to Leibniz's lively description of the mat-ter given in the *Extrait,* the publishing of the Socinian *Observations on the Learned Vindication of the Trinity and Incarnation* "opened everyone's eyes."[54] Even those who had originally greeted with favor Sherlock's *Vin-dication* now acknowledged that "Mr. Sherlock had gone to the opposite extreme, and that a wiser champion should take his place."[55] Sherlock, for his part, "understood, that he would do well to keep silent, and it was the opinion of the most politic, who feared for the success of the war, judging that the best thing was to let the Socinians be, since the orthodox are masters of pulpits and people. . . . But Dr. South, not at all wanting to suffer this blot of their Churches, could not refrain from stating in the end that he did not at all share the opinions of Mr. Sherlock and that the Socinians were right in saying that Tritheism was a consequence of his opinion."[56]

In 1693 an anonymous work by Robert South, which was destined to open another important chapter in the debate, was published: the *Animadversions upon Dr. Sherlock's Book, entituled A Vindication of the Holy and Ever-Blessed Trinity.*[57] As Nye points out, South's position is in the Aristotelian-Scholastic tradition.[58] South, defending the use of the traditional terms "essence," "substance," "nature," and "subsistence," harshly criticizes Sherlock's attempt to replace them with terms of his own invention.[59] The target of his attack is the two concepts around which Sherlock's doctrine of the Trinity revolves: self-consciousness and mutual consciousness. South's principal objection is that self-consciousness cannot be "the Formal Constituent Reason of Personality." Since it is an act of reflection on a person's acts, self-consciousness presupposes the subsistence of the person, namely, it presupposes an already formed personality and therefore cannot be the formal reason of it.[60] At the basis of South's confutation lies the principle of the priority of subsistence over all acts, in particular over all acts of knowledge in every self-conscious person. In other words, South insists on the "Priority of Being," with its primary modes and affections, over every act of knowledge ascribable to that being.[61] If this is generally valid both against the notion of self-consciousness and against that of mutual consciousness,[62] against the notion of mutual consciousness as the formal reason of a unity of nature among the persons of the Trinity he particularly notes that "Every *Act of Knowledge* supposes the *Unity* of the Thing, or *Being* from which that Act flows, as Antecedent to it, and therefore cannot be the *Formal Reason* of the said *Being*."[63]

Like Nye, South also remarks on the Cartesian origin of Sherlock's doctrine. In his opinion, the notion of self-consciousness stems from a misunderstanding of Descartes' "Cogito ergo sum."[64] But whereas Nye acknowledges in Descartes' original doctrine the identification of the nature of a mind or spirit with being "a thinking Being,"[65] South instead seems to release Descartes from the charge of having laid the foundation for Sherlock's theory, in which thought becomes the formal cause of the res cogitans. In fact, South seems to interpret the "Cogito" statement in the light of the principle of the priority of subsistence over acts: in Descartes' conception, he argues, thought remains simply the act of a preexisting subsisting "Being" that, starting from its effect, it is possible to identify as the cause. In South's view, Sherlock is therefore exclusively responsible for the unjustifiable leap from thinking considered as an effect to thinking considered as a cause.

The direct accusation of Tritheism finds its formulation and justification in chapter V of the *Animadversions*.[66] South denies that the persons of the Trinity are "three distinct Infinite Minds, or Spirits": in this case they would, in fact, be three gods, since "God and Infinite Mind, or Spirit, are Terms Equipollent, and Convertible."[67] Given the definition of "Mind" or "Spirit" as "Substantia Incorporea Intelligens [Intelligent Incorporeal Substance],"[68] three distinct Minds or Spirits would also be three distinct substances.[69]

After seven chapters of refutations, South reaches the apex of his presumed role as a champion of orthodoxy, expounding in the eighth chapter, "*The*

Ancient and Generally received Doctrine of the Church *concerning the* Article *of the* Blessed Trinity, *as it is delivered by* Councils, Fathers, Schoolmen, *and other later* Divines."[70] And here the problems begin. According to South, "every *Person* of the *Blessed Trinity* . . . is properly *The Godhead as subsisting with and under such a certain Mode, or Relation.*"[71] Nye has no doubt: in the balance between modalism and Tritheism, the Scholastic tradition (at least as it is presented by South) inclines toward modalism.[72] Leibniz summarizes Nye's caustic criticism of South's "Aristotelian Trinity" thus:[73]

> Doctor S[ou]th tells us that personalities are modes, and that modes or ways of being are neither substances nor accidents; that it is like a posture with regard to a body, which does not add any new entity. Moreover, he says that dependence, mutability, presence, absence, inherence, adherence are such modes, and they have no existence outside the thing they belong to. But in this fashion the three persons would not even be real entities [des realités]. . . . The doctor, having kept us in suspense for seven long chapters, in the end boils the whole thing down to nothing. There we are—all this fuss and insults against doctor Sherlock for having abandoned a Trinity of nothing, three postures of the same thing or three relationships. Not to mention that modes are changeable, and that persons are not. He will also say that God in posture A has engendered God in posture B, and that from postures A and B proceeds posture C. The Socinians will say that the controversy should end, and that it is futile to fight over postures.[74]

According to Nye, Ralph Cudworth too came out against the Scholastic doctrine of the Trinity, as being nominalist and Sabellian.[75] In *The True Intellectual System of the Universe* (London, 1678) the thesis of the famous Cambridge Platonist is that *"the* Platonicks *and* Pythagoreans, *at least, if not other* Pagans *also, had their* Trinity, *as well as* Christians."[76] The fact that some of the finest pagan minds came so close to a Trinitarian conception of God indicates, in Cudworth's view, that the Christian doctrine of the Trinity too is not as absurd as some people would have it. According to him, it is especially the genuine Trinity of Plato, unadulterated by the Platonists of later eras, that is very close to the Christian conception.[77] However, there are some differences between this "True and Genuine Platonick Trinity" (understood as the "Trinity of Divine Hypostases") and the Christian doctrine. Of these, the admission by Plato that the second and third hypostases are subordinated to the first is particularly important. This subordination, however, Cudworth points out, is introduced only to avoid a plurality of coordinated gods. In fact, the Platonists conceive of the three hypostases as being eternal, necessarily existing, infinite, omnipotent, and creative, and as partaking of a divine essence that is not unique but general and universal. Given these characteristics, without admitting a certain dependence and subordination one would inevitably end up falling into Tritheism.[78] Now, Cudworth continues, a certain subordination and dependence of the second and third persons on the first is admitted by the Christian doctrine of the Trinity as well.[79] In particular, the church fathers of the first three centuries seem to have upheld a subordinationism similar to that of the Platonists.[80]

To avoid Sabellianism, that is, the doctrine that the Father, Son, and Holy Spirit are only three different names for the same hypostasis, with only one essence, the church fathers also generally maintained that the divine essence shared by the persons of the Trinity is not singular but universal. This is clearly shown, argues Cudworth, even by the choice of the term "Homoousia" (and not "Tautoousia" and "Monoousia," which are too Sabellian) to indicate the shared participation in the divine essence.[81] At this point, without the admission of a certain dependence and subordination among the divine persons, that is, without the admission of a certain priority and posteriority in order and dignity, one could not hold that the three persons are only one God, any more than one can say that three men who share the same universal human essence are only one man.[82] Is there not, however, a form of Arianism hiding behind such subordinationism? Cudworth tries to refute this objection by insisting on the fact that, for the Platonists, as for the fathers of the early centuries, the second and third hypostases are not created by the first but partake of the same eternity, necessary existence, infinity, and omnipotence.[83] Since the Father is the root and source of the Son and Spirit, the three hypostases are one single principle and one single Creator; they are indissolubly united and enjoy a "Mutual Inexistence," or "Emperichoresis."[84]

Although on the one hand Nye appreciates Cudworth's criticism of the Sabellian position, on the other he does not fail to underline the weak points in the theory advanced by the Cambridge Platonist. According to the Antitrinitarian, the Platonic Trinity defended by the *True Intellectual System of the Universe,* starting from an initial Tritheism, ends up by falling back (despite Cudworth's intentions) into a Unitarian position. Seeing the undeniable Tritheistic consequences deriving from the admission of three persons each of which is omnipotent, infinite, eternal, and necessary, endowed with a divine essence that is not singular but general and universal, Cudworth would have the divine unity be guaranteed by the dependence of the second and third persons on the first. Now, objects Nye, such subordination, far from being able to guarantee the unity of the divine persons, only results in the admission of a single omnipotent God, namely, the Father, on whom the Son and Holy Spirit depend. And this, concludes Nye, is nothing but the position defended by the moderate wings of Arianism, despite Cudworth's protests to the contrary.[85]

The last doctrine of the Trinity examined by Nye is that expounded by Richard Hooker in *Of the Lawes of Ecclesiasticall Politie*.[86] Nye dwells in particular on what Hooker says in book V of the *Lawes*: "For the substance of God with this propertie *to be of none,* doth make the person of the Father; the very selfesame substance in number with this propertie *to be of the Father* maketh the person of the Sonne; the same substance hauing added vnto it the propertie of *proceeding from the other two,* maketh the person of the holie Ghost[.]"[87] In the first place, Nye points out the discrepancy between this conception and the commonly accepted orthodox doctrine. It clashes directly with the teaching of Peter Lombard, "the father of modern orthodoxy," according to whom the divine essence neither generates nor is generated, nor proceeds.[88] Moreover, Nye goes on, all the defenders of the dogma agree that the properties or characters of the Trinitarian relations are something positive and not a simple negation, as would be the case if the property of the Father is "to be of none."[89] But, aside from these differences within the Trinitarian field, Nye underlines the fact that Hooker's doctrine is self-contradictory, as it holds that the same numerically single substance, belonging to the Father, Son, and Holy Ghost, is simultaneously generated (in the Son) and ungenerated (in the Father), proceeds (in the Holy Ghost) and does not proceed (in the Father).[90] Moreover, it would also be false to say that God is "self-originated" or "self-begotten," as the correct expressions are "unoriginated" or "unbegotten."[91] Nye concludes his attack by remarking that, in Hooker's doctrine of the Trinity, the generation of the Son ends up by being the destruction of the Father. The property or characteristic of the Father (coinciding with being ungenerated) would, in fact, be destroyed within the divine substance by the characteristic of the Son, which is that of being generated.[92]

In the years immediately following the publication of Nye's *Considerations,* the controversy showed no signs of dying down.[93] Thomas Smith, replying in December 1694 to a letter in which Leibniz tells him he had heard of discussions arising in England regarding the inclination toward Tritheism and modalism, respectively, of the doctrines of Sherlock and Wallis,[94] admits that he is profoundly sorry for the rebirth on English soil of long-condemned ancient heresies.[95] Attempts at explanation such as those of Sherlock, with the introduction of new terms on the basis of which one would claim to have solved all the difficulties of the doctrine of the Trinity, instead of reducing the flames, only cause the fire to flare up further.[96] In Thomas Smith's opinion, Wallis was more cautious, although his replacement of the term "person" by the expression "three Somethings" was laughed at and harshly criticized.[97]

In November 1695, Thomas Burnett sent Princess Electress Sophie a report (translated into French by Leibniz) on the English Trinitarian polemics.[98] It is not by chance that in these letters of Thomas Smith and Thomas Burnett Sherlock's theories are still at the center of the debate. In fact, in 1694 Sherlock published anonymously a vibrant *Defence* of his doctrine of the Trinity.[99] Anything but convinced by Sherlock's *Defence*, South returns to the fray, publishing anonymously a book with the unequivocal title of *Tritheism Charged upon Dr Sherlock's New Notion of the Trinity* (London, 1695). The theses, attributed to Sherlock, that the nature of a Spirit consists in "Vital internal Sensation," that "The Trinity in Unity" can be explained "by Sensation and Continuity of Sensation," and that a man "feeling himself a distinct Person, can be the Reason of his being so" are all rejected on the basis of the same basic argument already used in the *Animadversions*: that is, the priority of subsistence over all acts.[100] This time, however, it is Jean Le Clerc who is accused of being the source of Sherlock's heterodox theses. The text singled out is the juvenile *Epistolae Theologicae,* published by Le Clerc in 1679 under the pseudonym Liberius de Sancto Amore.[101] The first harsh charge brought against Le Clerc is that of having denied that the mysteries are incomprehensible, and because of this denial of the "mysteriousness" of the Trinity the author of the *Epistolae Theologicae* is associated with Sherlock.[102] This is not all; the roots of Sherlock's specific doctrine of the Trinity are traced back to Le Clerc, inspired by Descartes' philosophy.[103] In the *Epistolae Theologicae,* in fact, it is asserted that the three divine persons are three distinct "Cogitationes" (or "distincti modi cogitandi [distinct modes of thinking]" or "distinctae series cogitationum [distinct series of thoughts]") in the single divine essence or nature.[104] In its turn, "Cogitatio" is defined as "whatever appears in our mind of which we are conscious,"[105] and this, maintains South, manifestly corresponds to Self-Consciousness. From these three distinct Cogitationes or Self-Consciousnesses of Le Clerc, Sherlock then passed to his three distinct spirits or minds. At this point, Le Clerc came to his aid once again, showing him the way to unite these three spirits thanks to his thesis that "Spirits can be united by cogitation alone"[106]—a thesis that, according to South, clearly recalls Sherlock's notion of mutual consciousness.[107]

These pages by South would seem to be the attempt to discredit Le Clerc lamented by Thomas Burnett in his letter to Leibniz of 22 September 1695.[108] Leibniz, for his part, though repeatedly expressing his esteem for Le Clerc,[109] has his reservations about Le Clerc's doctrine of the Trinity, and refers in particular to the juvenile *Epistolae Theologicae.*[110] In general, Burnett seems to appreciate South's writings, giving a flattering opinion of them in a letter dating from early 1696.[111] In the same letter, Leibniz is informed of an official position taken by the University of Oxford against Sherlock's terminology.[112] This time Sherlock's attempt at justification finds an answer in an anonymous publication by John Wallis.[113] In June of the same year, Thomas Burnett reports on the intervention of the bishops and King William III himself (the royal edict of 3 February 1696) by which they tried to put an end to the controversy by prohibiting any discussion of the Trinity except in the terms used in scripture and in the doctrinal articles of the Church of England. The shrill cry of the dispute of previous years was thus dying out; the Socinian treatises became ever rarer and more expensive, and Sherlock was let off the hook without ever having to admit defeat before his adversaries.[114]

Leibniz's Judgment

Leibniz opens his *Remarques* on Nye's *Considerations* by declaring that he has not seen what Wallis, Sherlock, and South have written on the Trinity.[115] And though having previously had occasion to appreciate Cudworth's *True Intellectual System of the Universe,* he does not now have it at hand.[116] He therefore prefers to abstain from a direct discussion of the doctrines upheld by the authors Nye criticizes, and to deal instead with the question of the Trinity.[117]

The first nonnegotiable point to be established is the Christian religion's absolute monotheism. Hence the refusal of every hypothesis that admits of three absolute, infinite, omnipotent, eternal, and sovereignly perfect substances, since three substances having these characteristics could not be anything but three gods.[118] Subordinationism, which conceives of the second and third persons of the Trinity as substances inferior to the supreme God and yet worthy of worship as gods, also is to be rejected, on account of its dangerous inclination toward polytheism and idolatry.[119] Leibniz here sinks his knife into one of the sores that afflict the debate even within the Antitrinitarian camp. If Stephen Nye accuses Cudworth's doctrine of this form of moderate Arianism, for their part the Antitrinitarians are not spared the criticisms of their adversaries for attributing divine honors to Jesus Christ.[120] Even Nye, stung to the quick by the works in which William Basset and Francis Fullwood accuse Socinus's followers of idolatry for having attributed the honors due to God to one whom they consider to be only a man,[121] feels obliged to point out that the "Socinians of England" honor Jesus Christ only as one exalted by God and put at the head of a church, not attributing to him anything more than what most Trinitarians ascribe to his human nature.[122]

If, therefore, on the one hand Leibniz rejects any hypothesis smelling of Tritheism or polytheism, on the other hand he also rejects modalism of a

Sabellian type, which considers the persons of the Trinity to be three names or three aspects of one and the same being.[123] This, in fact, would be a distortion of the meaning of the scriptures, just as unacceptable as "the violent explanations the Socinians give to passages of scripture."[124] Therefore, rejecting the position upheld by Wallis—though without naming him directly—Leibniz instead shares his opinion that the Socinians interpret the biblical passages in a distorted way. But just as Wallis proposes, he too does not waste time in long exegetical discussions. Instead he tackles directly what seems to him the key point, the question of possibility:[125] "The difficulty is that when one says that the Father is God, the Son is God, and the Holy Spirit is God; and that each one of these is not the other; and that, with all this, there are not three gods but only one God; it looks as though there is a clear contradiction, because, according to common sense, it is precisely in this that the notion of plurality consists, since if John is a man and if Peter is a man and if John is not Peter and Peter is not John, there will be two men. Either that or it must be admitted that we do not know what two means."[126] In other words, if one wishes to maintain the oneness of God, adhering to the indispensable principle that things which are identical to a third thing are identical to each other, it would seem that one has to affirm that there is no real difference between Father, Son, and Spirit, since all three would coincide with this one God. If, on the other hand, one wishes to maintain the distinctions among the persons of the Trinity, it would seem that one has inevitably to affirm the existence of three gods.

It is once again the distinction between God taken absolutely or essentially and God taken relatively or as a person that Leibniz puts forward as a solution to the apparent contradiction:[127] "Thus when in the Symbol attributed to St. Athanasius, it is said that the Father is God, that the Son is God, and that the Holy Spirit is God, and yet there is only one God, it must be admitted that if this word or term 'God' was always understood in the same way, both in naming three each of whom is God, and in saying that there is only one God, there would be an untenable contradiction. Therefore one must say that in the first case the word 'God' is understood as a person of the divinity, of which there are three, and in the second case as an absolute substance that is unique."[128] Continuing, Leibniz could not be more explicit in repeating one of the convictions on which his whole system is founded: the absolute validity of the principle of noncontradiction.[129] To admit that the dogma of the Trinity goes against this principle would be tantamount to declaring victory for the Socinians, who would rightly reject this dogma as false.[130]

Only after having assured the essential condition for faith in the Trinity, that is, the absence of a proven contradiction, can Leibniz pass on to the explanation of the mystery of the Trinity. His first approach to the problem is extremely cautious: relying on those same concepts of absolute and relative that are central to the distinction used to reject the charge of self-contradiction, Leibniz tries to stay as closely as possible to the terms of the scriptures and to the doctrine of the Trinity as handed down by church tradition.[131] However, he cannot stop there. And therefore we see him slowly unraveling the tangle: first he dwells on the epistemological status of the mysteries in a comparison with disciplines that are incapable of reaching the absolute certainty of demonstration, and then he gives a judgment (albeit with a grain of salt) on the theories criticized by Nye; lastly, he presents his own tentative interpretation of the traditional doctrine discussed previously:

> Nevertheless the objections of the Adversaries caused people to go further and led to an explanation of what is meant by person. In this, it has been more difficult to succeed since explanations depend on definitions. Now, those who give us the sciences are used to giving us also definitions. But it is not the same with Legislators, and even less with Religion. Therefore since the Holy Scripture and also the Tradition provide us with certain terms and they do not at the same time give us a precise definition of them, that forces us to make possible hypotheses when we want to explain things, in rather the same way as we do in Astronomy. And often the lawyers are obliged to do the same in order to give a term a meaning that can satisfy at the same time all the passages of the law as well as reason.[132]

The debate around the concept of person to which Leibniz refers has been seen to be one of the typical features of the English Trinitarian discussions.[133] Leibniz, without here entering into an exposition of his concept of person, instead offers some clarification of the type of knowledge that we can reach in the case of the mysteries. First of all, he repeats what he earlier stated in the *Remarque* to *Symbole et Antisymbole des Apostres:* we do not have a precise definition of the concept of person, in particular as applied to the divine sphere.[134] This fact, which also concerns other terms handed down by the scriptures and the tradition without adequate definition, prevents religion from reaching the status of a science, that is, a rigorously demonstrative discipline based on exact definitions. In this respect, Leibniz classifies jurisprudence and astronomy with religion.[135] Both in the case of the mysteries and in that of the problems dealt with by jurisprudence, it is not possible to proceed with the tools of rigorously demonstrative reasoning, typical of mathematics. Instead, it is necessary to have recourse to such procedures as the presumption of truth, the defense strategy, and reasoning by analogy.[136] Astronomy, in its turn, seems to be associated with religion for the type of certainty it can reach. Lacking precise definitions, that is, an exact knowledge of its objects of study, it can only draw hypothetical conclusions; that is, such conclusions are to be taken as valid until a proof to the contrary is given. After having proposed the parallel between the mysteries and the objects of jurisprudence, however, Leibniz points out an important difference between these two spheres: "The difference is that the explanation of the Mysteries of religion is not necessary; instead the explanation of the laws is necessary in order to judge of divergences. Therefore in matters [of the Mysteries] the best thing would be to stick exactly to the revealed terms insofar as possible."[137] Replying in July 1696 to the letter in which Thomas Burnett informed him of the intervention of the authorities to put an end to the Trinitarian controversies, Leibniz repeats: "You Sirs did well in making the disputes regarding the Trinity stop, and the safest thing is to stay with the terms of the scriptures and of the church. For to argue about terms on which there are no clear definitions is to play the game of morra in the darkness."[138]

Thus in these passages it seems that Leibniz intends to give up every attempt to explain the mystery of the Trinity; yet this intention is immediately belied, not only in the course of the *Remarques* themselves but also in all those texts where an explanation is, in fact, attempted. The above statements should thus be read in the light of what Leibniz writes on other occasions.[139] In general, it emerges that he does not at all intend to advise renouncing any explanation that goes beyond a strict exegesis of biblical passages. In his opinion, a rigorously textualist position would not be sufficient to refute the objections of the adversaries. Rather, his seems to be an appeal to prudence, when faced with attempts at explanation that, by introducing new terms in lieu of traditional ones, come to conclusions of doubtful orthodoxy. Given the guarantee of a long church tradition, Leibniz also approves of the use of terms, such as "person," which have no precise definition, and he does so because he does not feel it is right to renounce "everything that one adds to the mysteries beyond the express words of scripture."[140] It once again seems that Leibniz's attitude regarding the explanation of the mysteries should be basically referred to the position expounded in section 5 of the *Theodicy*'s "Preliminary Discourse," where the ambiguity deriving from the oscillation in meaning of the verb "expliquer," present in the texts of the period we are examining here, is finally eliminated thanks to his famous distinction between "expliquer" (to explain) and "comprendre" (to comprehend).[141] This seems to be the drift of what Leibniz, in October 1693, replies to Gerhard Meier, who, referring to Sherlock's attempts at demonstration, questions Leibniz on the principle that "one cannot and should not believe anything, except what takes the authority of truth from reason":[142] "As for the use of reason in Theology, I admit that nothing ought to be believed, unless some ground for belief is adduced, so that at least there is much force in the arguments, if not clearly a moral certitude. We believe [what] God [says] without arguments, but arguments are needed to know that it is God who has spoken."[143] If, on the one hand, one must not pretend fully to understand the revealed truths, that is, to demonstrate rationally what has been revealed by God ("Deo creditur sine argumentis"), nonetheless there must be some motives of credibility that justify faith in superrational propositions. That is, one must verify, by rational arguments, that what is said has the nature of an authentic revelation ("opus est argumentis ut sciamus Deum esse locutum").[144]

Having traced the limits within which the use of reason can and must be extended to the sphere of faith, Leibniz, though he is always well aware of the need to consult the sources directly,[145] does not refrain from giving a rapid judgment on the doctrines of the Trinity criticized by Nye. His first observation concerns the insufficiency of mutual consciousness as a guarantee of the union in one and the same individual nature of three persons conceived of as absolute substances, each endowed with its own nature, that is, as three Spirits, each of which possesses its own infinitude, knowledge, and omnipotence. If the perfect mutual consciousness of the thoughts of the different persons were sufficient to assure numerical unity, then God, who perfectly understands our thoughts, would be essentially united to us, to the point of constituting a single individual.[146]

Such a hypothesis errs therefore on the side of excess, attributing too much to the different persons and decidedly inclining toward Tritheism. On the other hand, however, the hypothesis hinging on a concept of personality like that indicated by Cicero's sentence "Tres personas unus sustineo," errs on the side of insufficiency, attributing too little to the persons of the Trinity and thus in the end reducing them to nothing.[147] In the same way, also the hypothesis that aims to ensure the difference between the persons of the Trinity by relations similar to modes, such as postures, presences, and absences, is completely insufficient to explain three different and simultaneously existing persons.[148] Giving his opinion once again in his correspondence, Leibniz points out Sherlock's inclination toward Tritheism and Wallis's bent toward modalism. Crediting, however, the orthodox intentions of the two authors, with a typical conciliatory spirit he tries to rescue the positive aspects of both theories, in search of a point of equilibrium between the proper need for unity expressed in Wallis's doctrine and the equally necessary emphasis on diversity in Sherlock's position.[149] Leibniz's solution, in fact, aims at salvaging both the oneness of the Godhead, which is inevitably compromised if the persons are conceived of as three absolute substances, and the character of substantiality and individuality of the persons of the Trinity, which is inevitably lost if they are reduced to mere relations within one divine essence. In Leibniz's view, although the persons of the Godhead are neither absolute substances nor mere relations, they are, however, constituted by or through relations ["per relationes constitui"].[150] These relations are conceived of as "substantial," that is, as essential to the ontological makeup of the persons of the Trinity: "One should then say that there are relations within the divine substance that distinguish the persons from each other; since these persons cannot be absolute substances. But one should also say that these relations must be substantial [substantielles] and that they are not sufficiently explained by simple modalities. Also one should say that the divine persons are not the same concrete being [le même concret], under different denominations or relations, as one man could be both a poet and an orator; but three different concrete relative beings in a single absolute concrete being [trois differens concrets respectifs, dans un seul concret absolu]."[151] Writing to Thomas Burnett and Basnage de Beauval, Leibniz repeats these ideas, once again advancing the distinction between absolute and relative as the key to the solution: "I do not dare say that the persons are substances taken absolutely, but I do not say either that they are relations and that they differ only as the King and the prophet in David; I will say only that they are different relative beings in the same absolute being [ce sont de differens estres relatifs dans un même estre absolu]."[152] The *Remarques* add another clarification: "One should also say that the three persons are not parts of the unique absolute divine substance. For the parts are themselves substances as absolute as the whole[.]"[153] That is to say, according to Leibniz the parts of a substance are substances in their own right that could (at least intelligibly) exist separately from the substance of which they are parts (as opposed to mere attributes or modes of a substance that could not exist without the substance in which they inhere). The persons of the Trinity, however, cannot exist one without the other and therefore are not 'parts' of the divine substance. Moreover, the persons of the Trinity cannot be conceived of as parts of the divine substance, since, in the case of the Trinity, each person expresses in his own way the entirety of the divine essence.

The next step is the frank admission that there is no example in nature that can satisfactorily correspond to what is affirmed of the divine persons.[154] But, Leibniz immediately adds, "It is not necessary to find it; and it is sufficient that what one wants to say does not imply any contradiction or absurdity. The divine substance has without doubt privileges that go beyond every other substance."[155] Between the lines one can see an implicit reference to the 'strategy of defense'; if, by definition, the mystery of the Trinity is not only beyond our powers of comprehension from the epistemological point of view but also beyond the ontological status of created substance from the metaphysical standpoint, it should come as no surprise that in nature there seem to be no examples capable of adequately accounting for the three-in-one relation existing between the persons of the Trinity. What is important, however, is that the doctrine of the Trinity does not involve any proven contradiction. Yet, Leibniz goes on, "Since we do not know all the creatures well enough, we cannot then be sure that there is not and that there cannot be any absolute substance apart from God, which does not contain multiple relative [substances]."[156]

This time it is Leibniz's conviction regarding the infiniteness of the created world that provides the reason why, on the basis of our always limited knowledge, one cannot rule out the possibility that there is, or may be, beyond God, a substance endowed with characteristics similar to those of the divine substance. Therefore one must not give up searching in nature for examples resembling the Trinity. Once again picking up the long tradition of the analogia Trinitatis, which goes back to Augustine in particular, Leibniz at once seizes the opportunity to present the closest analogy between the Trinity and the creatures that can be found in nature: "Our own Spirit gives us some image of this, and to make these notions more clear through something similar, I cannot find in the creatures anything more suitable to clarify this subject than the Reflection of the Spirits, when the same Spirit is its own immediate object, and acts on itself in thinking about itself and what it is doing. For this duplication [redoublement] gives an image or a shadow of two relative substances in the same absolute substance; namely, the one which thinks and the one which is thought; both these beings are substantial, both are concrete individuals and they differ in mutual relationships but they make up one and the same individual absolute substance."[157]

The analysis of the act of thinking, sketched out in *De Conatu et Motu, Sensu et Cogitatione*,[158] is here developed into an analysis of self-awareness. As he had already done in *De Scriptura, Ecclesia, Trinitate* and in *De Deo Trino*, Leibniz takes the mind that thinks itself as the example that comes closest to the plurality in unity of the God who is Three and One.[159] In *De Conatu et Motu, Sensu et Cogitatione*, we have seen that mens (mind) is defined as symbolum Trinitatis (a symbol of the Trinity) and that, in a sense specific to Leibniz, it is a symbol of the Trinity by virtue of a peculiar characteristic it has: the recomposition of unity in diversity thanks to the act of thinking, which in its turn is defined as the sensation of several things together or unity of what is manifold.[160] Now, the mind that thinks is indeed able to constitute a unity between itself and what is different from itself, that is, the object of thought, but the object of thought always remains "different" (*aliud*) from the thinking subject. In the case of self-awareness, the subject and object of thought are instead the same thing, though remaining distinct. This is what Leibniz expresses with the notion of "redoublement":[161] in an absolute individual substance (the same, identical spirit that thinks itself), there is a relation (in this case the mutual relation existing between thinking subject and object thought of) and therefore a diversity, and this is due to the fact that things related are somehow different.[162] Now, both the one who "understands" and the one who "is understood" are substantial beings, concrete individuals, but together they make up a single and identical absolute individual substance. In the case of self-awareness, the substance "that understands" and "that which is understood" together represent a form of identity in which the difference remains intact; this case can thus be taken as an image or shadow of the persons of the Trinity, that is, of how different substances can exist in a single absolute substance.

However, at this point an objection may arise: Doesn't this doctrine merely mask a new type of modalism? In concluding his *Remarques,* Leibniz seems to want to refute precisely this objection: "I do not dare, nevertheless, to take the comparison further, and I do not at all undertake to claim that the difference between the three divine persons is no greater than that between 'that which understands' and 'that which is understood' when a finite spirit thinks about itself, especially since that which is modal, accidental[,] imperfect, and mutable in us, is real, essential[,] accomplished, and immutable in God. It is enough that this duplication [redoublement] is like a trace of the divine personalities."[163] Leibniz is thus well aware that the analogy between the mind and the Trinity is, and must remain, just that: "an image," "a shadow," "a trace" of a mystery that transcends the created world. He, however, encouraged by the authority of the scriptures and the teachings of the church fathers, also proclaims the full force of this analogy: "Nevertheless the holy scripture, in naming the son the Word or Logos, that is the mental word [verbe mental],[164] would seem to indicate that nothing is more clear to explain these things, or easier to conceive, than the analogy of the mental operations. It is also for this reason that the fathers have linked the will to the Holy Spirit, as they have linked understanding to the son, and power to the father; distinguishing power, knowledge, and will; namely the father, the word and the love."[165]

Later on Leibniz also continued to take a keen interest in the teachings of the tradition concerning the Trinitarian nature of God, starting from the first gleams of pagan antiquity. Some ten years later, when he finally acquired a copy of Cudworth's *System,*[166] he turned his attention mainly to the many pages devoted to the presentation and comparison of the Platonic Trinity and the tradition regarding the Christian Trinity. A series of extracts and notes to the *System,* datable to about 1704,[167] add a few touches to the doctrine of the Trinity outlined in the *Remarques.* In commenting on the triad advanced by Proclus, composed of the one, the mind, and the soul,[168] Leibniz writes: "They correspond to the Father, the Logos, and the Spirit. But they are more correctly explained through power, knowledge and will, or love"[169]—thus referring again to the analogia Trinitatis put forward (in the wake of the teachings of the church fathers) in the passage of the *Remarques* quoted above. Further on he traces an analogy between the Trinity and created monads. Like the created monads, the true Trinity is composed not of substances but of principles; but while the created monads are composed of an active and a passive principle, the principles composing the Trinity are only active, since in God there is no passivity.[170]

9

The Case of Freke: On the
Mathematical Method in Theology

In December 1693, the envoy to London from the House of Braunschweig-Lüneburg, Wilhelm de Beyrie, reported on the latest scandal in the English Parliament: "Some days ago certain little books, in which the dogma of the Trinity is attacked as strongly as possible, were secretly distributed to each member of Parliament. Upon which, the Parliament ordered that they be burned by the executioner and that a search be made for the Author, the Printers and those who published them."[1] The one who caused the furor was the Antitrinitarian William Freke, the anonymous author of a little book divided into two parts, respectively entitled *A Dialogue By Way of Question and Answer, Concerning the Deity. All the Responses being taken verbatim out of the Scriptures* and *A Brief, but Clear Confutation of the Doctrine of the Trinity.*[2] Leibniz obtained a copy of the pamphlet[3] and, at the beginning of March, sent it to Princess Electress Sophie together with some reflections of his own.[4] The author, Leibniz explains to Sophie, is an Antitrinitarian, "but a very peculiar one," not so much a Socinian as an Arian. The Socinians, regarding Christ as a mere man, denied the preexistence of the Son of God before Mary gave birth to him. Freke, in rejecting this Socinian doctrine, was following the opinion of Arius, according to whom the Son of God, though a mere creature, nevertheless existed before the beginning of his life on earth.[5] Freke, however, then took another step, to conclude that the

Son and the Holy Spirit are angels, thus further departing from the Socinians, who consider the Holy Spirit to be only one of God's virtues. Moreover, according to Freke, the Son is the head of the whole universe, while the Spirit is at the head only of the good angels.[6] This once again raises the question of the adoration of the Son by both the ancient Arians and the modern Socinians.[7] At this point, Freke follows in the footsteps of Ferenc David: by refusing to attribute to the Son, a mere creature, the honors due only to God, Freke tries to avoid the charge of idolatry leveled by the Trinitarians against Arians and Socinians.[8] Leibniz concludes his observations with a severe judgment on the two parts of the pamphlet: "The Author of this little book, after having posed his questions, which he claims to resolve by the very words of scripture,[9] adds a supposed refutation of the Trinity[10] where, in my opinion, he shows more passion than penetration, and it seems that the transport that caused him to write is the reason why his argument is without any order, and even the style is not very refined."[11]

If not the quality of the arguments then perhaps the scandal aroused by the virulence of the Antitrinitarian's attack led Leibniz to think that a confutation of the pamphlet was advisable. The occasion to do so soon arrived. During the very days in which he was writing his brief remarks on the booklet for Sophie, Leibniz answered a letter sent to him in January 1694 by his nephew Friedrich Simon Löffler, who had to choose the subject of his dissertation to conclude his theological studies at the University of Leipzig.[12] Instead of discussing *De voluntate Dei antecedente et consequente*, as foreseen, Leibniz advised his nephew to confute Freke's pamphlet, and in this connection he sent him a series of extracts.[13] Löffler agreed and several times expressed his intention to translate the English text into Latin, putting off the writing of the dissertation to the beginning of the following year.[14] In December 1694, he told his uncle he intended to conduct the confutation by a "mathematical method," instead of sticking to the order followed by the English author in his pamphlet.[15] However, confessing his ignorance in the field, Löffler asked Leibniz for advice. The reply was not long in coming. At the beginning of 1695, Leibniz wrote to his nephew, praising his intentions. Although approving of the decision not to follow the order of arguments in Freke's book (which, as we have seen, he had already severely criticized in his remarks for Sophie), Leibniz is very cautious regarding the possibility of conducting the confutation by a mathematical method, on the ground that the reasoning was based more on the exegesis of passages from the scriptures and on invoking the authority of tradition than on strictly rational procedures. Insisting on the merely hypothetical nature of a demonstration in which one sometimes has to have recourse to historical facts, Leibniz warns his nephew against the temptation to promise more than he can deliver, as well as against the danger, run by many, of hiding what are mere paralogisms under the appearance of a demonstrative procedure.[16] The last piece of advice that Leibniz gives Löffler, regarding the advisability of referring in his dissertation to the history of the book he wishes to confute, closes with a remark that clearly indicates Leibniz's attitude toward controversies. Even in the most delicate and most burning issues one must aim at establishing the truth by means of reasoning and discussion, without resorting to repressive measures, which are, in the final analysis, ineffective. So it was with the decision of the English Parliament to burn Freke's book. The adversaries could, in fact, with reason reply that "it is easier to burn such things than to refute them: the truth, indeed, cannot be burned."[17]

Löffler set to work. Toward the end of January 1695 he sent Leibniz an outline of his dissertation, organized by a "mathematical method."[18] After a series of definitions, axioms, hypotheses, and postulates, Löffler indicates the three propositions he proposes to demonstrate: 1) "The Son of God is not an angel, but the supreme God"; 2) "The Holy Spirit is not an angel, but the highest God"; and 3) "God is One in a Trinity [of persons] [Unus est Deus in Trinitate]."[19]

To Leibniz's mind this attempt appeared disastrous; a few days after receiving the outline, he had ready a series of meticulous observations in which, point by point, he highlights the methodological errors in his nephew's reasoning.[20] The first thing to be contested is the terminology proposed by Löffler, namely, the incorrect definition (and consequently incorrect use) of axioms, hypotheses, and postulates.[21] And if Löffler starts on the wrong foot so far as the most basic methodological rules are concerned, the specific content of his outline is no better. The definitions proposed, Leibniz goes on, contain some statements that are superfluous, since they can be demonstrated, starting with the definitions themselves.[22] In their turn, the four axioms are either superfluous or present statements that, needing proof, are not axiomatic.[23] The hypotheses too, for their part, are either superfluous or imprecise.[24] And finally, the postulates are formulated in a negative way, unlike the customary practice of mathematics, and are (together with the first two definitions and the first hypothesis) completely useless, as they do not appear in the demonstrations.[25]

Starting from these premises, it is not surprising that Leibniz finds the demonstrations themselves full of difficulties.[26] To begin with, both the first and the second proposition to be proved would have to be demonstrated in two distinct proofs, since it is one thing to show that the Son and Holy Spirit are not angels, and another to prove that they are the supreme God.[27] In any case, the content of the first two demonstrations is also found wanting. There are two main objections underlying Leibniz's meticulous analysis of the arguments proposed by Löffler: 1) the scriptural foundation of the theses that are to be demonstrated is not sufficiently developed, first of all because of the lack of any clear rule of interpretation established beforehand; 2) some of the conclusions beg the question, since they are based on statements that are not conceded by the adversaries and that therefore must, in their turn, be proven.[28] Finally, the third proposition (nothing less than "God is One in a Trinity [of persons]") is not well demonstrated. For example, explains Leibniz, from the statement that "the father is God and the son is God, and the Holy Spirit is God" it does not follow that "God is one in a Trinity of persons," if it has not first been proved that we are dealing with three different persons, something that Sabellians and Socinians deny.[29] Seeing, however, that Löffler insists on following the form of the demonstrative method, despite Leibniz's warnings about the difficulty of the enterprise when one is dealing with theological matters, Leibniz decides to solve the problem at the root; putting aside his nephew's outline, he draws up a new one, enclosing it with his reply.[30]

Before we look at Leibniz's outline, a question arises: Is this an attempt by Leibniz to demonstrate the Trinity? If it is, how can this demonstration, conducted with a mathematical method, be reconciled with the position normally maintained by Leibniz that the mysteries cannot be demonstrated, since they are truths above (human) reason? Now, on close inspection, what Leibniz proposes to demonstrate is not the Three-in-One nature of God but the fact that the triune nature of God is revealed by the scriptures and upheld by ancient Christian tradition. Thus Leibniz's attempt seems to be not a "mathematical proof" of the Trinity but a peculiar form of biblical exegesis carried out with a "mathematical method," in reply to the Antitrinitarian exegesis of the biblical passages put forward by Freke.[31] In this connection one should also recall Leibniz's remark concerning the difficulty of applying the mathematical method to an argument based more on the exegesis of passages from the scriptures and the authority of tradition than on strictly rational procedures, as well as his insistence on the merely hypothetical nature of a demonstration in which one sometimes has to have recourse to historical facts.[32]

Leibniz's outline opens with the definition or explanation of terms.[33] There follow two axioms or, as Leibniz reminds Löffler, "universal propositions, which have no need of proof."[34] In particular, the second supplies a rule for interpreting the scriptures, the lack of which rule was one of the reasons for the failure of Löffler's demonstrations: in articles of faith necessary for salvation, the proper meaning of the words of scripture and the judgment of the universal church should not be abandoned without manifest need.[35] Leibniz's following argument should be read in the light of this axiom. First of all, he starts by showing that the scriptures and church tradition attribute to three different persons, the Father, Son, and Holy Spirit, characteristics that, in a strict sense, can be referred only to God. The various passages by which this conclusion is reached can be summed up as follows. So far as the Father is concerned, divinity is admitted by hypothesis, as it is not a matter of dispute.[36] The proof of the divinity of the Son, on the other hand, is reached on the basis of the following arguments. The holy scriptures, which by common admission are the word of God,[37] attribute to Christ characteristics such as eternity and being the Creator of all things. In lemmas 2, 3, and 4 it is shown, against the opinion of the Antitrinitarians, that such characteristics can be attributed only to God.[38] The scriptures also attribute to Christ such characteristics as, for example, being par excellence the Son of God and being generated before all the centuries. The second proposition foresees the demonstration of the fact that, once again against the opinion of the Antitrinitarians, such characteristics can properly be referred more to God than to a creature.[39] What has been said above about the scriptures is confirmed by the tradition of the universal church.[40] In particular, the church attributes worship to Christ,[41] something that, contrary to what the Socinians maintain, is shown to be owed only to God.[42] In the third proposition it is held that there is no need to abandon the proper meaning of the scriptures: only if one were faced with a proven contradiction would it, in fact, be necessary to depart from the literal sense of the biblical text.[43] Moreover, since here we are dealing with a matter that is fundamental for its direct implications regarding the absolute monotheism of the Christian religion, the conclusion to be drawn is that (by virtue of the rule of interpretation expressed in the second axiom), supreme Godhead is to be attributed to Christ.[44] Similar considerations hold for the Holy Spirit.[45] Now, given the oneness of God (demonstrated in the first lemma), and given that Father, Son, and Holy Spirit are different persons (as is established in proposition XV, against Sabellians and Socinians),[46] the statements of the scriptures regarding the divine characteristics of the Father, Son, and Holy Spirit can only be interpreted as the affirmation of a single God in three different persons.

The results of the entire argument are condensed by Leibniz in the outline of a demonstration of the last proposition:

> God is an absolute substance one in number [*Deus est unica numero substantia absoluta*], *with a Trinity of persons.* By *lemma* 1) it is shown that God is only one, that is, that there is only one such absolute substance; nevertheless there are three, to whom the supreme or true divinity belongs, the Father (by *hypothesis* 2), the Son (by *proposition* 7), and the Holy Spirit (by

proposition 14) and each of these is different from the others (by *proposition* 15), nor are there more, as all admit. They are, moreover, singular intelligent substances, essentially related [substantiae singulares intelligentes essentialiter relativae] by relations of paternity, generation and procession, according to the words of Scripture and the sense of the true Catholic Church, and for that reason they are said to be three persons of the divinity in the same absolute and most perfect singular substance, or (by *definition* 4) God, taken of course absolutely.[47]

The dogma of the Trinity should therefore be admitted not because the Trinitarian nature of God has been demonstrated but because it has been demonstrated that the Trinitarian nature of God is revealed by the scriptures and taught by tradition ("according to the words of Scripture and the sense of the true Catholic Church"), however incomprehensible this may be. The only sufficient reason for departing in this connection from the proper sense of the scriptures would be a proven contradiction between the affirmation of the oneness of God and the affirmation of the divine nature of three distinct persons. But, as we have seen in other texts and as is repeated here, in Leibniz's opinion there is no contradiction if one distinguishes between God taken absolutely and God taken relatively. In other words, there is no contradiction if one considers Father, Son, and Spirit as persons (that is, as intelligent singular substances), provided that they are also conceived as essentially related to one another, so that one cannot exist without the others and, together, they constitute a single absolute substance.[48] The distinction between God taken absolutely and God taken relatively is reiterated in the *Scholion*, where it is specified that Father, Son, and Spirit differ from one another only in the different relation of one to another, while they share all the attributes of the divine essence (such as, for example, eternity and omnipotence).[49]

Löffler, who was anxious to remain within the canons of orthodoxy, expressed concern especially about Leibniz's conception of the divine persons.[50] What Löffler feared was a dangerous sliding toward Tritheism by a description of the persons of the Trinity as "three substances," no matter how essentially related to one another they may be. Falling back on the authority of Abraham Calov and Michael Walther, he recalls the distinction between a person *in abstracto* (in the abstract) or taken formally (*formaliter sumta*) and a person *in concreto* (in the concrete) or taken materially (*materialiter sumta*). While a "person" in the abstract would be an "incommunicable subsistence" of the complete intellectual individual substance, a "person" in the concrete sense would be a "complete intelligent singular substance subsisting in an incommunicable way."[51] Now, the term *person* in a concrete sense or taken materialiter (that is, as "substance") can be referred only to

God as the sole and most singular divine essence, while the Father, Son, and Spirit can be understood only as persons in abstracto or formaliter, that is, as three incommunicable ways of subsisting of the only one most singular substance.[52] Although the expression "relative substance" (*substantia relativa*) is equivalent to what is meant by "mode of subsisting" (*modus subsistendi*), the use of the term *substance* (insists Löffler) might not seem very orthodox to some people.[53]

In his answer to Löffler's objections, Leibniz clarifies his conception of the persons of the Godhead.[54] If a description of the divine persons as "substances" (no matter how essentially relative they are to one another) could give rise to a suspicion of Tritheism, Löffler's proposal seems to Leibniz to err in the opposite direction, inclining toward modalism. Leibniz points out that in theological compendia the divine person is said to be "substantial subsistent" and not simply "subsistence" or "mode of subsisting"; the expression "mode of subsisting" should be referred more to personal relations than to the persons themselves.[55] But, adds Leibniz, this kind of distinction in the divine sphere concerns more our way of knowing than the thing itself. This is tantamount to saying that what is affirmed about the divine persons, far from being a definition in the strict sense, that is, one that is able to grasp the essential features of the thing in itself, is rather a description or explanation *quoad nos.*[56] Or, following the distinction between "comprehending" ("comprendre") and "explaining" ("expliquer"), it is not a question of understanding the 'how' of the divine persons but rather a question of explaining the terms just enough so that, on the basis of at least a confused knowledge of their meaning, one can believe.[57] It is therefore better to abstain from defining what the divine persons 'are' (that is, respectively, either substances or modes of subsisting), limiting oneself to explaining how they are understood *by us.*

And at this point, how, according to Leibniz, are they understood? By means of the consideration of three different modes of subsisting of the one absolute divine substance. These three different modes of subsisting, relative to one another and incommunicable (that is, exclusively characteristic of each of the divine persons), are not the persons themselves but that "by which" ("per quid") the persons are constituted. In other words, the divine persons are understood by us through the consideration of the different relations of one to the other in the one absolute divine substance.[58] Though repeating that, if correctly understood, it is perfectly legitimate to say that the divine person is a "subsisting [being] or singular substance [esse subsistentem seu substantiam singularem],"[59] in order to avoid misunderstandings Leibniz suggests making the following changes in the scheme he had previously sent to his nephew: "If you wish to change the definition of person in this way, as I said, you will still be able to change something in proposition XVI, where instead of the words: *They are, however, essentially relative intelligent singular substances* [*Sunt autem substantiae singulares intelligentes essentialiter relativae*], you can put: *They are, however, understood by means of relative incommunicable modes of being, or through relations* [*intelliguntur autem per modos subsistendi relativos incommunicabiles, seu per relationes*]; as also in the same place in the scholia, instead of the words: *they are in fact three different substances,* you can say: *they are in fact three different* [*entities*]*, or* etc. [*sunt enim tres diversi seu* etc.]."[60] It should be pointed out that, according to this passage, the modes of subsisting of the persons of the Trinity are understood as being equivalent to the relations among the persons.[61] We seem to be dealing here with one of the forms in which Leibniz conceives of relations in general: that is, relations are considered in this case not in an abstract sense but as individual properties of a subject (for example, the 'being a father' or 'subsisting as a father' of the first person of the Trinity).[62] When later on Leibniz explicitly writes that the persons of the Trinity are constituted *per relationes* (through or by relations),[63] this expression should apparently be interpreted as being equivalent to the explanation given here: the persons of the Trinity are constituted through different "modes of subsisting that are relative to one another and incommunicable" in the one absolute divine substance.

Perhaps better realizing the difficulty of the undertaking, Löffler hesitated.[64] He waited until August 1697 to announce the end of the drafting of the thesis, roughly summarizing for Leibniz the subjects dealt with.[65] The dissertation was discussed on 8 April 1698, with Joh. Benedict Carpzov as president of the commission.[66]

Leibniz, for his part, did not forget his attempt to apply the "mathematical method" (or, in other words, a rigorously demonstrative procedure) to the discussion of theological matters. He replied as follows to Johann Andreas Schmidt, a theologian and mathematician at the University of Helmstedt, who confided to him his oft-cherished plan to expound theology through a mathematical method:[67] "It would be nice to teach Theology by a Mathematical method, nor could anyone do it better than you, as you have worked in an excellent way in both fields. But I am afraid that it may not rightly be permitted to satisfy this desire, as long as Philosophy itself is not taught mathematically, the demonstrations of which Theology ought nonetheless to use in any case."[68] This cautious approach (already found in his correspondence with Löffler) is followed by the distinction between the possibility of applying the mathematical method to, respectively, natural theology and revealed theology.[69] If natural theology can reach the absolute or "metaphysical" certainty of mathematical demonstration, revealed theology, being founded partly on "history and its facts," and partly on the interpretation of texts, stops instead at "moral" certainty.[70] This moral certainty is provided not by the rigorously demonstrative procedures of mathematics but by that art of "weighing reasons" which, Leibniz complains, is insufficiently developed, and whose importance he underlines "even in the most important and most serious matters of life."[71] Therefore, reason has its tasks to perform in revealed theology as well; these tasks are specified in his reply to Johann Andreas Schmidt by the distinction between "unmediated" and "mediated" revelation. In the former case one must demonstrate the "authority"; that is, it is necessary to show the genuineness and divine provenance of the revelation; in the latter case (that is, every time the meaning of the revealed word is not clearly manifest) one must "demonstrate the meaning," that is, one can reach the truth only "by consequence or interpretation." But both in the "demonstration of the authority" and in the "demonstration of the meaning" it is not always possible to proceed by appealing to necessary truths. On the contrary, repeats Leibniz, it is necessary to use also arguments that stop at the level of moral certainty.[72] A use of rigorously demonstrative methods also in the sphere of revealed theology is therefore not ruled out,[73] provided it is clear from the start that it is not a question of reaching a demonstration of the revealed truth but a question of supporting, insofar as possible, the *demonstratio auctoritatis et sensus* (demonstration of the authority and the meaning). An example of this exegesis carried out with a mathematical method is the demonstration outline prepared for Löffler and offered by Leibniz to Johann Andreas Schmidt as an illustration of a theology sketched in a mathematical way: "I believe a certain Theology can be delineated in a Mathematical manner, in a preliminary way [prolusionaliter], so to speak, taking from philosophy many things, which must first be demonstrated in it. For what are axioms or Hypotheses in one science, can be themes [themata] in another. A few years ago a friend undertook an Academic dissertation in defense of the Trinity against the Socinians, which he wanted to write in a mathematical way. When he sent me the outline of his work, with his permission I changed many things, and so I sent it back to him. Nonetheless I think that I still have a copy of my scheme, which, if it seems to be worth it, I will seek out and send."[74] The basic attitude seems to be similar to that of the *preambula fidei* (preambles to faith). Part of theology can be delineated by following a strictly rational procedure. In it, philosophy has much weight, being called upon to demonstrate beforehand the foundation on which this theology intends to build. Leibniz, however, adds an important specification: *prolusionaliter.* That is, the strictly demonstrative part of theology does not cover the whole spectrum of the discourse on God.

10

Stillingfleet versus Locke and Toland:
On Clear and Distinct Ideas

The debates surrounding Nye and Freke did not exhaust Leibniz's attention to the English Trinitarian discussions. From the end of 1696 on, John Locke was in the eye of the storm. This time the polemic was triggered by the publication of *A Vindication of the Doctrine of the Trinity*[1] by the bishop of Worcester, Edward Stillingfleet, who exposed the danger for the mystery of the Trinity implicit in the epistemological doctrine set forth in Locke's *Essay concerning Human Understanding*.[2] Once again, Thomas Burnett of Kemney played a central mediating role: besides informing Leibniz on the development of the affair[3] and providing him with the various polemical writings that passed between Locke and Stillingfleet,[4] he attempted to put Leibniz in contact with Locke himself.[5] Although there was no direct correspondence between the two, several important writings by Leibniz on the controversy have survived, some of which reached Locke by way of Burnett.[6]

The correspondence between Leibniz and Burnett is rich in philosophical points of great interest. These range from the conception of substance to the discussion of the origin of ideas, from the problem of innate ideas to the ontological proof of the existence of God, from the hypothesis of thinking matter (with its consequences regarding the distinction between mind and body within the horizon of Descartes' philosophy) to the question of the immortality of the soul, from the discussion of the basis of certainty (with reference to Locke's doctrine of the concordance and discordance of ideas) to the distinction between necessary truths and truths of fact, from a recognition of the limits of knowledge to the problem of certainty in matters of faith. These subjects, discussed in a preliminary way in an exchange of letters with Thomas Burnett, were later picked up and developed in the *Nouveaux Essais*. It goes without saying that, given the range and complexity of the problems dealt with, we can here dwell only on the aspects most directly related to the subject of this book. First among these aspects is the very starting point of the controversy: that is, the bishop of Worcester's concerned denunciation of the denial of the mysteries (and in particular of the mystery of the Trinity) made by theological rationalism of the Socinian sort.[7] As Leibniz points out in his *Compte rendu*,[8] Stillingfleet, after having confuted the Antitrinitarian position on the basis of the scriptures and the ancient Christian tradition,[9] devotes the last chapter of the *Vindication* to a discussion of the Socinian objections to the Trinity advanced from the standpoint of reason. What the bishop proposes to examine is whether people must believe only that which they understand and that of which they have clear and distinct ideas.[10] In other words, it is the question of the submission of faith to reason that is subjected to analysis. The implications for the mysteries of the Christian faith in general and for the mystery of the Trinity in particular are obvious: if one must only believe what reason understands, then assent must be denied to everything that is, by definition, incomprehensible, that is, to everything that is traditionally gathered under the heading of 'mystery.' Hence the explicit proposal, advanced by John Toland and picked up by Deism, of a "Christianity without mysteries."[11]

Many of those in the Socinian and Unitarian movements had not yet themselves reached these extreme consequences of the Socinian approach to the relation between faith and reason. To cite only one representative example, suffice it to recall Stephen Nye's admission of the category of 'mystery': "There are (it may be) Mysteries, which we cannot comprehend how they should be. . . . [W]e do not reject the Doctrines of the *Trinity* and *Incarnation,* because they are *Mysteries;* but because they are *plain Contradictions* to Reason and common sense, and consequently *Untruths.*"[12] But is there really room in Socinian and Unitarian epistemology for the mysteries, understood as truths that surpass the limits of understanding of human reason? It would seem that there is not: although Faustus Socinus and his followers still make use of the category of mystery as that which is *supra rationem* (above reason), in a specifically Socinian sense supra rationem are the truths of faith that cannot be discovered by human reason without the aid of revelation but that, once they have been revealed, are immediately understood by reason, thus ceasing to be superior to reason.[13] If, therefore, Stillingfleet, like Leibniz, would agree in thinking that what involves a contradiction must be false and that reasons are needed in order to believe, what is objected to is the actual equation of the incomprehensible and the contradictory.[14] This equation is due to the priority assigned, in the final analysis, to human reason's capacity for understanding in the interpretation of the holy scriptures.[15] From these premises, Toland did nothing but draw the logical consequences, explicitly denying that there is anything "mysterious or superior to reason in the Gospel."[16] Now, insists Stillingfleet, anyone who (like the Antitrinitarians) makes reason the rule and measure of faith must provide an explanation of the nature and limits of such reason, and this the Unitarian texts do not do.[17] Toland, on the other hand, does attempt to provide this explanation,[18] basing his rejection of the mysteries in Christianity on his conception of reason and knowledge.

According to the author of *Christianity not Mysterious*, notes Leibniz, reason "is the Faculty of the soul that discovers the certitude of what is doubtful or obscure, in comparing it with what is clearly known. For one does not reason at all when one enjoys perfect evidence by an immediate perception, but when the spirit discovers agreement or disagreement . . . by the intervention of other mediating ideas, one calls this knowledge *reason or demonstration*."[19] Stillingfleet warns against this conception, since it presupposes that certainty always rests on clear and distinct ideas. If this is the case, it follows that every certainty of faith or reason comes to be lacking where there are no such ideas.[20] This is not all: according to Toland, ideas (on which all knowledge is based) come exclusively either from sensation or from the reflection of the spirit on its own operations. From these two sources, continues Stillingfleet, one cannot obtain the idea of substance, on which every possibility of explaining the Trinity is based.[21] In fact, the doctrine of the Trinity depends on the notions of *nature* and *person* and their reciprocal distinction.[22] Now, both these notions presuppose the idea of substance, since, says Stillingfleet, nature and substance "are of an equal extent"[23] and person is defined as "a compleat Intelligent Substance, with a peculiar manner of Subsistence."[24] If the notions of "nature" and "person" cannot come from sensation or reflection, their reciprocal distinction cannot be so derived either. As Leibniz explains in his *Compte rendu,* picking up the bishop's positions: "This difference between nature and person does not come to us from our simple ideas, but from reason, by which we judge also that, supposing that there is a distinction of persons in the divine nature, it must needs be, on account of the infinite perfection of the divine nature, that this distinction is not at all contrary to the unity of the divine essence."[25] To reduce the source of ideas to sensation and reflection, therefore, Stillingfleet goes on, is to banish substance (and with it the doctrine of the Trinity) from the sphere of rationality.[26]

It is at this point that the bishop directly attacks Locke's *Essay,* to the theses of which, bent to his own purposes, Toland clearly refers. Leibniz reports: "So I am not at all surprised, he says (p. 234 of the *Vindication*) that these gentlemen who follow this new way of reasoning, have banished substance from the world of reason; quoting on this matter some passages from the book that the renowned Mr. Locke published in English with the title *Essay on Human Understanding,* who says (in Book I, chapter 4, section 18) that we can have the idea of substance neither by the senses nor by reflection, and that substance means only an uncertain supposition of I do not know what."[27] Faced with such statements as this, while recognizing the good faith of the *Essay*'s author, Stillingfleet feels constrained to denounce the dangers inherent in Locke's *way of ideas.*[28] He contests the correctness of Locke's epistemology, proceeding to make a close analysis of the doctrine regarding the unknowability of substance.[29] If, by following this *way of ideas,* it is not possible to reach the idea of substance, then, according to the bishop, it is necessary to infer that ideas do not come only from sensation and reflection. The idea of substance as a substratum of modes and accidents is, in reality, one of the primary ideas that reason needs; from our very first conceptions, it is in fact repugnant to us to think that modes or accidents subsist by themselves.[30] The conclusion that the high prelate reaches, as summarized by Leibniz, is that "therefore one should not say that reason depends on clear and distinct ideas, and that it is false that simple ideas (coming from the senses or from reflection) are the only matter and foundation of our reasoning."[31]

In his *Letter* in reply to Stillingfleet, Locke rebuts the bishop's accusations point by point:[32] despite the bishop's acknowledgment of the abuse made by the author of *Christianity not Mysterious* of the doctrines of the *Essay,* Locke points out that Stillingfleet continues in effect to attribute to him theses and consequences that can be ascribed only to Toland, and he is particularly careful to underline that in the *Essay* there is not the least objection to the Trinity.[33] Turning to the specific charges brought against him in the *Vindication,* Locke first of all makes it clear that he never meant to banish substance from the rational sphere but maintained that this supposition of a *substratum* supporting the accidents, far from being a clear and distinct idea of substance, is instead an obscure, confused, vague, and relative idea: the obscure idea of a substratum that, nonetheless, we need to admit as the unknown cause of the union of simple ideas and the subsistence of the whole.[34] Moreover, it is not the existence of substance but the idea we have of it that is obscure and that has to be related to our habit of supposing a substratum. As proof of the fact that he has never doubted the existence of substance, Locke points out that he himself admitted positively that the senses make us sure of the existence of solid and extended substances, and reflection assures us of the existence of thinking substances.[35]

After a careful study of the writings of the two antagonists, Leibniz sent to Thomas Burnett a first series of observations.[36] In Leibniz's opinion, the cause of many of the misunderstandings between Locke and Stillingfleet regarding the idea of substance is the lack of a precise classification of ideas, such as is to be found instead in his *Meditationes de Cognitione, Veritate et Ideis*.[37] In particular, one should keep in mind the difference between what is "clear" and what is "distinct": "If I may dare to mix my thoughts with those of these outstanding men, I would distinguish between clear and distinct, as I have done other times in the Acta of Leipzig [*Acta Eruditorum*]. I call an idea clear when it suffices to recognize a thing, as when I remember a color sufficiently well to recognize it when it is brought to me; but I call an idea distinct when I know the conditions or requisites, in a word, when I have the definition of it, if it has one. Thus I do not have a distinct idea of all the colors, being often obliged to say that it is something, I know not what, that I sense very clearly, but that I am unable to explain."[38] Leibniz concludes: "I believe that one has a clear idea, but not a distinct idea, of substance, which in my opinion comes from the inner feeling that we have in ourselves, which are substances."[39] In line with the definition given above of a "clear idea" as that which suffices "to recognize a thing," Leibniz holds that we have a clear but not distinct idea of substance in that "people know very well how to recognize it and distinguish it from an accident, although they do not distinguish in it what is comprised in its notion."[40] He thus seems to imply that the description of the idea of substance proposed by Locke also falls into the category of "clear ideas": "M. Lock says very appropriately in his letter, that one judges of it as would a child in its mother's arms, *recognizing* that what carries it is supported by I know not what, whereas a more *distinct* knowledge would make us like a wise man, who would know even what the foundations of the buildings are, whether they are founded on rock or on gravel[.]"[41] Thomas Burnett objects that "this difference" between "clear" and "distinct" seems to be "more ingenious than philosophical," since, if knowing something distinctly requires an exact and rigorous knowledge of its complete nature, then not only God but even the most minute creatures would be beyond our capacities for distinct knowledge.[42] To him Leibniz replies, with some irritation, that it is necessary to distinguish also between distinct knowledge and adequate knowledge; he also points out that the difference between "clear" and "distinct" can be traced back to Descartes himself.[43] However, he is also moved to specify that "the knowledge of ideas, to be useful in reasoning," must be "not only clear, but also distinct."[44] It therefore seems possible to infer that a merely clear idea of substance is still not sufficient for reasoning. In any case, it remains a fact that Leibniz does not share Locke's doctrine of the unknowability of substance.[45] He is also not content, however, with the idea of substratum criticized by Locke, and in his letter to Thomas Burnett of 20/30 January he proposes as his contribution for arriving at a more distinct conception of substance the article that appeared in the *Acta Eruditorum* of March 1694, *De Primae Philosophiae Emendatione, et de Notione Substantiae,*[46] in which the notion of substance is redefined in terms of "force."[47]

It goes beyond the limits of this book to follow Locke and Leibniz further in the debate about substance. Instead, we still have to examine the issue of certainty, with particular reference to the sphere of faith. One of the key points in Locke's reply to the bishop of Worcester is that he has confused the thesis of the *Essay,* that simple ideas are the foundation of our knowledge, with the statement (ascribable only to the author of *Christianity not Mysterious*) that certainty always needs clear and distinct ideas, to which all knowledge is limited. Locke's defense is summarized by Leibniz as follows:

> Mr. the bishop of Worcester having said (*Vindic.* p. 252) that what he set out to prove was that certitude does not consist in clear and distinct ideas, but in the force of reason that is different from them, Mr. Locke replies (*Lettre* p. 87) that there is nothing in this which he does not agree with, in his opinion (combining *Lettre* p. 107, p. 117, p. 122) certitude being found in the perception of the agreement or disagreement of ideas. For example (*Lettre* p. 88) the idea of thought that is clear is joined at the same time to a clear idea of existence, and to an obscure idea of substance; and nevertheless one is still assured of the existence of this substance. . . . Mr. Locke protests (*Lettre* p. 90 and p. 116) that he has never said that clear and distinct ideas are the matter and foundation of our reasoning, nor even that this is founded only on clear ideas; but that he said only that simple ideas are the foundation of all our knowledge, although one cannot always deduce this knowledge (*Lettre* p. 100) from these ideas, without adding to them complex ideas that are not always clear.[48]

The distance between Locke and Toland on this point seems clear to Leibniz, who on 20/30 January 1699 writes: "He [Locke] declares . . . that he does not at all require that one should reject terms for which one has not a clear and distinct notion. And by this he makes it clear that he does not approve the use that the anonymous author [Toland] has made of his book."[49]

Thus Leibniz has no doubt about the fact that the intention of the bishop of Worcester "to show that we do indeed admit some things in philosophy, and with reason, although we do not at all have a distinct idea of them, and so too one must not reject the mysteries under the pretext that we do not have such ideas,"[50] is not "against M. Lock, but against the anonymous author."[51] In other words, the denial of the mysteries based on the acceptance of only what is clear and distinct is to be ascribed to Toland and not to Locke. Therefore, Leibniz repeats in his *Réflexions* on Locke's second *Reply,* "Monsieur Lock in his *Reply* to the late Monsieur Stillingfleet Bishop of Worcester acknowledges very clearly p. 46 seqq. that certitude does not always require clear and distinct ideas."[52] At this point, however, Leibniz advances a step: if it is true that certainty does not always require clear and distinct ideas, it does require that there should at least be something clear; and in the case of a rational, and not a sensorial, certainty, there must also be something distinct.[53] What are the consequences in the sphere of faith of such a doctrine of certainty? Leibniz's position would seem to imply that, in the case of faith as well, if one wishes to reach a certain degree of rational certainty, the clarity of ideas is not enough, that is, it is not enough to be able to recognize something without yet being able to know (distinguish) the "requisites" that are part of the notion of the thing itself: there must also be "something distinct," that is, one must know at least some of the requisites or 'ingredients' of the thing in question.[54] An explanation of Leibniz's position could come from his early work *Commentatiuncula de Judice Controversiarum.* In the *Commentatiuncula,* as we have seen, one of the conditions for being able rightly to believe ("hold true") a proposition that exceeds the limits of human understanding is an at least confused (or, according to Leibniz's mature classification of ideas, a clear, albeit not yet distinct) knowledge[55] of the meaning of the words. This is, however, only the first condition; the other indispensable condition is that there should be no proven contradiction.[56] If we reread what the young Leibniz wrote in the light of the above statements on certainty, it would seem possible to conclude that the element of distinction, which is necessary in order for there to be some degree of rational certainty, is given, in the case of the mysteries, by the absence of any proven contradiction. Put another way, if it is not possible to know all or many of the requisites of the notion in question, at least one requisite must be known, and this is the absence of a proven contradiction regarding the notion itself.

Having acknowledged that Locke's *way of ideas* does not, in itself, lead to the negation of what is above reason, it was only in 1701 that Leibniz was himself able to verify Toland's doctrine on the matter. The opening words of his *Annotatiunculae Subitaneae ad Tolandi Librum De Christianismo Mysteriis*

Carente[57] leave no doubt about Leibniz's eagerness to go to the bottom of the issue through a firsthand knowledge of the controversial work.[58] Having praised (with all due caution) the author's good intentions,[59] Leibniz cannot help pointing out that, starting from its very title, Toland's work "goes farther than is appropriate"; if, in fact, it is true that in Christian theology nothing must be admitted that is contrary to reason, that is, nothing absurd, the same is not true for what is above reason, that is, all that our reason is not able to comprehend. Leibniz's justification of this assertion hinges on the disproportion between the finitude of our intellect and the infinity inherent in every substance.[60] In other words, in the category of "what is above reason, that is, what cannot be comprehended by our reason," Leibniz puts not only issues relating to the divine sphere (and first of all the divine nature, as being infinite) but also the "complete notions" of substances. In fact, our finite intellect is not able to reach a "distinct consideration of infinite varieties" and must therefore rest content with a perfect understanding of only the "incomplete notions," such as those of numbers or figures. Thus, far from approving of the elimination of the superrational from the Christian religion, Leibniz seems to widen the sphere of what is above reason to include everything that goes beyond the narrow bounds of the abstract objects studied by mathematics.

This extreme (and in many ways surprising) position adopted by Leibniz should be placed in the framework of the classification of ideas and degrees of knowledge to which Leibniz, in the Locke-Stillingfleet debate, constantly refers: a classification that constitutes, also in the case of the *Annotatiunculae,* the underlying pattern for Leibniz's justification of what is above reason. The crucial point is the recognition that there are different degrees of the intelligibility of things and, as a consequence, of the fact that knowing is not identical to comprehending.[61] Leibniz observes that one can properly speak of "comprehending" only when one has ideas that are not only distinct but also adequate; when, that is, the elements that enter into the definition or resolution of the terms proposed are in their turn resolved until one reaches the primitive terms. The created reason of mankind, being finite, can only very rarely reach this degree of knowledge—namely, as has been seen, only in the case of "incomplete notions," such as that of numbers.[62] Knowledge, however, is broader than comprehension: it extends to include the many notions of which we have only clear, and not distinct, ideas; it then becomes restricted, on the basis of the increasing degree of adequacy, to distinct notions, and finally reaches the very few perfectly adequate notions. Precisely for this reason, whereas there is no scandal in believing "what cannot be comprehended,"[63] it is instead correct to affirm that "no one can believe anything but what he conceives of in his mind."[64] In order to believe, it is necessary somehow ("utcumque") to grasp the meaning of the terms,[65] although, even in the natural sphere, the "understanding of the words [intellectum verborum]" is very different from the "comprehension of the thing [comprehensionem rei]."[66] But what, more precisely, does this "utcunque" correspond to? Once again, Leibniz seems above all to be referring to a degree of knowledge that is at least clear, like that underlying sensorial certainty. But if a clear knowledge is enough to justify 'faith' in the objects of the senses, it is still not enough to justify faith in the revealed propositions, which can certainly not be reduced to the sphere of the senses. In order for there to be sufficient "motives of credibility," it is necessary that such clear knowledge be accompanied in the case of the revealed propositions by at least that element of distinctness that is provided by the absence of a proven contradiction or, in other words, by the possibility of defending the notion in question from the charge of contradictoriness.[67]

On the basis of this classification of the degrees of knowledge, within which there is room also for faith, Leibniz can reply to Toland's ambiguous statement that one must not call a mystery what one does not have adequate ideas of, or that of which one does not have a distinct vision of all the properties at one and the same time, because otherwise everything would be a mystery.[68] Pointing an accusing finger at this position, Stillingfleet noted that it seems we are faced with an internal inconsistency in Toland's discourse: while on the one hand the author of *Christianity not Mysterious* maintains that one should give assent only to what is understood on the basis of "clear and distinct" or "adequate" ideas, on the other he seems to affirm that we never have adequate ideas; we should therefore deduce, concludes the bishop, that no knowledge is possible.[69] Leibniz, who also took note, in his *Compte rendu*, of Stillingfleet's criticism, in his *Annotatiunculae* does not pause to show the possible inconsistency in Toland's writing—an inconsistency that would seem to stem from the lack of that explicit classification of ideas or degrees of knowledge on which Leibniz's argument is based.[70] Instead he prefers to go direct to the heart of the question, distinguishing between actual knowledge and possible knowledge.

If we understand by mystery that which goes beyond our actual knowledge, there are countless mysteries in the natural sphere. However, this is only a temporary situation: thanks to the continual advancement of knowledge, many of these mysteries can gradually be unveiled.[71] There are, however, many things that go beyond not only our actual knowledge but also our possibility of knowing. In the strong sense, a mystery is thus something that goes beyond the structural limits of finite reason such as humankind's.[72] And here, once again, Leibniz extends the sphere of mystery as such not only to the supernatural revealed truths but also to an adequate knowledge of what exists in nature. Human beings can only perfectly account for appearances (phenomena) and not for 'things in themselves,' since the comprehension of single substances is impossible for the finite intellect: "But to one who calls *Mystery* everything which is above any created reason, I dare say that no natural phenomena are above reason, although the comprehension itself of individual substances is impossible to the created mind because they involve the infinite. For this reason it is impossible to provide a perfect explanation [perfecta ratio] of the things of the universe. And nothing prevents certain divinely revealed dogmas from being of this kind."[73]

It is interesting to note that Leibniz continually insists on the parallel between mysteries in the supernatural sphere and what is commonly experienced and accepted as being above reason or incomprehensible in the natural sphere. In fact, it is again examples taken from the natural sphere that he uses to confute two of Toland's interrelated theses. First of all, Leibniz does not agree that, according to the scriptures and ancient Christian tradition, the mysteries are, properly speaking, only those truths that were unknown before revelation but that, once revealed, are perfectly intelligible. Truths such as the Incarnation, Leibniz points out, doubtless go beyond human reason even after they have been revealed.[74] Just as a blind man cannot judge of colors even if the theory of colors is explained to him, what revelation discloses is not only something unknown but also something that, although expressed by the Divine Word, nevertheless remains superior to our capacity of comprehension.[75] From this, however, it does not follow, as Toland maintains, that the revelation of incomprehensible truths is useless: even in the natural sphere, the discovery of things such as the magnetic needle remains extremely important even if we should never manage to explain its properties.[76] Moreover, Leibniz does not limit himself to marginal cases. As an example of the "many things" recognized by the philosophers of his time as being superior to human reason, he cites one of the central problems of post-Cartesian philosophy: the question of the union of soul and body.[77] But doesn't Leibniz perhaps think that he himself has brilliantly solved the problem with his doctrine of preestablished harmony? Apparently not, as we have seen. In the *Annotatiunculae* we find an anticipation of what Leibniz was to say a few years later in replying to Father Tournemine: the doctrine of preestablished harmony serves only to explain "the Phenomena" and not the metaphysical union, which at bottom remains a mystery.[78] Although the proposed doctrine therefore makes it possible to give a certain explanation of the union of soul and body, it does not penetrate to the metaphysical heart of the matter, on account of the incomprehensibility "of the inner workings of nature" ("interiorum naturae"), stemming from their intrinsic infinity ("ab influxu infiniti orientem"). Leibniz repeats that it is this infinity that explains why the finite intellect must often be content with clear and yet confused ideas, as it is not able to have a distinct vision of all the requisites.[79]

Leibniz's reply to Toland's final invitation to hope for an intelligible explanation of the doctrine of the New Testament contains in a nutshell Leibniz's position regarding the relation between revelation and knowledge. An intelligible explanation of the scriptures is not only something to hope for; to some extent, we already possess it, provided (and this marks the difference between Leibniz and Toland) we are content with a lower degree of intelligibility.[80] This is tantamount to saying that the scriptures are without doubt subject to an intelligible explanation, and revelation without doubt falls within the cognitive sphere, provided we realize that there are different degrees of knowledge, just as there are different levels of the intelligibility of things.[81] In conclusion, it seems that Leibniz's conception can be represented by a continuous line that goes from the lowest degrees of knowledge (characterized by clear and yet confused ideas) up to the perfect comprehension permitted by adequate ideas, which is mainly possible only to an infinite intellect such as God's. The difference, however, is merely one of degree: human reason is of the same nature as divine reason;[82] the mysteries are superior to reason not in an absolute sense but only in the relative sense of pertaining to humankind's limited reason in its mundane condition. Not only does God understand perfectly what, for human beings, is a mystery; Leibniz hypothesizes that there may be created intellects superior to humankind's that are capable of grasping what escapes us, and also that even human beings may reach this degree of knowledge in the next life.[83]

Incomprehensibility too, moreover, admits of differing degrees. The first degree is that of only temporary incomprehensibility: this is the case of natural phenomena governed by laws that can be discovered by the force of the unaided human intellect, thus resolving the mystery in the light of what is clear and distinct.[84] There is, then, an incomprehensibility "of fact." This is the case of truths that are not, in themselves, superior to reason but that require a revelation to be known, since they have to do with factual data (the example given is of the fall of Adam);[85] what Toland considers mysteries *tout court* could fall into this category: truths that were unknown before revelation but that, once revealed, are perfectly intelligible. Another incomprehensibility only "of fact" would seem to be that of the miracles, in that we are dealing with events made possible by a temporary exemption from the normal (or factual) laws of nature and therefore called by Leibniz "transitory mysteries" ("misteria transitoria").[86] Both the case of the miracles and the case of truths that depend on factual data knowable only through revelation would seem, in general, to be associated with that of the "truths of fact." Finally, there is the incomprehensibility of the mysteries in the strong sense, of which the highest example seems to be the Trinitarian nature of God. Here the incomprehensibility is one not only "of history" but also "of doctrine."[87]

Now, though it is easy to rebut the charge of contradiction for miracles or the mysteries connected to "truths of fact" (since the laws that God gave to nature are not necessary and there is no reason why their Author cannot modify them), it becomes more difficult for mysteries that seem to go against necessary truths and therefore appear to imply contradiction. But this is precisely the point that Leibniz is concerned to establish against Toland's sybilline equivalence between apparent contradiction and real contradiction.[88] In order to reject a dogma as irrational one must demonstrate that it entails a real contradiction. On the contrary, no one denies that the mysteries "seem" to imply contradiction, but this is because the matter has not yet been sufficiently discussed:[89] this is what the young Leibniz says, for example, in *De Demonstratione Possibilitatis Mysteriorum Eucharistiae* in speaking of the mysteries as what "seem impossible at first sight."[90] In the *Annotatiunculae* Leibniz underlines once again that in the case of supernatural truths it is not enough to follow appearances or resort to the calculation of probabilities, precisely because (as he later on affirms in the *Theodicy*) the mysteries go against appearances and (as he states in the *Commentatiuncula*) are improbable, though not impossible.[91] The example given by Leibniz here is that of a bet in which, although the probability of winning is greater than the probability of losing, if one loses the loss will be enormous, whereas if one wins the earnings will be minimal.[92] Just as in this example it is better to stick to what is, in general, more secure, albeit less likely, so too in the case of a conflict between the Word of God and appearances it is better to stick to God's Word; in fact, this does not involve any risk, unlike the case of what would happen if one chose to stray from the proper sense of the words on account of appearances.[93] And this, concludes Leibniz, "is all the more true as the Lord is wise and powerful";[94] that is to say, when the One speaking is he who, thanks to his power and wisdom, is able to perform what in normal circumstances would be extremely improbable.[95]

This statement brings us to the last aspect of the *Annotatiunculae* that has still to be examined: one that reveals a Leibniz who is very close to Locke or, seen from another perspective, a Locke who is much farther from the author of *Christianity not Mysterious* than Toland's use of the epistemological doctrines of the *Essay* would have us believe. The identity of the One who speaks is not indifferent to the position to be adopted with respect to the content of revelation. Against Toland's statement that the assent given to revelation (conceived of as a pure means of information) is based only on the "*Evidence* in things themselves" and not on the authority of the One who reveals them, Leibniz replies that the Revealer is not only a master "whom we believe only because he proves, or because he explains things by distinct concepts," but also a witness or an indefeasible judge.[96] On one condition, however: "after it is actually sure that the revealer is God himself."[97] In other words, to avoid fideistic outcomes, it is first of all necessary to verify the authenticity of the revelation. At this point one cannot help noticing how close Leibniz comes to Locke's doctrine in the *Essay:* where the witness is God himself (and this must be ascertained beforehand) one has "Assurance beyond Doubt, Evidence beyond Exception," whether the thing agrees or not with common experience and the ordinary course of events.[98] As for Locke, so for Leibniz, reason itself is the competent judge in the field of what is "according to reason." Translated into Leibniz's terms: "In doctrines which are supported by reason, as when a teacher teaches me Geometry . . . *the basis of my persuasion is not the authority of the speaker, but the clarity of the conception.*"[99] When, however, we enter into the sphere of what is above reason, in which the foundation of persuasion can no longer be "the clarity of the conception," it is right to accept (as also happens in the purely human sphere) an "evidence in persons [evidentia in personis]" instead of an "evidence in things [evidentia in rebus]," where by "evidence in persons" one means the authentic testimony of an authoritative and trustworthy witness.[100] Translated this time into Locke's terms, this means: where "the Evidence of Things" is lacking (that is, in the sphere of what is "above reason"), "there yet is Ground enough for me to believe, because God has said it."[101] Although at the time of the *Annotatiunculae* Leibniz surely had direct knowledge of the texts by Locke quoted above, we should recall that remarks similar to those just discussed are to be found already in the *Commentatiuncula,* dating from 1669 to 1671.[102] We may therefore conclude that Leibniz and Locke, as regards the relation between reason and revelation, independently reached similar positions, though starting from very different epistemological premises.

Finally, some last remarks should be reserved for Leibniz's attitude to the charge of Socinianism brought against Locke in several quarters.[103] During the Locke-Stillingfleet debate, Leibniz does not endorse the suspicion of Antitrinitarianism brought against Locke,[104] just as he does not endorse the suspicion that Locke wanted to admit into Christianity only what is clear and distinct, with the consequent denial of what is above reason.[105] In like manner, he does not comment on the explicit accusation that Locke wished to deny the dogma of the Trinity, a charge raised by the pastor John Edwards against Locke's *Reasonableness of Christianity*. In this anonymous tract published in 1695, in the wake of latitudinarian theology and the distinction between fundamental and nonfundamental articles of faith, Locke identifies Jesus of Nazareth's status as the Messiah as the only article of faith expressly required by Christ and the apostles to become a Christian. From Locke's statement that this is the essential core of revelation, Edwards unduly deduces that he wishes to deny the other revealed truths, on the basis of rationalistic premises of a Socinian kind.[106] Informed in June 1696 by Basnage de Beauval about the publication in Holland of a translation of *Reasonableness*,[107] Leibniz makes no mention of the negative presentation of the work's contents by the editor of the *Histoire des ouvrages des Savans*,[108] probably preferring to wait until he has the work in his hands before expressing any judgment. Although already in December of the same year Thomas Burnett tells Leibniz that he has bought for him a copy of *Reasonableness* and Locke's first *Vindication* against Edwards,[109] for the moment Leibniz refrains from commenting, perhaps also because Burnett himself asked him expressly not to name Locke as the author of the controversial work.[110] It was only in July 1705 that Leibniz broke his silence, replying to a fervent letter in which Lady Masham, shortly after Locke's death,[111] explicitly asked him for his opinion on *Reasonableness*:[112] "I have read other times the Reasonable Christianity of this illustrious Author and I very strongly appreciate those who manage to show the conformity of faith with reason. And, in my opinion, it ought to be taken as a maxim that what is unreasonable is the mark of falsity in Theology as well as in Philosophy."[113] Far from accusing Locke of theological rationalism of a Socinian kind for having wished to identify an essential core within revelation as a basis for tolerance and a center around which to reestablish harmony among the Christian confessions, Leibniz interprets Locke's argument as an expression of that conformity between faith and reason which, though it does not at all intend to deny the suprarational sphere, nevertheless rejects as false all that is proved to be irrational. As regards the relation between reason and revelation, we have seen that Leibniz and Locke are actually closer than their very different epistemological positions would lead us to expect. Moreover, Leibniz, by and large, shares with Locke a belief in the usefulness of identifying a core of basic truths on which to base religious harmony.[114] Although the basis Leibniz requires is much wider than that admitted by Locke, and includes among the articles of faith necessary for salvation the dogma of the Trinity,[115] there seem to be no texts in which Leibniz accuses Locke of Antitrinitarianism on account of this divergence.

Although in the very last years of his life Leibniz wrote that Locke had in-clined toward Socinianism, this was due not to his views on the Trinity but to questions of natural theology (such as the issue of the divine attributes) and to the problem of the immortality of the soul, in connection with possible materialistic outcomes (close to a certain Socinian metaphysics) opened up by Locke's hypothesis of thinking matter.[116] Toward the end of 1711, Leibniz writes to Malebranche that he has tried "to combat, en passant, certain lax philosophers, such as Mr. Lock, Mr. le Clerc, and the like, who have false and base ideas of man, the soul, the understanding, and even of the Divinity";[117] and in 1715 he adds that in Locke's theological writings many things are sus-pect.[118] But these negative judgments on Locke's theology seem likewise to re-fer to the abovementioned questions and not strictly to problems of revealed theology, such as the mysteries of the Trinity and the Incarnation.

PART IV

The Last Years (1706–1716)

11

Islam, Kabbalah, and the Trinity:
The Polemic regarding the Historical
Dissertations *by M. V. de La Croze*

Leibniz would certainly never have expected that, after so many explicit declarations of war against the Socinians, he himself, during the last decade of his life, would be the target of an accusation of Antitrinitarianism.

But let us proceed one step at a time. In 1707 Mathurin Veyssières de La Croze published a volume composed of three *Dissertations historiques*.[1] The polemical intention of the author was to show "which Heresies are more pernicious to the Church, those of Socinianism, or those of the Jesuits."[2] The plan begins to take shape in the first dissertation, dedicated to a comparison between Islam and Socinianism. The general thesis of the *Reflexions historiques et critiques sur le Mahometisme, et sur le Socinianisme* written by La Croze is that, in fact, the Muslim creed and the Socinian creed coincide, due to the fact that both reject the Trinitarian conception of God.[3] In the ensuing two dissertations, criticism is instead aimed at the Jesuits: the second attacks the theories of the Jesuit Father Jean Hardouin regarding the origin of the classical works of antiquity,[4] while the third, in examining the state of the Christian religion in the Indies, concludes that the claims made by the Jesuits for the conversions carried out in those lands are unfounded.[5] Only the first of these dissertations directly concerns us here. As La Croze argues, the Muslim idea that the Trinity is a corruption of monotheism coincides with the charge of Tritheism brought by the Socinians against the dogma of the

Trinity.[6] Moreover, in his opinion also the arguments supporting the rejection of the Trinity by Islam and the Socinians coincide: both parties insist on the supposed irrationality of this mystery[7] and on the specious affirmation that the biblical passages in which the divinity of Christ and the Holy Spirit most clearly emerge are interpolations of later ages.[8] In this connection, notes La Croze, the Anglican bishop George Bull amply proved, in his book in defense of the Council of Nicaea (325), that faith in the Trinity was present in the church right from the beginning. Therefore the Socinian thesis that the dogma of the Trinity was an invention of the council is totally groundless.[9] But the closeness of the followers of Socinus to those of Muhammed does not end with a theoretical agreement on points of doctrine: passing from Spain, to Italy, Poland, Lithuania, and Transylvania, La Croze gathers together examples of contacts and close relations between Antitrinitarians and Muslims.[10] Only the intransigence of the Muslims, who opposed any compromise on religion, prevented their complete alliance with the Socinians. Perhaps this very fact, surmises La Croze, may have led the Socinians to maintain so decisively the worship of Jesus Christ, a doctrine that was, on the other hand, proudly attacked by the Antitrinitarian Ferenc David.[11] Moreover, alongside the Muslims, the Antitrinitarians were also joined by a semi-Jewish sect, an exponent of which—Martin Seidel—asked for protection from the Socinians of Krakow, declaring that he had nothing at all to do with the Messianic doctrine, since all religion consisted in the Decalogue, which is inscribed in our conscience.[12] La Croze concludes that "Socinianism leads to Deism and to libertinism";[13] but an even more serious charge is made a few pages earlier, where Socinianism is said to be "an open door to Atheism, and to the denial of God," since Socinus denied the possibility of proving the existence of God by rational means, whereas "everything depends on reason in Socinianism."[14]

Before publishing his first dissertation, La Croze sent the manuscript to Leibniz for his opinion. Very much impressed by the undeniably profound erudition displayed in the essay, on 2 December 1706 Leibniz sent from Berlin a long letter in reply, in which he expressed (albeit with some reservations) his favorable opinion. Certainly flattered by the esteem of his illustrious correspondent, La Croze published the letter, unbeknownst to Leibniz, as an appendix to his *Reflexions historiques et critiques sur le Mahometisme, et sur le Socinianisme*.[15]

In Leibniz's letter, the tolerant attitude toward Islam is certainly very far from the animosity with which 'infidels' were treated at that time.[16] His opening words seem to echo the invocation expressed ten years before in a letter to Thomas Burnett: would that all were at least deists![17] In Leibniz's opinion,

Islam is a sort of Deism; it has the merit of having destroyed paganism in many regions of the earth and could be used to bring people "to the more sublime Religion of Christianity."[18] The truths of natural theology shared by Islam or, in general, by Deism, are thus to be understood as preambles on the way toward the fullness of faith, which can be reached only by passing on to the true revealed religion, represented by Christianity.[19] And indeed, immediately afterward Leibniz calls attention to the dogma that par excellence expresses the passage from natural to revealed theology: the dogma of the Trinity. This is the point of doctrine that prevents easy conversion from the adamantine monotheism of Islam to Christianity. Now, if Leibniz's program had even just a shade of Deism, a logical consequence would be, if not the elimination, at least the marginalization of the dogma of the Trinity as a nonfundamental truth, in view of the wider agreement possible regarding the truths of natural theology.[20] On the contrary, Leibniz is not willing to compromise on this point: conversion from Islam is to be attained not by shelving the dogma of the Trinity but by removing the Muslim opinion that Christians have multiple gods.[21] And here Leibniz, with a clear reference to the English Trinitarian polemics that some years before had involved William Sherlock, complains of the presence in Christian circles of doctrines that come perilously close to Tritheism.[22]

As for the Socinians, he shares La Croze's view that their creed agrees with Islamic doctrine on its main point, that is, in rejecting the Trinity and the Incarnation.[23] It is true that they consider Jesus Christ to be divine, unlike the Muslims, but, Leibniz goes on, it is precisely the Muslims who act coherently in refusing to worship (as Ferenc David also rightly proposed) one who is held to be a mere creature.[24] The case of the Christians is very different: "We worship formally and precisely only the eternal and the infinite; and the union of the Creator with the creature, however great it may be, must not alter this worship."[25] Here again we find the doctrine already upheld by Leibniz before.[26] Christians worship Jesus Christ only insofar as he is God, and if it is necessary to correct those who, out of ignorance, stray from this principle, confusing the Savior's divine and human natures, one must not, for this reason, reject the mystery of the union between divine and human nature or the mystery of the Trinity: "If some misinformed scholars, or some coarse person of the badly instructed people among the Christians, depart from this great principle of true worship, one must rebuke them and reprove them with zeal; but one must not for this reason destroy either the union of the Word with human nature, which is as close as possible, or the diversity of the three personalities [trois personalités] and of the two productions [deux productions], that the holy Scripture teaches us in God, without multiplying

God himself."[27] Leibniz does not seem to have any doubt that the mystery of the Trinity is not only sufficiently grounded in the scriptures but also (albeit remaining incomprehensible) sufficiently explained by the analogy with the creation: "There is something deep and incomprehensible in the Divinity, of which the Holy Scripture has given us some knowledge, through words borrowed from what one can find among the creatures that is analogous, but excluding the imperfections that one finds among the creatures."[28]

The Trinitarian nature of God is thus sufficiently revealed in the scriptures. Moreover, it appears that this doctrine has been taught by the church from the beginning, despite some inaccuracies found in the writings of the church fathers before the Council of Nicaea. These, Leibniz seems to imply, were unavoidable inaccuracies, due to the process of approaching a precise theological formulation of a doctrine already shared by the church.[29] Of these, the conception of some church fathers who were close to Platonism could be suspected of having encouraged the rise of Arianism, in conceiving of two distinct filiations of the Messiah before his earthly birth: with the first filiation, he was said to be the eternal only begotten Son of God; with the second, the Firstborn of the creatures. Thanks to this second filiation, the eternal Logos was endowed with a created nature that makes him an instrument of God in the production and direction of other natures. Now, whereas the fathers did not mean by this to deny the uncreated and consubstantial nature of the Son, the Arians instead kept only the second filiation, making the Son a mere creature.[30] Leibniz's source for this exposition of patristic theology before Nicaea appears to be George Bull's *Defensio Fidei Nicaenae,* to which La Croze also referred.[31] In chapters V to VIII of the third section, Bull defends the doctrines of the pre-Nicene fathers accused of having opened the way for Arianism, confuting the thesis that they denied the eternity of the Son. Leibniz refers to these chapters in a text that can help to throw light on some statements contained in the letter here under examination: it is a series of observations on J. G. Wachter's book *Elucidarius Cabalisticus sive reconditae Hebraeorum philosophiae Brevis et succincta recensio* (Rome, 1706).[32]

Wachter rereads, in the light of Kabbalistic speculations, Tatian's doctrine in the *Oratio ad Graecos* concerning the generation of the Son.[33] Leibniz reports: "Tatianus, in his *Oration to the Greeks,* professes himself to be a follower of the Barbarian (that is, Hebrew) philosophy. In the very lord of the universe, by the power of the word, now himself, now the word that was in him (the internal word) came to be. As, moreover, he wanted, the word sprang forth from its simplicity, not brought forth in vain, but the first-born work of his spirit (the external word). We know this to be the starting-point of this world (Adam Cadmon, the first-born). . . . These things [were said by]

Tatianus, where only the Hebrew words of Ensoph and of Adam Cadmon are lacking."[34] The firstborn Tatian is speaking of would thus correspond with the *Adam Kadmon,* or primordial man, of the Kabbalah. This concept was already present in the antique Kabbalah and was used at times to indicate the totality of the divine emanation in the ten *Sefirot* or 'spheres,' while at other times it indicated a single *Sefirath.* In the Kabbalah of Isaac Luria (1534–1572) it took on a new and central meaning. The *Ein-Sof,* namely, God, conceived in terms close to Neoplatonism as infinite, eternal, necessary Being, with an act of contraction (*zimzum*) produces a space full of light, described anthropomorphically as Adam Kadmon, the first creation, whose ten numerations or Sefirot constitute the cosmic structure.[35] Leibniz does not here comment on the parallel between the Kabbalistic doctrine of Adam Kadmon and the patristic doctrine of the generation of the Son, limiting himself to pointing out that Tatian's doctrine, as given above, does not in any case make him a precursor of Arianism.[36] Arius's heresy consists, in fact, in having confused the Firstborn with the only begotten Son,[37] or, according to what Leibniz wrote to La Croze, in having eliminated the first filiation that makes the Son the only begotten, eternal and consubstantial with the Father, and keeping only the second filiation, which makes the Son the first among the creatures. It is at this point that Leibniz mentions the chapters of the *Defensio Fidei Nicaenae* in which Bull shows that Tatian and some other church fathers before Nicaea maintained a sort of birth of the Son before the creation of the world, and that a procession of the Logos from the Father for the creation of the world was admitted also by some authors who came after Nicaea.[38] Now, Bull notes, even Athanasius attributes a triple nativity to the Son: the first as the only begotten Son of God, residing with the Father from all eternity; the second as the Firstborn of the creatures in view of the creation of the world; and the third as the Son of the Virgin Mary in the mystery of the Incarnation.[39] This explanation, Bull goes on, is not to be despised, inasmuch as it contains the key for correctly understanding the thought of the early church fathers unjustly accused of Arianism.[40]

Although, as mentioned above, in Tatian's case Leibniz does not comment on the proposed parallel between the Son and Adam Kadmon, he still seems interested in establishing points of contact between the Kabbalah and Christianity. This is not surprising, in view of Leibniz's typical conciliatory spirit, always ready to search out and accept every fragment of truth, wherever it may be found.[41] Thus, just as he does not hesitate to define the other great monotheistic religion, Islam, as a sort of Deism, which can be used for the spread of Christianity, so too in the case of the Kabbalistic doctrine he does not scorn possible parallels, in view of the conversion of the Jews. For this

reason Leibniz lends his ear to those thinkers who, in a more or less orthodox way, saw in the Kabbalah proofs of the truth of Christianity and, in
particular, of the distinctive doctrines of the Christian revelation: the Incarnation and the Trinity.[42] Among his contemporaries, two names stand out:
Christian Knorr von Rosenroth (1636–1689) and Franciscus Mercurius van
Helmont (1618–1699), two eminent exponents of the Christian Kabbalah,
with whom Leibniz entertained cordial personal relations.[43] The former,
through the monumental compendium of the Kabbalah known as *Kabbala
denudata*,[44] furnishes the main source for non-Jewish Kabbalistic literature
until the end of the nineteenth century, and the first extensive presentation
of the Lurianic Kabbalah to the Christian world. Described by Leibniz as
"perhaps the cleverest man in Europe for his knowledge of the most hidden
matters of the Jews,"[45] in the annotations to the *Elucidarius Cabalisticus*
he is defended against the accusation of Wachter that his work does not re-
veal the true Kabbalah.[46] Van Helmont, on the other hand, in close contact
with Rosenroth, played an important role in linking the Kabbalah to the
philosophical speculations of the Cambridge Platonists.[47] He also exerted a
decisive influence on Anne Viscountess Conway, editing, among other things,
the translation and posthumous publication of the *Principia Philosophiae
Antiquissimae et Recentissimae de Deo, Christo et Creatura*, composed by
Conway in English between 1672 and 1677.[48] This work, conceived in the
context of the Christian Kabbalah, was much appreciated by Leibniz.[49]

The points of contact between the Kabbalistic doctrine of the primordial
man (Adam Kadmon) and the Christian doctrine of the generation and Incarnation of the Son of God were emphasized in particular in the essay von
Rosenroth published as an appendix to the second volume of the *Kabbala
denudata*, that is, the *Adumbratio Kabbalae Christianae, id est, Syncataba-
sis hebraizans, sive brevis applicatio doctrinae hebraeorum cabbalisticae ad
dogmata Novi Foederis, pro formanda hypothesi, ad conversionem Judeo-
rum proficua*.[50] This text, an anonymous work by van Helmont, is a sort
of manifesto of the seventeenth-century Christian Kabbalah, the intents of
which are already stigmatized in the title: the application of the Kabbalah to
Christianity is aimed at the conversion of the Jews. Within this program, the
identification of Adam Kadmon with the Christian Messiah clearly became
a strong point, something that could not fail to attract Leibniz's attention.
During his stay at Sulzbach in 1688, while he was perusing the *Kabbala
denudata*[51] with von Rosenroth, Leibniz wrote to Landgraf Ernst von Hessen-Rheinfels: "I also find a very skillful man at Sulzbach . . . his name is
Mr. Knorr de Rosenroth. He passes the time . . . digging up the Kabbalistic
Antiques of the ancient Jews where he has found excellent things regarding

the Messiah that the modern Jews ignore, or try to suppress, or divert from their real meaning."[52] It is not by chance that in Leibniz's notes of this period taken from his conversations with von Rosenroth we find a reference to the figure of Adam Kadmon, the Messiah, that very closely resembles the three generations of the Son proposed by Athanasius, defended by Bull and represented by Leibniz in his letter to La Croze:[53] "The infinite Being consists in an indivisible point, and the light emanated or the sphere of activity sends his light according to his liking. The first to be born of the creatures, the Messiah, inasmuch as it is a creature (created), is called Adam Kadmon; he receives the first rays of the light and sends them to the creatures. . . . [T]he Messiah has descended. . . . The Messiah has taken a body; one must therefore distinguish three things in him, his divinity, his rank, as the first-born among the creatures, and finally the one that was born, in time, of a virgin."[54] Leibniz again dwells on the figure of the Messiah and on the distinction between the different generations in reading the *Elucidarius Cabalisticus* and annotating the passages in which the distinction between the first two generations is expressed by the concepts of "internal Logos" (namely, the Word existing in God from all eternity) and "external Logos" (namely, the Word that proceeds from God as the Firstborn of the creatures in view of the creation of the world).[55] Leibniz speaks of the three generations of the Son as having "nothing to do with faith, but not being contrary to faith" in one of the marginal notes to his copy of the *Elucidarium*.[56] An explicit comparison between Adam Kadmon and Origen's doctrine of the preexistence of souls, of which the first was that of the Messiah, is found in the letter to La Croze.[57]

Nevertheless, the search for points of contact does not stop Leibniz from criticizing those aspects of the Christian-Kabbalistic conception of the Messiah considered incorrect or insufficiently founded. In January 1695, Leibniz returned to Lorenz Hertel a manuscript commentary by Caspar Calvör regarding *Seder Olam sive ordo seculorum,* an anonymous work attributed to van Helmont.[58] In his accompanying letter, Leibniz, among other things, criticized the conception of the Messiah as an intermediate being between God and the creatures, and thus neither infinite nor finite, a conception that leads to the heterodox thesis of the inferiority of the Son to God. To refute this thesis, appeal is made to a mathematical argument: there is no middle between finite and infinite that is not, in its turn, either finite or infinite. This is illustrated by the case of the proportional middle line between a finite line and an infinite line—a line that, in its turn, must be infinite.[59] In short, Leibniz seems to mean that the correct conception of the Messiah is that which recognizes him as the true God, equal to and consubstantial with the Father, and not as an 'intermediary' inferior in nature to the Absolute

Being.[60] Likewise, the theory that God needed an instrument for his work of creation is judged to be unsustainable, since it would involve an infinite regress.[61] Lastly, the idea of the preexistence of a celestial body of Christ, before the Incarnation, is considered frankly fanciful.[62] All this is topped off by the explicit condemnation of the pantheistic and emanationist aspects of the Kabbalistic doctrine.[63] With specific regard to the mystery of the Trinity, the fact that Leibniz simply reports without comment Wachter's objections to the interpretation of Pico della Mirandola and J. F. Buddeus that the first three Sefirot of the Kabbalistic tree foreshadow the Trinity suggests that he tacitly kept his distance from these two authors.[64]

But let us turn from the Kabbalah to the letter to La Croze. The tolerant attitude adopted by Leibniz toward Islam is extended to the Antitrinitarians as well. This time, however, his motivations are different. We are not dealing here (as in the case of Islamic monotheism) with a recognition of the positive aspects of the doctrine espoused, we are dealing with a more general rule of behavior with regard to those who have gone astray. Leibniz's interpretation of the modern Antitrinitarians' intentions reflects what was, in effect, the judgment on the movement expressed by some of its illustrious exponents.[65] Intending to proceed along the way opened first by the Lutherans in Germany and then by the Calvinists in France, they wished to do nothing but carry the Reformation forward. If the intentions were good, in Leibniz's opinion the results were undoubtedly negative: the Christian religion, far from being purified, was almost destroyed.[66] Although he identifies the ultimate roots of modern Antitrinitarianism in the Protestant Reformation, Leibniz refuses to saddle the Reformation with the errors of the Antitrinitarians.[67] What is important to stress here, however, is the clarity with which the position held by these Antitrinitarians is condemned as erroneous. At the same time, it is acknowledged that error as such is not a ground for punishment. If one has a certain right to take those measures that are strictly necessary to prevent the propagation of the error, Leibniz uses a very strong word to describe the rigor exerted against the Antitrinitarians: inexcusable.[68] Here an interesting position takes shape with regard to the justification and appropriate degrees of punishment: the intentions of the one who errs should be kept in mind; the error as such cannot be punished, only corrected; consequently, the punishment must not be an end in itself (as it would be in a rigorously retributionist conception) but must serve to correct the one who errs; and lastly, the repressive measures meant to prevent the propagation of the error must be as limited as possible. Leibniz's tolerant tone is crowned by the denial that a painful death (like that which was the lot of some Antitrinitarians) must inevitably be seen as a divine punishment,[69] together with an acknowledgment of the moral rectitude found among the Antitrinitarians and the Muslims.[70] At any rate, in the end the Socinians come off worse in the comparison between Socinianism and Islam. In fact, in Leibniz's view, their audacity goes even further than that of the Muslims: not content with combating the most important mystery of revealed theology, they weakened even natural theology, denying our natural knowledge of God and maintaining a conception of God unworthy of his greatness.[71] In sum, concludes Leibniz, "the Socinians seem to trim both natural and revealed Religion, in theory and in practice, and remove from it much of its beauty."[72]

In January 1708 the fuse begins to burn. Writing from Berlin on the 19th of that month, La Croze promptly informed Leibniz: "I do not know if you have seen what a Jesuit disguised as a doctor of the Sorbonne has said against my Dissertations in the 14th Volume of the Bibliothèque Universelle. Nothing more feeble and more miserable. This beast has dared to accuse you of Socinianism on the most pitiful evidence. Nevertheless there are some people here that have the nerve to find this nice. I will reply as modestly as possible, and I will see if Mr. Le Clerc will insert my reply in his Bibliothèque Choisie."[73] La Cloze is referring to the scathing article printed in 1708 in the fourteenth volume of the *Bibliothèque choisie* published by Jean Le Clerc, in which "un docteur de Sorbonne" harshly attacks the *Dissertations historiques*.[74] In large part the article deals with the polemic raised by the theories of the Jesuit Father Hardouin, criticized by La Croze in the second *Dissertation historique*.[75] At the beginning, however, the anonymous author dwells on the *Reflexions historiques et critiques sur le Mahometisme, et sur le Socinianisme,* expressing the cutting judgment that so hurt La Croze. According to the "docteur de Sorbonne," La Croze wrote this dissertation "to cleanse himself of any suspicion of Socinianism."[76] In reality, however, in the doctor's view, La Croze embraced the Unitarian creed, which is identical, as regards Jesus Christ, to that of the Socinians.[77] The proof on which such a heavy accusation is based is the fact that La Croze, in his *Dissertations historiques,* approved the Trinitarian doctrine presented by Bull in his *Defensio Fidei Nicaenae.* Now, continues the doctor, this doctrine is very far from orthodoxy. It is, in fact, a form of modalism, in that it reduces the Trinity to a *nonnulla distinctio* (certain distinction) between wisdom and charity in God. Although such a conception may satisfy Islam and Judaism, it has nothing to do with the Christian Trinity.[78] It is therefore extremely blameful "that a man of spirit, as is Mr. *De Leibniz,* would appear not to have any other God, nor any other Trinity, than those of the ones [La Croze and Bull] previously mentioned; above all in his letter, that is addressed to this Author [La Croze], and that this latter took care to have printed at the end of his first Dissertation; because this letter is a kind of approval, almost in all its parts, with praise."[79]

La Croze did not remain inactive. On 9 February 1708 he wrote to Leibniz: "I have sent to Holland a Response to the Jesuit who censured my Book. I told him nothing regarding myself. But I spoke to him as he deserved regarding what he said about you."[80] On 18 February Leibniz broke his silence, judging the charges to be so devoid of foundation as not to deserve a reply: "I am surprised that Mr. *le Clerc* has published the letter of the doctor of Sorbonne, before having given a review of your book. This letter does not contain anything, and hardly deserves a reply. Finally I have read it and I do not understand anything of what he says about me, and I think that other people would also not understand anything of it. I have not said that I completely approve of Mr. *Bull;* and Mr. *Bull* is strongly praised by the Protestants. I think that you could include a kind of review of your book in your reply that would make the best parts of the book known, disregarding the rest of the letter. I will think about writing a note to Mr. *le Clerc.* If he refuses you, another will not refuse you."[81] A few days later, on 29 February, Leibniz wrote again, saying that the flimsiness of the arguments used by the doctor seems to confirm his idea that the best thing is simply to let the matter blow over; he hopes also that at least he will not be directly involved in La Croze's reply.[82] Irritated by Leibniz's obvious reluctance to be drawn into the polemic, La Croze replies drily on 12 March 1708: "I was delighted to see that you hardly care about the insults of the supposed doctor of the Sorbonne. As far as I am concerned, I feel that I am still treated considerably well, seeing where this comes from; for I am almost certain that the author of these opinions is a Jesuit. There are some traits that can only come from an author of the Society [of Jesus]. I recognise their morals, and their Sophisms. I will give the order to omit what regards you in the answer I sent to Amsterdam. It's enough, Sir, that you wish it. I have nothing to reply."[83] Whether the promised correction was never communicated or whether it was never made, the fact is that La Croze's anonymous reply, published in the fifteenth volume of the *Bibliothèque choisie* also cites Leibniz.[84] The tone is very bitter, conceding nothing to ceremony.[85] Speaking in the third person, La Croze counterattacks that the author of the *Dissertations historiques* has never in the least been suspected of Socinianism, and that as regards the mystery of the Trinity he has no ideas other than those commonly taught by the Roman Church. As for Bull and Leibniz, the supposed doctor speaks with very little respect for those who are wiser and more erudite than he is, launching unproved accusations and thus making himself hateful and blameworthy.[86]

Although Leibniz, after pondering the idea of sending a few lines to Le
Clerc, in the last analysis decided not to take a position publicly, there remains among his manuscripts the draft of a reply, in two distinct versions.[87]
In the second in particular, Leibniz dwells on the charge of Antitrinitarianism
brought against him. Recapitulating the circumstances that led him to write
his letter to La Croze, he first of all takes care to distance himself from the
virulent animosity displayed by the latter against the Society of Jesus:

> I have learned that a doctor of the Sorbonne that I do not have the honour
> of knowing attacks me in a little piece inserted in the 14th Volume of the
> "Bibliothèque Choisie," where this Doctor criticizes the *dissertations His-*
> *toriques,* the first Volume of which appeared last year in Rotterdam. The
> learned author of these dissertations gave me the first volume to read in
> manuscript, wherein he talks about the Unitarians, and I wrote him a letter
> about this, which he did me the honor of adding to his work. I read the two
> other dissertations only after they were printed, and I did not even know
> that they would appear with the first. I find in them several wise and useful
> remarks; and I am surprised that the doctor talks about them with contempt.
> But I admit having a better opinion of the jesuits and of the Missionaries of
> the orient, than this knowledgeable Dissertator seems to have of them: and
> I have also made this known in some other published works. However, I do
> not expect my friends to follow my opinions. Judgments must be even freer
> than the will[.][88]

Leibniz then passes to examine the charges, showing that the argument on
which they are based contains a clear non sequitur:

> But here is what they accuse me of. The doctor of the Sorbonne claims that
> Mr. Bull, the famous English author, in his defense of the Council of Nicaea
> reduces the dogma of the Trinity to merely saying that God has wisdom and
> charity, and among these three things there is a *nonnulla distinctio.* The Au-
> thor of the dissertation approves the book of Mr. Bull pp. 61, 62, and I in my
> letter approve almost all the parts of the dissertation with praise. Therefore
> I approve this opinion of Mr. Bull. He appears to have gone a bit too far in
> his inferences. . . . In encouraging the author to publish it, I did not agree
> with all his opinions, and this author only admires, in the book by Mr. Bull,
> the justification of the Council of Nicaea; if this English doctor has some
> opinions like the ones expressed in this Critique, I wash my hands of them.
> I nevertheless doubt that one may find them, but that is what I do not have
> the leisure to examine at the moment[.][89]

In the first version, after expressing an opinion regarding the work of the
missionaries in the East and the theories of Father Hardouin,[90] Leibniz further clarifies his position with regard to Bull's doctrines:

I wanted to say these things regarding the learned dissertations in question to remark that I admire them, but that I do not agree with everything that they have brought forward. It is the same with some writings by the famous Mr. Bull, the English Theologian. I have praised his work where he has made it clear that the notion of the Trinity was dominant before the great council of Nicaea. The Doctor of the Sorbonne complained of me regarding this, that I am in I don't know what bad opinion of this author. Since Mr. Bull's book is generally admired, and I have the impression that it deserves to be, I have praised what has been considered praiseworthy, which is the main thing. If he has mixed in some extraordinary opinions I do not remember it, and I do not want to get involved in this, even less to approve it.[91]

At any rate, the general tone is very different from that of La Croze, offering a glimpse into the thoughtful tranquillity with which Leibniz, now sixty-two years old and far removed from some of the fiery words of his early years, considers the controversies of his time:

I am more the type to excuse than to accuse people, and to praise rather than to blame; and I prefer to note the good in people to benefit from it, and to encourage them, rather than to point out their defects and do them wrong. . . . There are many true and certain things, but sometimes this truth is only known in a confused way until one begins to doubt it. And it is then that it becomes developed and demonstrated as it should be. . . . One should hope that the quarrels against learned people would remain as far as possible within the bounds of civility, and one should also avoid offending those one contradicts. . . . The Skeptics are never liked by the experts in a scientific field or a doctrine, whatever it may be; they only satisfy the ignorant, who bow to skepticism because it seems to console their ignorance. However, insightful objections are always useful, and serve to better clarify the truth: but those who only object, and who doubt only for the purpose of doubting, damage their own reputation in the company of well educated people and harm those who are not educated, by seducing them, and by teaching them to neglect to learn.[92]

Whereas Leibniz seems to wish to forget the matter and shelves his reply, La Croze's troubles are not over. On 15 April he complains to Leibniz: "Mr. de Beauval has made a very unfaithful extract of my Dissertations in his Histoire des Ouvrages des Savans. He makes me look as ridiculous as possible. At the beginning I was incensed by it; but now I am glad of it. I have been deceived once, I won't be twice. I'm not to the liking of the century. The best thing I can do now is to let other people write. This is also the decision that I took, and I will firmly keep to it."[93] In fact, despite La Croze's declared decision to withdraw into a dignified silence, what follows in the letter betrays his desire to involve his illustrious correspondent in the dispute: "I would like you to take a look at the extract of Mr. de Beauval. He praises your letter: but he attributes to you an opinion that you might not approve."[94] Next is an account of the wrongs received, which closes with an improbable declaration of serene detachment from all afflictions: "Mr. le Clerc has also, reluctantly, inserted my reply in his Bibliothèque choisie. I have not yet seen it: but I have heard that there is something against me. Two days ago I saw a letter that he wrote to a Minister in Berlin, in which he treats me with contempt. I am, therefore, being mistreated by everyone. That does not affect me."[95]

Perhaps unwillingly, perhaps worried by the possibility (hinted at by La Croze) of fresh attacks, Leibniz returns to the affair. Replying to the letter he had recently received, he allows himself a bit of irony in talking about La Croze's complaints: "I have not yet seen the last Histoire des ouvrages des Savans: therefore I do not know what opinion Mr. *de Beauval* attributes to me: he is wrong if he goes beyond my expressions; and, in this case, I will be forced to explain myself. I do not understand why he mistreats you; could it be that he, Mr. *le Clerc* and Mr. *Bernard,* although normally hardly united with one another, conspire against you? . . . If my opinion has any importance, I would advise you, Monsieur, not to care about the pieces which ridicule you, and to continue always on your path. Other capable people will be just with you."[96] Without reacting to La Croze's covertly irritated reply,[97] on 19 May 1708 Leibniz was able to give his opinion regarding Basnage de Beauval's review.[98] Reassured about the actual lack of any direct attack on himself,[99] he tries to sweeten the pill for poor La Croze, against whom the publisher of the *Histoire des Ouvrages des Savans* certainly did not spare polemical broadsides.[100] Thus, Leibniz finds the sarcastic "lamentations" used by Basnage when talking of the Preface to the *Dissertations historiques*[101] "a bit sharp,"[102] while he gives a positive spin[103] to the judgment (anything but flattering) that La Croze, having "the reputation of a Scholar," would assume "also the authority of one."[104] Although admitting that some statements do not do justice to La Croze,[105] Leibniz in general is conciliatory.[106] La Croze, however, finding no comfort in this, repeats that his resentment is well founded, and he even exacerbates it: now even the Socinians attack him because of what he wrote against them![107] This time Leibniz seems to decide that it is time to end the affair once and for all, and in his later letters he avoids commenting on the disputes unleashed by the *Dissertations historiques.*

12

The Socinians Again

Around 1706, Leibniz encountered unawares an old acquaintance: the Socinian Andreas Wissowatius.[1] In a book entitled *Vernünfftige Religion / Das ist Gründlicher Beweiss / dass man das Urtheil gesunder Vernunfft auch in der Theologie, und in Erörterung der Religions-Fragen gebrauchen müsse* (Rational Religion, That Is, a Thorough Proof That the Judgment of Sound Reason Must Also Be Used in Theology and in the Discussion of Religious Questions), the adversary he had fought in his youth lay hidden under the pseudonym of Arsenius Sophianus. The work, published in 1703 in Halle,[2] is actually the translation into German of Wissowatius's *Religio Rationalis,* which appeared posthumously in Amsterdam in 1684.[3] Evidently unaware of the Latin original as well, Leibniz read and annotated the German version edited by Johann Gottfried Zeidler (1655–1711).[4] The work is focused on one of the issues to which, as we have seen, Leibniz continually returns: the problem of the use of human reason in theology. It is therefore not surprising that in these years, immediately preceding the publication of the *Theodicy,* Leibniz should dwell with intense interest on the theses held by Sophianus. What is prima facie much more surprising is the positive judgment he makes regarding a work that he himself recognizes as having a Socinian origin.[5] Does Leibniz perhaps privately approve of the Socinian approach to the relation between faith and reason, right at the moment when he is thinking of publicly fighting against it in the "Preliminary Discourse" of the *Theodicy*? A more careful reading of what exactly he approves and disapproves of in the book of Sophianus-Wissowatius leads us to discard this hypothesis, at the same time revealing Leibniz's freest and most unprejudiced face: a Leibniz who is willing to recognize and appreciate whatever seems to him to be true, no matter what its source—even from an adversary he otherwise tenaciously fought against.

Instead, he does not spare his criticism of the author of the "Vorrede"— in all probability Zeidler himself, who (in his turn hiding behind the pseudonym Synesius Philadelphus) prefixed to the work a preface in which, as Leibniz immediately noticed, a clear pietist orientation can be seen.[6] Faced with Synesius's statement that "humankind has its greatest misfortune after the Fall precisely in reason, and at times is worse than the beasts,"[7] Leibniz cannot help but fall into the opposite camp and make common cause with Sophianus-Wissowatius, according to whom the human intellect, even after the Fall, conserves its capability to judge rightly—a thesis repeated in the *Theodicy*.[8] Likewise, he cannot but disapprove of the idea that pagan logic and metaphysics are to be rejected as not belonging to true wisdom: in his view, although they are not necessary to everybody, this does not diminish their validity.[9] Moreover, Leibniz regards it as a patent exaggeration to say that one could not correctly explain even one word of the Bible by means of these sciences.[10] Finally, he rejects as unacceptable Synesius's view that there are no orthodox or pseudo-orthodox Christians, since each person understands the mysteries in a different way.[11] "I do not see," Leibniz predictably comments, "how one person can be orthodox, and his opposite not be pseudo-orthodox. One of two people contradicting each other must be in error."[12]

Wissowatius's treatise is much closer to Leibniz's way of thinking on the matter of faith and reason. As we have already seen in connection with his youthful polemic against the Socinians, Leibniz is willing to go a long way with his adversaries: all the way to asserting the conformity between faith and reason, with its various implications.[13] The doctrine expounded by Wissowatius in *Vernünfftige Religion* and Leibniz's observations regarding it give us an opportunity to see more precisely what the two thinkers have in common and where exactly Leibniz differs from the followers of Socinus. It should first of all be pointed out that *Die Vernünfftige Religion* is very far from being an expression of the most radical rationalistic fringes of Socinian thought. Wissowatius's aim is much more moderate than the programmatic elimination of mysteries and the supernatural from the Christian faith, as pursued by the Socinian Joachim Stegmann Sr. and by John

Toland.[14] What Wissowatius sets out to prove is, as he announces in the very title of *Vernünfftige Religion,* the necessity of using reason in theology and, in particular, in religious discussions, an aim that cannot help but meet with Leibniz's approval. Far from wishing to eliminate the mysteries, Wissowatius is instead concerned to rebut the thesis that the acknowledgment of the need for rational analysis in the solution of controversies necessarily means subordinating faith to reason. No, he replies, Christians who acknowledge the necessity of reason also acknowledge the necessity of revelation, inasmuch as the truths of the Christian religion could not be discovered by human reason independently.[15] Many of the arguments used by Wissowatius in support of the use of reason in matters of faith can certainly be included among the tasks assigned by Leibniz to reason in the sphere of faith: Wissowatius, like Leibniz, insists on the fact that reason has to prove the authenticity of the revealed text and the reliability of the testimony on which faith is based;[16] with reasoning that is very similar to the statement of the young Leibniz that "believing is to hold as true [credere est verum putare]," and in order to consider something true it is necessary to know the meaning of what is being stated,[17] Wissowatius also upholds the need for a certain degree of understanding of the meaning of the divine word in order to be able to believe in its truth;[18] and finally, a thesis undoubtedly shared by Leibniz is that the truths of faith are never against reason and that a supposed revelation which is proved to be self-contradictory or impossible cannot be true.[19] Therefore true faith is not and cannot be blind; on the contrary, it must be supported by what Leibniz would call "motives of credibility."[20]

To put it briefly, many of the statements made by Wissowatius on the relation between faith and reason—supported by quotations that, in disaccord with the Enthusiasts, range from classics such as Tertullian, Augustine, and Thomas Aquinas to the more moderate passages of Faustus Socinus, Johannes Crell, and Joachim Stegmann, from the Catholics Francisco Suarez, Valeriano Magni, and Thomas White to the Lutherans Balthasar Meisner and Andreas Kesler, from the Reformed thinkers Rudolf Goclenius and Johann Amos Comenius to the Remonstrants Simon Episcopius and Étienne Courcelles—by their closeness to Leibniz's viewpoint justify his overall appreciation of the book as expressed in his notes to *Vernünfftige Religion,* as well as his remark that the author of the treatise "seems to be a learned man, and one who has read good books."[21] It should also be pointed out that, although it is certainly possible to recognize in *Vernünfftige Religion* the typical signs of Socinian rationalism,[22] Leibniz (rightly or wrongly) does not read in it the intent to subordinate faith to reason, by assigning priority to reason in the interpretation of the text. In proof of this, there is the explicit comparison and contrast he notes between the doctrine of Sophianus-Wissowatius and the theological rationalism proposed by Lodewijk Meyer in *Philosophia S. Scripturae Interpres:*[23] according to Leibniz, Meyer's book, which argues for the role of reason as the supreme judge in religious controversies and as the absolute norm in the interpretation of the scriptures, is "to be held against Sophianus."[24]

Leibniz especially praises the biblical examples given by Wissowatius in *Vernünfftige Religion,* in which the use of reason rightly leads one to abandon the literal meaning of the scriptures in favor of a metaphorical interpretation or, again, those examples in which the sacred text itself provides proof in support of his theses.[25] However, by far the most analytical part of Leibniz's observations is devoted to the register of the *Grund-Regeln* or universally true common notions, put forward by Wissowatius.[26] Although Leibniz diligently copies out all eighty-one Grund-Regeln,[27] and once again expresses a generally positive judgment, it is just at this point that he shows his dissent. "The register of the fundamental rules on pp. 26 is very fine," writes Leibniz, "even though it appears that one or the other is meant to support the point of view of the Socinians, since the teaching of the universal Church is not laid out clearly."[28] His first example regards the mystery of the Trinity: "For example three times one is three: that is commonly known; but when one says there are three, each one of which is God, and yet there is just one God, the word God is not being taken in the same way in this argument: at the beginning it means a divine person, or something relative, [whereas] at the end it means a substance or something absolute."[29] Leibniz is, of course, careful not to disagree that "three times one is three" is a universally valid truth, just as he is careful not to claim an exception to this rule for the Trinity. His line of defense is the one we are familiar with, hinging on the distinction between God taken relatively and God taken absolutely:[30] if one understands properly the term "God" that appears in the propositions "God is the Father," "God is the Son," and "God is the Holy Spirit" and the term "God" that appears in the proposition "God is One," one sees that the dogma of the Trinity does not contradict the necessary truth that "three times one is three."

Instead, Leibniz contests the universal validity of the twentieth rule proposed by Wissowatius,[31] again introduced as an implicit objection against the mystery of the Trinity: "That something infinite can only be one (p. 28) is not established. In the immense space there are countless straight lines, each one of which is infinite."[32] This is followed by a remark intended to ward off any suspicion of Tritheism from the conception of the divine persons: "That a person is a substance (pp. 28) one does not grant, and takes the word differently; otherwise one would fall back upon three Gods."[33] Why does Leibniz here deny that the persons of the Trinity are substances, when he maintained the contrary in other texts?[34] The statement should be read together with the related Grund-Regel proposed by Wissowatius, according to which "A person is a complete / singular / intelligent substance"[35] ["Persona est substantia completa singularis intelligens]."[36] In Wissowatius's definition of person as "complete substance" ("substantia completa"), Leibniz sees the insinuation that the doctrine of the Trinity entails the affirmation of three absolute substances, something that Leibniz has always denied: if the persons of the Trinity can be understood as substances, it must be clear that they are three relative substances in a single absolute substance.[37] Replying a little later to another Socinian, moved perhaps also by Wissowatius's implicit objection, Leibniz feels it advisable to spell out that only the *subsistens absolutum* can properly be called "substance."[38] But already around 1678, in *Il n'y a qu'un seul Dieu* and in *Symbole et Antisymbole des Apostres,* Leibniz had insisted (in words that reflect the much later remarks on *Vernünfftige Religion*) on the fact that the term "person" must be understood in the divine sphere only by analogy and that therefore "those who believe in three divine persons do not understand this word 'person' in the usual way, otherwise three divine persons would be three Gods."[39]

Two other Grund-Regeln that implicitly undermine the dogma of the Trinity are later attacked by Leibniz. In both cases he rejects the charge that the generation or procession of the divine persons necessarily implies a subordination, and thus the inferiority of the second and third persons to the first. To Wissowatius's assertion that "Any person who comes from another [von einer andern ist] / is not the highest God,"[40] Leibniz simply replies "Nego" ("I deny"),[41] leaving the actual confutation to other texts.[42] His reply to the Grund-Regel that what generates is always prior to the generated is more detailed.[43] Leibniz objects that this is not true in all cases: if, for example, the sun were eternal, its rays also would be eternal.[44]

In its turn, the mystery of the Incarnation too is defended against the charge of impossibility contained in the statement that *disparata* (that is, things opposed to one another, such as God and man) cannot simultaneously be predicated of the same thing or of one another.[45] Leibniz reiterates the line of defense that goes, so to speak, from the actual to the possible: just as soul and body, though disparata, are nevertheless united, so too it is possible for God and man to be joined in Christ.[46] The notes continue, confuting one after the other the further objections of a Socinian nature to be found in the Grund-Regeln, specifically regarding the doctrine of the Eucharist, the relation between necessity and divine liberty, God's justice, immortality, and the substantiality of the soul when separated from the body.[47] Suffice it here to make one last general remark, which returns to the point where the round of criticisms against the otherwise appreciated Grund-Regeln started. As we have seen, Leibniz points out that some of them do not reflect "the teaching of the universal Church."[48] It is right here, in the recognition of the authority of tradition and of the universal church as regards the determination of what is an authentic revelation (and therefore by definition in conformity with reason, even if it surpasses our capacity for understanding) that there is a key difference between Leibniz's position and that of the Socinians. This is, in fact, the weak link in the reasoning of moderate Socinianism, aimed at safeguarding what is "above reason": a weak link that inevitably breaks in the most radical form of Socinianism, which quite coherently ends up denying the existence of superrational truths in the Christian religion. Leibniz, in other words, agrees to "consider true," or to accept the presumption of the truth of, such dogmas as the Trinity and the Incarnation (which are and remain incomprehensible to human reason even after having been revealed) on the ground that they are taught by the ancient Christian tradition and by all the major Christian confessions ("the universal Church"). With regard to these dogmas, reason has a 'negative' task: that is, the task of rebutting the alleged proofs brought against what is presumed to be true. The Socinians, on the contrary, refuse to accept the judgment and authority of what Leibniz calls "the universal Church." They entrust reason with the positive task of judging the mysteries, which, once revealed, must be understood by human reason or else be rejected as self-contradictory.

Leibniz's differences with respect to the Socinian theses found in Sophianus-Wissowatius's book, expressed in the detailed confutation of some of the Grund-Regeln, do not prevent Leibniz from voicing his appreciation of what he considers valid in the book. The final judgment on *Vernünfftige Religion* is thus emblematic of an ecumenism that though on the one hand is willing to pass over the barricades of the official churches when truth is perceived in the enemy camp, on the other has very precise ideas regarding what is and remains unacceptable: the book deserves a new edition, concludes Leibniz, but it is necessary to leave out the "Vorrede," and "several Socinian things must be omitted."[49]

In comparison with his judgment on Sophianus-Wissowatius, Leibniz's treatment of Christoph Stegmann is much more critical.[50] Stegmann is the other Socinian whose work attracted Leibniz's attention in this period. The work in question is the manuscript *Metaphysica Repurgata,* dating from 1635. Leibniz saw it early on in his life,[51] but he obtained his own copy only much later,[52] probably around 1708. The intermediary this time is one of the exponents of Socinianism: Samuel Crell.[53] On 1 December 1707, Crell wrote to Leibniz: "I delivered Stegmann's Metaphysics, finally described at length, to my friend Kirch [Gottfried Kirch (1639–1710)], directing it to you. I am sorry that it was not done more quickly. But partly the expectation of another copy, and partly other impediments drew out this affair to this point."[54] On 7 June 1708, Crell wrote again, announcing the shipment of another Socinian treatise, this time one that Leibniz had never seen: the *Animadversiones in Philosophiam* by Christophorus Ostorodt.[55] Apparently Leibniz was anxious to put his hands on these two works, to judge by the warmth with which, on 12 July, he thanked his correspondent: "You pile benefit on benefit, when you deliver to me Ostorodt's Animadversiones in Philosophiam, after Stegmann's Metaphysics. I saw Stegmann's work time ago, but have never seen Ostorodt's[.]"[56] Leibniz's enthusiasm must not deceive us: the dissatisfaction he had already expressed regarding Stegmann's metaphysics[57] (discreetly shared by Samuel Crell)[58] returns with vigor in the series of observations dating from around 1708.[59] At the center of Leibniz's text is his defense of the wisdom and justice of God, and of the immateriality of the soul, against the materialistic metaphysics of Stegmann.[60] However, some interesting passages are dedicated to the Trinity, the denial of which is presented at the beginning of the text as the most characteristic element in Socinian theology.[61] And in fact, in his *Metaphysica Repurgata,* Stegmann aims to show, among other things, the self-contradictoriness of the dogma of the Trinity. The first argument to which Leibniz replies is based on the difference between universal and singular.[62] Leibniz writes: "He denies that a singular essence is common to several things, and establishes that this involves a contradiction. And in truth he would rightly dispute the orthodox Theologians if they were to hold that God is one exactly in the same sense in which these theologians hold that the father is God, the son is God, and the Holy Spirit is God; and that the father, son and holy spirit are different. For the word 'God' is being used in another sense when we say that God is one, than when we say that there are three, any one of whom is God."[63] Once again it is the distinction between God taken absolutely and God taken relatively that removes the apparent contradiction.[64] It is true that it would be contradictory to predicate the singular divine essence (or, in other words, God taken absolutely or essentially) of a plurality of individuals. Since there is only one God taken absolutely, it would be wrong to say, "The Father is God (taken absolutely); the Son is God (taken absolutely); the Holy Spirit is God (taken absolutely)."[65] The contradiction, however, does not exist, inasmuch as in these three propositions the term "God" indicates "a certain person of the divinity" and not "God taken absolutely or, as they commonly say, essentially, of whom there are three persons, in a single essence in number."[66]

Stegmann's second series of arguments against the dogma of the Trinity hinges on the concept of relation. Leibniz summarizes: "Then the author discusses Relations in divine matters, which are plainly of a different kind, and by our way of thinking constitute the persons [nostro concipiendi modo constituunt personas]; and he says that every relation is an Accident."[67] By stating that the ontological nature of every relation is that of accident, Stegmann aims to show the erroneousness of the theological doctrine whereby the divine persons are "subsistent relations."[68] If, objects Stegmann, they are relations, they cannot be persons. From an ontological point of view, a person is a substance. On the contrary, the nature of a relation is that of being an accident, that is, an entity nonsubsisting by itself, which inheres in another and which, in the last instance, inheres in a subject or substance.[69]

Leibniz's reply, instead of trying to reinforce the ontological status of relations, goes even farther than the Socinian Stegmann along the way of weakening it. "But the relation between the center and the circumference," writes Leibniz, "is not an accident of the circle."[70] This statement should be read in the light of Leibniz's general theory of relations, according to which a relation considered as such, outside the subjects (or as a 'bridge' between two or more individual things), is a purely mental entity and thus, properly, not an accident (which is an intrinsic property, quality, or modification of the subject).[71] That Leibniz understands relations in this sense becomes clear both from the paragraph before and from the one following this. In fact, he criticizes Stegmann's doctrine that a relation is a type of accident, defined as "respective quality."[72] Leibniz replies: "But I would prefer to distinguish between Relation and quality. For it is something that is not produced per se, but results when something else is produced. Nay, in truth, Relations, which are nothing but respects, are not Things but truths. . . . I prefer to consider Relations as truths resulting from the constitution of things rather than as Beings [pro Entibus]."[73] In other words, in the framework of the ontological division of the "objects of our thoughts" into "substances, modes, and relations" proposed by Theophile in the *Nouveaux Essais,* relations are 'second intentions' of the intellect that result when two or more substances, with their modifications (modes, qualities) are thought simultaneously.[74] In this sense relations as such are "truths" that result from the constitution of things, that is, from the simultaneous presence in thought of two or more substances with their modifications ("qualities"). But at this point what happens to the persons of the Trinity? Given the ontological weakness of relations qua relations, to conceive of the persons of the Trinity as relations would certainly not guarantee the characteristics of subsistence and distinct individuality required by any nonmodalist theology of the Trinity. Now, Leibniz goes on,

Stegmann rightly denies that the persons of the Trinity are relations, "for we do not say that persons are relations, but that they are constituted through relations [per relationes constitui]."[75] Persons are therefore not relations, but what does it mean to say that they are constituted "per relationes"?[76] Hasn't Leibniz just stated, both before and after this, that relations "result" from the existence of two or more individuals with their qualities ("For a relation . . . is something which is not produced per se, but results when something else is produced")? Relations are thus not a cause but an effect. What Leibniz seems to mean is that the distinctiveness of the divine persons is constituted by the ways in which they relate to each other. The very fact that there is a relation indicates the existence in the correlates of different intrinsic properties that are the foundation of the relation itself (fundamentum relationis) (for example, in the case of the relation of paternity, the *vis generandi* in the subject of the relation).[77]

However, Stegmann's objections do not stop here. In fact, the Socinian continues: "If the divine person were a relation, necessarily there would be as many persons in God as there are relations to be found in him"[78] Leibniz replies: "But not all are constitutive."[79] What he seems to mean is that not all relations are essential relations, that is, relations founded in essential properties that are constitutive of the correlated subjects.[80] Stegmann's last objection reiterates the charge that the idea of subsistent relation is in fact self-contradictory. Every subsistent entity is a substance; now, since a relation is an accident, it cannot at the same time be subsistent, that is, it cannot at the same time be a substance.[81] This time Leibniz does not pause to point out that a relation as such is not, properly speaking, an accident. Instead, he directs his attention to the statement that "every subsistent is a substance."[82] According to him, only what subsists absolutely is properly called substance, that is, a being that subsists per se.[83] The case of the subsistens relativum, such as the persons of the Trinity are, is different ("sed aliud est subsistens absolutum, quod proprie substantiam dicimus; aliud relativum ut personae in divinis").[84] Leibniz seems to mean that the subsistens relativum, strictly speaking, does not subsist per se (like the subsistens absolutum), since an essential characteristic of its ontological structure is its being *ad aliud,* that is, being in relation: as Leibniz writes in De Scriptura, Ecclesia, Trinitate and in the Examen Religionis Christianae, the divine person "essentially involves relation" and therefore cannot exist without the others.[85]

Despite the attempt to make the relations of the Trinity fit as closely as possible into the framework of his general theory of relations, Leibniz remains aware that also in this case one can reason only by analogy: relations "in divine matters . . . are plainly of a different kind."[86] What he means more precisely can be inferred from one of his very last reflections, dating from the end of 1715 or even 1716: the series of notes to the book by the Jesuit Aloys Temmik, *Philosophia Vera Theologiae et Medicinae Ministra.*[87] Leibniz writes: "Socrates qua warm activates the sense of touch, qua singing that of hearing, qua white that of sight, but there are not three Socrates, nor three things [res], but just three predicates. But in divine matters, when God qua Father generates and spirates [spirat], God qua Son is born and spirates, God qua Holy Spirit is spirated and proceeds, there is in this greater diversity, and different persons are constituted. Nevertheless, the diversity of predicates, or formal diversity, is a kind of rudimental indication and foreshadowing of the diversity of persons."[88] Further on he repeats: "Socrates qua white activates the sense of sight, qua singing that of hearing, qua warm that of touch, as I pointed out above. One can reflect on whether this as such makes a different subsistence in divine matters."[89] In Socrates we can formally distinguish different modes of being. However, these modes of being are not sufficient to ground a diversity of persons, as happens in the Trinity. The formal diversity or diversity of predicates to be found in the creatures is, however, a "foreshadowing [adumbratio]" of the diversity of persons in the Trinity. Thus, in *De Deo Trino* Leibniz wrote, in commenting on the proposed analogy between the Trinity and the mind that thinks itself: "What happens in the created Mind in some way occurs in God in the most perfect manner."[90] Or, again, with explicit reference to the relations of the Trinity: "One should then say that there are relations within the divine substance that distinguish the persons from each other, since these persons cannot be absolute substances. But one should also say that these relations must be substantial [substantielles] and that they are not sufficiently explained by simple modalities. . . . [T]hat which is modal, accidental[,] imperfect, and mutable in us, is real, essential[,] accomplished, and immutable in God."[91]

The fact that Leibniz here speaks of "modalities" with reference to relations suggests that in this case he does not mean relations as such, outside subjects, but relations as relational accidents, as modes of being of the subject.[92] These modes of being of the subject (in which, properly speaking, relations are founded) are raised in the mystery of the Trinity to the ontological status of substantiality, but precisely because they are analogous to relational accidents they correspond to substances that are essentially related to one another. Now, this constitutive being ad aliud of the divine subsistence or personality is not a limitation but on the contrary a "new perfection." In fact, Leibniz writes in his *Notationes* to Temmik: "The created subsistence consists in the negative, as to be sure it is a being [ens] not tied to another. But the uncreated personality is a new perfection."[93]

The reference is to the doctrine expounded by Temmik regarding the *ens subsistens*.[94] After having established that *substantia* and *subsistentia* are distinct, in that "just as substance indeed underlies [substet] the accidents, so subsistence underlies [substet] the operations,"[95] Temmik writes that the personality or created subsistence consists "in the negative," that is, it consists in the negation of bonds, obligations, or subjection to other persons.[96] The personality of the divine persons is, instead, a positive perfection; if it consisted in the negation of subjection to another person, since God is only one, there would be only one person.[97]

Finally, another facet of the Socinian doctrine that Leibniz encountered in this period deserves mention: the Christology developed by Samuel Crell along lines that are in many ways independent of traditional Socinian doctrines. Crell's position on the matter is summarized in the seventh of the *Praecipua Capita Christianae Theologiae, in quibus Samuel Crellius à Socino dissentit:* "Not only was the Holy Spirit given to Jesus Christ the Son of God without measure, but also the Majesty and Divine presence . . . it is strictly united with his humanity and inseparable from it."[98] In a long passage dedicated to the divine nature of Christ in his letter to Leibniz of 7 June 1708, after having approved Leibniz's statement that the union of the Word with human nature is "as close as possible,"[99] Crell states: "I, who maintain that it is not the divinity of some eternal Son, produced or generated by another, but the divinity itself of the most high and first God of all, which is most strictly united with Christ the man, seem to me to feel more sublimely about the divinity of Christ than those who hold that some eternal Son, produced by another, and therefore a creature, is endowed with a divine nature. That dwelling of God the Father in Christ, or his very close union with Christ, is not sterile, but produces divine qualities in Christ."[100] In his reply, Leibniz does not dwell on the possible *distinguo*,[101] content for once to be able to write that the doctrine proposed by this (albeit *sui generis*) exponent of Socinianism is not so very far from orthodoxy.[102]

13

The Curtain Call

The famous "Preliminary Discourse on the Conformity of Faith with Reason" prefixed to the *Theodicy* can certainly be considered Leibniz's literary manifesto of the relationship between faith and reason. Into it flow thoughts matured in the course of a lifetime: in a single overview—sometimes hurried, sometimes in a more focused way—Leibniz considers characters, works, and positions discussed in previous years, starting from his very earliest writings. Although the direct antagonist of Leibniz in this case is Pierre Bayle, there are many fronts in Leibniz's battle, aimed at establishing the extent, as well as the limits, of the use of reason in theology.[1] In this context, among the principal motives that inspired the "Preliminary Discourse" are the Trinitarian discussions generated by the spread of Socinian rationalism, as Leibniz clearly declares in section 16: "The question of the use of Philosophy in Theology was greatly debated by Christians, and it was found difficult to agree on the limits of such use, when the details of the matter were discussed. The Mysteries of the Trinity, the Incarnation and the Last Supper gave the greatest cause for dispute. The new Photinians fought against the first two of the Mysteries, having recourse to certain Philosophical Maxims[.]"[2]

Bayle's position (at least his ostensible one) is well known. Human reason is incapable of resolving the problem of evil, in the face of which the following question remains without an answer: If there is only one God, immensely good, all-knowing and all-powerful, why does evil exist in the world?[3] The fact that reason cannot give an answer to this and similar questions, stirring up instead only doubts, is nothing but a consequence of its weakness and incapacity to arrive at the truth. If reason brings up insoluble objections against the truths of faith, this must not, however, lead to the rejection of faith. The well-known outcome is of a fideistic character: faced with the irreconcilability of faith with reason, one must silence reason, since it is a weak and imperfect instrument, and one must trust faith blindly.[4] It is just this thesis of the opposition between faith and reason that, according to Leibniz, is to be refuted before one can confront the problem of evil. Between faith and reason there is conformity, in that both have truth as their object, and two truths cannot contradict one another. Truth is only one: there are no truths of faith that are in contrast with truths of reason, because in the last analysis both come from God.[5] To the controversy specifically directed against Bayle is added a more general attack against the so-called Averroistic doctrine of double truth[6]—a doctrine that, about a century earlier, had newly been the object of violent controversy in the nearby University of Helmstedt.[7] Against Bayle and against the supporters of a double truth, one philosophical and the other theological, Leibniz confirms his usual position: one cannot demonstrate the contrary of truth; there are no insoluble objections against truth, because that would go against the principle of noncontradiction, which is the foundation of all logic and the ultimate criterion of the distinction between truth and falsity. If one were to demonstrate that an article of faith, a dogma, involves contradiction, one would have demonstrated in an incontrovertible way that this presumed article of faith is false and is simply the invention of some theologian.[8]

At this point, though, another front is opened, against which Leibniz in the *Theodicy* unleashes his final attack: the Socinian front. The Socinians represent the opposite pole compared to the (at least ostensible) position of Bayle and the supporters of the irreconcilability of philosophy and theology.[9] Although the submission of faith to reason is, according to Leibniz, unacceptable, the way to fight it is not to oppose faith to reason.[10] A common, indispensable starting point for both Leibniz and the Socinians is the conformity between faith and reason. For this reason, Leibniz insists, in section 22 of the "Preliminary Discourse," "Certain Authors have been too quick to agree that the Holy Trinity is contrary to this great principle, which holds that two things that are the same as a third are also the same as each other; that is to say, if A is the same as B, and if C is the same as B, then A and C must also be the same as each other. For this principle is an immediate consequence of the principle of non-contradiction, and is the foundation of all Logic; and if it ceases, there is no way to reason with certitude. . . . And one can say generally that it is necessary to be on guard never to abandon the necessary and eternal truths, in order to support the Mysteries, lest the enemies of religion take therefrom the right to deny both Religion and the Mysteries."[11]

But can one save this conformity without falling into the Socinian position once again? In the "Preliminary Discourse," Leibniz recapitulates all the passages of a by now well-rehearsed strategy, adopted in his very early writings and insistently reused in the following years. The first move is to recall the traditional distinction between "against reason" and "above reason,"[12] grounding it on the distinction between necessary truths and truths of fact: only what goes against absolutely certain and indispensable truths is against reason (and therefore impossible); what contrasts only with experience can be, instead, above reason.[13] The first example of these truths superior to the human capacity of comprehension is the Trinity, but the ambit of these truths is not restricted to the mysteries of faith. On the contrary, it embraces also the 'mystery' of universal harmony and the distinct knowledge of an infinity of things.[14] The mysteries, therefore, precisely because they exceed the limits of the human intellect, are by definition incomprehensible truths. This does not mean, though, that they are against reason: their impossibility would have to be positively demonstrated, since their incomprehensibility and their dissimiliarity to what we are used to observing in nature is not a sufficient reason to reject them as irrational.[15] In the *Nouveaux Essais* Leibniz establishes explicitly that, in the case of a contrast between the literal meaning of the sacred scripture and "a great appearance of *Logical impossibility,* or at least a recognized *physical impossibilty,*" unless it concerns a clear attribution of imperfection to God (as in the case of anthropomorphism), one must stick to the letter: once again, the impossibility must be demonstrated, for in order to abandon the literal sense of the scriptures an apparent contradiction based on what happens in nature is not sufficient.[16] In other words, Leibniz reproaches both Bayle and the Socinians with two types of confusion. In the first place, they confuse 'above' and 'against' reason. By removing this distinction, Bayle goes so far as to affirm that one must believe as superior to reason even that which is against it. On the opposite side, the Socinians end up in fact by denying the superrational sphere, since finite human reason rejects as irrational all that it cannot comprehend. The second type of confusion is the undue shift from improbability to impossibility, that is to say, from what is against likelihood to what is against reason.

Against this defense by Leibniz of the mysteries as supernatural truths, an objection can be raised, which is precisely the objection formulated by

Bayle in the *Dictionaire historique et critique* and reported by Leibniz in sections 72 and 73 of the "Preliminary Discourse": "It is evident that reason will never attain to what is above it. Now, if it could supply answers to the objections that are brought against the dogma of the Trinity and that of hypostatic union, it would attain to these two mysteries, it would subject them to itself, and would submit them to the strictest examination by comparison with its first principles, or with the aphorisms stemming from common notions; and so proceed until finally it had concluded that they agree with the natural light. It would therefore do what surpasses its power; it would go beyond its limits, which is formally contradictory. . . . [I]f some doctrines are above reason, they are beyond its range, it cannot attain to them."[17] It is the same objection that, years later, in 1773, Lessing too insinuates in his ironic comment on the *Defensio Trinitatis:*[18] to bring onto the field, in defense of the mysteries, the shield of incomprehensibility, is equivalent to placing the mysteries outside the radius of action of natural human reason. Certainly in this case reason cannot raise any objection, except at the price of the absolute separation and incommensurability between faith and reason. And it is exactly this conclusion that, as we have seen, the first publisher of the *Defensio Trinitatis* draws: "Reason is not the tribunal with jurisdiction over divine matters."[19] How, then, can reason judge what by definition exceeds its limits of comprehension?

The line of argumentation adopted by Leibniz in order to be able to maintain the conformity between faith and reason in the case of superrational truths now comes into play, a line of argumentation that, it is worth repeating, marks the difference between Leibniz's position and that of the Socinians. Since both the truths of faith and the truths of reason come from God and God cannot contradict himself, from the start one assumes that every authentic revelation is in conformity with reason, even though because of our limited capacities of judgment we are not able to comprehend *how.* The next passage is at this point Leibniz's recognition of the value of the ecclesiastical tradition: there are dogmas that the entire Christian church has for centuries believed and announced as divine revelations. One is rationally justified in holding these dogmas as true (and in maintaining their possibility) until the opposite is demonstrated. The concept of presumption plays a central role here. As we have seen, for something that has not yet been positively demonstrated or, even more, something that cannot be positively demonstrated, a presumption of truth can be invoked and held as valid until one has proof of the opposite.[20] Or again, considered from another perspective, "every time Logical necessity is not demonstrated, one can presume in a proposition only physical necessity."[21] The second aspect of Leibniz's procedure comes into play at this point: the by now familiar 'strategy of defense' that finds in the "Preliminary Discourse" its most explicit formulation and also its definitive consecration as the way to save the conformity between faith and reason without subjugating faith to reason. To the objection of Bayle, mentioned above, Leibniz replies by saying that the burden of proof falls on the opponents of the mysteries and not on their defenders: it is the opponent that must make it evident that the mystery is false; the supporter, admitting the mystery on the basis of the revelation guaranteed by church tradition, recognizes from the beginning that it is impossible to make it something evident; his only task is to respond to the adversary by forcing him to prove in good form all his utterances or, at most, by pointing out the equivocation concealed in the objection, without this involving a positive argumentation in favor of the thesis being attacked.[22] To respond to the objections, it is thus by no means necessary to submit the mysteries to the examination of reason in the attempt to make them comprehensible; they are simply taken as true (presumed true) until their falsity is proven. It is in this sense that reason can attain to what is superior to it: not by "penetrating inside the matter" but by showing that the objections brought up to now have not been able to demonstrate its impossibility.[23]

What has been said so far helps us to understand better the famous section 5 of the "Preliminary Discourse," which in a few lines expresses the kernel of Leibniz's doctrine on the relationship between faith and reason.[24] The section opens with the distinction between "explaining," "comprehending," "proving," and "supporting," a distinction that is often later repeated and confirmed:[25] the mysteries can be explained, but they cannot be comprehended; they can be (actually they have to be) supported against objections, but they cannot be proven. It is clear that "supporting against objections" recalls the 'strategy of defense,' which has its basis in the fact that the mysteries cannot be "proved *a priori*, or by pure reason."[26] That is to say, the mysteries cannot be proven by the analysis of the notion in question, obtaining a distinct knowledge of all the elements that compose it. An analysis of this type, pushed to its last terms, would, in fact, coincide with comprehension;[27] but this is by definition impossible in the case of the mysteries, since they are truths superior to human reason. Just as the mysteries cannot be proven a priori, likewise one cannot even "make it understood *how* they come about" or "push reasoning as far as the how of the mystery,"[28] as this would coincide once again with "comprehending" the mysteries.[29] The unprovability of the mysteries does not, however, take away the necessity for "proofs of the truth of Religion" or "motives of credibility" in order for us legitimately to believe (or to consider true) the mysteries.[30] These are proofs that cannot give an "absolute" certainty (as would be the case with a priori proofs) but can give a "moral" certainty, based on positive truths or truths of fact,[31] truths whose necessity is only moral, as they are dependent on the free choice of God.[32]

In the "Preliminary Discourse" too the "motives of credibility" can be organized into the three broad categories already found in the early *Commentatiuncula de Judice Controversiarum*:[33] 1) the historical and philological verification of the authenticity of the revealed scripture and of the authenticity of the testimony;[34] 2) at least a confused knowledge of the meaning of the divine word; and 3) the absence of a proven contradiction. While the third condition refers once again to the strategy of defense, the second coincides with the "explanation" of the mysteries "so much as is necessary to believe them," which is described in section 5 of the "Preliminary Discourse." To be able to believe, Leibniz specifies, referring to the Trinity and the Incarnation, that at least an "analogical understanding" of the meaning of the mysteries is necessary, since one cannot consider as true "words entirely devoid of meaning" or "sine mente soni [sounds without meaning]."[35] This explanation is in any event very far from being comprehension, and, Leibniz constantly reminds us, it marks a limit to human knowledge, leaving beyond the possibility of adequate knowledge not only supernatural truths but also an infinity of natural truths.[36] Once the "credentials," represented by the motives of credibility, have been presented before the court of reason, the latter must give way to revelation as a new light superior to it.[37] From beginning to end, from his first writings to the last, the faith of which Leibniz speaks is a faith that has its reasons, without thereby being subjected to reason.

In the *Theodicy* proper, Leibniz refers to the Trinity only in section 150 of the second part. It is, however, an important passage, in which one of Leibniz's fundamental metaphysical doctrines—the distinction between divine intellect and will, on which, respectively, the essence and existence of things depend—is reinterpreted in terms of the Trinity. The discussion of the Manichean doctrine of the two principles in fact gives Leibniz an opportunity to repropose his typical solution to the problem of evil in the world through the familiar thesis according to which, while the divine intellect contains the ideas of infinite possible worlds, the divine will, holding firmly only to good, gives existence to our world precisely because it is the best of all possible worlds. This discussion is also the occasion to reinterpret, perhaps in a less familiar way, this same doctrine in a Trinitarian sense:

> There are actually two principles, but they are both in God, that is, his Understanding and his Will. The understanding furnishes the principle of evil, without being tarnished by it, without being evil; it represents natures as they are in the eternal truths; it contains in itself the reason wherefore

evil is permitted; but the will is turned only to good. Let us add a third principle, that is, power; it precedes both the understanding and the will; but it acts as the former shows it, and as the other commands. . . . Many have even believed that there was therein a secret relation with the Holy Trinity: that Power relates to the Father, that is to say, to the source of Divinity; wisdom to the Eternal Word, which is called logos by the most sublime of the Evangelists, and will or Love to the Holy Spirit. Nearly all the expressions or comparisons taken from the nature of the intelligent substance tend to this.[38]

The inverse approach is found in the *Examen Religionis Christianae,* written more than twenty years before. In this case it is the traditional distinction between power, knowledge, and will (posse, scire, velle) in the Trinity that is reinterpreted in the light of the distinction between the essence of things (dependent on the divine intellect) and the existence of things (dependent on the divine will): "Antiquity was accustomed, and in my view wisely and [in a way] accommodated to our capacity, to illustrate the mystery [of the Trinity] by analogy to the three principal faculties of the mind or the requisites of action which are Posse, Scire, Velle; so that Power was ascribed to the Father, as the source of divinity; wisdom to the Son, as Word of the mind; and will or love to the Holy Spirit. For from the virtue or power of the divine essence proceed the Ideas of things or the truths which wisdom comprehends [complectitur], and which then at last according to their perfection become the objects of the will; and from this is also made manifest the order of the divine persons."[39]

With these examples in mind, a similar application of the analogia Trinitatis can be easily identified in the *Monadology,* in the passage where Leibniz writes: "There is in God *Power,* which is the source of all, then *Knowledge,* which contains the detail of ideas, and finally *Will,* which makes changes or productions according to the principle of the Best. And that is what corresponds to what in created Monads constitutes the subject or Basis, the perceptive Faculty and the Appetitive Faculty."[40] This time the analogy is left tacit; but, as the two passages taken, respectively, from the *Theodicy* and the *Examen Religionis Christianae* suggest, the association of Father, Son, and Holy Spirit with power, knowledge, and will or love is a commonplace so well established in theology as to represent—precisely here, at the heart of Leibniz's metaphysics—a clear allusion to the Trinity. Leibniz himself bears witness to this fact: when Bisterfeld derives, from the theological tradition, a metaphysical doctrine very similar to the one expressed in the passage from the *Monadology* quoted above, Leibniz recognizes immediately the implicit allusion to the Trinity. In *Philosophiae Primae Seminarium,* Bisterfeld writes, in fact, that the patristic and Scholastic authors "wisely attributed wisdom to every being [ens], and they established this very useful and very profound axiom: To every being [ens] belongs power, wisdom, and love."[41] In his copy of the book, Leibniz writes "Pater" ("Father") above the word "potentia" ("power"); "Filius" ("Son") above the word "sapientia" ("wisdom"); and "Sp[iritus] S[anctus]" ("Holy Spirit") above the word "amor" ("love").[42]

The traces of the classic doctrine of the analogia Trinitatis, disseminated throughout Leibniz's writings, thus reemerge powerfully at the apex of Leibniz's metaphysics, in the *Monadology*. Leibniz's defense of the mysteries of the Christian faith, and particularly his defense of the Trinitarian mystery, seems to have deep roots, roots that do not cling superficially to the dictates of court orthodoxy but instead penetrate to the heart of Leibniz's philosophy. In his search for a metaphysical explanation of the structure of the universe and for a solution to the classic problem of how to reconcile unity and multiplicity, identity and diversity, Leibniz operates in the setting of traditional Christian theology—a tradition that, not least for strong pragmatic reasons, he unflinchingly supported. The Trinity—the perfect identity in diversity of Three in One—offers a perfect model of harmony, defined by Leibniz as *diversitas identitate compensata* (diversity compensated by identity).[43] It is therefore not by chance that the Trinitarian conception of God proved to be a subject of serious reflection and constant defense by Leibniz. In it he acknowledged a truth above (human) reason handed down by the millennia-old tradition of the universal church, a truth that, as such, could be cleared of the charge of contradiction and could even be reflected in some aspects of his metaphysics.

Abbreviations

A	Leibniz, G. W. *Sämtliche Schriften und Briefe.* Edited by the Academy of Sciences of Berlin. Series I–VIII. Darmstadt, Leipzig, Berlin, 1923ff. Cited by series, volume, and page. "N." followed by an Arabic numeral indicates the number assigned to the text by the publishers.
VE	Leibniz, G. W. *Vorausedition zur Reihe VI—Philosophische Schriften—in der Ausgabe der Akademie der Wissenschaften zu Berlin.* Edited by the Leibniz-Forschungsstelle of the University of Münster. Münster, 1982–1991. "N." followed by an Arabic numeral indicates the number assigned to the text by the publishers. The Arabic numeral by itself indicates the page.
GP	Leibniz, G. W. *Die Philosophischen Schriften.* Edited by C. I. Gerhardt. 7 vols. Berlin: Weidmannsche Buchhandlung, 1875–1890. Reprint, Hildesheim: Olms, 1960–1961. Cited by volume and page.

DUTENS	Leibniz, G. W. *Opera omnia, nunc primum collecta, in classes distributa, praefationibus et indicibus exornata.* Edited by L. Dutens. 6 vols. Geneva: De Tournes, 1768. Cited by volume, part (if relevant), and page.
GRUA	Leibniz, G. W. *Textes inédits d'après les manuscrits de la Bibliothèque Provinciale de Hanovre.* Edited by G. Grua. 2 vols. Paris: PUF, 1948.
LBr	Leibniz-Briefwechsel. Hanover, Niedersächsische Landesbibliothek.
LH	Leibniz-Handschriften. Hanover, Niedersächsische Landesbibliothek.
Leibn. Marg.	Books with annotations by Leibniz. Hanover, Niedersächsische Landesbibliothek.
Berlin AK d. W. Hschr.	Berlin Akademie der Wissenschaften Handschriften.
DENZ.	*Enchiridion symbolorum definitionum et declarationum de rebus fidei et morum.* Edited by H. Denzinger. Revised by A. Schönmetzer. 33th ed. Freiburg im Breisgau: Herder, 1965.
P.L.	*Patrologiae cursus completus. Series latina.* Edited by J. P. Migne. 217 vols. Paris: J. P. Migne and Garnier, 1878–1890.

Notes

Introduction

1. See *Meditationes de Cognitione, Veritate et Ideis* (A VI, 4, 589; GP IV, 425).
2. GP III, 444.
3. *Defensio Trinitatis*, 1669 (A VI, 1, 522).
4. See *Remarques sur le livre d'un Antitrinitaire Anglois* (c. 1693), in Antognazza, "Inediti leibniziani sulle polemiche trinitarie," 550.
5. *Commentatiuncula de Judice Controversiarum*, 1669–1671 (A VI, 1, 550).
6. *Ibid.*
7. *Theodicy*, "Preliminary Discourse," § 29 (GP VI, 67).
8. Ibid., § 5 (GP VI, 52).
9. See chapter 13.
10. See chapter 13.
11. See chapter 1.
12. *Demostrationum Catholicarum Conspectus*, 1668–1669 (A VI, 1, 499).
13. A IV, 1, 532.
14. A II, 1, 162.
15. A VI, 1, 479.
16. A VI, 2, 283.
17. A II, 1, 174.
18. A VI, 3, 116.
19. Piro, "Leibniz e il progetto degli 'Elementa de mente et corpore,'" 114.
20. Piro, *Varietas Identitate Compensata*, 9. Cf. also Buzon, "L'harmonie: Métaphysique et phénoménalité," 95–120. According to Leinkauf, "Diversitas Identitate

Compensata," the concept of harmony as *diversitas identitate compensata* is the hermeneutical key to Leibniz's philosophy in general, besides being a basic theorem of thought from the fifteenth to the seventeenth centuries.

21. Cf. *De Scriptura, Ecclesia, Trinitate* (A VI, 4, 2289; VE, 433) and *Sceleton Demonstrationis* (A I, 11, 234).

22. GP III, 34–35: "Moreover, from the combination of Wisdom and Goodness comes the choice of the best series of things, and thus the admirable harmony and perichōrēsis of all things arises, which causes all things to be most appropriately connected." See also the *Synopsis* of the *Tractatio de Deo* (GRUA, 475): "Origin of things. Ultimate reason [ratio] of things. He views all possible things, and chooses the best. Perichōrēsis of things." In another text, composed around 1708, Leibniz appeals to the "perichōrēsis rerum" against the Epicurean negation of final causes (DUTENS II, 132).

23. GP II, 412: "It is very true that there is no part of nature that we can comprehend perfectly, and the perichōrēsis of things itself proves this. No creature, no matter how noble, can simultaneously perceive distinctly or comprehend an infinite number of things; nay, indeed, if it comprehended a part of nature, it would also comprehend the whole Universe on account of the same perichōrēsis I spoke of." The term *perichōrēsis* occurs also in GRUA, 797.

24. GP III, 34–35.

25. See GP VI, 64.

26. *Notae ad Joh. Henricum Bisterfeldium*, 1663–1666 (A VI, 1, 153). See, in this connection, chapter 1.

27. See *De Scriptura, Ecclesia, Trinitate* (A VI, 4, 2289; VE, 433); *Examen Religionis Christianae (Systema Theologicum)* (A VI, 4, 2365; VE, 2419); *Sceleton Demonstrationis* (A, I, 11, 234); *Remarques sur le livre d'un Antitrinitaire Anglois*, 549.

28. *Ad Christophori Stegmanni Metaphysicam Unitariorum*, in Jolley, "An Unpublished Leibniz MS on Metaphysics," 188. See chapter 12 and R. M. Adams's review of the Italian edition of this book in the *Leibniz Review* 10 (2000): 53–59, esp. 56–57.

29. Cf. Piro, *Varietas Identitate Compensata*, 100–101.

30. *Ad Christophori Stegmanni Metaphysicam Unitariorum*, 188.

31. I owe the idea of Leibniz's treatment of the Trinity as a concrete, complex system to Adams's review of the Italian edition of this book in the *Leibniz Review* 10 (2000): 57. Adams also pointed out the consistency of Leibniz's conception of the Trinity with his nominalism or conceptualism, as well as some theological and philosophical problems opened by it.

32. DUTENS V, 147.

Chapter 1. Leibniz's Program: The Plan of Catholic Demonstrations

1. The *Demonstrationum Catholicarum Conspectus* was composed around 1668–1669. It was probably written down in the spring of 1668; Leibniz later took it up again, annotating and completing his first draft. In this period he was already among the retinue of Baron Johann Christian von Boineburg (1622–1672). The meeting with Boineburg, formerly first counselor of the elector of Mainz, was decisive for him. Boineburg took him under his protection and introduced him to the Catholic court of Mainz, where Leibniz resided from 1668 to 1672 in the service of Johann Philipp von Schönborn (1605–1673).

2. The project of the *Demonstrationes Catholicae* has been authoritatively defined by Heinrich Schepers as Leibniz's greatest plan ("*Demonstrationes Catholicae*—Leibniz' grosser Plan," paper presented at VI. Internationaler Leibniz-Kongress, first plenary session, 18 July 1994; unpublished).

3. Known as *Systema Theologicum*, this text dates probably from the period between April and October 1686. First published in 1819, it has recently been republished in A VI, 4, N. 420; VE, N. 512 under the title *Examen Religionis Christianae (Systema Theologicum)*. The title comes from the phrase found on the last sheet of Leibniz's manuscript ("Examen religionis Christianae," LH I, 2, 1 Bl. 30v). Against the widespread view that the *Examen* was conceived by Leibniz as the basis for the reunification of the churches, Adams, "Leibniz's Examination of the Christian Religion," 517–546, points out that this hypothesis is not plausible, given the text's clear bias in favor of Catholic doctrine.

4. Johann Friedrich (1625–1679), son of Duke Georg von Braunschweig-Lüneburg, in 1651 abandoned the Lutheran faith to embrace Catholicism. Leibniz came into contact with him in 1671, first by correspondence and then meeting him in person near Frankfurt, probably in October 1671. This was shortly before Leibniz's departure for Paris, where he stayed for four years (1672–1676); at the end of this Parisian sojourn Leibniz accepted the duke's proposal to enter his service. There are two different drafts of the letter of autumn 1679 to the duke. The first—*Konzept* A: LBr f 12 Bl. 150–151, 161–162 (*links*)—is published in A II, 1, N. 213; the second draft—*Konzept* B: LBr f 12 Bl. 150–151, 161–162—is published in A I, 2, N. 187; lastly, in the final part of Bl. 162 there is the text of another letter by Leibniz, again addressed to Duke Johann Friedrich: it would seem to be another short draft of the same letter we are here dealing with (published in A I, 2, N. 186).

5. Cf. A I, 2, 225; A II, 1, 488.

6. Cf. A II, 1, 488, and A I, 2, 224–225. Leibniz comes back to these subjects in his correspondence with Landgraf Ernst von Hessen-Rheinfels (1623–1693), who, having converted to Catholicism in 1651, strove for the reconciliation of the churches. In particular, in a letter of January 1684, speaking of the reasons that prevent him from becoming a Catholic, Leibniz writes (A II, 1, 538): "There are some philosophical opinions, for which I believe I have a demonstration, and which it would be impossible for me to change in my present state of mind," hastening, however, to add in the following letter (A II, 1, N. 245): "I can assure you that the philosophical doubts I mentioned in my previous letter hold nothing against the Mysteries of Christianity such as the Trinity, the Incarnation, the Eucharist, and the resurrection of bodies. I do think these things are possible, and since God has revealed them I hold them to be true. Some day I want to devote an essay to some points of controversy between Catholics and Protestants, and if it is approved by judicious and moderate people, I would be very happy, but it is absolutely necessary that one hide that the author is not a Catholic. Just this prejudice makes the best things suspect."

7. Cf. A I, 2, 225, and A II, 1, 488.

8. Belonging to the same period as the *Conspectus*, the *Confessio Naturae contra Atheistas*, dating from the spring of 1668, was first published, unbeknownst to Leibniz, in Spizelius, *De Atheismo Eradicando . . . Epistola*, 125–135. The aim of the *Confessio Naturae* is to prove the existence of God and the immortality of the soul, as Leibniz himself writes in the letter to Jakob Thomasius of 20/30 April 1669 (A II, 1, 24). In the first part ("That the reason of Corporeal Phenomena cannot be given without an

incorporeal Principle, i.e. God," A VI, 1, 489), Leibniz proposes a proof of the existence of God based on consideration of the structure of bodies. The second part aims instead at proving the immortality of the soul ("The immortality of the human soul demonstrated by a continuous sorites," A VI, 1, 492).

9. A II, 1, 488. Cf. also A I, 2, 225.

10. Regarding this paragraph, which is fundamental for the presentation of the relation between faith and reason in Leibniz's thought, see chapter 13.

11. In particular, on the relation between the mysteries of the Trinity and the Incarnation and truths of fact, see chapter 4.

12. *De Demonstratione Possibilitatis Mysteriorum Eucharistiae;* A VI, 1, 515. For a discussion of this text, see chapter 4.

13. A II, 1, 488–489: "The *third part* deals with the Church, where I have very convincing proofs that the Hierarchy of the Church is by right Divine, and I distinguish exactly the limits of its secular and Ecclesiastic power." Cf. also A I, 2, 225.

14. *Demonstrationum Catholicarum Conspectus* (A VI, 1, 494): "The *Prolegomena* will contain the Elements of Philosophy. That is, the first principles of Metaphysics (of Being [de Ente]), Logic (of Mind [de Mente]), Mathematics (of Space [de Spatio]), Physics (of Body [de Corpore]), Practical Philosophy (of the City [de Civitate])." Cf. also A I, 2, 225–226, and A II, 1, 489.

15. See also A II, 1, 489.

16. See also ibid. and A I, 2, 225–226.

17. See in particular the works by Dascal: "Strategies of Dispute and Ethics," 108–115; "La balanza de la razon," 363–381; "Nihil sine Ratione: Blandior Ratio," 276–280. Cf. also Antognazza, "The Defence of the Mysteries of the Trinity and the Incarnation: An Example of Leibniz's 'Other' Reason," 283–309.

18. The development of this new part of logic does not seem to be required by natural theology: for such truths as the existence of God and the immortality of the soul, Leibniz believes it is possible to reach absolute certainty based on proof.

19. A I, 2, 225–226: "It would also be necessary to advance *metaphysics*, in order to have some clear notions of God, the soul, the person, and the nature of substance and accidents. For I establish by demonstration and intelligibly explain the substantial forms that the Cartesians claim to have eliminated as inexplicable chimeras, to the detriment of our religion, whose mysteries would be nothing but impossibilities if the nature of the body consisted only in extention, as Descartes claims." See also A II, 1, 489–490. In particular, the notions of person and substance (besides that of God, obviously) are directly involved in the mysteries of the Trinity and the Incarnation. The problem of accidents and substantial forms is, on the other hand, related to the discussion of the Eucharist and Transubstantiation. In this connection, see, for example, two letters from Leibniz to, respectively, François de La Chaise (A II, 1, 512; probably May 1680) and Ernst von Hessen-Rheinfels (A II, 1, 532; 3 November 1682). The Trinity, the Incarnation, and the Eucharist are the mysteries Leibniz most frequently defended. Even when he refers in general to the defense of the mysteries, these three are the most representative cases. On the metaphysical consequences of Leibniz's conception of the Eucharist, see Fouke, "Metaphysics and the Eucharist in the early Leibniz," 145–159.

20. A II, 1, 489: "And unless one has some familiarity with the profoundest *physics*, one cannot meet the difficulties that arise against the history of creation, the flood, and the resurrection of bodies." See also A I, 2, 226.

21. A II, 1, 489: "Finally the *true morality* must be demonstrated, to know what is justice, justification, freedom, pleasure, beatitude, beatific vision." See also A I, 2, 226.

22. A II, 1, 489: "There is nothing so in harmony with *political truth*, and the happiness of the human race, even here below and in this life, as what I have put forward, an inviolable and irresistible power of the sovereign over external goods and the inner empire that God exercises through the Church on people's souls." See also A I, 2, 226.

23. To judge by what Leibniz himself affirms, he undertook the study of mathematics on the one hand to test his ability to reason rigorously, thus lending credit to his proofs in the theological field, and on the other to forge the tools needed for these proofs. See A II, 1, 490. Cf. also A I, 2, 226.

24. A II, 1, 490–491: "Finally, to render my demonstrations absolutely incontestable, and as certain as what can be proved by an arithmetical calculation, I would give a taste of this new Writing or characteristic, however one wishes to call it. . . . Now, wherever it is received, true religion, which is always the most reasonable, and in a word all that I have advanced in my work of Catholic Demonstrations, will be easily established; and it will be just as impossible to resist the solid reasons as it is impossible to argue about arithmetic." See also A I, 2, 226–227. These confident statements by Leibniz regarding the possibility of reaching, in the *Demonstrationes Catholicae*, the absolute and irresistible certainty of mathematics seems in reality applicable only to that part of the *Conspectus* dedicated to natural theology. As we have seen, as regards revealed theology (which includes the mysteries), in this same letter Leibniz explicitly admits the human impossibility of going beyond the threshold of moral certainty.

25. A strong reminder of the importance of theological reflection (and in particular of revealed theology) in the development of Leibniz's thought has recently come from the following works: Beeley, *Kontinuität und Mechanismus;* Goldenbaum, "Leibniz as a Lutheran," 169–192; Goldenbaum, "Transubstantiation, Physics and Philosophy at the Time of the Catholic Demonstrations," 79–102; Mercer, *Leibniz's Metaphysics.*

26. A II, 1, 493.

27. After the *Prolegomena*, the *Conspectus* provides for four parts: *Part I. Demonstration of the Existence of God* (see A VI, 1, 494); *Part II. Demonstration of the Immortality and Incorporality of the Soul* (see A VI, 1, 494–495; these two parts are gathered together in a single part in Leibniz's presentation of the *Conspectus* to Duke Johann Friedrich: see A II, 1, 488, and A I, 2, 225); *Part III. Demonstration of the Possibility of the Mysteries of the Christian Faith* (see A VI, 1, 495–499); *Part IV. Demonstration of the Authority of the Catholic Church. Demonstration of the Authority of Scripture* (see A VI, 1, 499–500).

28. Concerning the problems raised by a positive "demonstration of the possibility of the mysteries" and the peculiar nature of Leibniz's 'demonstration,' see in particular the Introduction and chapter 4.

29. A VI, 1, 495.

30. Daniel Hofmann was born at Halle around 1538. A strictly Lutheran theologian, he was one of the first professors called to teach at the University of Helmstedt, founded in 1576 by the duke of Braunschweig-Lüneburg, Julius (1528–1589). Involved in various animated disputes both with exponents of other Christian confessions and with other Lutherans, he died in 1611 at Wolfenbüttel. Paul Slevogt was born in April 1596 at Poffendorf, near Weimar. He studied at the University of Jena, where in 1625 he was

given the chair of Greek and Hebrew and later that of logic and metaphysics. He was dean of philosophy several times and rector of the university; he died in 1655.

31. The professors were, in particular, Johann Caselius, Oven Günther, Duncan Liddel, and Cornelius Martini. A more extended treatment of the matter can be found in Antognazza, "Hofmann-Streit," 390–420.

32. Hofmann, *Propositiones de Deo, et Christi Tum Persona Tum Officio*.

33. Cf. in particular ibid., the fifteenth thesis.

34. *Declaratio*, in Grawer, *Libellus de Unica Veritate*, 138–142. See ibid., 139.

35. The book examines various questions from philosophical and theological standpoints. Introducing his work, Slevogt explicitly refers to the controversy that broke out at Helmstedt regarding Hofmann's theses (cf. Slevogt, *Pervigilium de Dissidio Theologi et Philosophi*, 9).

36. See § 13 of the "Preliminary Discourse" (GP VI, 58).

37. See A VI, 1, 532. On the *Refutatio Objectionum Dan. Zwickeri*, see chapter 2.

38. Regarding the question of double truth, cf. *Sessio* VIII (Mansi, ed., *Sacrorum Conciliorum Nova et Amplissima Collectio*, vol. XXXII, 842).

39. See *Nouveaux Essais*, book IV, chap. 17, § 23 (A VI, 6, 494). Also important in this connection are the preceding paragraph, containing some clarifications of what Leibniz means by "above Reason" (see A VI, 6, 492–493), and the following chapter, "De la Foy et de la Raison et de leur bornes distinctes" (see A VI, 6, 495–502). Hofmann and Slevogt are mentioned also in *De Religione Magnorum Virorum* (1687–1694; GRUA, 35–44; A VI, 4, N. 421; VE, N. 524) in the context of the debate on double truth.

40. A VI, 1, 495.

41. See also, for example, what the young Leibniz wrote, again in this case to Duke Johann Friedrich, toward the second half of October 1671 (A II, 1, 163). Another unequivocal passage is found, some years later, in *De Deo Trino* (A VI, 4, 2291; VE, 661).

42. As is well known, for Leibniz only that which is not self-contradictory can exist: therefore the actual existence of something is in itself proof of its noncontradiction. This type of argument, which starts from the actual existence in nature of a certain kind of relation, to conclude that it is possible that a similar relation exists in the divine sphere as well, is used by Leibniz also in defense of the mystery of the Incarnation against the charge of self-contradiction. The attempt to explain how this relation is possible comes only later (see A VI, 3, 371; on this text see chapter 7).

43. A VI, 1, 495.

44. A VI, 1, N. 16. These arguments are dealt with in particular in the replies to Wissowatius's second and third objections. On the *Defensio Trinitatis* see chapter 2.

45. *De Conatu et Motu, Sensu et Cogitatione* was published for the first time in A VI, 2, 280–287. *Trinitas. Mens*, published in GRUA, 559, can now also be found in A VI, 2, 287–288. For a commentary on these two texts, probably composed between spring and autumn 1671, see chapter 3.

46. A VI, 1, N. 15/4. On this text see chapter 4.

47. See in particular *De Scriptura, Ecclesia, Trinitate* (1680–1684*), A VI, 4, N. 403; VE, N. 112; *Origo Animarum et Mentium* (March–June 1681*), A VI, 4, N. 275; VE, N. 81; *De Mundo Praesenti* (spring 1684–winter 1685/86*), A VI, 4, N. 301; VE, N. 107; *De Persona Christi* (1680–1684*), A VI, 4, N. 405; VE, N. 147; *De Deo Trino* (1680–1684*), A VI, 4, N. 404; VE, N. 148; *Examen Religionis Christianae (Systema Theologicum)*, A VI, 4, 2365; VE, 2419; *Remarques sur le livre d'un Antitrinitaire Anglois*, 550.

48. A VI, 1, 495.

49. The expression "plurality in unity" in reference to the trinitary being of God is used by Leibniz in *De Scriptura, Ecclesia, Trinitate* (A VI, 4, 2289; VE, 433).

50. Born around 1605 in Siegen, the most important town in the very small German principality of Nassau-Dillenburg, Bisterfeld completed his studies at the flourishing academy of Herborn, under the guidance of the chief philosopher of the school, Johann Heinrich Alsted (1588–1638). The events of the Thirty Years' War, however, seriously undermined the academy's ability to survive. Alsted was thus led to accept, in 1629, the invitation to direct the new Calvinist academy of Alba Julia (Transylvania). He moved there together with the young Bisterfeld, who later married his eldest daughter. For the rest of his career, until his death in 1655, Bisterfeld taught philosophy and theology at Alba Julia, combining his teaching activity with frequent diplomatic trips as a representative of the prince of Transylvania. Bisterfeld's isolated geographical position partly explains his obscurity. A second, related reason is the extreme rarity of most of his more interesting philosophical and theological writings. For a more complete exposition of the considerations regarding the relation between Leibniz's thought and that of Bisterfeld given in this chapter, see Antognazza, "Immeatio and emperichoresis," 41–64, and Antognazza, "Debilissimae Entitates? Bisterfeld and Leibniz's Ontology of Relations," 1–22.

51. Bisterfeld, *Philosophiae Primae Seminarium*, 132.

52. A VI, 1, N. 17 (Niedersächsische Landesbibliothek, *Sammelband* Leibn. Marg. I) publishes, under the title of *Notae ad Joh. Henricum Bisterfeldium*, the series of underlinings and marginal notes in Leibniz's copy of the following posthumous works by Bisterfeld: Bisterfeld, *Philosophiae Primae Seminarium*; Bisterfeld, *Elementorum Logicorum Libri Tres . . . Accedit, Ejusdem Authoris, Phosphorus Catholicus . . . Cui Subjunctum Est, Consilium de Studiis Feliciter Instituendis*.

53. For an indication of the most important studies, see Antognazza, "Immeatio and emperichoresis," 42–44.

54. Cf. Kabitz, *Die Philosophie des jungen Leibniz*, 6–8. Regarding the importance of the concept of harmony for Bisterfeld, Massimo Mugnai notes that Leibniz himself, referring to the *Phosphorus Catholicus* in *De Arte Combinatoria*, recognizes in the idea of the universal relation of all things to all things the foundation of Bisterfeld's philosophy. Summarizing the influence of this idea on Leibniz's thought, Mugnai concludes (Mugnai, "Der Begriff der Harmonie," 72): "It is very revealing that the description of the harmony found in *De arte combinatoria* coincides almost completely with that of Bisterfeld, and it is even more significant that the concept of harmony defined in Leibniz's early work remains unaltered in its essential contents in the later development of Leibniz's thought."

55. Cf. Bisterfeld, *Philosophiae Primae Seminarium*, 185–186: "Both the variety and the connection of relations is plainly wonderful. . . . [T]he whole of Logic is nothing else but a mirror of relations. This variety takes on the wonderful connection of relations which the Greeks called emperichoresis circumincession, and we are wont to call immeatio: which is nothing else but the varied concourse, combination, and complication of relations. This governs throughout the entire Encyclopaedia and especially in the deeper anatomy of things. See our Logic chapter 3. But what is truly wonderful is that both the variety and the connection of relations from beginning to end is founded in the worshipful mystery of the Most Holy Trinity." A more complete explanation of the

concept of immeatio, and in particular of its derivation from the relations of the Trinity, can be found in the first book, third chapter of *Elementorum Logicorum Libri Tres*, to which Bisterfeld himself refers in the passage just quoted. Immeatio is defined as "the concourse of relations [relationum concursus]." It is the key and kernel of all logic. On account of its rarity, continues Bisterfeld, the term immeatio requires an explanation both of its origins and of its use (Bisterfeld, *Elementorum Logicorum Libri Tres*, 6–7): "I. Immeatio is the mutual union and communion of things. The Theologians first observed this in the Most Holy Trinity, and they called it emperichōrēsis, that is to say, mutual interexistence, and by the industry of these some more acute philosophers were stimulated and detected immeatio to be spread throughout nature, and also throughout the picture of nature, the Encyclopaedia. Hence: 2. Immeatio is either real or mental, and in either case it is most efficacious. Real immeatio is the mutual union and communion of things occurring in nature: which will be most outstanding in more sublime things, say divine and spiritual things. . . . 3. Mental immeatio is the mutual union and communion of human thoughts." On the origin of the concept of immeatio see Antognazza, "Bisterfeld and Immeatio," forthcoming.

56. Cf. Muller, *Dictionary of Latin and Greek Theological Terms*, 67–68, 102.

57. See Bisterfeld, *Philosophiae Primae Seminarium*, 132 and 186.

58. On the title page of Bisterfeld's *Phosphorus Catholicus*, Leibniz simply writes: "Ingeniosissimus Libellus" (A VI, 1, 160). On the title page of *Philosophiae Primae Seminarium*, his positive judgment is spelled out as follows (A VI, 1, 151): "A very distinguished little book, whose equal in this kind I have not seen." Two of Leibniz's very first works—the *Dissertatio de Arte Combinatoria* (1666; A VI, 1, N. 8) and the *Nova Methodus Discendae Docendaeque Jurisprudentiae* (1667; A VI, 1, N. 10)—contain further praises of the *Phosphorus Catholicus* (see A VI, 1, 199 and A VI, 1, 279). His opinion of these writings remained high in the following years: two decades later, writing from Hanover to his brother Johann Friedrich, occupied with settling matters of inheritance, Leibniz includes in the list of books that he wishes to keep for himself the works by Bisterfeld that he read as a young man (see A I, 4, 681).

59. One of the passages underlined, for example, is the statement quoted above (Bisterfeld, *Philosophiae Primae Seminarium*, 132): "Unless we wish to do manifest violence to the truth, it must be said that the universal harmony of all things is founded in the holy Trinity, and that this itself is the source, norm and end of every order. When this is acknowledged and affirmed, the whole of nature and Scripture is pure light; when this is ignored, or denied, there is nothing but darkness and horrendous chaos." Another passage, also quoted above (Bisterfeld, *Philosophiae Primae Seminarium*, 186), says: "What is truly wonderful is that both the variety and the connection of relations from beginning to end are founded in the worshipful mystery of the Most Holy Trinity."

60. A fourth example is discussed in chapter 13.

61. See Bisterfeld, *Philosophiae Primae Seminarium*, 128–129, and A VI, 1, 158.

62. Bisterfeld, *Philosophiae Primae Seminarium*, 124.

63. See ibid., 116–117, and A VI, 1, 157.

64. See Bisterfeld, *Philosophiae Primae Seminarium*, chap. VIII, "De Ordine," 123–132 (especially 130–131).

65. See Bisterfeld, *Philosophiae Primae Seminarium*, 38, and A VI, 1, 153. On the analogia Trinitatis implicit in this passage, see the Introduction. On the concept of habitudo in Bisterfeld and Leibniz see Antognazza, "Debilissimae Entitates," 6–8, 13.

66. For a concise presentation, see Antognazza, "Die Polemik des jungen Leibniz gegen die Socinianer," 17–24, and Antognazza, "Die Rolle der Trinitäts- und Menschwerdungsdiskussionen für die Entstehung von Leibniz' Denken," 56–75.

67. See on this point the Introduction.

68. A VI, 1, 495.

69. Leibniz will come across the Socinian Andreas Wissowatius again much later, around 1706, reading and commenting on the German translation of Wissowatius's *Religio Rationalis*. Some of Leibniz's notes on *Die Vernünfftige Religion* are published in GRUA, 69–72. On this text see chapter 12.

70. A VI, 1, N. 17.

71. See A II, 1, 24. In this letter, dating from 20/30 April 1669, Leibniz takes sides in the dispute between ancients and moderns, Scholastics, and reformers, affirming that he found more truth in Aristotle than in Descartes (see A II, 1, 15): the new physics does not contradict Aristotelian philosophy and does not lead to the consequences the Cartesians would like it to. On p. 21, there is also a curious grouping together of Socinians and Cartesians, united by their shared nonacceptance of the ancients (in the case of the Socinians, and the church fathers; in the case of the Cartesians, Aristotle and his Greek interpreters).

72. See in A II, 1, 171 some passages of the long letter written to Antoine Arnauld at the beginning of November 1671, in which Leibniz refers in particular to the mystery of Transubstantiation. See also chapter 4.

73. Samuel Przypkowski was born around 1592. He received his early education in the Polish Socinian communities, continuing his studies at Altdorf and then at Leiden. In 1616 he returned to Poland, becoming one of the most important exponents of Polish Socinianism. Forced, together with the other Socinians, to abandon Poland, he settled in Prussia. He died in exile in 1670.

74. *Symbole et Antisymbole des Apostres*, in Antognazza, "Inediti leibniziani sulle polemiche trinitarie," 535–538.

75. *Ad Christophori Stegmanni Metaphysicam Unitariorum*, in Jolley, "An Unpublished Leibniz MS on Metaphysics," 161–189. On this text see chapter 12. Christoph Stegmann (who was born around 1598 and died in 1646) was the younger brother of the more famous Joachim Stegmann, with whom he shared the Socinian faith. The *Bibliotheca Anti-Trinitariorum* reports on three of his works, including the unpublished *Metaphysica Repurgata* (cf. Sand, *Bibliotheca Anti-Trinitariorum*, 133–134; cf. also Zedler, *Grosses Vollständiges Universal-Lexicon aller Wissenschafften und Künste*, vol. XXXIX, 1469; Jöcher, *Allgemeines Gelehrten-Lexicon*, vol. IV, 794).

76. Thomas Burnett of Kemney (or Kemnay) (1656–1729) plays a very important role in providing Leibniz with precious information on the English Trinitarian polemics. Thanks to his mediation, Leibniz comes into possession of the polemical writings exchanged by Locke and Edward Stillingfleet (see chapter 10) and is able to see the famous work by Servetus, *De Trinitatis Erroribus Libri Septem* (cf. chapter 11, note 68).

77. Sophie von der Pfalz (1630–1714), the wife of Ernst August von Hannover (brother and successor of Duke Johann Friedrich), became Leibniz's great protector after the death of Johann Friedrich.

78. Friedrich Simon Löffler was born in 1669 in Leipzig, where he studied theology. He died in 1748. Some letters sent by Leibniz to Löffler in the early months of 1695 (N. 96, N. 160, N. 161, N. 162, N. 163, N. 209 in A I, 11) are particularly important. See chapter 9.

79. Thomas Smith was born in London in 1638 and pursued theology and Oriental studies at Oxford. He became a Presbyter in the Anglican Church in London, and he died in 1710.

80. See in this connection chapter 9.

81. See *Extrait* and *Remarques sur le livre d'un Antitrinitaire Anglois*, in Antognazza, "Inediti leibniziani sulle polemiche trinitarie," 539–550. On these texts see chapter 8.

82. See chapter 12.

83. A VI, 1, 495.

84. See *De Scriptura, Ecclesia, Trinitate* (A VI, 4, 2290; VE, 434); *De Deo Trino* (A VI, 4, 2292; VE, 662).

85. See *Examen Religionis Christianae (Systema Theologicum)* (A VI, 4, 2364; VE, 2418).

86. A VI, 1, 495.

87. See *Defensio Trinitatis* (A VI, 1, 529). See chapter 2.

88. See in particular *Examen Religionis Christianae (Systema Theologicum)* (A VI, 4, 2366; VE, 2419).

89. A VI, 1, 496.

90. A VI, 4, 2290; VE, 434: "Perception itself or Love is the Holy Spirit; for if God perceives himself, that is the same as loving himself. Then it proceeds from the Father and son, since the Lover and the beloved are not indeed prior to love in time, but in the nature of things."

91. See chapter 2.

92. See DENZ, 800.

93. A VI, 1, 496: "Chap. 11. That the internal Actions [Actiones ad intra] are divided, but the external works [opera ad extra] are undivided."

94. Chapter 22, "Regarding the incarnation of the Son of God," is canceled; Leibniz, in revising his plan, must have considered it better to shift the entire discussion of the problem of the Incarnation to chapters 26–33. Chapter 22 is, in fact, out of place here, coming between two chapters dealing with sin (see ibid.).

95. Ibid. In the margin Leibniz adds: "In which way in the feeding of 5,000 the part is greater than the whole. Explained by the nature of vegetation and increase. Boyle's experiment about the tree growing in a vase of water, in the Sceptical Chymist." Leibniz is referring to the Latin translation of the work by Boyle *The Sceptical Chymist*, published in London in 1661 (*Chymista Scepticus*, 1662). Boyle rejects both the theory of the Aristotelians according to which all mixed bodies result from the composition of the four elements—earth, water, air, and fire—and the theory of the followers of Paracelsus (*Spagyrici Vulgares*) according to which there are three basic elements: salt, sulfur, and mercury. The experiment mentioned by Leibniz is found in the second part of the book, where Boyle describes the growth of a mint plant in a vase of water (cf. Boyle, *Chymista Scepticus*, 54ff.). Leibniz, with this remark, seems to mean that in nutrition new elements are produced, different from those one started with. This 'creation,' however, is not at all miraculous but is explained by the natural processes of growth. It is no accident that Leibniz here makes reference to a book that, though it cannot be considered a chemistry treatise in the modern sense, nevertheless marked a basic turning point in the history of science.

96. See the initial part of the *Confessio Naturae* (especially A VI, 1, 490). A similar position is to be found, almost twenty years later, in § X of the *Discours de Métaphysique*

(cf. A VI, 4, 1542–1543; VE, 1699) and, even later, in the *Système nouveau de la nature et de la communication des substances* (1695) (GP IV, 478). On Leibniz's distinction between physics and metaphysics, science and philosophy see Antognazza, "Leibniz and the Post-Copernican Universe," 309–327 (especially 312–315).

97. *De Incarnatione Dei seu de Unione Hypostatica*, probably written in 1669 and 1670, was published entire for the first time in A VI, 1 N. 18. On this text see chapter 3.

98. A VI, 1, 497.

99. Cf. Anselm, *Cur Deus Homo*, 1098, in P.L., vol. CLVIII, 359–432. This work speaks of "necessary reasons" designed to show that the Word had to become incarnate (cf. "Praefatio" in P.L., vol. CLVIII, 361). Anselm's thesis is that sin, being an offense against God, requires infinite satisfaction in order to be expiated. Now, since God could not properly forgive without satisfaction or leave man without reparation, and since no creature would be able to expiate sin worthily, a God-man was necessary. *Cur Deus Homo* was later mentioned by Leibniz in an extract from Twisse, *Dissertatio de Scientia Media* (GRUA, 354). This is the only other reference to Anselm's work that I have managed to find.

100. Cf. in particular *De Demonstratione Possibilitatis Mysteriorum Eucharistiae* (A VI, 1, 515).

101. Cf. in particular *De Persona Christi* (A VI, 4, 2295–2296; VE, 659) and *Examen Religionis Christianae* (*Systema Theologicum*) (A VI, 4, 2366; VE, 2419).

102. The followers of Arius (256–336) deny that the Son is of the same substance as the Father: he is not truly God but a creature of a superior order, raised to the condition of Son of God by a special act of grace. Even if he can be called God, according to the Arians it must always be remembered that he is not really God but is so only in an improper and moral sense. Arianism was condemned by the First Council of Nicaea (325), in which it was affirmed that Jesus Christ is the true Son of God, of the same substance as the Father and therefore truly God (see *Symbolum Nicaenum*, DENZ. 125–126).

103. The Nestorians (from Nestorius, patriarch of Constantinopole, who died in 451) maintain that in Christ there are two natures and two persons, connected by a moral union. The Nestorian heresy was condemned by the Council of Ephesus (431), which established that Christ, man-God, is a single person: the hypostatic union is physical, not moral.

104. Eutychianism, whose name comes from Eutyches of Constantinopole (who flourished in the fourth and fifth centuries), is a form of Monophysitism, a heresy according to which only one nature (*physis*) is recognized in the incarnate Word. Both Eutychianism and Monophysitism were condemned by the Council of Chalcedon (451), which declared that in Christ human nature and divine nature are united (personally) but not confused, changed. or altered.

105. Ubiquitism, i.e., the attribution of ubiquity to the humanity of Jesus Christ by reason of the hypostatic union, is maintained by the Lutherans as a consequence of the *communicatio idiomatum* (namely, the communication, in the unity of the person of Christ, of the properties of one nature to the other nature). On Leibniz's opposition to the doctrine of communicatio idiomatum, see in particular chapter 7.

106. Leibniz is referring to the controversy that broke out between the Lutheran theologians of Giessen and Tübingen regarding the doctrine of *kenōsis* by which the Lutherans, fixing on Paul's words in Phil. 2:7 "*heauton ekenōsen*" ("[he] emptied himself"), try to explain the union of human and divine nature in Christ through a free exinanition

of the divinity. While the theologians of Giessen held that Jesus voluntarily stripped himself of his divine qualities, refusing to use them although he rightfully possessed them, the theologians of Tübingen maintained that he, though actually possessing them, used them only in secret. In 1623 Thummius, of the school of Tübingen, published *Tapeinōsigraphia Sacra, Hoc Est, Repetitio Sanae et Orthodoxae Doctrinae de Humiliatione Christi Theanthrōpou.* Leibniz mentions this controversy again in his *Defensio Trinitatis* (see A VI, 1, 524), without taking a position on one side or the other.

107. The doctrine of the Theopaschites, expressed by the formula "one of the Trinity suffered in the flesh," is another logical consequence of the communicatio idiomatum, in the opposite direction from ubiquitism; in this case, in fact, a property of human nature (suffering) is attributed to the divine nature.

108. The Third Council of Constantinople (680–681) condemned Monothelitism, which teaches the existence in Jesus Christ of only one will, and declared that in Christ, as there are two natures, so there are two wills, although there is only one person.

109. A VI, 1, 497. The followers of Julianus of Halicarnassus are called by this name in a pejorative sense by their adversaries, the Severians (from Severus of Antioch). In the controversy regarding the corruptibility of the body of Christ that, in the sixth century, opposed Severians and Julianists, the latter maintained the incorruptibility of the body of Christ from the first moment of the Incarnation.

110. In particular, in one of his replies to Wissowatius's second argument, Leibniz again mentions the dispute between the theologians of Tübingen and Giessen to which chapter 30 of the *Conspectus* refers (cf. *Defensio Trinitatis;* A VI, 1, 524).

111. Among the texts in which, after his early period, Leibniz deals with the problem of the Incarnation, the most important ones are the following: *De Scriptura, Ecclesia, Trinitate* (A VI, 4, N. 403; VE, N. 112); *Il n'y a qu'un seul Dieu* (A VI, 4, N. 396; VE, N. 113); *Symbole et Antisymbole des Apostres; De Persona Christi* (A VI, 4, N. 405; VE, N. 147); *Examen Religionis Christianae* (*Systema Theologicum*) (A VI, 4, N. 420; VE, N. 512). On Leibniz's Christology, see in particular chapter 7.

112. Although it remained unpublished until the ninenteenth century, in the seventeenth and eighteenth centuries Bodin's book circulated in manuscript form and was read by many illustrious personages. After a first, partial edition of 1841 (Guhrauer, *Das Heptaplomeres des Jean Bodin*), it was published in its entirety by L. Noack in 1857 (Bodin, *Colloquium Heptaplomeres*). Recently there has been a critical edition by G. Gawlick and F. Niewöhner (Wiesbaden: Harrassowitz, 1996).

113. This is perhaps the copy that Boineburg possessed. It seems that Leibniz, however, managed to obtain a copy of the *Colloquium,* sent to him by a Swedish minister (see Leibniz's letter to Polycarp Leyser of 5 May 1716, LBr 559 Bl. 12–13; see also Polycarp Marci's letter to Leibniz of 13 December 1690, A I, 6, 309). Leibniz's copy (which probably corresponds to the *Codex Hanoveranus Lat. II,* whose existence is attested in 1840) has not been rediscovered. At the Herzog August Bibliothek of Wolfenbüttel there are two copies of the *Colloquium* (dating from 1727) "cum Variantibus Lectionibus c. c. academiae Juliae Seu Conringii, Thomasii, Leibnitii, Molani, Kochii et Scholiis e Schedis Polykarpi Leyseri" (*Cod. Guelf 89.1 Extravagantes* and *Cod. Guelf. 220. 2 Extravagantes*).

114. Cf. Leibniz to Jakob Thomasius, 20/30 April 1669 (A II, 1, 24); Leibniz to Gottlieb Spitzel, 12/22 December 1669 (A I, 1, 81); Leibniz to Antoine Arnauld, early November 1671 (A II, 1, 176); *Justa Dissertatio,* winter 16 71–1672 (A IV, 1, 372).

115. Cf. Leibniz to Sebastian Korthold, 21 January 1716 (DUTENS V, 337) and 19 March 1716 (DUTENS V, 338); Leibniz to Lorenz Hertel, May 1716 (in Burckhard, *Historia Bibliothecae Augustae*, part III, 347).

Chapter 2. The Early Polemic against the Socinians

1. Wissowatius (or Andrzej Wiszowaty) was born in 1608 to a family belonging to the middle Polish nobility. Educated right from the start in a Socinian environment, from 1619 to 1629 he attended the famous school of Raków. From 1642 on he devoted himself to pastoral activities in various Polish Socinian circles. Meanwhile, the persecution of the Socinian Church began. In 1655 Wissowatius lost all his possessions, including his library and the manuscripts of his works. After the edict of 1658 that ordered all Antitrinitarians to leave Poland within two years, he was one of the last Socinians to cross the border. After a stay of two years in Hungary and Transylvania, in 1663 he moved to Mannheim, where he remained for three years. Forced to leave this city too, in order to continue his work on behalf of Socinianism he spent the last part of his life in Amsterdam, where he devoted himself mainly to writing and publishing. It was in this period that he wrote most of his works, one of the most important of which is *Religio Rationalis* (see chapter 12). He died in Amsterdam in 1678. The main source for Wissowatius's biography is *Anonymi Epistola Exhibens Vitae ac Mortis Andreae Wissowatii*, published a few years after his death in the *Bibliotheca Anti-Trinitariorum*, 219–263 (see ibid., 145–149, for a bibliography of Wissowatius's works, many of which have been lost). The anonymous author of the *Epistola* is probably Wissowatius's son, Benedykt, who, after Sand's death in 1680, edited the posthumous edition of the *Bibliotheca*. Further biographical and bibliographical information can be found in: Bock, *Historia Antitrinitariorum, Maxime Socinianismi et Socinianorum*, I, 1010–1029; Wilbur, *A History of Unitarianism: Socinianism and Its Antecedents*; Ogonowski, "Andrzej Wiszowaty," in Wissowatius, *Religio Rationalis: Editio Trilinguis*, 9–23.

2. Born in Danzig in 1612 to a Lutheran family, Zwicker studied medicine at Königsberg, where he had occasion to come into contact with Antitrinitarian ideas. Converted to Socinianism by his colleague Florian Krause, he did not have any particular pastoral role within the active Socinian community of Danzig. He polemicized with some authoritative members of the Socinian Church, who even accused him of fanaticism. Although he shared with the Socinians an aversion to the dogmas of the Trinity and the Incarnation in the name of reason, he preferred not to feel tied to any church, professing to be an independent both in religion and in politics. In 1643, forced with other Socinians to leave Danzig, he settled in Moravia. In 1657 he moved to Holland. There, presumably in Amsterdam, his *Irenicum Irenicorum, Seu Reconciliatoris Christianorum Hodiernorum Norma Triplex* was published anonymously in 1658. In it Zwicker tries to show that, according to reason, the scriptures, and tradition only the Father is the highest God; by recognizing the authenticity of this primitive faith, the reconciliation of all Christians could be achieved. He died in Amsterdam in 1678. Further information about Zwicker can be found in Bock, *Historia Antitrinitariorum*, I, 1045–1069; Caccamo, "Ricerche sul socinianesimo in Europa," 573–607 (cf. in particular 598–601); Kolakowski, *Chrétiens sans Église*, 225–227; Pintacuda de Michelis, *Socinianesimo e tolleranza nell'età del razionalismo*, 139–140; Bietenholz, *Daniel Zwicker, 1612–1678*. For further bibliographical information, see *Allgemeine Deutsche Biographie*, XLV, 534–535. The bibliography

of Zwicker's works is given in pp. 151–156 of the *Bibliotheca Anti-Trinitariorum* and in Bock, *Historia Antitrinitariorum,* I, 1048–1069.

3. The *Defensio Trinitatis* probably dates from the spring of 1669.

4. The *Refutatio* was probably composed in 1669 and 1670.

5. A VI, 1, 521: "In truth it is not now up to me to present arguments, but to reply."

6. Ibid., 522.

7. The importance of Leibniz's use of the 'strategy of defense' with reference to the mysteries of faith is pointed out clearly and convincingly by Marcelo Dascal in his article "La razon y los misterios de la fe segun Leibniz," 193–226; republished in English translation ("Reason and the Mysteries of Faith," 93–124). We shall return to Dascal's theses in chapter 4. The presence in Leibniz of "defense strategies" is mentioned by Varani, *Leibniz e la "Topica Aristotelica."*

8. Angelelli, "The Techniques of Disputation in the History of Logic," 800–815 (see especially 806–813).

9. Cf. ibid., 806–807.

10. Cf. ibid., 808. As we shall see, this is what Leibniz does: before replying, he repeats the arguments proposed by Wissowatius, reformulating them in what he considers to be a more correct manner.

11. Ibid.

12. Cf. ibid., 809–810.

13. *Defensio Trinitatis;* A VI, 1, 520.

14. Cf. Olaso, "Leibniz y el arte de disputar," 7–31. I quote from the French version ("Leibniz et l'art de disputer" in *Akten des II. Internationalen Leibniz-Kongress,* IV, 207–228). According to Olaso, Leibniz, taking his cue from Roman law, accepts as a method of dispute the kind of presumption that dispenses with proofs until the contrary is proved. This is a concept that Leibniz often uses in the main points of his system, although he left only incidental reflections on it (cf. ibid., 215–217). On the "presumption of possibility" see the masterly chapter by Adams in *Leibniz: Determinist, Theist, Idealist,* 192–213.

15. The following considerations on the use of the concept of "presumption" in the sphere of supernatural truths are developed in Antognazza, "The Defence of the Mysteries of the Trinity and the Incarnation."

16. See in this connection the passage of the *Defensio Trinitatis* quoted above in which Leibniz writes (A VI, 1, 522): "Moreover, something is presumed to be possible, until the contrary is proved."

17. A VI, 1, N. 12.

18. This is a variant published in A VI, 2, 567. Cf. Olaso, "Leibniz et l'art de disputer," 217.

19. See A I, 2, 225–226, and A II, 1, 489.

20. A VI, 1, N. 22. For a detailed discussion of the *Commentatiuncula,* probably composed in the years 1669–1671, see chapter 4.

21. Cf. *Commentatiuncula,* §§ 33–34. In the *Theodicy* Leibniz does not tire of repeating that the mysteries go against appearances and are not at all likely.

22. See *Commentatiuncula,* § 33.

23. Ibid., § 20.

24. *Elementa Juris Naturalis;* A VI, 2, 567.

25. *Nouveaux Essais,* book IV, chap. 14, § 4 (A VI, 6, 456).

26. Ibid.; A VI, 6, 457.

27. GP VI, 69. See also GP III, 444. Cf. Olaso, "Leibniz et l'art de disputer," 227.

28. *Commentatiuncula*, § 32.

29. *De Demonstratione Possibilitatis Mysteriorum Eucharistiae*; A VI, 1, 515.

30. Leibniz writes in *Raisons que M. Jaquelot m'a envoyées pour justifier l'Argument contesté de des-Cartes qui doit prouver l'existence de Dieu, avec mes reponses,* 20 November 1702 (GP III, 444): "The possibility is always presumed and must be held as true until one proves its impossibility. This Argument has the effect of transferring the burden of proof to the adversary, i.e. asking the adversary to furnish proof." Cf. Dascal, "La razon y los mysterios de la fe segun Leibniz," 224. On the *onus probandi* cf. also Gil, "Du droit à la Théodicée," 157–173.

31. Marcelo Dascal insists on the need for such a balance in his article, cited above.

32. See chapter 1.

33. A VI, 1, 532.

34. See, for example, § 39 of the "Preliminary Discourse" of the *Theodicy* (GP VI, 73).

35. See, for example, *Remarques sur le livre d'un Antitrinitaire Anglois,* 547: "I know that there are some scholastic authors who believe that the principle of Logic or Metaphysics *quae sunt eadem uni tertio, sunt eadem inter se* [things which are equal to a third thing are equal to each other] has no place in the Trinity. But I do not agree with them at all, and I believe that this would mean to concede victory to the Socinians, in overturning one of the first principles of human reasoning, without which one would no longer know how to reason about anything, or be certain of anything."

36. The importance given to tradition regarding, in particular, the dogma of the Trinity seems to emerge as early as the *Dedicatio* of the *Defensio Trinitatis* (A VI, 1, 518). At the end of the *Defensio Trinitatis*, it is stated again that the mystery of the Trinity is a doctrine accepted for centuries in the entire Christian world (see A VI, 1, 530). The acknowledgment of the church's authority is, moreover, unequivocally expressed in the fourth part of the *Conspectus*, which clearly provides for the *Demonstratio Autoritatis Ecclesiae Catholicae* (see A VI, 1, 499–500). Subsequently, Leibniz several times stressed the importance of tradition (cf., for example, *De Scriptura, Ecclesia, Trinitate*; A VI, 4, N. 403; VE, N. 112).

37. See *Defensio Trinitatis* (A VI, 1, 522): "Moreover, something is presumed to be possible, until the contrary is proved."

38. See *Commentatiuncula de Judice Controversiarum* (A VI, 1, 553). On this point see also chapter 4.

39. Ogonowski in his article "Leibniz und die Sozinianer," 393, notes: "The designation of *superrational truth* applies also to Socinian theology." Between Leibniz's way of conceiving of these truths and that of the Socinians there is, however, a radical difference: while for the Socinians these are truths that, once revealed, can be comprehended, according to Leibniz they remain incomprehensible even after revelation (cf. ibid., 391–393).

40. See *Commentatiuncula de Judice Controversiarum*; A VI, 1, 553. In this sense, what Leibniz writes regarding the mystery of the Trinity in the *Remarques sur le livre d'un Antitrinitaire Anglois,* 549, is very clear: "It is necessary to admit that there is no example in nature that corresponds sufficiently to this notion of divine persons. But it is not at all necessary to be able to find one; and it is sufficient to be able to say that there is no contradiction, or absurdity."

41. Where "to explain" is distinguished from "to comprehend" in the sense indicated by Leibniz in § 5 of the "Preliminary Discourse" of the *Theodicy.*

42. Leibniz refers to this letter in the complete title of the work. The original text of the letter to Boineburg has not been found. There is, instead, a copy, with the title handwritten by Boineburg, conserved in Hanover (LH I, 6, 3a Bl. 4–5). From this, other copies were made (cf. in particular LH I, 6, 3a Bl. 8–11). The *Bibliotheca Anti-Trinitariorum,* 147, indicates, among the manuscripts left by Wissowatius, a text entitled *De S. Trinitate Objectiones Quaedam,* corresponding, according to Bock, *Historia Antitrinitariorum,* I, 1025, to the letter sent by Wissowatius to Boineburg.

43. Boineburg, in fact, accused the Socinian doctrine regarding the worship of Christ of being contradictory, since Jesus, considered a mere creature, was nevertheless accorded worship as a divinity. Wissowatius, in the belief that he had replied exhaustively to this charge in a previous missive addressed to Boineburg, now sends in his turn a series of objections aiming to prove the contradictory nature of the doctrine of the Trinity upheld by Christians (see *Wissowatius ad Baronem Boineburgium,* A VI, 1, 519). Leibniz affirms that he has not seen Boineburg's objections and Wissowatius's replies regarding the question of the divinity of Christ and the worship due to him. He therefore abstains from taking any position on this previous phase of the controversy (*Responsio ad Objectiones Wissowatii contra Trinitatem et Incarnationem DEI Altissimi,* A VI, 1, 519). Shortly afterward, however, in *De Incarnatione Dei,* Leibniz attacks the Socinian doctrine on the worship of Christ, judging it incoherent and idolatrous, in that worship is bestowed on him who is considered a mere creature. On the contrary, the Christian doctrine is much more coherent, since divine worship is granted only to God (see chapter 4). In later years he returned to this subject several times, confirming his position (cf. for example *De Scriptura, Ecclesia, Trinitate,* A VI, 4, 2290; VE, 434; Leibniz to Ernst von Hessen-Rheinfels, A I, 3, 318; *Examen Religionis Christianae,* A VI, 4, 2367 and 2385–2386; VE, 2420–2421 and 2436–2437).

44. Leibniz himself acknowledges that Wissowatius has presented the most difficult problems to solve (see A VI, 1, 518 and 530).

45. See ibid., 519.

46. A IV, 1, N. 1.

47. See A VI, 1, 518.

48. On pp. 213–223 there is Wissowatius's letter; on pp. 226–239 the *Dedicatio* and Leibniz's replies. The same texts can be found in Leyser, *Amoenitatum Literarium Reliquiae,* 213–223 and 226–239. There seems to be no basis for the claim that there was an edition in 1671 (cf. Bock, *Historia Antitrinitariorum,* I, 1025).

49. Fontenelle, "Éloge de M. Leibnitz," 94–128. Published also in DUTENS I, xix–liii. Fontenelle says of the *Defensio Trinitatis* (DUTENS I, xliv): "*M. Leibniz* shows, in a writing entitled *Sacrosancta Trinitatis per nova inventa Logica defensa* that ordinary Logic has great defects, so that in following it his adversaries may have had some advantages, but if one reforms it, they lose all these advantages, and consequently true Logic is favorable to the faith of the orthodox."

50. See *Acta Eruditorum* (1717), 322–336 (the *Defensio Trinitatis* is mentioned on p. 326).

51. First published under the pseudonym L. de Neufville in Leibnitz, *Essais de Théodicée,* vol. 1, 1–120. It reappears in the edition of the *Theodicy* published in Amsterdam in 1747, from which I quote. Louis de Jaucourt's judgment, both on the

Defensio Trinitatis and, in general, on Leibniz's position regarding the mystery of the Trinity, is interesting (Jaucourt, *Vie de M. de Leibnitz,* 58–59): "In his writings he tried to show that it was only by means of a very defective logic that Wissowatius could draw some advantage from this dispute, but that good logic favored the orthodox faith. Moreover, it was not that M. Leibnitz was of the opinion that one must prove the Trinity by philosophical reasons; no, he was very far from this position: he admitted only the Word of God as the foundation of this Mystery, and he wisely believed that, regarding this dogma, the best thing would be, without wishing to go into explanations, to simply stick to the revealed words, since there is no example in Nature which sufficiently well corresponds to the notion of the divine Persons. He even had no problem in saying that it was very wrong to go further, and to claim to explain the word *Person* and other such things; in which, moreover, success is found more fruitless since explanations depend on definitions. That is roughly a summary of his ideas on this subject." In summarizing Leibniz's position regarding the Trinity, Jaucourt seems implicitly to refer also to the *Remarques sur le livre d'un Antitrinitaire Anglois,* published for the first time in 1718 by Feller in *Otium Hanoveranum.* Although, on the one hand, Jaucourt rightly grasps Leibniz's detachment from any attempt to *demonstrate* the Trinity ("to prove the Trinity by philosophical reasons") and likewise rightly reports Leibniz's full awareness of the inadequacy of any example drawn from nature, as also of every definition of such terms as "person," on the other hand, it seems he does not sufficiently appreciate that Leibniz does not renounce the attempt to approach an explanation of the mystery of the Trinity through analogy with what happens in nature.

52. Leyser, *Apparatus Literarius Singularia Nova Anecdota,* 210–211: "God gave us reason, so that by it we could judge of human and finite things, not divine matters, arising from infinity. . . . Let us use this reason as God intended us to. Reason is not the right tribunal for divine things [Ratio non est forum competens rerum divinarum]. . . . It is said that the mystery of the Trinity is above reason and not contrary to it. I do not question the received distinction. Yet I assert that the mystery of the Trinity is against reason."

53. Jakob Carpov, a Lutheran theologian born in Goslar in 1699, studied theology, philosophy, and law at Jena. In 1737 personal problems forced him to leave Jena; he settled in Weimar, where he died in 1768. A follower of Wolff, he was the first who tried to construct an entire theological system in a strictly mathematical and deductive form, applying Wolff's philosophy to theology.

54. Carpov, *Revelatum Sacro-Sanctae Trinitatis Mysterium Methodo Demonstrativa Propositum,* 194–232 (see in particular p. 194, the brief introduction to Wissowatius's letter with the relative replies).

55. DUTENS I, 10–16.

56. In *Zur Geschichte und Litteratur,* 371–418. Lessing bases his edition on a manuscript copy, once conserved at Wolfenbüttel, now lost. He maintains that he is the first to publish, together with Leibniz's replies, Wissowatius's letter, although he must have been familiar with the previous editions. Zbigniew Ogonowski hypothesizes that this behavior should be related "to the project (which Lessing entertained after 1770) of undertaking the edition of selected morsels of Reimarus. Everything seemed to be a preparation of the ground for the battle which, as we know, was for some time to occupy the attention of all the best German intellectuals of the period." (Ogonowski,

"Andrzej Wiszowaty," in Wissowatius, *Religio Rationalis: Editio Trilinguis,* 14). *Des Andreas Wissowatius Einwürfe wider die Dreieinigkeit* can be found also in various collections of Lessing's works, including Lessing, *Gesammelte Werke,* vol. VII, 489–535, from which I quote.

57. See Lessing, *Des Andreas Wissowatius Einwürfe,* 524.

58. Ibid., 532.

59. GP IV, 111–125.

60. A VI, 1, N. 16: N. 16/1 *Dedicatio;* N. 16/2 *Wissowatius ad Baronem Boineburgium;* N. 16/3 *Responsio ad Objectiones Wissowatii.* See also in A VI, 2, 573–577, "Untersuchungen und Erläuterungen zu Band VI, 1."

61. *Theologiae Cursus Completus,* vol. VIII, 751–758.

62. See Baur, *Die christliche Lehre von der Dreieinigkeit und Menschwerdung Gottes,* vol. III, 575.

63. See ibid., 574–577. The judgment expressed by Rhode in "Mainz und der europäische Osten," 64–65, is critical both of Leibniz and of Wissowatius. Also Ludwik Chmaj, in his essay devoted to Andreas Wissowatius as an activist and religious thinker (Chmaj, *Andrzej Wiszowaty jako działacz i myśliciel relijny*) deals briefly with the *Defensio Trinitatis* (see 36–38). For Chmaj both Leibniz and Wissowatius deceive themselves in believing that their arguments are clear and evident and that they stem directly from reason: in reality, they are based on metaphysical foundations that, as such, are, in Chmaj's opinion, completely arbitrary. Instead, Olgierd Narbutt, in a brief paper dedicated to Wissowatius's syllogisms seen from the perspective of Leibniz's criticism, underlines the fact that Leibniz manages to discover the errors inherent in Wissowatius' reasoning (cf. Narbutt, "Sylogizmy Wiszowatego w świetle krytyki Leibniza," 413–416).

64. Trapnell in *The Treatment of Christian Doctrine,* 95, opens his presentation of the *Defensio Trinitatis* by declaring that he follows the "order" proposed by Leibniz, but not the "procedure." In my opinion, however, it is in the "procedure" that the entire value of Leibniz's text lies. In the chapter devoted to Leibniz (see ibid., 78–122), Leibniz's main other writings dealing with the Trinity and Incarnation are briefly examined. Unfortunately, however, the discussion is compromised by a series of misrepresentations and misunderstandings of the original texts.

65. The centrality of this problem in the *Defensio Trinitatis* was grasped by Wolff. In his *Elogium Leibnitii,* 326, Leibniz's work is presented in these terms: "*The Holy Trinity defended by a novel, discovered Logic,* in which he showed the errors (hitherto unobserved) regarding the copula in Syllogisms."

66. A VI, 1, 530.

67. Ibid., 518.

68. Ibid., 520.

69. Ibid.

70. Johannes Raue (or Rauen) was born in Berlin in 1610. After studying at the University of Wittenberg, in 1633 became a 'tutor' at the college of Erfurt, and from 1636 to 1639 he was a professor at the University of Rostock. In 1639 he was called to the Academy of Sora-Soroe (Denmark) where he taught geography and chronology, and later eloquence and logic. Finally, he entered the service of Prince Friedrich Wilhelm von Brandenburg as a librarian. He died in Berlin in 1679. Raue's writings include: *Subita et Necessaria Defensio adversus Sex Primas Lectiones V. Cl. Joh. Scharfii; Invitatio ad*

Sacrae Eloquentiae Studium; Tractatus de Propositionibus Modalibus contra Scharfium; Obtestatio Publica ad D. Georgium Kruquium de Rationibus, Quas Habeat adversus Logicam Novissimam; Prior Fundamentalis Controversia pro Logica Novissima: Addita Sunt et Labyrinthus Logicorum circa Hanc Praecipue Materiam, et Filum Ariadnaeum. On the problem of the copula there is a lively debate between Raue and Johannes Scharff (1595–1660). Antoni Korcik, in an article entitled "La Defensio Trinitatis contra Wissowatium de Leibniz en rapport avec la polémique de Scharff avec Rauen," 181–186, deals with this debate, seeing in it the starting point for the controversy between Leibniz and Wissowatius (see ibid., 182). A concise presentation of Raue's logic can be found in Angelelli, "On Johannes Raue's Logic," 184–190. The originality and interest of Raue's logic are pointed out several times by Roncaglia, *Palaestra Rationis* (on Raue see in particular 143–145).

71. See Raue, *Subita et Necessaria Defensio*, 125–126.

72. Ibid.

73. Ibid., 127.

74. Ibid.

75. See what Leibniz writes at the end of the *Defensio Trinitatis* on the nature of the copula as the beginning of the thread that makes it possible to solve the difficulties advanced by Wissowatius (A VI, 1, 530).

76. See Raue, *Prior Fundamentalis Controversia pro Logica Novissima*, 385–387. Cf. Angelelli, "On Johannes Raue's Logic," 188.

77. See Angelelli, "On Johannes Raue's Logic," 188–189; Roncaglia, *Palaestra Rationis*, 143. Raue writes, with regard to the *commune tertium* (common or shared third term) (Raue, *Prior Fundamentalis Controversia pro Logica Novissima*, 166–167): "Every one to whom *being a philosopher* is attributed, is the same one to whom *being a student of nature* is attributed. Here those things which are attributed are two terms and that to which they are attributed is the *common Third Term*. To this common third term the *Term of the Predicate* is therefore attributed because indeed the *Term of the Subject* is attributed to it."

78. For the commune tertium as a "single substratum" and the necessity of "hooks" so that the copula can function, see Roncaglia, *Palaestra Rationis*, 143. Roncaglia, however, seems to identify these "hooks" with the two auxiliary copulas.

79. Raue, *Prior Fundamentalis Controversia pro Logica Novissima*, 387.

80. Ibid.

81. Ibid.

82. Ibid., 403–404.

83. Ibid., 404.

84. Ibid., 403.

85. See A VI, 1, 520. Raue writes (ibid., 274–275): "We should see, which is the essential predication, and which the accidental. It is essential when something belongs to something by reason of its essence. . . . To be sure, the predication is accidental, when something belongs to something only in utterances concerning its existence, or only insofar as one exists with the other."

86. Where "omnis" (every), as we have seen Raue point out, includes the demonstrative or definitive pronoun.

87. See Scharfius, *Manuale Logicum* ("Praecognita de Copula Propositionis," f. 9v). Cf. Roncaglia, *Palaestra Rationis*, 144–145.

88. A VI, 1, 182–183.

89. The reference is to Raue's conception of the copula, about which Leibniz has just spoken (*Defensio Trinitatis;* A VI, 1, 520: "Which also Ioh. Raue of Berlin partly noted in his most original speculations on the copula").

90. I.e., "omnis" (every).

91. A VI, 1, 520. Cf. what Raue writes in *Subita et Necessaria Defensio,* 154: "*When it is commonly said,* He who [Ille, qui] redeems us is our Messiah. *This means:* Everyone who [Omnis Ille, qui] redeems us, *etc. Indeed it means that the Universal sign is omitted.*"

92. A VI, 1, 520.

93. Ibid.: "I reply with a distinction: by *all things,* either the Creatures are meant, or also the Son with them."

94. Ibid.

95. See what the Fourth Lateran Council (1215) states (DENZ. 800).

96. A VI, 1, 520.

97. This is a note made by Leibniz directly on the copy of Wissowatius's letter, published among the *Lesarten* in A VI, 2, 575.

98. This is made clear by a note that Leibniz later added next to the reformulated major premise (A VI, 1, 520): "This major premise is denied."

99. See in this connection chapter 5.

100. *De Lingua Philosophica;* A VI, 4, 889; VE, 360. For a further discussion of this text, composed between the end of 1687 and the end of 1688, see chapter 5.

101. A VI, 1, 520.

102. See ibid., 521.

103. See ibid.

104. Ibid. Among others Augustine, *De Trinitate,* book I, chap. 6, and book VI, chap. 10; Thomas Aquinas, *Summa Theologica,* part I, quest. XXXIX, art. VIII; Bonaventure, *Sermo de Trinitate,* in Bonaventure, *Opera Omnia,* vol. IX, 352; Comenius, *De Christianorum Uno Deo, Patre, Filio, Spiritu Sancto,* 48.

105. A VI, 1, 521.

106. Ibid.

107. Cf. Dascal, "La razon y los misterios de la fe segun Leibniz," 218.

108. Leibniz rejects this charge by making a distinction between the meanings of the term "God" in the following propositions: "There is only one God" and "The Father is God, the Son is God, etc." In the first case the meaning is "God taken absolutely," and in the second "God taken relatively" (see in particular *Notationes Generales,* A VI, 4, 552–553; VE, 185–186; *De Trinitate,* A VI, 4, 2346; VE, 274; *Circa Geometrica Generalia,* in Mugnai, *Leibniz' Theory of Relations,* 147; *Remarques sur le livre d'un Antitrinitaire Anglois; Nouveaux Essais,* A VI, 6, 498; *Essais de Théodicée,* GP, VI, 63–64). For a discussion of this point, see chapter 5.

109. See A VI, 1, 521.

110. Ibid.

111. See Mt 24:36 and Mk 13:32.

112. Wissowatius's original formulation reads as follows (A VI, 1, 522): "Whoever did not know the day of judgment, is not the most high GOD. The son did not know the day of judgment. Therefore the Son is not the most high GOD."

113. A VI, 1, 522.

114. Ibid.: "For it is possible, on our hypothesis, that he who [ille qui] does not know the day of judgment, namely a man, and he who is [ille, qui est] the most high GOD, are the same."

115. Ibid.

116. Ibid. And it is just the fact that Wissowatius did not manage to prove the contrary, i.e., the impossibility that in the one person of Jesus Christ there is a union of human nature and divine nature, that Leibniz aims to show in the rest of his reply. To Wissowatius's objection (ibid., 523–524): "GOD and man are different things, but different things cannot properly be predicated either both of a third thing or of one another. . . . As it is absurd that iron is wood, and the soul is the body," Leibniz replies by denying such an impossibility (see ibid., 523): by applying the "method of the copula" (ibid.) to the propositions "iron is wood" and "the soul is the body" we shall see that (ibid.) "the case may arise in which it is correct to say that something which is iron (i.e., partially) is also wood (i.e., partially) and something which is soul (partially) is also body (partially). Nor is it absurd that the same entity both is and is not the most high GOD according to different aspects." He also denies the validity of Wissowatius's statement that a part cannot properly be predicated of a composite whole (see ibid., 524), provided that a *reduplicatio* (reduplication) is implied (ibid., 523): "I do not see why the part cannot properly be predicated of the whole, provided a reduplication is given or understood. For properly the Whole is nothing other than single parts predicated of it with union. E.g., Man is soul and body. For whatever soul and body are, in any case man is soul, and at any rate the same man is body [illud utique anima est, et idem utique corpus est]. If therefore we may form this proposition: Man is soul and body, what prevents us from rewriting the compound sentence as two simple sentences: man is soul, and man is body? Likewise, therefore, from our hypothesis, Christ is one entity formed of GOD and man, one will be able to say: Christ is GOD and man, and so: Christ is GOD, and Christ is man."

117. Ibid., 526: "The most high GOD is singular, nor is it predicated of many. But this does not stand in the way of the Trinity. For *he who* is [*is qui* est] the most high GOD (or the person of the most high GOD) can nonetheless be predicated of many, because *he who* is the most high GOD, or the person of the divinity, is universal and not singular. From this it also appears that even if they are three, of whom each is that which is [quidlibet est id quod est] GOD, yet they are not three GODS. For there is not three times one GOD, each being distinct from the others, but there is three times one, of whom each is that which is GOD, or three times a person. Therefore there are not three GODS, but three persons."

118. *Dissertatio de Arte Combinatoria* (A VI, 1, 183).

119. A VI, 1, 526.

120. Burgelin writes in "Théologie naturelle et théologie révélée chez Leibniz," vol. IV, 16: "In a monadological perspective, the trinity of persons in God can seem singularly embarrassing." Skelly, *Leibniz's Revelation-Inspired Metaphysics*, writes along similar lines; in his opinion the Trinitarian conception of God is in contrast with Leibniz's monadology.

121. A VI, 1, 526.

122. As I have already mentioned, later, in *De Scriptura, Ecclesia, Trinitate*, Leibniz in referring to the Trinity uses the expression "plurality in unity" (VE, 433). See also *Sceleton Demonstrationis* (A I, 11, 234).

123. The reference is to the remark (marked by the letter *u*) with which Leibniz closes his reply to the second argument (see A VI, 1, 525–526): "The son is no less necessary to the father than the father is to the son. For if properly the father is that which understands, the son is that which is understood, and the holy spirit is the act of understanding, and in eternal and divine matters actuality [esse] and potentiality [posse] are the same thing, there will not be that which understands in GOD which does not actually understand; moreover, the act of understanding cannot exist without that which is understood. On the contrary, in GOD nothing which could be understood is not understood, and thus does not have that which understands corresponding to it. Therefore as the second person cannot exist without the first, so the first cannot exist without the second." We find here the same parallel between operations of the mind and the Trinity that we have already seen operative in the *Conspectus:* in analogy with the necessary implication between the subject of intellection ("intellectivum"), the object of intellection ("intelligibile"), and the act of intellection ("intellectio"), Leibniz draws the conclusion of the necessary implication of the persons of the Trinity. This is, however, only an analogy, which aims to show the actual existence in nature of a case similar to the one whose possibility one wishes to uphold.

124. Ibid., 526–527.

125. *Monadology* (GP VI, 607); see also *Theodicy,* § 10 of "Preliminary Discourse" (GP VI, 56): "There are necessarily simple substances and without extention, scattered throughout nature," and § 1 of *Principes de la Nature et de la Grace, fondés en raison* (GP VI, 598): "A *simple Substance* is one that has no parts." Both the *Principes* and the *Monadology* date from 1714. See, respectively, GP VI, 598–606 and 607–623.

126. *Monadology,* § 13 (GP VI, 608).

127. Ibid.

128. *Monadology,* § 16 (GP VI, 609).

129. *Principes,* § 1 (GP VI, 598): "Compounds [Les composés] or bodies are Multitudes; and simple substances, Lives, Souls, Spirits are Units."

130. See *Principes,* § 2 (GP VI, 598): "The Monads, not having parts, cannot be formed or destroyed"; *Monadology,* § 6 (GP VI, 607): "The Monads begin and end only abruptly, that is to say, they do not begin except by creation, and end by annihilation, whereas what is compound [composé] begins or ends in parts."

131. A VI, 1, 526.

132. A VI, 1, 479. This passage probably dates from the second half of 1671.

133. Leibniz writes in the *Remarques sur le livre d'un Antitrinitaire Anglois,* 549: "The three persons are not parts of a single absolute divine substance."

134. See A VI, 1, 526–527.

135. See, for example, the remark with which Leibniz ends his reply to the second argument (ibid., 525–526), which he himself refers to here (ibid., 526: "supra lit. u.").

136. See, e.g., *Examen Religionis Christianae (Systema Theologicum),* A VI, 4, 2365; VE, 2419; *Remarques sur le livre d'un Antitrinitaire Anglois; Theodicy,* § 54 of the "Preliminary Discourse"; *Lettre de Monsieur de Leibniz à l'Auteur des Reflexions sur l'Origine du Mahometisme,* DUTENS V, 481–482.

137. A VI, 1, 527.

138. A VI, 4, 1507; VE, 417.

139. See A VI, 1, 527.

140. See ibid., 528–529. In particular, in the sixth argument Wissowatius raises the problem of the generation of the Son by the Father: the difficulties involved in such generation would lead to excluding, as being contradictory, that he who has been generated can be God (*Wissowatius ad Baronem Boineburgium;* ibid., 528). In his reply, Leibniz makes it clear that the generation of the Son is "before all time" (ibid., 528 and 529). In the generation of the Son, there is neither beginning nor end in a temporal sense; the priority of the Father over the Son is logical and not temporal (ibid., 528): "Prior esse natura non tempore," where the term *natura* must not be taken in the sense of an ontological superiority of the Father over the Son. It is rather the case (following an example proposed by Leibniz many years later) of the same kind of logical priority that the lover and the beloved have with respect to love (*De Scriptura, Ecclesia, Trinitate;* VE, 434): "The lover and the loved one are indeed not prior in time, but in the nature of the thing."

141. *Wissowatius ad Baronem Boineburgium;* A VI, 1, 530.

142. The *Refutatio* was published for the first time in 1930 in the *Sämtliche Schriften und Briefen* (A VI, 1, N. 17; see also "Untersuchungen und Erläuterungen zu Band VI, 1" in A VI, 2, 577). The title *Refutatio Objectionum Dan. Zwickeri* is not Leibniz's.

143. See *Commercii Epistolici Leibnitiani*, 1314–1320 (in particular, 1316).

144. A VI, 1, 531.

145. Ibid.

146. Ibid.

147. See in particular the concluding syllogism, in which Zwicker sums up the contents of his work (Zwicker, *Tractatus*, 8).

148. Ibid., 4.

149. Ibid.

150. Ibid.

151. A VI, 1, 531.

152. A VI, 1, N. 15/2. In this writing Leibniz aims to "show the possibility of the Transubstantiation of bread and wine into the body of Christ" (A VI, 1, 508). On *De Transsubstantiatione* cf. Mercer, *Leibniz's Metaphysics*, 82–89.

153. A VI, 1, 511. See also A VI, 1, 508.

154. A VI, 1, 511.

155. An accident, Leibniz writes, is "whatever is not Substance" (A VI, 1, 509) or, on the basis of the definition of substance given previously, what does not have in itself the principle of action.

156. A VI, 1, 531.

157. Cf. *De Transsubstantiatione* (A VI, 1, 511): "For the Suppositum is a Substantial individual (just as a Person is a rational substantial individual)."

158. A VI, 1, 531.

159. Zwicker, *Tractatus*, 4.

160. Ibid.

161. Zwicker, *Tractatus*, 4–6.

162. A VI, 1, 532.

163. Ibid.

164. Ibid.

165. See §§ 2–3 of the "Preliminary Discourse" of the *Theodicy*. See also § 345 of the *Theodicy* and § 11 of the *Principes de la Nature et de la Grace*.

Chapter 3. The Inquiry into the Mind

1. A II, 1, 114.

2. Cf. A II, 1, 108. *De Usu et Necessitate Demonstrationum Immortalitatis Animae* was published together with the appendix *De Resurrectione Corporum* in A II, 1, N. 59.

3. A II, 1, 114.

4. See ibid.

5. Ibid.

6. On this point see also chapter 4.

7. See A VI, 1, 494.

8. *De Ratione Perficiendi et Emendandi Encyclopaediam Alstedii* (A VI, 2, 395). Alsted's *Encyclopaedia* came out in 7 volumes at Herborn in 1630. For Alsted see Hotson, *Johann Heinrich Alsted*. With particular regard to his relations with Leibniz see Hotson, "Alsted and Leibniz," vol. I, 356–363; Antognazza and Hotson, *Alsted and Leibniz on God, the Magistrate and the Millennium.*

9. A II, 1, 173.

10. A II, 1, 113.

11. See *De Incarnatione Dei seu de Unione Hypostatica.*

12. The opening sentence (A VI, 1, 533), "On the incarnation of the Son of GOD or the Hypostatic incarnation, the following things are to be noted," was later canceled.

13. The title *De Incarnatione Dei seu de Unione Hypostatica*, under which the text appears in the edition prepared by the Berlin Academy of Sciences, is not Leibniz's. Moreover, he did not replace the canceled title with a new one. Mercer highlights the importance of *De Incarnatione Dei* for Leibniz's reflections on the problem of substance (cf. *Leibniz's Metaphysics*, 144–157).

14. See *De Persona Christi* (A VI, 4, 2295; VE, 658).

15. *Symbole et Antisymbole des Apostres*, 538: "Also those who speak of the divine nature of Jesus Christ understand nothing else but the fullness of the word or of the Divine Wisdom, which dwells in him who was born of Mary; this habitation is called personal union since it is very perfect"; *Il n'y a qu'un seul Dieu* (A VI, 4, 2211; VE, 435): "*There is a very close union between the divine and human natures in Jesus Christ*. This union does not consist only in the concord or conformity of feelings, but also in a real influence, presence and intimate operation." See also *De Scriptura, Ecclesia, Trinitate* (A VI, 4, 2291; VE, 434); *De Persona Christi* (A VI, 4, 2294–2297; VE, 658–660).

16. See, for example, *Examen Religionis Christianae (Systema Theologicum)* (A VI, 4, 2366; VE, 2420).

17. In Christ there would be two natures and two persons, connected by a moral union.

18. See, e.g., the *Conspectus*, chap. 28 (A VI, 1, 497).

19. Tournemine, "Conjectures sur l'union de l'âme et du corps," 231–237. R. J. Tournemine (1661–1739), editor of the *Mémoires de Trévoux*, remarks that both occasionalism (criticized by Leibniz) and the system of preestablished harmony do not manage to establish a true union between soul and body (see ibid., 234). Leibniz's reply ("Remarque de l'Auteur du Systeme de l'Harmonie préetablie sur un endroit des Mémoires de Trévoux du Mars 1704"), in its turn included in the *Mémoires de Trévoux* of March 1708, was also published in GP VI, 595–596, from which I quote.

20. GP VI, 595. See also a brief note written around 1710 in which Leibniz refers specifically to the Incarnation (in Robinet, *Malebranche et Leibniz,* 413–414).

21. On the *vinculum substantiale* see Adams, *Leibniz,* 299–305; Rutherford, *Leibniz and the Rational Order of Nature,* 276–281, and Look, *Leibniz and the "vinculum substantiale."*

22. GP II, 461.

23. See *Remarque de l'Auteur du Systeme de l'Harmonie préetablie sur un endroit des Mémoires de Trevoux du Mars 1704.* Leibniz writes in § 55 of the "Preliminary Discourse" of the *Theodicy* (GP VI, 81): "although I do not hold that the soul changes the laws of the body, nor that the body changes the laws of the soul, and I have introduced the pre-established Harmony to avoid this disorder, I do not fail to admit a true union between the body and the soul, which occurs in the suppositum. This union is metaphysical, whereas a union of influence would be physical." The paragraph goes on to reiterate the analogy between "the union of the Word of God with human nature" and "the union of the Soul with the body."

24. *Remarque de l'Auteur du Systeme de l'Harmonie préetablie sur un endroit des Memoires de Trévoux du Mars 1704;* GP VI, 596: "It is like in the *Mysteries,* where we also try to *elevate* what we understand of the ordinary development of Creatures to something more sublime that can correspond to them in relation to the Divine Nature and Power, without being able to conceive in them anything sufficiently distinct and sufficiently appropriate to form an entirely intelligible Definition." Cf. Adams, *Leibniz,* 303–307.

25. Kabitz, *Die Philosophie des jungen Leibniz,* 150–153. Kabitz omits some parts of Leibniz's manuscript. *De Incarnatione Dei seu de Unione Hypostatica* was first published in its entirety in A VI, 1, N. 18 (see also A VI, 2, 577–578: "Untersuchungen und Erläuterungen zu Band VI, 1").

26. Cf. Kabitz, *Die Philosophie des jungen Leibniz,* 81–88.

27. A VI, 1, 534.

28. A VI, 1, N. 15/2.

29. A VI, 1, 534.

30. Ibid., 533.

31. Ibid., 534.

32. Ibid., 533.

33. A VI, 1, 508 and 511.

34. Ibid., 508: "Whatever has the principle of action in itself, if it is a body, has the principle of motion in itself. For every Action of the Body is motion. For every Action is a variation of the essence [variatio essentiae]. Therefore every Action of the body is a variation of the body's essence. The essence or definition of Body is being in space. Therefore a variation of the body's essence is a variation of existence in space. A variation of existence in space is motion. Therefore every Action of the body is motion. QED."

35. See this chapter, p. 39.

36. A VI, 1, 508.

37. In the part devoted to the demonstration of the existence of God, we read (A VI, 1, 494): "Demonstration from this principle, that there is no origin of motion in bodies."

38. See *Confessio Naturae;* A VI, 1, 490.

39. See ibid.

40. Ibid. This definition seems to be equivalent to that of "esse in spatio" given in *De Transsubstantiatione* (see A VI, 1, 508).

41. See A VI, 1, 490–491. Nor would it be a valid explanation to say that the body is moved from eternity, because no reason would be given as to why it is in this state from eternity and not, rather, at rest. Nor is an infinite regress possible in searching for the causes. There is, in fact, no explanation until one arrives at the ultimate reason (ibid., 491).

42. A II, 1, 20: "For Mind gives motion to matter so that it may obtain a good and pleasing figure and state of things for itself. For Matter in itself is lacking in motion. The principle of all motion is Mind, which also Aristotle rightly saw."

43. *De Transsubstantiatione*; A VI, 1, 509: "5.) Therefore no body, taken without a concurring mind, is Substance. 6.) Whatever is not Substance, is an *Accident or Species*. 7.) Therefore a body, without a concurring mind, is an Accident or Species."

44. It should be pointed out that the accident is defined in *De Transsubstantiatione* as "whatever is not substance" or "a being subsisting through itself [ens per se subsistens]" (cf. A VI, 1, 509).

45. Ibid.

46. Cf. the fourth condition (A VI, 1, 534): "The immediacy of its action."

47. A VI, 1, 533.

48. Ibid.: "Two minds cannot be joined hypostatically, unless one is perfect and one is imperfect." In line with this thesis, Leibniz later contests one of the postulates on which Jean Le Clerc (using the pseudonym Liberius de Sancto Amore) rests his explanation of the hypostatic union in the first of the early *Epistolae Theologicae* (cf. "Epistola I. De Unione Hypostatica Duarum Christi Naturarum," 1–14). Le Clerc writes (ibid., 6): "POSTULATES. I. Spirits are thinking substances. II. God is infinite Spirit. III. Things are not united except through that by which they come together. IV. Those things between which there is some agreement [convenientia] can be united. V. Things can be united more closely when there is greater agreement between them. . . . VIII. There is greater agreement between two finite spirits than between a finite and an infinite one. IX. In the case of God, since he is a spirit, there is some agreement with finite spirits." Making appeal to the fifth and the eighth postulates, Le Clerc therefore demonstrates the proposition "Two creatures can be more closely united to one another than the creature with God" (ibid., 7): "By postulate 5 things can be united more closely when there is greater agreement between them. But by postulate 8 there is greater agreement between two finite spirits than between a finite spirit and God. Therefore two creatures, etc." Leibniz, in his copy of the *Epistolae* (Niedersächsische Landesbibliothek, T-A 3553), underlines the fifth postulate (p. 6), noting in the margin: "False: a concave and a convex can be more closely united than two convex surfaces." Again, on p. 7, after having underlined the sentence "things can be united more closely when there is greater agreement between them," he writes: "Male [wrong]." In other words, if it is true that there is more agreement between two finite spirits (or, to use the words of *De Incarnatione Dei*, two imperfect minds) than between a finite and an infinite spirit (an imperfect mind and a perfect mind), it is, however, false that things between which there is greater agreement can be united more closely, as is shown by the example of concave and convex. And, in fact, the hypostatic union is possible not between two imperfect minds but between a perfect mind and an imperfect mind.

49. A VI, 1, 533: "Now it is to be inquired whether God is hypostatically united to all bodies or to all the World, or can be to some or to none."

50. Ibid.: "I think the world or bodies are not united hypostatically to God."

51. Ibid., 534.

52. Ibid., 533: "Moreover, God cannot act otherwise on bodies (if we exclude annihilation and creation) than by conferring motion; while, then, they are moved, they are continuously created, as has been demonstrated by me." This conception is already present in the *Demonstrationum Catholicarum Conspectus*, where Leibniz plans to give a demonstration of the existence of God "from this principle, that motion cannot arise without continuous creation" (A VI, 1, 494). It is then clarified in the letter to Jakob Thomasius of 20/30 April 1669, where Leibniz writes (A II, 1, 23): "Properly speaking, motion does not exist in bodies, as a real thing in them, but it has been demonstrated by me that whatever is moved is continuously created, and that bodies in any instant when they are in motion are something, but in any time between the instants when they are in motion are nothing." As Kabitz rightly points out, behind this conception lies the idea that bodies do not have in themselves and of themselves any cohesion and that such cohesion cannot be reached even by movement, as it is interrupted by pauses. Movement is, in fact, according to the young Leibniz the cause of the size and shape of bodies; but since it, too, is interrupted by pauses, its conservation, as also the conservation of bodies, requires a continuous, new creation by God (cf. Kabitz, *Die Philosophie des jungen Leibniz*, 87 and 61–62). It should be pointed out that the idea of conservation in being as continuous creation by God is present also in Descartes (*Meditationes de Prima Philosophia*, in Adam and Tannery, eds., *Oeuvres de Descartes*, VII, 48–49). In the *Principia Philosophiae*, Descartes makes the conservation of the same quantity of movement in the universe depend on God and the constancy of his will (cf. part II, xxxvi). The doctrine of conservation as continuous creation is again advanced also by the Dutch Cartesian Raey in *Clavis Philosophiae Naturalis*. Leibniz, in the abovementioned letter to Thomasius, says he has read Raey, but in such a way that he scarcely remembers what he said (cf. A II, 1, 19). Lastly, it should be noted that already in the *Theoria Motus Abstracti*, probably composed in the winter of 1670–1671, Leibniz modified his conception, abandoning the idea that movement is interrupted by pauses (A VI, 2, 265): "Motion is continuous, or interrupted by no pauses."

53. A VI, 1, 533. Leibniz states in a variant (A VI, 2, 578): "For a Hypostatic union it is required that one be the instrument of the other."

54. A VI, 1, 534: "And indeed, whoever creates acts on the thing, and does not act by means of the thing, and so the thing is not his instrument of action."

55. Ibid.: "In truth, the instrument of God is the mind, united to God, by which God acts on bodies otherwise than by creating. Therefore the hypostatically united is nothing else but what is the immediate instrument of a thing having the principle of action in itself."

56. A VI, 4, 2295; VE, 658. *De Persona Christi* probably dates from 1680–1684.

57. A VI, 1, 534.

58. Ibid.

59. Having ruled out the hypostatic union between God and bodies, since, as we have seen, God can act on bodies only by creating, Leibniz emphasizes that this is precisely the point of distinction between the action of the mind and the action of God on the

body (A VI, 1, 534): "The mind does not act on the body by creating, but by moving; God creates."

60. Ibid.

61. Ibid., 535.

62. These are, respectively, *Trinitas. Mens* (first published in GRUA, 559, now found also in A VI, 2, N. 42/5) and the last part of *De Conatu et Motu, Sensu et Cogitatione* (first published in A VI, 2, N. 42/4).

63. Cf. in particular the two works dealing, respectively, with 'abstract' motion (*Theoria Motus Abstracti*; A VI, 2, N. 41) and 'concrete' motion (*Hypothesis Physica Nova*; A VI, 2, N. 40), probably composed in the winter of 1670–1671 and both published in the spring of 1671.

64. Francesco Piro's exposition of Leibniz's early doctrine on the mind and body in "Leibniz e il progetto degli 'Elementa de mente et corpore,'" 106–116, is, despite its brevity, very precise and well documented. Cf. also Piro, ed., "G. W. Leibniz: Harmonia e conatus," 204–220.

65. A II, 1, 172.

66. A II, 1, 113.

67. A II, 1, 108.

68. Hobbes, *De Corpore*, part III, chap. XV, 2, in Hobbes, *Opera Philosophica*, vol. I, 177.

69. A II, 1, 108. See also the letter written by Leibniz to Heinrich Oldenburg on 29 April (9 May) 1671; A II, 1, 102: "*Conatus* is, moreover, motion through a point in an instant."

70. A VI, 2, 265. See also Leibniz to Lambert van Velthuysen (May 1671); A II, 1, 98: "*Conatus* is the beginning of motion"; Leibniz to Arnauld (early November 1671); A II, 1, 173: "Conatus is to motion as point is to space."

71. See A VI, 2, 266: "*No conatus without motion lasts beyond the moment except in minds*. For what in the moment is conatus, that is in time the motion of the body: here is opened the door for the pursuit of the true difference between body and mind, which up to now no one has explained. For every body is a momentary mind, but lacking in *memory*, because it does not retain beyond the moment simultaneously its own conatus and another contrary one (for there must be two, an action and a reaction, or a comparison and then a *harmony*, for *sensation* to exist, and without which there is no sensation, *pleasure* or pain): therefore, it lacks memory, it lacks the sense of its own actions and passions, it lacks thought." In this text it seems that one can identify an early conception of Leibniz's monadology. Cf. Garber, "Motion and Metaphysics in the Young Leibniz," 160–184, and Moll, "Die erste Monadenkonzeption des jungen Leibniz," 53–62.

72. A VI, 2, 266.

73. *De Conatu et Motu, Sensu et Cogitatione*; A VI, 2, 285.

74. Ibid., 282 and 285.

75. Ibid., 282.

76. Ibid., 282 and 285.

77. See the quoted passage taken from the *Theoria motus abstracti*; A VI, 2, 266. See also the letters written by Leibniz to Heinrich Oldenburg on, respectively, 11 March and 29 April (9 May) 1671: "Every body is a momentary mind, and hence without awareness, sense, or memory. If, indeed, in a single body two contrary conatus could

simultaneously endure beyond the moment, every body would be a true mind" (A II, 1, 90); "Every body is an instantaneous mind; the mind preserves the conatus without there being motion, [but] the body does not preserve [it]" (A II, 1, 102).

78. A II, 1, 173: "Every body can be understood as a momentary mind, but lacking in memory."

79. See *De Transsubstantiatione*; A VI, 1, 490.

80. See his letter of early November 1671 to Arnauld, in which Leibniz claims to have demonstrated, as regards motion, two very important propositions (A II, 1, 172): "First, a body at rest has no cohesion or consistency, contrary to what Descartes thought, and, therefore, whatever is at rest can be set in motion and separated by any motion at all. I advanced this proposition a long time ago, and I found that a body at rest is nothing, nor does it differ from empty space. . . . The second is that every motion in the plenum is circular and homocentric, nor can motion in a straight line, or in a spiral, ellipse or oval be understood in the world; indeed, neither can a circular motion with different centers, unless we admit a vacuum. . . . From the latter proposition, [we see that] the essence of a body does not consist in extension, i.e. size and shape, because empty space is necessarily different from a body, although it still is extended. From the former, [we conclude that] the essence of body has more reason to be regarded as consisting in motion, since the notion of space is summed up by size and shape, i.e. extension." Cf. also farther on (A II, 1, 175): "Since for the first time it was discovered by me that the essence of the body does not consist in extension, as Descartes thought . . . , but in motion, and therefore the substance or nature of a body, even according to Aristotle's definition, is the principle of motion (for there is no state of absolute rest in bodies); and indeed, the principle of motion or substance of the body lacks in extension." It should be pointed out that Leibniz here uses the term *substantia* (substance), as the equivalent of *natura* (nature) or "principle of action": that is, as the equivalent of what in *De Transsubstantiatione* was called *forma substantialis,* not to be confused with substantia taken in the sense of *suppositum* (= *ens per se subsistens* = that which has the principle of action in itself). See *De Transsubstantiatione*; A VI, 1, 511.

81. See A VI, 1, 490.

82. See Leibniz to Johann Friedrich, 21 May 1671; A II, 1, 108: "For just as Actions of Bodies consist in motion, so do Actions of minds consist in *conatus.*"

83. The *Conspectus,* the first part of which is devoted to the demonstration of the existence of God, provides for a "demonstration from this principle: that there is no origin of motion in bodies" (A VI, 1, 494).

84. A VI, 2, 287.

85. See, respectively, chapters 1 and 2.

86. See *Conspectus*; A VI, 1, 495.

87. A VI, 1, 527.

88. A VI, 1, 490.

89. A II, 1, N. 11.

90. A VI, 2, 161: "*All bodies are homogeneous, i.e. they differ only in size, shape and motion.*"

91. A VI, 1, 495.

92. A VI, 2, N. 42/3. *De Materia Prima* probably dates from the years 1670–1671; the fragment is therefore a little earlier than, or contemporaneous with, *Trinitas. Mens.*

93. A VI, 2, 279: "Aristotle's prime matter is the same as Descartes' subtle Matter. Each is infinitely divisible. Each is, in itself, lacking in form and motion, and each takes its form from motion. Each receives motion from the mind." In this case *forma* (form) seems to be equivalent to *figura* (shape).

94. Ibid., 280.

95. *Specimen Demonstrationum de Natura Rerum Corporearum ex Phaenomenis* (probably the second half of 1671); A VI, 2, 307: "Space is the same thing as the possibility of bodies."

96. A VI, 2, 280: "Prime matter, if at rest, is nothing, and it is as some Scholastics obscurely said, that Prime matter takes its existence from the form."

97. See Augustine, *Confessiones*, book XIII, chap. 11.

98. A VI, 2, 287.

99. Ibid., 287–288.

100. This reading seems to be justified also on the basis of a note, later canceled, in which Leibniz writes: "*Mind* is referred to the eternal verities" (A VI, 2, 287).

101. Ibid., 288.

102. A VI, 1, 526. See also *Demonstrationum Catholicarum Conspectus*; A VI, 1, 495.

103. A VI, 2, 288. As for the absolute being in action of God, clarification may once again come from the *Defensio Trinitatis*, where Leibniz mentions the identity of *esse* and *posse* in the divine nature (A VI, 1, 526): "For if properly the father is that which understands [intellectivum], the son is that which is understood [intelligibile], and the holy spirit is the act of understanding [intellectio], and in eternal and divine matters actuality [esse] and potentiality [posse] are the same thing, there will not be that which understands in GOD which does not actually understand; moreover, the act of understanding cannot exist without that which is understood. On the contrary, in GOD nothing which could be understood is not understood, and thus does not have that which understands corresponding to it."

104. Leibniz's words seem to echo what Augustine writes, for example, in *De civitate Dei*, book XI, chap. 26.

105. See Augustine, *De Trinitate*, book IX, chap. 6, in Augustine, *Opera*, vol. XVI, "Therefore, the mind itself and love and news of it are what might be called three things, and these three are one, and as they are perfect they are equal."

106. A VI, 2, 288. In the following years, Leibniz came back several times to this conception, clarifying and specifying its meaning. See for example the following texts: *De Mente* (October 1676) (GRUA, 266); *De Origine Rerum ex Formis* (April 1676*) (A VI, 3, 519); *Dialogue entre Theophile et Polidore* (summer–autumn 1679*) (A VI, 4, 2234; VE, 39); Leibniz to Arnauld (9 October 1687) (GP II, 125); *Parallele entre la raison originale ou la loy de la nature . . . et le Christianisme ou la loy de la nature rétablie* (after 1704) (GRUA, 47); *Theodicy,* "Preliminary Discourse," § 61 (GP VI, 84).

107. A series of observations made by Leibniz on several occasions from spring to autumn 1671 are published under this title in A VI, 2, N. 42/4.

108. A VI, 2, 286.

109. Ibid., 286.

110. Ibid., 286.

111. Ibid., 285.

112. Ibid., 286.

113. Ibid., 286.

114. Ibid., 282.

115. Ibid., 283.

116. Ibid., 283.

117. See *Remarques sur le livre d'un Antitrinitaire Anglois*, 550: "I find in the creatures nothing more appropriate for clarifying this subject than the Reflexion of Spirits, when one and the same Spirit is its own immediate object, and acts on itself in thinking of itself and what it does. For this doubling [redoublement] provides an image or shadow of two respective substances in a single absolute substance; i.e., what thinks and what is thought; both of these beings are substantial, each is a concrete individual; and they differ by some mutual relations, but they form only one and the same absolute individual substance." On this point see also chapter 8. See also *De Scriptura, Ecclesia, Trinitate* (A VI, 4, N. 403; VE, N. 112); *Origo Animarum et Mentium* (A VI, 4, N. 275; VE, N. 81); *De Mundo Praesenti* (A VI, 4, N. 301; VE, N. 107); *De Persona Christi* (A VI, 4, N. 405; VE, N. 147); *De Deo Trino* (A VI, 4, N. 404; VE, N. 148); *Examen Religionis Christianae (Systema Theologicum)* (A VI, 4, 2365; VE, 2419).

Chapter 4. The Relation between Revelation and Knowledge

1. *Remarque de l'Auteur du Systeme de l'Harmonie préetablie sur un endroit des Mémoires de Trévoux du Mars 1704;* GP VI, 596.

2. See chapter 3, note 19.

3. First published in A VI, 1, N. 22. See also A VI, 2, 581–582: "Untersuchungen und Erläuterungen zu Band VI, 1."

4. A VI, 1 N. 15/4. See also A VI, 2, 572–573: "Untersuchungen und Erläuterungen zu Band VI, 1."

5. Cf. Dascal, "La razon y los misterios de la fe segun Leibniz."

6. *Meditationes de Cognitione, Veritatie et Ideis* (GP IV, 422): "Knowledge is *clear,* therefore, when I have that from which I can recognize the thing represented, and this [clear knowledge] is in turn either confused or distinct. It is *confused* when I cannot enumerate one by one the traits which are sufficient to distinguish the thing from others, although the thing really has those traits and requisites into which its notion can be resolved." See also *Nouveaux Essais,* book II, chap. 29.

7. See Dascal, "La razon y los misterios de la fe segun Leibniz," 214.

8. See ibid., 219.

9. See ibid., 219–220 and 225.

10. See chapter 2.

11. The question "De Judice Controversiarum" (Of the Judge of Controversies) is one of the classic topics in the theology of Leibniz's time. We briefly dwell here only on those writings that can most directly be linked to the *Commentatiuncula.*

12. Meyer (1630–1681) was part of the inner circle of Spinoza's friends. Born into a petit-bourgeois Lutheran family, he studied philosophy and medicine in Leiden. Probably around 1654 he became a friend of Spinoza, later becoming one of the main publishers of his works. Spinoza's influence was thus added to the basic Cartesianism that characterizes Meyer's thought. Leibniz came to know about the controversy aroused by the publication of *Philosophia S. Scripturae Interpres* through his and Boineburg's extensive correspondence: see Leibniz to Daniel Wülfer, 19 December 1669, A I, 1, 80;

Leibniz to Gottlieb Spitzel, 7 April 1671, A I, 1, 133; Johann van Diemerbroeck to Leibniz, 18 (28) August 1671, A I, 1, 166; Lambert van Velthuysen to Leibniz, probably May 1670, A II, 1, 42; "*Erici Mauritii* Epistola ad *Boineburgium* de Itinere Suo Belgico: *Kilonii d. 14. Mart. 1670*," in *Commercii Epistolici Leibnitiani*, 1311; "Excerpta ex Literis *Io. Fabricii*, Ioannis Filii, ad *Boineburgium* de Itinere Suo Belgico: *Hamburgi d. 10. Aug. 1670*," ibid., 1315. Leibniz's brief judgment on Meyer's work is severe; he expresses it in a note to his copy of the *Nova Methodus Discendae Docendaeque Jurispruden-tiae* (Frankfurt: Johann Davidis, 1667). After having mentioned, in § 65, *Philosophia S. Scripturae Interpres* as the work of an "Anonymous Arminian Author . . . published in Belgium," he adds (A VI, 1, 338): "But it, however, must be read with great caution, and in some instances he adopts perverse rules of interpretation. Afterward it was discovered that the author was Ludwig Meyer, a doctor and friend of Spinoza; what things the learned Theologians objected to this book could be collected." A fuller description of the terms of the debate is found in § 14 of the "Preliminary Discourse" of the *Theodicy*, at the conclusion of which Leibniz observes (GP VI, 59): "One speaks then in Holland of *rational* and *non-rational Theologians*, a partisan distinction often mentioned by Mr. Bayle, who finally comes out against the former; but it does not seem that precise rules have yet been given, to which both parties agree or disagree regarding the use of reason in the explanation of the Holy Scriptures." In his reference to Bayle, Leibniz seems to be pointing to chapter CXXX of the *Réponse aux Questions d'un Provincial* (Rotterdam, 1704–1707). It should be noted that the main question animating the debate between "Rational" and "Anti-Rational" theologians described by Bayle in chapters CXXX and CXXXI is precisely the question of the Trinity.

13. The place of publication that appears on the title page of the first edition (Hamburg) is false. The direct connection between Leibniz's reading of the *Tractatus* and the writing of the *Commentatiuncula* has recently been shown by the illuminating study by Goldenbaum, "Die Commentatiuncula de judice," 61–107. Among the volumes belonging to Boineburg's library, Goldenbaum found a copy of the first edition of the *Tractatus Theologico-Politicus* annotated by the young Leibniz (notes published in Goldenbaum, "Die Commentatiuncula de judice," 105–107).

14. This edition was preceded by a Belgian version in 1667. Again in 1673, Meyer's work was reprinted in Amsterdam with the same title as in 1666. In 1674 another edition (identical to the Leiden edition of 1673) was published in which Meyer's work follows the *Tractatus* by Spinoza (*Tractatus Theologico-Politicus Cui Adjunctus Est Philosophia S. Scripturae Interpres ab Authore Longe Emendatior*). The third Latin edition was published in 1776. On Meyer's work, see Bordoli, *Ragione e scrittura tra Descartes e Spinoza*.

15. As is pointed out by Kolakowski, *Chrétiens sans Église*, 749, "historians agree in supposing that the great reflections on the Bible that Spinoza wrote while preparing the *Tractatus theologico-politicus* were used by Meyer for his study, which in this way benefitted from his intimacy with the philosopher."

16. See Spinoza, *Tractatus Theologico-Politicus*, 1670, chap. XIV, in Gebhardt, ed., *Spinoza Opera*, vol. III, 179.

17. See the *Philosophiae Descriptio* proposed by Meyer in the second section of chapter V (Meyer, *Philosophia S. Scripturae Interpres*, 40).

18. See ibid., chap. IV, § 1.

19. See ibid., "Prologus."

20. See ibid., 44: the true interpreter of the holy scriptures is "one who can dig out the truths of the passages contained in them. . . . Therefore since . . . Philosophy is the true, certain, and undoubted understanding of things, deduced from known principles by the light of nature, and demonstrated apodictically: by this both the truths of the passages of Scripture can be certainly brought to light, and the things brought to light can be demonstrated, as well as the explanations made of them by others, whether in truth it is advisable, or not, to explore them further, and show undoubtedly what are the traits of this or that. Wherefore it very clearly follows that this is a certain and infallible Norm both for interpreting the holy Books and for exploring the interpretations."

21. Of these, the dogma of the Trinity; see ibid., 47.

22. See ibid., 39–40.

23. See ibid., chap. XVI.

24. See ibid., "Prologus." The danger, for the mysteries of faith, of Descartes' criterion of truth was noted by the young Leibniz, as is shown by some remarks contained in his first long letter addressed to Arnauld (see A II, 1, 171). What place can there be for truths *superior* to human reason (and of which it does not, and cannot, have clear and distinct ideas) in a philosophy whose first principle is that of admitting as true only that which is clear and distinct? The adoption of the principle of noncontradiction as the criterion of truth, as reposed by Leibniz (see, for example, A II, 1, 444), instead makes it possible to admit the mysteries into the cognitive sphere: even if we do not and cannot have a clear and distinct knowledge of them, they are nonetheless truths inasmuch as they comply (until the contrary is proved) with the principle of noncontradiction.

25. See Meyer, *Philosophia S. Scripturae Interpres*, 102–103.

26. Ludwig van Wolzogen was born at Amersfoort in 1633. Professor of church history at Utrecht, as well as a pastor and preacher for the Walloon community, he was part of the circle of Cartesianizing Cocceians of Utrecht. He then moved to Amsterdam, where he continued his activity as a professor and preacher; he died on 13 November 1690.

27. For an indication of some of the numerous works published against Wolzogen see Burmann, *Trajectum Eruditum*, 457–462.

28. One who was particularly active against Wolzogen was Jean de Labadie (1610–1674), on whose initiative the Walloon church of Middelburg denounced him to the Walloon synods of Flushing and Naarden (see Labadie, *Extrait de quelques propositions erronées et scandaleuses*). Wolzogen's book, however, was declared orthodox (see Labadie, *Quatorze remarques importantes*). Labadie, who refused to recognize the sentence and to present his apologies to the accused, abandoned the synod, thus leaving the Reformed Church. In 1669 a group of professors of theology (including Coccejus and Desmarets) came to the defense of Wolzogen, attesting to his orthodoxy (cf. *Jugemens de plusieurs professeurs et docteurs en théologie*, collected by Wolzogen himself, who was the author of the preliminary letter and the preface). According to what is related by Burmann in *Trajectum Eruditum*, in the opposite camp, again in 1669, the *Theologorum Quorumdam Judicium de Libro Ludovici Wolzogen de Scripturarum Interprete* was published; in it Wolzogen's work is energetically censured.

29. See § 33; A VI, 1, 553.

30. Adrian van Walenburch was born in 1609 in Rotterdam and died in 1669 at Wiesbaden; from 1661 on he was the auxiliary bishop in Cologne. He was succeeded by his brother Peter (1610–1675), one of the most outstanding men in the circle of

collaborators of Johann Philipp von Schönborn (1605–1673). On Peter Walenburch and his activity in the court environment of Mainz see in particular Wiedeburg, *Der junge Leibniz*, vol. I, part I, 79–92, and Jürgensmeier, *Johann Philipp von Schönborn*, 172–176.

31. Leibniz certainly had direct knowledge of the treatises of the Walenburch brothers, as can be seen from the references to them contained in the fragment *De Unitate Ecclesiae Romanae*, probably composed between the autumn of 1669 and 1671 (see A VI, 1, N. 21). Regarding the Walenburch brothers, cf. also Leibniz's letters to Simon Löffler of 20/30 April and 25 September (5 October) 1669 (A I, 1, N. 34 and N. 35); the letter to Joh. Andreas Bose of 25 September (5 October) 1669 (A I, 1, N. 36); the letter to Daniel Wülfer of 19 December 1669 (A I, 1, N. 37); the letter to Phil. Jakob Spener of 11/21 December 1670 (A I, 1, N. 60). Already in the *Nova Methodus* (New Method) (1667) Leibniz refers to the Walenburchs' work *De Praescriptionibus Catholicis* (Antwerp, 1666; in *Tractatus de Controversiis Generales Contracti*, Cologne, 1667). In later years too Leibniz mentions Peter van Walenburch several times, declaring that he discussed religious matters with him for hours (see the letter written by Leibniz, probably at the beginning of 1681, to Ernst von Hessen-Rheinfels; A I, 3, N. 223). Some extracts made by Leibniz from the first treatise contained in A. and P. van Walenburch, *Tractatus Generales de Controversiis Fidei* (A VI, 4, N. 422; VE, N. 7), probably date from the first half of 1677.

32. Van Walenburch, *Tractatus Generales de Controversiis Fidei*, "Tractatus Primus," 2. I quote here from the abridged version of the first treatise (see *ibid.*, 2–15; the fuller version is published on pp. 111–225). The "Examen Primum" ("First Examination") criticizes the Protestant doctrine whereby the articles of faith necessary for salvation are to be proved by reference to scripture alone, as they are said to be contained in it in a clear and evident manner (see ibid., 2). The third Treatise is dedicated specifically to the problems raised by the distinction between fundamental and nonfundamental articles of faith (*De Articulis Necessariis, Fundamentalibus, seu Essentialibus: Eorundemque Oppositis Erroribus*, in Van Walenburch, *Tractatus Generales de Controversiis Fidei*).

33. Ibid., treatise III, section III, 23: "In that period the Protestants read the Holy Scriptures diligently: nevertheless, they did not find a catalogue of necessary articles, which are proved sufficiently as such by Scripture alone. In establishing the necessary articles, Lutherans do not agree with Lutherans, nor Reformed with Reformed." The problem becomes particularly acute for centrally important dogmas of Christian doctrine, such as the Trinity and the divine nature of Jesus. See in particular *De Unitate Ecclesiae et Schismate Protestantium, Aliorumque*, book VII ("In what way the unity of the Church is to be found"), chap. XV ("The Reformed cannot prove with certainty the Most Holy Trinity from the Holy Scripture"), in van Walenburch, *Tractatus Generales de Controversiis Fidei*, treatise IX, 252–253.

34. See van Walenburch, *Tractatus Generales de Controversiis Fidei*, treatise III, section XVI, 30: "*Without the tradition of the unwritten Word of God, and the witness of the Church, it is not possible to know what the necessary articles are. . . .* Without tradition, and the witness of the Church, no one can know the true meaning of the necessary articles[.]" The question regarding the interpretation of scripture and the judge of controversies is dealt with in particular in the "Examen Secundum" ("Second Examination") of the first treatise. See in particular § 1 ("Regarding the interpreter of the Holy Scripture, and the judge of controversies") and § 2 ("On the Interpretation of the

Holy Scripture"), 3–4 (abridged version) and 137–139, in Van Walenburch, *Tractatus Generales de Controversiis Fidei.*

35. Ibid., 4. See ibid., 137.

36. Van Walenburch, *Tractatus Speciales, de Controversiis Fidei,* treatise I, chap. VII, 3.

37. See in particular van Walenburch, *Tractatus Generales de Controversiis Fidei,* treatise I, "Third Examination."

38. Ibid., treatise I, chap. VII, 3: "When Protestants say that the true meaning of the divine Word is to be sought from the Holy Spirit, the author of the Holy Scriptures, they assert the very same thing as what the Catholic Church teaches, . . . It is not therefore principally the Church that judges of the meaning of the Holy Scripture, but the Holy Spirit presiding in the Councils, residing in the Church, declaring the meaning of its words from the beginning of the universe. . . . Hence, moreover, it is clear how unjustly the Roman Catholic Church has been attacked, as if it set up men as Judges of God, and of His Word; as if it elevated men above the authority of the Holy Scripture; since the Holy Spirit present in the Church, using the Pastors as its organs, and opening up its meaning to the faithful, bestows authority on the Church."

39. See *Commentatiuncula,* §§ 1–2 (A VI, 1, 548).

40. Ibid.

41. Ibid.

42. Ibid., 548–549.

43. Ibid., 549. It should be noted that this formulation resembles, almost literally, one of the principles attributed by the Walenburchs to their adversaries (Van Walenburch, *Tractatus Generales de Controversiis Fidei,* 137: "Nothing is to be believed, as being necessary for salvation, that is not contained in Scripture").

44. See *Commentatiuncula,* § 9; A VI, 1, 549: "Moreover, in other laws this is not the case, because in a Republic it is necessary to decide about matters which are not contained in the laws; this is not necessary in questions of faith."

45. Ibid.

46. *Commentatiuncula,* § 11; A VI, 1, 549.

47. Ibid.

48. Ibid.: "Which is otherwise in questions removed from practice, of GOD one and triune, the nature and person of Christ, of the presence of Christ and bread in the last supper, of predestination, and other controversial matters."

49. Ibid., § 12; A VI, 1, 549.

50. Ibid., § 7.

51. This sentence is found in a later text: *De Scriptura, Ecclesia, Trinitate,* dating from 1680–1684 (see A VI, 4, 2289; VE, 433). In any case, we are dealing with a conviction that is certainly already operative, as is shown, for example, by the *Defensio Trinitatis.*

52. See *Commentatiuncula,* §§ 13–19. For a comparison with Spinoza's *Tractatus Theologico-Politicus* cf. Goldenbaum, "Die Commentatiuncula de judice," especially 80–89.

53. See in particular *Commentatiuncula,* § 13; A VI, 1, 549.

54. Ibid., 549–550: "But you will say that the Holy Scripture cannot be the judge, at least, of its own authenticity. So it is, for it cannot be the judge whether the text (e.g., there are three who bear witness) is authentic. This therefore must be proved by reason and history, as generally the very divinity of the Holy Scripture, which Scripture itself

cannot prove, because in such matters self-witness is not permitted. For even if it calls itself the word of GOD, yet this must be proved by others."

55. See ibid., § 20; A VI, 1, 550: "But there is still a not inconsiderable difficulty. For faith regards the meaning, not the words; therefore it is not sufficient for us to believe that whoever said that 'This is my body' was saying the truth, unless we also know what he said. For indeed we do not know what he said if we keep only to the words, ignoring their force and power."

56. Ibid., A VI, 1, 550.

57. The comparison with the parrot is found in chapter XIII of Spinoza's *Tractatus Theologico-Politicus*, against which Leibniz is here directing his criticism. Cf. Goldenbaum, "Die Commentatiuncula de judice," especially 80, 90–93.

58. A VI, 1, 550–551.

59. Leibniz adopts the same position in the *Theodicy* (§ 54 of the "Preliminary Discourse"; GP VI, 80): "It is not necessary to require always what I call *adequate notions*, which contain nothing that has not been explained, since even sensible qualities such as heat, light, sweetness, do not supply us with such notions. So we agree that the mysteries receive an explanation, but this explanation is imperfect. It suffices that we have some analogical understanding of a mystery, such as the Trinity or the Incarnation, so that in receiving them we do not pronounce words entirely devoid of meaning."

60. See Dascal, "La razon y los misterios de la fe segun Leibniz," 214.

61. A VI, 1, 550: "It is not always necessary for faith to know what sense of the words is true, *as long as we understand it*" (my italics).

62. Ibid.: "Nor do we positively reject it."

63. In the paragraphs following, Leibniz exemplifies what was said above, applying it to the case of the Eucharist. It is thus shown that, for there to be faith, there must necessarily be a certain degree of understanding of Christ's words "this is my body," even though an adequate knowledge of their meaning is not required.

64. A VI, 1, 551.

65. See ibid., § 29; A VI, 1, 551–552. By this Leibniz certainly does not want to maintain that in philosophy, as in the sphere of the mysteries, one does not arrive at clear and distinct knowledge. As he was later to point out in the *Meditationes de Cognitione, Veritate et Ideis*, there are notions that cannot be defined, but this does not mean, in and of itself, that they correspond to confused knowledge. (GP IV, 423: "Nevertheless we also have a distinct knowledge of an undefinable notion when it is *primitive* or known of itself, that is, when it cannot be reduced to elements and can only be understood through itself, and therefore lacks component elements.") What Leibniz in the *Commentatiuncula* wishes to call attention to is the fact that in philosophical discourse *also* confused notions are used. It should also be pointed out that the "blind cogitation" spoken of in § 27 of the *Commentatiuncula* (A VI, 1, 551) is extended in the *Meditationes de Cognitione, Veritate et Ideis* to other procedures resorted to in algebra and in arithmetic (see GP IV, 423). In § 30 of the *Commentatiuncula* (A VI, 1, 552), Leibniz reiterates that the faith of most Christians is based on the acceptance of propositions of which one has only a confused knowledge. But, once again, what is true for the man in the street is true also for philosophers and theologians trying to explain mysteries such as the Trinity (see A VI, 1, 552).

66. See *Commentatiuncula*, § 32; A VI, 1, 522: "I therefore conclude: if anyone thinks that a distinct knowledge of the meaning of the mysteries of faith is necessary for

salvation, I will show him that scarcely one Christian in a thousand, nay even more, not even he who thinks this way, has ever had such distinct knowledge. And consequently an apprehension of the formula expressed in the Holy Scripture, with a confused knowledge of the meaning by the intellect, and some disjunctive assent or opinion on its part, is sufficient for Salvation. For I challenge those who deny that faith exists together with the fear of its opposite or that it is an opinion, if they are telling the truth, to try to explain why such faith has room for the notion of 'more or less.' However, that it does admit of it, the witness of Christ shows."

67. See ibid.

68. Stimulated by Locke's reflections, Leibniz later comes back to these thoughts. In fact, he says in book IV of the *Nouveaux Essais,* in the character of Theophile (A VI, 6, 493): "In effect the great mysteries are made known to us by the testimony of God that one recognizes through *motives of credibility,* on which our Religion is founded." It should be pointed out, en passant, that when Theophile, immediately afterward, approves the affirmation of Philalethe that "Faith is a firm assent, and properly governed assent cannot be given except on the basis of good reasons," saying, "I heartily congratulate you, Monsieur, when you wish to found faith on reason; otherwise why should we prefer the *Bible* to the *Koran* or the ancient books of the Brahmins?" these words can certainly not be understood as the submission of faith to reason. The "faith based on reason" is faith based on the motives of credibility. The priority of the text (once its "credentials" have been presented) over reason is, moreover, asserted clearly both in the *Commentatiuncula* (see § 34) and, after the *Nouveax Essais,* in the "Preliminary Discourse" of the *Theodicy* (§ 29; GP VI, 67).

69. A VI, 1, 552: "(§ 33.) So much for the Textuals. The *Rationals* are pure or mixed." In ordering the positions of the Socinians, Reformed, and Evangelicals (or Lutherans) on the basis of the priority to be given, in the examination of doubtful cases, to the text or to reason, Leibniz seems to identify the Socinians (characterized by the assertion of the priority of reason over the text both in theory and in practice) with the *Rationales meri* (pure Rationals); the Reformed (supporters of the priority of the text over reason only in theory, but not in practice) with the *Rationales mixti* (mixed Rationals); the Evangelicals with the *Textuales* (Textuals). See ibid.: "The Reformed in practice, and the Socinians in theory and practice say one should stand more by reason, and it is better for words to be forcibly interpreted, rather than that something improbable should be admitted by reason. On the contrary, the Evangelicals in practice and theory, and the Reformed in theory, say that one must rather stick to the proper meaning of the words, even if it is improbable to reason (as long as it is not impossible), rather than that the words should be interpreted forcibly or metaphorically. And it is just in this that lay the state of the controversy between the Philosopher interpreter of scripture and Wolzogenium. I say the Reformed in theory, but not in practice, because in the supper they say that the presence of the body of Christ is not only improbable to reason, but is indeed impossible." It should be noted that, while the core of the controversy between Lodewijk Meyer and Ludwig van Wolzogen (cf. supra) is located in the problem of whether to assign priority to reason or to the text, Leibniz does not comment on Meyer's remark that the Socinians are still too moderate in their recourse to reason as regards the interpretation of the scriptures. Meyer himself, as we have seen, actually claims for himself a position in which the primacy of reason is much more radically recognized than it is by the Socinians, who instead, in the range of positions

presented here by Leibniz, seem to incarnate the most extreme rationalist wing. Moreover, it seems possible to detect a veiled criticism of the Reformed thinkers, on account of the inconsistency between what they say in theory about the primacy of the text and the position then adopted in practice as regards the real presence in the Eucharist: its exclusion as impossible (and not just improbable) is carried out, Leibniz seems to suggest, by following the rule of the priority of reason.

70. Ibid.

71. See ibid., 552–553: "When the meaning of a text is doubtful, likewise when reason can determine nothing certain, as is the case in things of fact, and a conflict arises between the text and reason, it is indeed not absolute, but probable, in this way: The real presence of the body of Christ, likewise the Trinity in GOD, is probable according to the text (for from the text nothing except what is probable can be gathered) but improbable (N.B., although not impossible, for we certainly do not concede this to the Socinians and the Reformed) according to reason; then it is asked, whether it is better to side with reason or the words of the text."

72. The reference is clearly to the mystery of the Trinity.

73. A VI, 1, 553.

74. Cf. Kabitz, *Die Philosophie des jungen Leibniz* (see in particular 133–134).

75. Around 1693, Leibniz returns to these ideas, clarifying them, in reference once again to the mystery of the Trinity, in *Remarques sur le livre d'un Antitrinitaire Anglois*, 549–550: "One must admit that there is no example in nature that corresponds sufficiently to this notion of the divine persons. But it is not at all necessary to find one; and it is sufficient that what one says of it implies no contradiction or absurdity. Divine substance no doubt has privileges that surpass all other substances. However, as we do not know all the creatures well enough, we cannot assert that there is not, and that there cannot be outside God, any absolute substance that contains in itself several respective substances."

76. A VI, 1, 553: "My opinion is that it is appropriate that we rather stand by the meaning of the text, even if it is improbable to reason, as long as it is possible, and this on condition that it is GOD who is speaking. For he, since he is wise, will not give us words by which we may be deceived. [Yet this is what] he would give, if that sense which is in the highest degree suitable to the text according to the rules of interpretation . . . were false. And since he is powerful, he can carry out whatever he promised."

77. Ibid.

78. Ibid., 553–554. It should be noted that here Leibniz takes into consideration an article of faith in which, even for the Socinians, the condition "provided that it is possible" posed in § 34 may be considered to be met. Therefore the problem of impossibility is not posed (as would instead be the case for the mystery of the Trinity), and the question is reduced to a case of improbability. Now, Leibniz would seem to be saying, the Socinians, even when the possibility is not in doubt, give reason priority in interpretation. In fact, when faced with what is improbable according to reason, they opt for a metaphorical interpretation of the scriptures, unlike the 'Catholics.'

79. See ibid., § 33; A VI, 1, 552–553: "The Trinity in GOD is probable according to the text (for from the text nothing except what is probable can be gathered)."

80. See ibid., § 7.

81. See for example the *Dedicatio* of the *Defensio Trinitatis* (A VI, 1, 518). The acknowledgment of the church's authority was later explicitly confirmed many times, even as regards the specific case of the dogma of the Trinity (see chapter 6).

82. See A VI, 1, 554. Secular controversies fall into the category of practical controversies for which, according to Leibniz, absolute infallibility is not required, as a practical infallibility is sufficient. For the idea of a logic of probability contained in this part of the *Commentatiuncula*, see Kabitz, *Die Philosophie des jungen Leibniz*, 25–31. Cf. also Wiedeburg, *Der junge Leibniz*, 216–222.

83. See A VI, 1, 554: "In religious controversies when it is a question of the foundation of faith, it is necessary to have some infallible judge, i.e. either some man provided with the gift of infallibility by GOD, according to the supporters of the Papacy; or, with the Evangelicals, the text taken *in terminis*, to which nothing is added and nothing is taken away."

84. A VI, 1, 499.

85. If, even in the *Commentatiuncula*, Leibniz's position cannot be totally reduced to the solution of the Textuals, even less is it to be identified with a rationalist position, as is maintained by Kabitz, *Die Philosophie des jungen Leibniz*, 116–119. The fact that our limited reason is able to provide reasons for believing in the mysteries, i.e., it is able to establish that the mysteries *can* be believed since they do not entail any proven contradiction, does not change the fact of their *being believed*, i.e., the fact that these are 'believed' truths, not 'seen' or 'demonstrated' ones.

86. This is the last of a group of four texts that can be connected to the discussions between Leibniz and Boineburg on the question of the Eucharist, collected in the *Akademie Ausgabe* under the title *Demonstratio Possibilitatis Mysteriorum Eucharistiae*. The other three texts probably date from 1668. *De Demonstratione Possibilitatis Mysteriorum Eucharistiae* must surely be related to Leibniz's first letter to Arnauld (early November 1671) in which the theses presented in the fragment regarding the mystery of the Eucharist reappear almost word for word (see A II, 1, 175–176).

87. In this connection Leibniz's intention is to show that the doctrine of the real presence upheld by the Confession of Augsburg and the doctrine of transubstantiation as held by the Catholic Church do not, in the final analysis, differ significantly from one another. The differences regard merely secondary matters (such as the duration of the real presence or transubstantiation and the Eucharistic worship; see A VI, 1, 516).

88. A VI, 1, 515.

89. GP IV, 425.

90. *Theodicy,* "Preliminary Discourse," § 5 (GP VI, 52).

91. A VI, 1, 515.

92. *Theodicy,* "Preliminary Discourse," § 28 (GP VI, 67).

93. This case clearly shows that, in Leibniz, the expression "truths superior to reason" always implies that we are dealing with human reason.

94. A VI, 1, 515.

95. See § 33 (A VI, 1, 552): "Reason can determine nothing certain, as is the case in matters of fact."

96. See *Commentatiuncula,* § 33.

97. A VI, 1, 515.

98. See *De Usu et Necessitate Demonstrationum Immortalitatis Animae* (A II, 1, 114). This text, included with the letter sent by Leibniz to Duke Johann Friedrich on 21 May 1671, and *De Demonstratione Possibilitatis Mysteriorum Eucharistiae* date from the same period. See also Leibniz to Johann Friedrich (second half of October 1671); A II, 1, 163.

99. A VI, 1, 515.
100. Ibid.
101. Ibid.

Chapter 5. The Conformity of Faith with Reason

1. See chapter 1, note 3.

2. See A VI, 1, 495: "*Demonstratio Possibilitatis Mysteriorum Fidei Christianae.*" In the letter in which Leibniz presents his plan of the *Demonstrationes Catholicae* to Duke Johann Friedrich (autumn 1679), this part is defined as "Revealed theology" (see A II, 1, 488).

3. A VI, 1, 495.

4. A VI, 4, N. 397; VE, N. 1. On the *Hofmann-Streit*, see chapter 1.

5. A VI, 4, 2214; VE, 2.

6. A VI, 4, 2215; VE, 3.

7. A VI, 4, 2213, 2215, 2217–2218; VE, 1, 3, 5.

8. A VI, 4, 2214, 2217; VE, 2, 5.

9. A VI, 4, 2213, 2215–17; VE, 1, 3–5.

10. A VI, 4, 2213; VE, 1.

11. In the long concluding passage of the *Dialogus*, Theologus himself warns against the abuses of reason in the theological sphere (see A VI, 4, 2218–2219; VE, 6). In a writing entitled *Specimen Demonstrationum Catholicarum seu Apologia Fidei ex Ratione* (1685*), Leibniz maintains the legitimacy and necessity of using reason to defend faith against the attacks carried out by a perverse use of the very same reason (see A VI, 4, 2324; VE, 1101–1102).

12. See *Dialogus* (A VI, 4, 2215, 2217; VE, 3, 5). See also *Examen Religionis Christianae* (A VI, 4, 2362; VE, 2416–17).

13. To the statement by Theologus that, if it is true that human principles cannot prove anything certain in the divine sphere, then it is also not possible to prove rationally the existence of God (see A VI, 4, 2215; VE, 3), Misosophus replies that even the proof of the existence of God belongs to the sphere of revelation (see A VI, 4, 2215; VE, 3). Theologus's reply is that even revelation requires rational instruments (A VI, 4, 2215; VE, 3): "But I said to you that revelations and miracles should be examined by reason."

14. See A VI, 4, 2213–2214; VE, 2. See also an observation by Leibniz of October 1676 (A VI, 3, 367): "The truth of the Christian religion must not be proved by miracles, but by the excellence and sanctity of the doctrine itself as promulgated by Christ."

15. In the *Examen Religionis Christianae*, Leibniz emphasizes the role played by the motives of credibility as a safeguard against superstition and credulity (A VI, 4, 2361–2362; VE, 2416): "Further, revelation must be marked by some traits (which are commonly called motives of credibility) from which it is clear that what is contained in it and is shown to us is the will of God and not the illusion of an evil spirit or our perverse interpretation; . . . this requires caution, lest reverence degenerate into superstition and faith be given to some old wives' tales." See also Leibniz to Ernst von Hessen-Rheinfels, 3 November*, 1682 (A II, 1, 532): "One believes nothing either in religion or anything else, except by true or false reasons that lead us to it; *it is necessary that there be motives of credibility* [*necessaria sunt motiva credibilitatis*]"; *Annotatiunculae Praeparatoriae*

ad Opuscula Apologetica, 1685* (A VI, 4, 2298; VE, 1741): "There would be no obligation of believing unless God himself, speaking through reason in us, supplied the signs by which the word of God is discerned from the word of the impostor."

16. *De Deo Trino*; A VI, 4, 2291; VE, 661. In different terms, the same idea is presented to Ernst von Hessen-Rheinfels in a letter of early March 1684 (A II, 1, 539): "I can assure you that the doubts of philosophy of which I spoke in my previous letter have nothing contrary to the Mysteries of Christianity, such as the Trinity, the Incarnation, the Eucharist, and the resurrection of the bodies. I consider these things possible, and since God has revealed them I hold them to be true." That is to say: not the truth (depending on revelation) but the noncontradictoriness of the dogmas can be proved by reason. See also *De Usu et Necessitate Demonstrationum Immortalitatis Animae*; A II, 1, 114.

17. See *Dialogus*, A VI, 4, 2215; VE, 3: "Yet our religion would be poor if arguments were lacking, nor would it be any better than Islam or paganism."

18. See A VI, 4, 2214; VE, 2: "M[isosophus]. Once having admitted the analysis of faith by reason, every future faith will be human, not divine. T[heologus]. Very serious authors who wrote about the analysis of faith met this difficulty excellently. For the human analysis of faith as regards the motives of credibility, which is done in history and in reason by examining and confirming histories, is one thing; quite another thing is the divine analysis of faith, which is made in the operation of the Holy Spirit working in our hearts." See also *Examen Religionis Christianae* (A VI, 4, 2362; VE, 2416): "Meanwhile, beyond human reasons for faith or motives of credibility a certain internal operation of the Holy Spirit is required which, being called divine faith, as such works [efficit] and strengthens the soul in the truth."

19. See A VI, 4, 2214; VE, 2: "The human analysis of faith as regards the motives of credibility . . . is done in history and in reason by examining and confirming histories"; *Examen Religionis Christianae*, A VI, 4, 2362; VE, 2416: "Accordingly, it is necessary that right reason as the natural interpreter of God can judge of the authority of the other interpreters of God, before they are admitted; where, in truth, they once made faith, so to speak, to its legitimate person, now reason itself must pay obeisance to faith. This can be illustrated by the example of the governor, who is in the name of a prince in a province or garrison; he is not given to fearing a successor, nor admits him except after he has carefully inspected the papers of his mandate, lest in such guise an enemy should creep in; where in truth once he knew the will of the lord, now he submits himself and his whole garrison without dispute." As we have seen with regard to the *Commentatiuncula* and as clearly appears from the passage of the *Examen Religionis Christianae* just quoted, this first task takes place prior to any analysis of the content of the revelation. Once the 'credentials' of the revelation have been preliminarily verified by rational instruments, human reason must give way to it, recognizing its own limitations. An example similar to the one proposed in the *Examen Religionis Christianae* is to be found in the *Theodicy*, "Preliminary Discourse," § 29 (GP VI, 67). As regards the preliminary need for philological, linguistic, and historical studies to establish "the authority of the sacred text," see also *De Schismate*, second half of 1683 (A IV, 3, 235).

20. See *Dialogus*, A VI, 4, 2217; VE, 5 and *De Deo Trino*, A VI, 4, 2291; VE, 661. In particular, on the role of defense entrusted to reason, see also A VI, 4, 2213, 2215; VE, 1, 3.

21. A VI, 4, 2215; VE, 3.

22. A VI, 4, 2215, 2217; VE, 3, 5.

23. A VI, 4, 2216; VE, 4.

24. See A VI, 4, 2215; VE, 3. See also *Reunion der Kirchen*, end of 1683; A IV, 3, 283.

25. This is the objection implied by Misosophus's statement (A VI, 4, 2216; VE, 4): "I believed that *no word was impossible for God*, and that therefore contradictory things were not impossible for God."

26. A VI, 4, 2216; VE, 4.

27. Ibid.

28. A VI, 4, 2216–2217; VE, 4.

29. See, for example, *Reunion der Kirchen*, end of 1683 (A IV, 3, 282–283), and *Conferentia ad Apologiam Catholicae Veritatis*, autumn 1685* (A VI, 4, 2343; VE, 14).

30. See *De Non Violando Principio Contradictionis in Divinis contra Honoratum Fabri* (A VI, 4, 2341; VE, 1832): "This principle must be applied wherever [one is dealing with] truth and falsehood." In a note commenting on the *Conversations chrétiennes* of Malebranche, composed around 1678, Leibniz criticizes the Cartesian doctrine of evidence, reproposing instead as a more certain criterion of truth the principle of noncontradiction (A II, 1, 443–444): "Descartes supposes: that a clear and distinct knowledge is the mark of truth and that we must admit nothing except what is clearly and distinctly known. . . . I reply *first of all* that clear and distinct knowledge is a matter to be approached with prudence, and that one has to have some signs of it. . . . In a word, I do not know of any other propositions that are clearly and distinctly known except those whose contrary contains a contradiction, or *is reduced* to propositions containing a contradiction. And this *reduction* must be made by an incontestable chain of reasoning, that is to say, it must be demonstrated by way of contradictories. . . . Descartes' principle that whatever I clearly and distinctly perceive is true is not very useful when one does not know the mark of what is truly clear and distinct, but mine, which is the one used by everyone, never fails: that is to say, that everything that contains a contradiction is false, and that everything that is contradictory to what is false, is true." See also *Specimen Demonstrationum Catholicarum seu Apologia Fidei ex Ratione*, 1685* (A VI, 4, 2327; VE, 1104).

31. The occasion arises from the discussion of the theory of *virtualitates* (*De Non Violando Principio Contradictionis in Divinis contra Honoratum Fabri*; A VI, 4, 2340; VE, 1831): "They want such virtualities to be the divine nature and the person of the word [personam verbi (that is, the second person of the Trinity)], which although in reality [realiter] they are the same identical thing, yet likewise are in relation to contradictory predicates as if they were really distinguished. Some people want these to be found in created things." Against this second statement, the Jesuit father Honoratus Fabri speaks out: virtual distinctions cannot be allowed in the natural sphere as they are contrary to the principle of noncontradiction, without which no knowledge would be possible. The supernatural sphere is different: here, one must accept on faith many things that are greater than our capacity for understanding (see A VI, 4, 2340–2341; VE, 1831–1832; Fabri's position is picked up and criticized in the *Nouveaux Essais*, book IV, chap. XVIII, § 9; A VI, 6, 498). Fabri's reasoning implies the equivalence between "against reason" and "above reason," which is a direct consequence of the negation of the absolute validity of the principle of noncontradiction. Now, Leibniz points out, if one abolishes the distinction between 'above' and 'against' reason, the way is made clear for every absurdity that would claim to be revealed. In other words,

there is no longer any possibility of discerning true from false in the religious sphere: to cite the two most striking examples, it becomes impossible to demonstrate the existence of God, or to defend the dogma of the Trinity (see A VI, 4, 2341; VE, 1832). All positions—the atheist or the theist, the Trinitarian or the Antitrinitarian—would be equally valid or, seen from the opposite standpoint, equally without foundation. "It is therefore wiser and saner to say," concludes Leibniz, "that neither in divine nor in created things can contradictory propositions be admitted." (A VI, 4, 2341; VE, 1832).

32. See *De Non Violando Principio Contradictionis in Divinis*; A VI, 4, 2341–2342; VE, 1832: "And altogether the Mystery of the Holy Trinity is to be explained thus so as to avoid a real contradiction, or indeed we will desert to the Antitrinitarians. Nay, regarding the principle of human reasoning *things that are equal to a third thing are equal to one another*; (since it is founded on the principle of non-contradiction), it is to be said altogether that it is not violated indeed even in divine matters, otherwise in every haughty argumentation anything could be asserted about God with impunity; nor will syllogisms be made in Theological matters, nor will modes and figures [of the syllogism] belong there. Therefore we must beware lest by asserting such things we confirm a heresy, and altogether we must explain the mystery of the Trinity in such a way that such stumbling blocks are avoided." See also *De Trinitate* (A VI, 4, N. 416; VE, N. 75).

33. *Circa Geometrica Generalia*, 1678–1680* (in Mugnai, *Leibniz' Theory of Relations*, 139–147); *De Deo Trino*, 1680–1684* (A VI, 4, N. 404; VE, N. 148); *Notationes Generales*, summer 1683–beginning 1685* (A VI, 4, N. 131; VE, N. 58); *De Trinitate*, autumn 1685* (A VI, 4, N. 416; VE, N. 75); *Examen Religionis Christianae* (*Systema Theologicum*), April–October 1686* (A VI, 4, N. 420; VE, N. 512); *De Lingua Philosophica*, end 1687–end 1688* (A VI, 4, N. 186; VE, N. 97).

34. See *Notationes Generales* (A VI, 4, 552; VE, 185): "*The Father is God, the son is God, the Holy Spirit is God; and the father is neither the son nor the Holy Spirit, and the Son is neither the father nor the Holy Spirit, and the Holy Spirit is neither the father nor the son*, (that is, of these three none is identical to another of them) and yet they will not be three, but still one."

35. See ibid.: "If *B* is *A*, and *C* is *A*, yet *B* and *C* are the same, then it is said that there is only *One A*; if in truth *B* and *C* are not identical, there is a *plurality of As*. Hence it is clear that the definition of One and many presupposes the definition of 'same' and 'different' as more simple [concepts]. If *B* is *A* and *C* is *A*, and *B*, *C* are not the same, there are said to be *two As*. If, besides, it is added that *D* is *A*, and none of these *B*, *C*, *D* is identical to another of them, it will be said that there are three *As*, and so forth. The symbol attributed to Saint Athanasius seems to be in conflict with this definition . . . clearly, if God is taken in the same sense, when it is said *the father is God*, etc., as when it is said: *God is One*, then, at any rate, either this implies a manifest contradiction or the concept men have of one and many is changed, which is not to explain the mystery, but to talk nonsense."

36. See *Examen Religionis Christianae* (A VI, 4, 2364–2365; VE, 2418): "Moreover, the Sacred Monuments of the Christians teach that the most high God (who by reason itself is established to be only one in number) is nonetheless triune in persons. . . . But this is to be received in such a way that every suspicion of Tritheism is avoided. Therefore when it is said, *the Father is God, the Son is God, the Holy Spirit is God*, and these three are different from one another (so that the Father is not the Son or the Holy Spirit, nor is the Son the Holy Spirit or the Father, nor is the Holy Spirit the Father or the Son),

this is to be understood in such a way that nonetheless there are not three gods, but only one, albeit triune in persons. Indeed, the Antitrinitarians say that this is contradictory, and the plural number means nothing else than that three different things, each of whom is God, are said to be three gods, nor can several different things in number be one in number."

37. *Notationes Generales,* A VI, 4, 552; VE, 185 (see note 35); *De Deo Trino,* A VI, 4, 2291–2292; VE, 661 (see note 47) and *Circa Geometrica Generalia,* 147: "If B is A, and C is A, and B is not C, nor is C B, it will be said that there are *two* As. But if B is A, and C is A and D is A; and B is not C nor D, and C is also not B nor D, and D is neither B nor C, it will be said that there are *three* As. And so on. And generally when there is not only one A, they are said to be *many*. And this is the origin of *Numbers;* and this very expression is observed in Athanasius' symbol, although there its use seems to contradict this definition."

38. *Circa Geometrica Generalia,* 147.

39. Cf. Muller, *Dictionary of Latin and Greek Theological Terms,* 106 and Ratschow, *Lutherische Dogmatik zwischen Reformation und Aufklärung,* part II, 59–75, 82–113. One of the main sources from which Leibniz draws this distinction seems to be two theological works by Johann Heinrich Alsted (*Distinctiones per Universam Theologiam Sumptae; Quaestiones Theologicae Breviter Propositae et Expositae*) in which the distinction between God taken absolutely or essentially or ousiōdōs and God taken relatively or personally or hypostatikōs appears several times applied to various cases and in diverse contexts (cf. *Distinctiones,* § 1, § 3, § 16, § 20, § 22, § 30, § 32, § 61, § 62, § 63, § 66, § 67, § 69, § 79, § 84, § 86, § 93; *Quaestiones,* § 5, § 109, § 118, § 121, § 126). Almost all these passages are underlined by Leibniz in his copy of the two works (cf. Antognazza and Hotson, *Alsted and Leibniz on God, the Magistrate and the Millennium*).

40. On reduplicative propositions and Leibniz's use of reduplicative operators (first of all *quatenus*) see Mugnai, *Leibniz' Theory of Relations,* 104–110. Cf. also Angelelli, "On Identity and Interchangeability in Leibniz and Frege," 94–100; Mugnai, *Astrazione e realtà,* 80–86; Burkhardt, *Logik und Semiotik in der Philosophie von Leibniz,* 228ff.

41. See *Notationes Generales* (A VI, 4, 552–553; VE, 185): "It should therefore be known that when we say: *There is only one God,* we mean God taken absolutely, or, as is commonly said, essentially, of whom there are three persons, in one essence in number; when indeed we say *The Father is God, the Son is God,* etc., we do not mean God taken absolutely, containing all persons or triune in persons, nor even can it be said that the father or the son is triune in persons, but we mean God taken relatively or, as they say, personally, or one or another person of the Godhead." In a passage of the *Examen Religionis Christianae,* later replaced, Leibniz writes (A VI, 4, 2364; VE, 2418): "It is necessary, for the sake of avoiding contradiction, that this word God be taken with a somewhat variable meaning, and understood a little differently when we say *The Father is God or the son is God* from when we say *There is only one God,* for the father cannot be said thus to be one in number, as simultaneously to be triune in persons, or that three persons, so to speak, constitute him; for it would be absurd and unheard of in the Church to say that in the father there is the father, son and Holy Spirit, or that the father is constituted by the father, son and Holy Spirit. Therefore, in the former expression, by the word *God* we mean a person of the Godhead, and in the

latter that absolute substance which is only one in number, but which contains [complectitur] three persons of the Godhead." The final version, much more concise, goes (A VI, 4, 2365; VE, 2418–2419): "But these [the Antitrinitarians] ought to think that the Church does not want the Father, for example, or the Son to be triune in persons, but to be one person of the Godhead. Therefore, though the persons are multiplied, God, who is triune in persons, is not multiplied, nor therefore are there three gods on account of there being three persons."

42. See *Notationes Generales* (A VI, 4, 552; VE, 185).

43. Ibid.: "If *A* is *B* and *B* is *A*, then *A* and *B* are said to be *identical*. That is, *A* and *B* are the *same thing*, if one can always be substituted for the other (except for those cases in which we are not speaking of the thing in itself but of the way of conceiving it, in which they differ. Thus *Peter* and *The Apostle who denied Christ* are the same, and one term can take the place of the other; except when I consider this very way of conceiving, which some call reflexive, as for example, when I say *Peter insofar as he was the Apostle who denied Christ, just so far he sinned,* I cannot substitute *Peter* in each case, viz., I cannot say *Peter insofar as he was Peter sinned*)." This text, like the two cited in the following note, are used by Mugnai, *Leibniz' Theory of Relations,* 108–109, to illustrate one of the two uses made by Leibniz of reduplicative operators (in particular quatenus), i.e., in the determination of "those particular contexts which violate the principle of substitutivity *salva veritate* . . . Leibniz recognizes that there are limits to the application of the principle of substitutivity, and identifies them in those contexts where a given property is predicated of a subject according to a particular mode of consideration (*modus considerandi*)."

44. *Specimina Calculi Rationalis*, April–October 1686* (A VI, 4, 810; VE, 1935): "*A* ∞ *B* means *A* and *B* are *the same*, that is, they can be substituted for one another everywhere. (Unless it is prohibited, which occurs in them when some term is asserted to be considered in a certain respect, as, for example, although a three-sided figure [trilaterum] and a triangle [triangulum] are the same thing, yet if you say *a triangle as such has 180 degrees,* the term three-sided figure cannot be substituted for it. There is, in this sentence, something material.)" See also *Principium Scientiae Humanae,* winter 1685–1686* (A VI, 4, 672; VE, 1003–1004): "Moreover, reduplicative propositions are to be excepted; in them we try to speak about some term in such a strict fashion that we cannot wish to substitute it. For they are reflexive and behave with respect to thoughts as material propositions do with respect to words." Cf. Mugnai, *Leibniz' Theory of Relations,* 108–109.

45. A VI, 4, 2346; VE, 274. The distinction between God taken absolutely or essentially and God taken relatively or personally as a way of rejecting the charge that the dogma of the Trinity is contradictory, can be found not only in the texts cited but also in the following writings: *Remarques sur le livre d'un Antitrinitaire Anglois* (1693*), 547; *Sceleton Demonstrationis* (26 January (5 February) 1695), A I, 11, 234; *Nouveaux Essais,* book IV, chap. 18, § 1 (A VI, 6, 498); *Vernünfftige Religion* (1706*), GRUA, 70; *Ad Christophori Stegmanni Metaphysicam Unitariorum* (1708*), 184; *Theodicy,* "Preliminary Discourse," § 22 (GP VI, 63–64).

46. See chapter 2.

47. See *De Deo Trino,* A VI, 4, 2291–2292; VE, 661: "*There are three persons of the Divinity, of whom there is one essence in number.* We do not demonstrate this Mystery of faith by reason, but we only illustrate it and defend it against objections. Now, the

most powerful of the objections is this: if three [entities] are different from one another, and any one of them is God, it follows that there are three Gods. For if the father is God, and the son is God, and the Holy Spirit is God, and the father is not the son, nor the Holy Spirit; and the Son is not the father or the Holy Spirit, and lastly the Holy Spirit is not the father or the son; either it will have to be said that there are three gods or that we do not know what one and many mean, and therefore in just such a manner it may even be denied that father, son and grandson are three men; or, the reason will have to be adduced as to why we call these three men, and deny that those are three gods. We shall reply, although the father is not the son, yet the father is he who is [est is qui est] the son, namely, the one God in number. This cannot be said of two men, father and son, and this is the real reason for the difference."

48. A VI, 4, 889; VE, 360. The reference to Johannes Raue's doctrine of the copula is explicit in the passage immediately prior to the one cited (see A VI, 4, 889; VE, 359).

49. A VI, 4, 2346; VE, 274. The explanation given in the *Notationes Generales* (A VI, 4, 553; VE, 186) is less clear, although it can be brought back to the one expounded above: "In the same way the Holy Trinity is not in conflict with this principle that things which are identical to a third thing are identical to each other, for when the father and son are said to be the same God, there *God* does not mean either the triune God, nor a person of the Godhead, but the same or One God is said to partake of the numerically same divine essence [ejusdem numero divinae essentiae]."

50. See one of the marginal notes to Temmik, *Philosophia Vera Theologiae et Medicinae Ministra* (in Mugnai, *Leibniz' Theory of Relations*, 163): "In divine matters there is one individual in many which is not in the creatures."

51. See *Remarques sur le livre d'un Antitrinitaire Anglois*, 547: "It is also necessary to say that the three persons are not parts of the single absolute divine substance"; *De Deo Trino*, A VI, 4, 2293; VE, 662: "Those who conceive the persons of the Holy Trinity as individuals of the same species and the common Essence as a universal commit a most serious mistake."

52. Or, alternatively, *The Son is God; The Holy Spirit is God.*

53. See *De Trinitate*, A VI, 4, 2346; VE, 274: "Therefore those statements are rightly to be explained as not entailing any manifest contradiction, yet both statements are appropriate, since there is no reason why we should say one is more appropriate than the other, for in human affairs there is no example of this way of speaking, which would allow us to reason about the property on the basis of use." See also *Origo Animarum et Mentium* (A VI, 4, 1461; VE, 293): "There is no contradiction in these matters, because men do not sufficiently consider what is identity and diversity [idem et diversum]."

54. See *Dialogus inter Theologum et Misosophum* (A VI, 4, 2218; VE, 5–6). One cannot help but think of Leibniz's reading of Bayle's work (cf., for example, *Theodicy*, "Preface"; GP VI, 39: "M. Bayle wants to make reason be silent, after having made it talk too much"). See also Leibniz to Ernst von Hessen-Rheinfels, 3 November* 1682 (A II, 1, 532): "To wish to renounce reason in religion, is in my opinion an almost certain sign either of an obstinacy approaching enthusiasm, or, what is worse, of hypocrisy."

55. See *Dialogus inter Theologum et Misosophum* (A VI, 4, 2218; VE, 6).

56. See *Specimen Demonstrationum Catholicarum seu Apologia Fidei ex Ratione* (A VI, 4, 2323–24; VE, 1101). It should be noted that this is an inverse procedure with respect to that adopted in the *Theodicy*: there the conformity between faith and reason is deduced from a consideration of the common derivation both of revelation and of

reason from the one God (cf. "Preliminary Discourse," §§ 29, 39, 61); here the common derivation both of the order of nature and of the order of grace from the one God is inferred by observing the conformity between faith and reason.

Chapter 6. Sola Scriptura? *The Interpretation of the Scriptures and the Authority of Tradition*

1. It should be pointed out that the principle of *scripture alone* does not mean that Protestants deny the usefulness of the tradition as regards in particular the interpretation of difficult passages or decisions regarding matters not explicitly defined in the biblical text. Leibniz himself makes this clear in writing to Ernst von Hessen-Rheinfels in August 1683 (A I, 3, 319): "The authority of the ancient Church is without doubt of great weight in matters which the Holy Scripture has not defined in clear terms. The Protestants themselves often make use of the Fathers not only against the Socinians but even against themselves, and I remark that the Calvinists refer to the old times, when they argue against the Lutherans regarding Ubiquity and the Communication of the traits or properties of the natures [of Christ]."

2. Van Walenburch, *Tractatus Generales de Controversiis Fidei*, first treatise, 2. See chapter 4.

3. See A I, 8, 163–164. In his letter of reply (1/11 October 1692; A I, 8, 172) Leibniz defends the Protestants, vindicating the refinement of their theology and noting that the principle of faith advanced by Bossuet ("Yesterday one believed so: therefore even today one has to believe the same") referred not to the entire ecclesiastical tradition but to the latest opinion, with the consequent danger of a canonization of the dominant abuses.

4. See *De Scriptura, Ecclesia, Trinitate*, 1680–1684* (A VI, 4, 2288–2289; VE, 433): "I am afraid that we cannot satisfactorily evince the Holy Trinity from scriptures, without invoking the tradition, yet it is given much more clearly by joining Scripture with tradition. It is nonetheless certain that the Holy Scripture is much more in favor of the Trinity and is sometimes violently twisted by the Antitrinitarians"; *Positiones*, autumn 1685–February 1686* (A VI, 4, 2352; VE, 1834): "Moreover, we see that there are Dogmas that have been accepted in the Church for so many centuries, especially as regards the Trinity and the incarnation, that if they were false, they would be very dangerous, nor yet can they be evinced sufficiently from the holy books"; Leibniz to Ernst von Hessen-Rheinfels, 4/14 August 1683 (A I, 3, 318): "It is true, as V. A. remarks, together with many able Controversialists, that it is difficult to refute the Socinians with only the passages of the Holy Scripture. . . . As for the rest, the replies of the Socinians to certain passages of the Holy Scripture, especially to the beginning of the Gospel of St. John, seem to me forced"; *De Unitate Ecclesiae*, second half of 1683 (A IV, 3, 221): "Certainly, if we plainly reject the authority of the Church, almost at once the Antitrinitarians will win, for no prudent person would deny that the passages of holy scripture are liable to many exceptions." The same statement is found also in *De Romanae Ecclesiae Dogmatibus*, 1685* (VE, 438). In *Reunion der Kirchen* (end of 1683) and in *De Deo Trino*, Leibniz underlines that the Antitrinitarians do violence to the scriptures. See, respectively, A IV, 3, 282: "Truth cannot fight against truth. This principle, nonetheless, is not to be abused, nor is philosophy, with the Antitrinitarians, to be made the interpreter of Scripture, as if it were permitted to force the words of scripture in order to adapt them to natural reason"; and A VI, 4, 2292–2293; VE, 662: "The Antitrinitarians, besides that they are

compelled to force the words of the holy Scripture by a very constrained interpretation, and to stray from the old traditions of the Church, induce themselves into consequences that are barely tolerable."

5. See *De Schismate*, second half of 1683 (A IV, 3, 236–237): "Anyhow, some think the Holy Trinity is a slight question, and whether the Christ we adore is an omnipotent and eternal GOD, or a mere man surrounded with the great glory of GOD, and yet the doubting of indifferent matters must be put forth also for this very controversy, where once it derived from the canon of the Church. Certainly it is most unsafe to waver and to play the sceptic in affairs of salvation, where every danger is to be held great for the very magnitude of the thing which we put in peril." The fact that the Trinity is an article of faith necessary for salvation appears also in the argumentation presented in *Sceleton Demonstrationis* (A I, 11, N. 163; see chapter 9).

6. See *Positiones* (A VI, 4, 2352; VE, 1834): "There are Dogmas that have been accepted in the Church for so many centuries, especially regarding the Trinity and incarnation, that if they were false, they would be very dangerous." See also *De Unitate Ecclesiae*; A IV, 3, 220–221.

7. See *De Scriptura, Ecclesia, Trinitate* (A VI, 4, 2289; VE, 433): "In disputing against the Socinians and Anabaptists refuge should be taken in the traditions and authority of the Church"; *De Schismate* (A IV, 3, 236–237): "It is clear [that one must] either take refuge in the liberty of indifferent matters in religion or be brought back to the discipline of the Catholics. . . . Certainly it is most unsafe to waver and to play the sceptic in affairs of salvation, where every danger is to be held great for the very magnitude of the thing which we put in peril. Therefore, as far as I can see, one thing remains: after vain agitations of the soul, I think refuge should be sought in all matters in the haven of the Church, in which alone true tranquillity is to be had, when we are not safely indifferent, nor do we hope for security from a private examination after so many infelicitous examples in such difficulty of judging."

8. See *De Scriptura, Ecclesia, Trinitate* (A VI, 4, 2289; VE, 433); *De Unitate Ecclesiae* (A IV, 3, 222); *De Romanae Ecclesiae Dogmatibus* (VE, 439).

9. See *Positiones* (A VI, 4, 2352; VE, 1834); *De Unitate Ecclesiae* (A IV, 3, 220–221); Leibniz to Ernst von Hessen-Rheinfels (4/14 August 1683; A I, 3, 318).

10. See *Il n'y a qu'un seul Dieu*, 1678–1686* (A VI, 4, 2211–2212; VE, 435–436): "Everything that is said of the Trinity and the incarnation has to be explained in a way so as not to offend the divine perfections or the honor given to the sovereign being. . . . However, the best thing is to remain faithful to the terms that God himself has revealed. And it is for this reason that it would be a good thing if Theologians avoided all those expressions that Scripture and the perpetual tradition of the Catholic Church do not authorize." In *De Scriptura, Ecclesia, Trinitate*, the "great question" underlying the doctrine of the fundamental and nonfundamental articles is discussed in the following terms (A VI, 4, 2288; VE, 433): "Whether all things in which it is not possible to err without danger to one's salvation, are held to be defined in the Holy Scripture, is a great question: It seems to me that the first undoubted point is that the authority of the Holy books themselves is received through the tradition of the Church, hence I am afraid that we cannot satisfactorily evince the Holy Trinity from the scriptures, without resorting to the tradition, but it is accounted for much more clearly by joining Scripture with the tradition." See also the critique conducted in *De Deo Trino* against the Antitrinitarians (A VI, 4, 2292–2293; VE, 662).

11. See for example *Reunion der Kirchen*, dating back to the end of 1683 (A IV, 3, 283).

12. See *De Schismate* (A IV, 3, 245).

13. See *Specimen Demonstrationum Catholicarum seu Apologia Fidei ex Ratione*, 1685* (A VI, 4, 2323–2324; VE, 1101); *De Schismate* (A IV, 3, 245).

14. See a note in the margin of the text of *De Scriptura, Ecclesia, Trinitate* (A VI, 4, 2286–2287; VE, 431): "If I had been born in the Roman Church I would not go out of it; actually I would even believe everything which I now believe. The authority of the Pope, which greatly deters many, certainly deters me least of all, for I think that nothing can be understood to be more useful to the Church than the correct use of it." The problem of the Roman Church, Leibniz specifies in the immediately preceding lines, regards not dogmas but religious practices (*praxes*).

15. See *De Schismate* (A IV, 3, 241–242). In the *Justa Dissertatio* (winter 1671–1672; A IV, 1, N. 15), written by the young Leibniz to convince Louis XIV to abandon the project of invading Holland, undertaking instead an expedition to Egypt, the Socinians are defined as "extremi Reformatorum" (cf. A IV, 1, 372: "The Socinians are the extremists among Reformed Christians, beyond whom it is impossible to go without becoming Muslims").

16. See *Annotatiunculae Praeparatoriae ad Opuscula Apologetica*, 1685* (A VI, 4, 2298; VE, 1741); *De Schismate* (A IV, 3, 245–246).

Chapter 7. On the Triune God *and* On the Person of Christ

1. One of the innumerable examples of Leibniz's deep knowledge of the theology of the church fathers is the long series of extracts from the fathers on the subject of the human nature of Christ (LH I 9, 12 Bl. 377 and 395; unpublished).

2. A VI, 4, 2364; VE, 2418. For the difference between the Latin and Greek traditions regarding the procession of the Spirit, see chapter 1. In *De Scriptura, Ecclesia, Trinitate* (A VI, 4, 2289; VE, 433) the dogma of the Trinity is presented in the following terms: "God is certainly to be held as being one in number, nor are there three Gods, but three persons of the Godhead; therefore we do not say that the Father, the son and the Holy [Spirit] are Gods, but persons of the godhead." In *De Persona Christi* (A VI, 4, 2295; VE, 658) and in *De Deo Trino* (A VI, 4, 2291; VE, 661), respectively, the following very brief formulations are given: "in the Trinity there are three persons, one nature"; "*There are three persons of the Godhead, of which persons there is one essence in number.*"

3. On Leibniz's concept of person in the context of the theology of the Trinity, cf. Antognazza, "Leibniz e il concetto di persona nelle polemiche trinitarie inglesi," 207–237 (in particular 233–237); Antognazza and Hotson, *Alsted and Leibniz on God, the Magistrate and the Millennium*, 44–53.

4. A VI, 4, 2365; VE, 2419.

5. A VI, 1, 511.

6. See in this connection the definition of divine person given in *Sceleton Demonstrationis*, 26 January (5 February) 1695 (A I, 11, N. 163). See chapter 9.

7. *Examen Religionis Christianae* (A VI, 4, 2365; VE, 2419): "Furthermore, a person in general is a substance, single in number, and incommunicable, which in God essentially involves relation and constitutes, with its correlatives, an absolute

substance single in number." *De Scriptura, Ecclesia, Trinitate* (A VI, 4, 2289; VE, 433): "Moreover, the person of the divinity is some singular uncreated substance, subsisting per se, but which involves an essential relation, so that its existing alone implies [a contradiction]."

8. *Examen Religionis Christianae* (A VI, 4, 2365; VE, 2419).

9. See *De Deo Trino* (A VI, 4, 2291; VE, 661): "*There are three persons of the Godhead, of which persons there is one essence in number.*"

10. See A I, 11, 228, 234 and 312. For a detailed discussion of these texts see chapter 9.

11. See *Ad Christophori Stegmanni Metaphysicam Unitariorum*, 188. For this text, see chapter 12.

12. See *Persona: Paraphrase zu Valla* (A VI, 4, 2540; VE, 664): "'Person' means that quality by which one man differs from another man both in soul and in body and in external qualities, as Hector is the person of a son to Priam, the person of a father to Astyanax, the person of a husband to Andromache, the person of a brother to Paris, the person of a friend to Sarpedon, and [the person of] an enemy to Achilles. If, moreover, we believe Valla, there are in the divinity persons and indeed qualities, not substances—the father, the son and the holy spirit. But thus the false and Greek definition of quality is to be rejected, which [holds that a quality] may be absent before the corruption of the subject, for Light and Heat are never absent from the sun. These things are in Valla *bk.* 6." The text is Valla, *De Elegantia Linguae Latinae Libri Sex*, book VI, chap. 33: "In Boetium de Persona." On the similarity of this position to that held by John Wallis in the course of the Trinitarian polemics in late seventeenth-century England, see chapter 8. Around 1678, Leibniz also dwells on the justification of the plurality of persons in God given by Malebranche in the *Conversations chrétiennes* (A II, 1, 454): "God acts only for his glory; all the creatures cannot render him an honor worthy of him. . . . Now, a person cannot honor himself. Therefore there are several persons in God."

13. See *Extraits de D. Petau*, c. 1691–1695 (GRUA, 332–338).

14. Ibid., 338. On Leibniz's doctrine regarding the relationship between concretum (e.g., 'man') and abstractum philosophicum (e.g., 'humanity') in the context of Scholastic philosophy see Mugnai, *Introduzione alla filosofia di Leibniz*, 54–61.

15. Cf. *Remarques sur le livre d'un Antitrinitaire Anglois* (c. 1693), 549: "The divine persons are not the same concrete [being], under different names or relations, as would be a man who is both a poet and an orator; but they are three different respective concrete [beings], in a single absolute concrete [being]"; Leibniz to Thomas Burnett of Kemney, late January 1696 (A I, 12, 368): "I do not dare to say that the persons are substances taken absolutely, but I would also not say that they are relations and that they differ only like the King and the prophet in David; I would only say that they are different relative beings in a single absolute being."

16. This is what Leibniz writes, in the context of the theology of the Trinity, in *Ad Christophori Stegmanni Metaphysicam Unitariorum*, 188: "Relations . . . are not Things [Res] but truths. . . . I hold that relations are rather truths resulting from the constitution of things, than Beings [Entia]." Cf. also *Notationes Quaedam ad Aloysii Temmik Philosophiam*, in Mugnai, *Leibniz' Theory of Relations*, 156: "Relations . . . are not Beings [Entia] . . . but they are truths"; *Leibniz's Marginal Notes and Remarks to Temmik's Text*, in Mugnai, *Leibniz' Theory of Relations*, 161: "Relations seem to be nothing but truths." On these texts, see in particular chapter 12.

17. A VI, 4, 2365; VE, 2419. On this point see also chapter 8.

18. See *De Scriptura, Ecclesia, Trinitate,* 1680–1684* (A VI, 4, N. 403; VE, N. 112); *Origo Animarum et Mentium,* March–June 1681* (A VI, 4, N. 275; VE, N. 81); *De mundo praesenti,* spring 1684–winter 1685–1686* (A VI, 4, N. 301; VE, N. 107); *De Persona Christi,* c. 1680–1684* (A VI, 4, N. 405; VE, N. 147); *De Deo Trino,* 1680–1684* (A VI, 4, N. 404; VE, N. 148).

19. A VI, 4, 2292; VE, 661.

20. See *De persona Christi* (A VI, 4, 2295–2296; VE, 659): "The Mystery of the Trinity is very well illustrated by the analogy of the Mind regarding itself [in se reflexa]." The expression "in unitate pluralitatem" ("plurality in unity") is found in *De Scriptura, Ecclesia, Trinitate* (A VI, 4, 2289; VE, 433).

21. See *De Scriptura, Ecclesia, Trinitate* (A VI, 4, 2289; VE, 433): "In created things there is nothing that better illustrates this plurality in unity than what we experience in ourselves, when the Mind perceives itself. Wherein there is some difference between the person perceiving and the person perceived, which are nevertheless one individual."

22. A VI, 4, 1461; VE, 292–293.

23. On the fundamentum relationis cf. Mugnai, *Leibniz' Theory of Relations,* especially chaps. II and III.

24. See *De Deo Trino* (A VI, 4, 2292; VE, 661): "Nevertheless it cannot wholly and in every respect be said that one is the other, since they are correlated entities"; *Origo Animarum et Mentium* (A VI, 4, 1461; VE, 293): "[T]he two between which there is a certain relation are in a certain manner different."

25. See *De Mundo Praesenti* (A VI, 4, 1507; VE, 417).

26. Cf. a series of Leibniz's notes (dating from after 1677) on the *Confessions* of Augustine (*Metaphysica S. Augustini;* A VI, 4, 1682; VE, 1743): "He endeavors to explain the Trinity by these three: Being, power, and will. *Confessions,* book 13, chap. 11." In reality the triad is being, knowledge, and will, as Leibniz himself says correctly in a second series of notes (*De Rerum Creatione Sententiae;* A VI, 4, 1682; VE, 1744). A peculiar reinterpretation in a combinatory sense of the general analogia Trinitatis that embraces the whole of creation, finding its highest point in man and in the mind, is found by Leibniz in an exchange of letters between Q. Kuhlmann and A. Kircher (published in 1674) and in the text by Weigel, *Universi Corporis Pansophici Caput Summum,* 1673. See, respectively, *Aus und zu einem Briefwechsel Kuhlmann-Kircher,* probably dating from the winter of 1674–1675 (A VI, 3, N. 14; see in particular 207 and 212) and *Universum Corpus Pansophicum,* first half of 1683* (A VI, 4, N. 237/4; VE, N. 320/4).

27. A VI, 4, 2292; VE, 662. See also *Symbole et Antisymbole des Apostres* (composed around 1678), 538: "And those who believe there are three divine persons do not understand this word 'person' in the ordinary sense, otherwise the three divine persons would be three gods. But they understand it as one may say that there are different things in the same substance of the soul, such as power, wisdom or the inner word, and will"; *Il n'y a qu'un seul Dieu,* 1678–1686* (A VI, 4, 2211; VE, 435): "*It is certain that there is only one God.* That is why those who say that there are three divine persons do not understand, or ought not to understand, the word 'person' as one does among people, otherwise there would be three gods. Therefore they compare the three persons of a single same substance with three faculties that are found in a single soul, as are the power of acting, knowledge, and will"; *Examen Religionis*

Christianae (A VI, 4, 2365; VE, 2419): "The ancients were used to illustrating this mystery—and, as seems to me, wisely and appropriately for our understanding—by the analogy of the three chief faculties of the Mind, or requirements for action, which are power, knowledge, and will; thus power is ascribed to the Father as the source of divinity; wisdom to the son as the Word of the mind, and will or Love to the Holy Spirit. For by virtue of the divine essence or power come forth [promanant] the ideas of things or truths which wisdom embraces, and thence lastly in accordance with its perfection they become objects of the will, whence also the order of the divine persons is disclosed." On this singular rereading of the traditional doctrine that sees the distinctions among posse, scire, and velle in the Trinity, in the light of the fundamental distinction between the essence and existence of things (respectively dependent on the divine intellect and will), see chapter 13.

28. *De Deo Trino* (A VI, 4, 2292; VE, 662): "For the Father multiplies the person of the Godhead, while he thinks himself, and while he loves himself. Therefore the Son is generated from the Father, the Holy Spirit proceeds from the father and son, since the intellect presupposes the power of acting, and the will presupposes both the power of acting and the power of understanding, although, on the other hand, understanding and being understood, loving and being loved, are common to all three persons. Yet only the son is generated by essential primitive intellection, only the Holy Spirit proceeds by essential primitive love, by means of which several persons of the one God reflecting on himself arise, just as, in our mind thinking itself, all things are shared both by the mind thinking and by the mind thought (since they are one) except for a certain distinction arising from this reflection of the mind on itself; indeed, thus also in the person of the mind manifesting or thought the act of understanding [intellectio] of the person thinking is expressed, but in some derivative way."

29. See *Origo Animarum et Mentium* (A VI, 4, 1461; VE, 293): "Therefore, there is in the Mind a certain Two-ness [Binitas], but since in God the very act of understanding [intellectio] is something perpetual and subsisting, for that reason we cannot have a proper idea of the Trinity; nevertheless, we can not less precisely point out [demonstrare] the Trinity in God than the two-ness in us." "Demonstrare" should be understood here in the broad sense of "showing" or "indicating," as is proved not only by Leibniz's continually repeated conviction of the superrationality of the mystery of the Trinity but also, in this very passage, by the affirmation that "we cannot have a proper idea of the Trinity."

30. We read in a marginal note to *De Scriptura, Ecclesia, Trinitate* (A VI, 4, 2289–2290; VE, 433–434): "The Word, or that which is thought, is the image of the father, since the father perceiving the word perceives that which he himself is, namely, that Mind that thinks itself. The perception itself or Love is the Holy Spirit; in fact for God to perceive himself is the same as loving himself."

31. On relations conceived of in the abstract as "mere ideal things" cf. Mugnai, *Leibniz' Theory of Relations*.

32. See *Ad Christophori Stegmanni Metaphysicam Unitariorum,* 188: "[Stegmann] denies that persons are relations, and rightly so, for we do not say that persons are relations, but that they are constituted through relations [per relationes constitui]."

33. For example, Leibniz writes to Des Bosses in April 1714 (GP, II, 486): "The relation common to each [David and Solomon] is a merely mental thing." Cf. Mugnai, *Leibniz' Theory of Relations,* 46.

34. The marginal note to *De Scriptura, Ecclesia, Trinitate* continues as follows (A VI, 4, 2290; VE, 434): "On the other hand, [the Holy Spirit] proceeds from the Father and the son, because the Lover and the beloved are prior to love not in a temporal sense, but in the nature of the thing. The Greeks admit that the Spirit proceeds from the father through the son."

35. See *Ad Christophori Stegmanni Metaphysicam Unitariorum*, 188.

36. The letter to Des Bosses quoted above goes on (GP II, 486): "The foundation of which are the modifications of the individuals."

37. See *De Deo Trino* (A VI, 4, 2292; VE, 662): "The father is the origin of all. . . . For the Father multiplies the person of the Godhead"; *Examen Religionis Christianae* (A VI, 4, 2365; VE, 2419): "So that power is ascribed to the Father as if the source of divinity." The order of the trinitarian processions is logical and not temporal, as Leibniz himself is careful to point out in *De Scriptura, Ecclesia, Trinitate* (A VI, 4, 2290; VE, 434).

38. See *De Deo Trino* (A VI, 4, 2293; VE, 662–663): "It is no less absurd to consider the Holy Spirit only as some attribute of God, for in what manner is it sent or how are we ordered to baptize through it just as also through the Father and son. Finally, it is the height of absurdity to take the choirs of angels for the Holy Spirit, as a certain Neo-Arian did." The Neo-Arian Leibniz is talking about would seem to be William Freke, author of *A Dialogue By Way of Question and Answer, Concerning the Deity*, in which he upholds the position reported here. In his correspondence with Friedrich Simon Löffler of 1694–1695, dedicated precisely to the confutation of Freke's pamphlet, Leibniz refers several times to the Antitrinitarian as a "Neo-Arian" (see chapter 9). These considerations would lead to a postponement of the date of composition of *De Deo Trino* (which the *Akademie Ausgabe* places around 1680–1684) to at least 1693, the year in which Freke's book was published.

39. A VI, 4, 2292; VE, 661. See also later (A VI, 4, 2293; VE, 662): "For it was demonstrated above that God is one in number, and it is enough to dispel all difficulties that we keep before our eyes the *similitude* given a little before of the multiplication of persons as in a mind thinking itself." My italics.

40. See *Symbole et Antisymbole des Apostres*, 537–538: "One does not very well know what it is that person, nature and union are in these divine matters. . . . And those who believe there are three persons do not understand this word 'person' in the ordinary sense, otherwise three divine persons would be three gods"; *Il n'y a qu'un seul Dieu* (A VI, 4, 2211–2212; VE, 435): "We do not understand sufficiently well what the terms Person, Nature, and Union mean with regard to God."

41. In *Il n'y a qu'un seul Dieu* (A VI, 4, 2212; VE, 435), right after having stated that "we do not understand sufficiently well what the terms Person, Nature, and Union mean with regard to God," Leibniz adds: "It is permitted to give them a reasonable meaning, one worthy of God." See also *De Persona Christi*, 1680–1684* (A VI, 4, 2295; VE, 658): "It is clear . . . how wisely conceived are the formulas the Church uses, and I do not see how we could speak more soberly and in accordance with the meaning of the scriptures, the analogy of faith and *hypotypōsin tōn hygiainontōn logōn*, and I add also the force of expression, than by using the terms of nature and person, as has been said." In *Examen Religionis Christianae* we read (A VI, 4, 2366–2367; VE, 2420): "The words 'person' and 'nature' are quite appropriately applied."

42. *Il n'y a qu'un seul Dieu* (A VI, 4, 2212; VE, 435–436): "it would be a good thing for Theologians to stop using all those expressions that scripture and the perpetual tradition of the Catholic Church do not authorize."

43. See chapter 8.

44. Cf., for example, a brief reference to the Incarnation in a series of notes dating from 1691–1695 (GRUA, 343), as well as the extracts from the *Conversations chrétiennes* of Malebranche (A II, 1, 447): "It may even be that the main design of God in the creation is the incarnation of his son, and that the order of Nature serves only as an occasion for the order of grace, the obedience and the sacrifice of the incarnated word has pleased more than the rebellion of man has displeased. *O certainly necessary sin of Adam. . . . O happy fault that deserved to have such and so great a savior.* God acts for his glory, and the chief of his designs is that from which he draws more glory, and he takes more glory in his son than in all the rest of his works." See also ibid., 448, 451, 453, 454, Leibniz's collection of similar arguments advanced to justify the Incarnation.

45. See *Examen Religionis Christianae* (A VI, 4, 2365–66; VE, 2419–2420); *De Persona Christi* (A VI, 4, 2295; VE, 659). The issue of *De Persona Christi* is touched upon also in *Unvorgreiffliches Bedencken über eine Schrift genandt "Kurze Vorstellung"* (early 1998–early 1999*); LH I 9, 2, Bl. 106–167; LH I 9, 4, 174–315 (final draft with many corrections in Leibniz's hand); LH I 7, 5, Bl. 95–99.

46. See *De Persona Christi* (A VI, 4, 2294–2295; VE, 658): "*On the person of Christ. In Christ there is one person, but two natures, divine and human.* A little above it was shown that the Word, i.e. the Son, is the second person of the Godhead; the same son is a man, who is called the Christ. Hence the person of Christ is itself that second person of the Godhead, which took on the flesh in time. Therefore, there is one person, who is both man and God, and two natures, one divine and eternal, the other human and assumed, which subsists in the personality or subsistence [subsistentia] of the word as an arm in the subsistence of the body."

47. Cf. *De Persona Christi* (A VI, 4, 2295–2296; VE, 659): "Furthermore, just as the Mystery of the Trinity is very well illustrated by the similitude of the Mind reflecting on itself, so the Mystery of the incarnation is very well illustrated by the Union of Mind and body, as also the Holy Fathers (Justin the Martyr, Athanasius, and Augustine) recognized. For they remain two natures and make one person; perhaps it can even be said not inappropriately that the body is sustained by the subsistence [subsistentia] of the soul, or matter by the subsistence of the form, so that there is no other subsistence of a composite than that of the form, from which also some Scholastics do not seem to shrink away." See also *De Scriptura, Ecclesia, Trinitate* (A VI, 4, 2290; VE, 434): "As for the person of Christ, the union of natures cannot be better explained than is done by the Holy Fathers by the union of soul and body"; *Examen Religionis Christianae* (A VI, 4, 2366–2367; VE, 2420): "The Holy Fathers illustrate very well the mystery of the Incarnation by comparison with the union of soul and body, for just as the soul and body are one man, so God and man are one Christ. But there is this difference, that the soul takes something from the imperfections of the body, whereas the divine nature cannot suffer any imperfection. But the words 'person' and 'nature' are used quite appropriately; for just as several persons have the one nature of Godhead, so on the other hand one of the persons of the Godhead embraces more than one nature, i.e. divine and human."

48. The passage from *De Persona Christi* (A VI, 4, 2296; VE, 659) quoted in the previous note goes on as follows: "And it seems proper that the person of man and

of the separate soul are called the same. . . . Therefore the union of natures does not consist in the communication of properties [communicatio idiomatum], but in one subsistence. Therefore the Word bestows his subsistence on humanity." Cf. also GRUA, 338: "If it were imagined that he was a man before the assumption, nothing would be detracted from him by changing him with regard to nature, or detracting personality from him, but something would supervene; and so humanity or nature is not an abstractum philosophicum."

49. See A VI, 3, 370–371. This is an extract from one of Spinoza's three letters to Oldenburg, seen by Leibniz probably on the occasion of his visit to London in October 1676. The subjects discussed in these letters, of which Leibniz made a copy, are the same as those of the *Tractatus Theologico-Politicus*. Leibniz's copy, with numerous annotations, is published in A VI, 3, N. 26 (*Epistolae Tres D. B. de Spinoza ad Oldenburgium*). The three letters can also be found in Gebhardt, ed., *Spinoza Opera*, vol. IV: Epistle LXXV (December 1675–January 1676), 311–316; Epistle LXXVIII (7 February 1676), 326–329; Epistle LXXIII (November–December 1675), 306–309. The letter we are interested in here is this last one, indicated in Leibniz's copy as *Epist. 3tia* (3rd Epistle).

50. A VI, 3, 371.

51. Cf., for example, a comment by Leibniz inserted in a series of extracts from Boyle, *The Excellency of Theology compar'd with natural philosophy*, 1674, dating from December 1675–February 1676. Commenting on the sentence (A VI, 3, 227) "The way in which the soul is affected variously by the passions of the body is such a difficulty as that of any mystery in theology," Leibniz writes: "The difficulty of the union of soul and body is just as difficult as the difficulty of the incarnation, and the difficulty of action on it is just as [difficult] as that of the incarnation."

52. See chapter 4. An interesting reinterpretation by Leibniz of the classic analogy between the Incarnation and the union of soul and body in man can be found in a letter to Sophie dated 18 November 1702 (in *Die Werke von Leibniz*, ed. by Onno Klopp, vol. VIII, 397): "Mr. Comte de Fleming establishes the incarnation of God without thinking about it. For just as an active [principle] joined to an animal makes a man, so too the divinity joined to a man would make a man-god." See also GP VI, 521.

53. Also the statement contained in chapter 9 of the *Conspectus* (A VI, 1, 495) seems to go in this direction: "Why no other than the Second person of the Deity was incarnated, is given a harmonious explanation."

54. See *Il n'y a qu'un seul Dieu* (A VI, 4, 2211; VE, 435): "*It is also true that Jesus Christ was a real man;* against those who believe that divinity in him took the place of the soul."

55. See *Examen Religionis Christianae* (A VI, 4, 2366; VE, 2420): "Therefore, we learn from the divine revelation that the Word or only-begotten Son of God, when the pre-established time had come, assumed all human nature, consisting in soul and body."

56. *De Persona Christi* (A VI, 4, 2295; VE, 658). The passage continues: "From which it is clear how beautifully all things harmonize in the Catholic faith, both what is said about the Trinity and what is said about the incarnation, and how wisely conceived are the formulas the Church uses." Further on Leibniz uses the following statement as the title for one of the paragraphs of *De Persona Christi* (A VI, 4, 2295; VE, 659): "*The Mystery of incarnation is very beautiful.*"

57. *Il n'y a qu'un seul Dieu* (A VI, 4, 2211; VE, 435): "*There is a very close union between the divine nature and humanity of Jesus Christ. This union does not only*

consist in the agreement or conformity of feelings, but also in a real influence, presence and intimate operation." See also *Symbole et Antisymbole des Apostres,* 538: "Also those who speak of the divine nature of Jesus Christ understand nothing else but the fullness of the word or Divine Wisdom which lives in one who was born of Mary; this habitation [inhabitation] is called a personal union, because it is very perfect." In § 55 of the "Preliminary Discourse," Leibniz repeats that the Incarnation is the closest possible union between Creator and creature. Referring to the analogy of the union of soul and body, he seems to want to avoid using the term *influence* used in *Il n'y a qu'un seul Dieu,* as this might make one think of a "physical" union, whereas both in the case of the union of soul and body and in that of the Incarnation, the union is "metaphysical" (GP VI, 81): "Although I do not hold that the soul changes the body's laws, nor that the body changes the soul's laws, and I have introduced the pre-established Harmony to avoid this disorder, I do not fail to admit a true union between the soul and the body, which makes it a suppositum. This union is metaphysical, whereas a union of influence would be physical. But when we speak of the union of the Word of God with human nature, we must be content with a knowledge by analogy, such as the comparison of the union of the Soul with the body is capable of giving us; and we must also be content to say that the incarnation is the closest union that can exist between the Creator and the creature, without any need of going further."

58. See *Symbole et Antisymbole des Apostres,* 537–538: "One does not very well know what it is that person, nature and union are in these divine matters. . . . The difference consists only in the mode of the union of the humanity of Jesus Christ with the Word that is divine wisdom. And as no one can boast to understand the manner of this union, one disputes only about formulas"; *Il n'y a qu'un seul Dieu* (A VI, 4, 2211–2212; VE, 435–436): "We do not sufficiently understand what the terms Person, Nature, and Union mean with regard to God. . . . [T]*he safest thing is to hold on to the formulas that God himself has revealed.* And it is for this reason that it would be a good thing for Theologians to stop using expressions that scripture and the perpetual tradition of the Catholic Church do not authorize"; *Examen Religionis Christianae* (A VI, 4, 2367; VE, 2421): "Regarding the mode of the Union of Natures, many subtle questions are raised, which it would be better not to broach." In *De Scriptura, Ecclesia, Trinitate* (A VI, 4, 2290–2291; VE, 434) Leibniz writes: "It is sufficient that we believe that by the incarnation . . . the fullness of divinity dwelled in humanity by a true union."

59. See *De Persona Christi* (A VI, 4, 2295; VE, 658–659): "For those who maintain that there are two persons either make of Christ a Being by aggregation, like a society, composed of a man or God dwelling in a man, as the devil dwells in the possessed, or certainly they make two Christs or sons, one of man and the other of God, and they ought to deny either that the one Christ is a man or that Christ is God; but those who maintain there is one nature ought, on the other hand, either to deny one of the two or to say that divinity is humanity."

60. A VI, 4, 2296; VE, 659. Leibniz returns to the subject of the communicatio idiomatum in the context of the discussions in the Protestant camp in his *Tentamen Expositionis Irenicae Trium Potissimarum inter Protestantes Controversiarum* (LH I 9, 7 Bl. 355–356; September 1698) and in the defense of the *Tentamen Expositionis Irenicae* (1698–1699*) published in Schrecker, "G.-W. Leibniz: Lettres et fragments inédits," 86–89.

61. It should be pointed out that Leibniz, though he rejects the communicatio idiomatum and consequent ubiquitism, nonetheless admits the real presence. See *De Scriptura,*

Ecclesia, Trinitate (A VI, 4, 2290; VE, 434): "I do not see what advantage ubiquity brings, since Christ is not [present] in the supper in the same way in which he is everywhere, but in a peculiar way."

62. See *De Persona Christi* (A VI, 4, 2296; VE, 659): "The attributes and operations of one Nature are not to be ascribed to the other nature. Thus it is to be said, aganist the Theopaschites, that the Godhead did not suffer; against the Ubiquitists that humanity is not omnipresent; and against the Monothelites that the operation or volition of the Godhead and humanity is not single"; *De Scriptura, Ecclesia, Trinitate* (A VI, 4, 2290; VE, 434): "More appropriately it is said that the Godhead did not suffer, nor is humanity omnipresent." On the disputes that arose around the Monothelites, accused of Eutychianism by their adversaries, against whom, in their turn, the upholders of Monothelitism launched the charge of Nestorianism, cf. Leibniz to Jacques-Bénigne Bossuet, 1/11 October 1692 (A I, 8, 173–174) and Bossuet to Leibniz, 27 December 1692 (A I, 8, 216).

63. See *Examen Religionis Christianae* (A VI, 4, 2367–2368; VE, 2421): "Regarding the mode of the Union of Natures, many subtle questions are raised, which it would be better not to broach. Among other things, [there is the question] of the *communicatio idiomatum,* [namely,] whether indeed and to what extent the properties of one nature can be attributed to the other, as if this were necessary. It is sufficient that what otherwise belongs to the individual natures should be attributed rightly in the concrete instance [Sufficit concreto recte tribui]; for it is correctly said that God suffered in Christ, and the man is omniscient and omnipotent; but to attribute, in virtue of the union, omnipotence, ubiquity and (as follows with equal justification) eternity to humanity, and to ascribe nativity and passion to the divinity, is in either case to talk nonsense, as it is either *akyrologia* or a contradiction." In *De Persona Christi,* after having affirmed the contradictoriness of the attribution of what belongs to one nature to the other, Leibniz adds (A VI, 4, 2296; VE, 659): "But God was born, and a virgin gave birth to God." See also the following very brief comment by Leibniz on the thesis of D. Petau (*Theologica Dogmata*) according to which, in Christ, it is preferable to consider that it is not the *abstracta* (divinity, humanity) that are joined, but the *concreta* (God, man) (GRUA, 338): "Divine and human nature are not in fact abstracta, but concreta, i.e. Beings [*Entia*]." Leibniz seems to mean that in the Incarnation divinity and humanity are not considered as such, that is, as *abstracta,* but as *concreta (God, man).*

64. *De Persona Christi* (A VI, 4, 2296; VE, 659). Note the use of a formulation similar to that used in the *Defensio Trinitatis* in the wake of the logical doctrine of Johannes Raue. On this issue see chapter 2.

65. On the distinction between *communicatio idiomatum in abstracto* and *in concreto,* and on *praedicatio verbalis,* see Muller, *Dictionary of Latin and Greek Theological Terms,* 72–74, 153, 237. Cf. also Sparn, "Das Bekenntnis des Philosophen," 162.

66. *De Persona Christi* (A VI, 4, 2296; VE, 659–660): "Therefore the union of natures does not consist in the communicatio idiomatum, but in subsistence. And so the Word bestows its subsistence on humanity, not its essence, nor essential properties, which are indeed common also to the other persons of the Godhead." Cf. also Leibniz to Jacques-Bénigne Bossuet, 1/11 October 1692 (A I, 8, 173–174): "The personal union . . . means that the human nature does not have its own proper subsistence, as it would have naturally without that. . . . There are a thousand difficulties in philosophy regarding the commingling of God with creatures. . . . And the difficulty becomes even greater

when God joins with a creature that is united to him personally, and that has only in him its subsistence or its suppositum."

67. The passage from *De Persona Christi* (A VI, 4, 2296; VE, 660) quoted in the previous note proceeds as follows: "And certainly, if the Hypostatic union consisted in the communication of properties, also the father would be united hypostatically to the son, to whom he communicated his attributes."

68. *De Scriptura, Ecclesia, Trinitate* (A VI, 4, 2291; VE, 434): "Just as certainly neither does the soul communicate, by union with the body, its force of willing or understanding to the body itself, nor does it take from the body extension and other attributes of that kind. There are, however, some operations that cannot be understood except by the union of both."

69. See *Examen Religionis Christianae* (A VI, 4, 2366; VE, 2420): "There is this difference, that the soul takes something from the imperfections of the body, but the divine nature cannot suffer imperfection."

70. See *De Scriptura, Ecclesia, Trinitate* (A VI, 4, 2290–2291; VE, 434): "It therefore suffices that we believe that by the incarnation all perfections that fall into human nature were communicated to humanity"; *De Persona Christi* (A VI, 4, 2296; VE, 660): "All the perfections of which a creature is capable are seen to be ascribed to the Human nature of Christ, excepting those that are in contrast with his task as a redeemer"; *Examen Religionis Christianae* (A VI, 4, 2367–2368; VE, 2420–2421): "Nor is it clear why . . . the external assumption of human nature should be considered unworthy of God; [such human nature] receives perfections from the deity, but in truth does not give back imperfections to the deity. . . . Meanwhile, from union with the word, so much perfection, knowledge and power must be said to be attributed to that very humanity in itself as can befall a man insofar as he is a man."

71. Cf. in this connection chapter 30 of the *Conspectus* (A VI, 1, 497).

72. See *Examen Religionis Christianae* (A VI, 4, 2368; VE, 2421): "Which also is affirmed more carefully of the state of spoliation, except that then when the body remains passible, the suppressed glory sometimes appears only by some rays shining as through a cloud."

73. See *De Persona Christi* (A VI, 4, 2297; VE, 660).

74. See ibid. Cf. Biel, *Epitome et Collectorium ex Occamo super Quatuor Libros Sententiarum*, 14, 1. 3.

75. See *Il n'y a qu'un seul Dieu* (A VI, 4, 2211–2212; VE, 435–436); *Symbole et Antisymbole des Apostres*, 538; *De Scriptura, Ecclesia, Trinitate* (A VI, 4, 2290; VE, 434); *Examen Religionis Christianae* (A VI, 4, 2386; VE, 2437–2438).

76. See *Examen Religionis Christianae* (A VI, 4, 2385–2386; VE, 2436–2437).

77. See *De Scriptura, Ecclesia, Trinitate* (A VI, 4, 2290; VE, 434); *Examen Religionis Christianae* (A VI, 4, 2367; VE, 2420–2421); *De Unitate Ecclesiae*, second half of 1683 (A IV, 3, 221); *De Schismate*, second half of 1683 (A IV, 3, 241); Leibniz to Ernst von Hessen-Rheinfels, 4 to 14 August 1683 (A I, 3, 318) and 10 January* 1691 (A I, 6, 159).

Chapter 8. Between Tritheism and Modalism

1. A I, 12, 367.

2. The little book has thirty-five pages in all. Nye also published another series of *Considerations*, which came out in London the following year (*Considerations on the*

Explications of the Doctrine Trinity. Occasioned by four Sermons). When using the short title *Considerations* I refer to the book of 1693.

3. Both the *Extrait* and the *Remarques sur le livre d'un Antitrinitaire Anglois* are published in Antognazza, "Inediti leibniziani sulle polemiche trinitarie," 539–550.

4. *Remarques sur le livre d'un Antitrinitaire Anglois,* 546.

5. Cf. Leibniz to Thomas Burnett, end of January 1696; A I, 12, 367.

6. On English Unitarianism in the seventeenth century the following texts remain fundamental: Colligan, *The Arian Movement in England;* McLachlan, *Socinianism in Seventeenth-Century England;* Sina, *L'avvento della ragione;* Tulloch, *Rational Theology and Christian Philosophy in England in the Seventeenth Century;* Wallace, *Antitrinitarian Biography;* Wilbur, *A History of Unitarianism.* There is a useful, though not always precise, work by Bianchi, "Some Sources for a History of English Socinianism," 91–120.

7. Nye was born around 1648 and died in 1719.

8. The term *Unitarian* seems to have been introduced into England by Henry Hedworth (1626–1705), who in 1673 used it in *Controversy Ended.* On this text cf. McLachlan, *Socinianism in Seventeenth-Century England,* 309ff.

9. A second edition, corrected and enlarged, appeared in 1691.

10. Nye, *Considerations,* 3.

11. See ibid., 4. Leibniz summarizes in his *Extrait* (539): "However, the Trinity is opposed to this great article."

12. See Nye, *Considerations,* 4–7.

13. *Extrait,* 539. See Nye, *Considerations,* 5–6. The reference is to Bellarmino, *Secunda Controversia Generalis de Christo Capite Totius Ecclesiae,* book II, chap. VI, in Bellarmino, *Disputationes de Controversiis Christianae Fidei.*

14. In fact, Leibniz adds (*Extrait,* 539): "They [the Hebrews] would have understood it like the Unitarians, that is to say, in the natural sense."

15. Ibid.

16. See Nye, *Considerations,* 7–10. John Wallis (1616–1703), the famous English mathematician, called by Leibniz himself "one of the greatest Geometricians of the century" (*Remarques sur le livre d'un Antitrinitaire Anglois,* 548), took an active part in the theological debate on the question of the Trinity.

17. Published separately in London by Tho. Parhurst between 1690 and 1692, these writings were finally collected by the same publisher under the general title of Wallis, *Theological Discourses; containing VIII Letters and III Sermons Concerning the Blessed Trinity* (London, 1692).

18. See the following anonymous pamphlets by Nye: *Doctor Wallis's Letter Touching the Doctrine of the Blessed Trinity; Answer to Dr. Wallis's Three Letters Concerning the Doctrine of the Trinity; Observations on the Four Letters of Dr. John Wallis, Concerning the Trinity and the Creed of Athanasius.* The Antitrinitarian William Freke too took up his pen against Wallis, with the anonymous publication of *The Arrian's Vindication of Himself, against Dr. Wallis's Fourth Letter on the Trinity.*

19. See Nye, *Considerations,* 7–10; *Extrait,* 539–541. The Trinitarian doctrine of Sabellius (third century A.D.) upholds the absolute unity of the divine substance, of which the three persons are only 'modes' of appearing. Hence the name 'modalism.'

20. See Nye, *Considerations,* 7–8. Leibniz summarizes thus (*Extrait,* 539–540): "John Wallis, doctor of Theology at Oxford, says that those who conclude that there

are three Gods, since there are three divine persons, grossly deceive themselves, taking the person for a God, when it is only a Mode. . . . The three persons, as Mr. Wallis says, are only three relations of God toward the creatures, whose Creator, redeemer and Sanctifier he is."

21. See Nye, *An Answer to Dr. Wallis's three Letters,* 20. For a specific treatment of the debate on the concept of person in the framework of the English Trinitarian polemics, see Antognazza, "Leibniz e il concetto di persona nelle polemiche trinitarie inglesi."

22. See Wallis, *A Second Sermon Concerning the Trinity,* 55.

23. Ibid., 59–60.

24. Leibniz notes in the *Extrait,* 540: "When one says that there are three persons, this is not like saying that there are three men or three angels, but like when Cicero says, that I, one alone, can sustain three persons, or three personages: sustineo unus tres personas." As we shall see below, in the *Remarques* Leibniz criticizes the reduction of 'person' to 'personage.'

25. Wallis, *A Second Sermon Concerning the Trinity,* 60.

26. See ibid., 61. See also Wallis, *An Explication and Vindication of the Athanasian Creed,* 40–41, 62–64; Wallis, *A Fifth Letter,* 15–19; Wallis, *A Sixth Letter,* 3–6; Wallis, *A Seventh Letter,* 16 and 19; Wallis, *An Eighth Letter,* 10–11.

27. See, for example, Wallis, *An Explication and Vindication of the Athanasian Creed,* 39; Wallis, *A Fifth Letter,* 18–19; Wallis, *A Seventh Letter,* 13–15, 21; Wallis, *An Eighth Letter,* 12–13, 16; Wallis, *A Second Sermon,* 63.

28. See Wallis, *A Fifth Letter,* 17–19; Wallis, *A Second Sermon,* 56.

29. See Nye, *Considerations,* 9, and *Extrait,* 540: "The Church teaches three subsisting persons, and Mr. Wallis gives a trinity of external denominations, or accidental predications." In the lines just before this, Leibniz summarizes as follows one of Nye's strongest objections against the conception of the persons of the Trinity advanced by Wallis (*Extrait,* 540): "If the three persons, as Mr. Wallis says, are only three relations of God towards the creatures, whose Creator, redeemer, and Sanctifier he is, there is nothing to prevent there from being many other persons, since God has a thousand other relations with the creatures. Moreover, persons are eternal, but the relations with the creatures could not be prior to the creatures. And how can one say that the creation has engendered redemption from all eternity?"

30. See Nye, *Observations on the Four Letters of Dr. John Wallis,* 8: "We may call this Explication, *Dr. W's Three New Nothings.*"

31. See ibid., 10. See also Nye, *Considerations,* 8, and *Extrait,* 540.

32. See Nye, *Considerations,* 10. See also the *Extrait,* 541.

33. William Sherlock was born around 1641. He succeeded John Tillotson (1630–1694) as the dean of St. Paul's (1691); his writings aroused lively controversy. He died in 1707.

34. A second edition was published in London in 1691.

35. Published anonymously, without any indication of the place or date of issue, the *Brief Notes* probably came out in London in 1689 or 1690. It seems that Th. Firmin saw to their publication. A few weeks after Sherlock's attack in the *Vindication,* the *Brief Notes* were reprinted with a few typographical variants in pp. 10–17 of *The Acts of Great Athanasius* (London, 1690). I quote from this edition.

36. Cf., for example, ibid., 14, where the author plays on the name of Athanasius ("not S. *Athanasius,* but (drawing the S a little nearer) *Sathanasius*") and is ironic

about his counting ability ("This is not the first time in this Creed, that *Athanasius* has discover'd *He could not count*").

37. See Sherlock, *Vindication*, 45–100.

38. Ibid., 48.

39. See ibid. This division between the bodily and spiritual spheres shows signs of the strong influence of Descartes on Sherlock's doctrine. As we shall see later, Nye quickly recognizes it.

40. Ibid., 48–49.

41. See ibid., 66.

42. Ibid., 68.

43. See ibid., 67: "They are distinguished, just as Three finite, and created Minds are, by Self-consciousness . . . each Divine Person has a Self-consciousness of its own, and knows and feels itself (if I may so speak) as distinct from the other Divine Persons . . . as *James* feels himself to be *James,* and not *Peter,* nor *John;* which proves them to be distinct Persons."

44. See ibid., 66: "It is plain the Persons are perfectly distinct, for they are Three distinct and infinite Minds, and therefore Three distinct Persons; for a Person is an intelligent Being, and to say, they are Three Divine Persons, and not Three distinct infinite Minds, is both Heresie and Nonsense."

45. See ibid., 68: "As the self-consciousness of every Person to itself makes them distinct Persons, so the mutual consciousness of all Three Divine Persons to each other makes them all but One infinite God: as far as consciousness reaches, so far the unity of Spirit extends, for we know no other unity of a Mind or Spirit, but consciousness: In a created Spirit this consciousness extends only to itself, and therefore self-consciousness makes it One with itself, and divides and separates it from all other Spirits; but could this consciousness extend to other Spirits, as it does to itself, all these Spirits, which were mutually conscious to each other, as they are to themselves, though they were distinct Persons, would be essentially One: and this is that essential unity, which is between Father, Son, and Holy Ghost."

46. Ibid., 66.

47. Nye, *Considerations,* 12. The complete title of the edition Nye refers to (including, as we have seen, the *Brief Notes*) is the following: *The Acts of Great Athanasius. With Notes, By way of Illustration, On his Creed; And Observations on the Learned Vindication of the Trinity and Incarnation, by Dr. William Sherlock* ([London,] 1690). I quote from this edition. The anonymous *Observations on the Learned Vindication of the Trinity and Incarnation, by Dr. William Sherlock,* is followed by other little books directed against Sherlock's *Vindication.* Nye is once again in the vanguard with the anonymous publication of *Some thoughts upon dr. Sherlock's Vindication of the doctrin of the holy Trinity, in a letter* (London, 1690). *A Vindication of the Unitarian, Against a Late Reverend Author On the Trinity* was also published in 1690. This time the anonymous author was William Freke. The following year Pierre Allix published, again anonymously, *A Defence of the Brief History of the Unitarians, Against Dr. Sherlock's Answer in his Vindication of the Holy Trinity.*

48. See Sherlock, *Vindication,* 66, 67, 73, 84.

49. See *Observations,* 21. This is not all: according to the *Observations,* Sherlock explicitly admitted that "each of these Persons is *a* God" (ibid., 24), thus proving, by his use of the indeterminate article, that we are talking about several individuals of the

same type. The incriminating passage is to be found on p. 98 of the *Vindication:* "We must allow each Person to be a God, but each distinct Person is not a distinct God; there is but One Godhead, which can no more be distinguished than it can be divided from itself." If, therefore, Sherlock's intention was certainly not to affirm a plurality of gods, without doubt the language chosen lays itself open to attacks by his adversaries.

50. See Nye, *Considerations*, 12. Cf. *Extrait*, 540–541. The *Observations* contain, on 27–28, the same type of objection.

51. See Nye, *Considerations*, 10. After his criticism of the doctrine of the *res cogitans*, Nye does not spare his blows against the conception of the *res extensa*. It should be noted that already in 1690, in the anonymous tract *Some Thoughts upon Dr. Sherlock's Vindication*, Nye interpreted Sherlock's doctrine of the Trinity as an application of Descartes' philosophy to the theological sphere (see p. 1).

52. Leibniz provides a summary as follows in the *Extrait*, 541: "Just as the Trinity of Mr. Wallis is Ciceronian, one can say that that of Doctor Sherlock is Cartesian; for he derives it from the Cartesian principle, I think therefore I am; so that the unity of these three Divine subsisting spirits, who have thought, and each of whom is aware of his own thoughts, in his opinion consists only in the perfect knowledge that each one has also of the thoughts of the others. It will be like a Senate of three Gods, who perfectly understand one another."

53. Leibniz reports (ibid., 543): "There is too much scurrility in Dr South's book against Dr Sherlock. . . . he is wrong to speak with scorn of such an able man, and to treat him always like an ignorant person." Cf. Nye, *Considerations*, 19.

54. *Extrait*, 541.

55. Ibid.

56. Ibid.

57. I quote from the second edition (printed for Randal Taylor [London, 1693]). The first edition, published at Worcester College, Oxford, also came out in 1693. In the same year a letter is addressed to South attacking the *Animadversions* (*Letter to the Reverend Doctor South* [London]). It would seem to be an early reply to South by Sherlock himself.

58. See Nye, *Considerations*, 11, and *Extrait*, 541–542.

59. See the second chapter of the *Animadversions*.

60. See ibid., 71.

61. See ibid., 106.

62. See ibid., 97 and 107.

63. Ibid, 97.

64. See ibid., 88.

65. See Nye, *Considerations*, 10.

66. In 1695 South devoted an entire volume to this charge (*Tritheism Charged upon Dr Sherlock's New Notion of the Trinity*). We shall return to this text later.

67. South, *Animadversions*, 119; cf. also ibid., *Argument* I, 119–122.

68. See ibid., 122.

69. See ibid., *Argument* II, 122–124.

70. See ibid., the title of the eighth chapter.

71. Ibid., 242.

72. This is Nye's interpretation of the attempts at explanation that trace their origin to Peter Lombard, who in his turn was influenced by Abelard. Leibniz sums it up in the

Extrait, 541–542: "The Scholastics reformed the Platonic or Tritheistic Trinity of the Fathers in approaching the jargon of Sabellius. Peter Lombard Bishop of Paris, called the master of sentences, is the author of it. . . . It is also said that a Unitarian was the true father of it, and that Peter Lombard took his ideas from a book by Abelard on the Trinity. One may call it the Trinity of properties." See Nye, *Considerations,* 11. On pp. 23–24 Nye again insists on interpreting the doctrine of the Fathers in a Tritheistic way, against South's interpretation of it.

73. See Nye, *Considerations,* 11, and *Extrait,* 541. Nye observes that also the so-called Trinity of properties is to be referred to this "Aristotelian Trinity" (Nye, *Considerations,* 11): "To this Trinity (of *Aristotle* and the *Schools*) we must reckon the *Trinity of Properties;* which . . . is so variously explained, as to make even divers *sorts* of Trinities: yet I refer all the *Property-Trinities* to . . . *the Trinity according to Aristotle;* because they are all grounded, on the abstracted or Metaphysical and Logical Notions, of that Philosopher."

74. *Extrait,* 543. Cf. Nye, *Considerations,* 19–26, and South, *Animadversions,* 241. Leibniz's attention dwells briefly also on Nye's stinging words against submission to the ecclesiastical authorities (*Extrait,* 543): "Doctor S[ou]th on p. 240 submits to the judgment of the Church of England. . . . Mr. Milbourne in his book against the Socinians makes the same compliment to his good and Reverend Mother, the Anglican Church. This shows that they have not at all a religion of their own and that they bend as the wind blows." Cf. Nye, *Considerations,* 20. The references are, respectively, to South, *Animadversions,* 240, and to the work by the Anglican presbyter Milbourne, *Mysteries in Religion Vindicated* (see the second page of the "Epistle Dedicatory"). Nye replies to Milbourne with the text (published anonymously in London in 1692) *An Accurate Examination of the Principal Texts Usually alledged for The Divinity of our Saviour.* The polemic between Milbourne and Nye is mentioned in a letter of 4 (14) August 1697, sent by Friedrich Simon Löffler to Leibniz (see A I, 14, 397).

75. Leibniz reports (*Extrait,* 542): "[Cudworth] speaks of the Trinity of the Schools only with scorn, both as nonsense and as a Sabellian Trinity, which is only made up of names." Cf. Nye, *Considerations,* 25. On the relation between Cudworth's thought and that of Leibniz, see in particular the works of Wilson: *Leibniz's Metaphysics* (especially 160–173); "Nostalgia and Counterrevolution," 138–146.

76. See Cudworth, *The True Intellectual System,* "Preface," **2. The parts directly concerning the Trinity are to be found in chap. IV. For the question of the Trinity see in particular pp. 558–632.

77. See ibid., "Preface," **2 and 619–621.

78. See ibid., 589–590, 592, and 596–597.

79. See ibid., 599–600.

80. See ibid., 595–596.

81. See ibid., 612–613.

82. See ibid., 601–605.

83. See ibid., 575 and 577–580.

84. See ibid., 588–591 and 616–619.

85. Leibniz sums up Nye's criticism thus in the *Extrait,* 542–543: "The doctrine that Doctor Cudworth proposes in his Intellectual System is a Platonic Trinity. He admits three equally eternal persons, but by no means equal in power and dignity. There are

three eternal, infinite, necessary, spirits, of the same nature, but different with regard to their individual or numerical unity. And therein lies the sense of the Homoousios, or the consubstantiality of the Fathers . . . which otherwise it would have been necessary to use the terms tauto-ousios, or mono-ousios. So Mr. Cudworth and Mr. Sherlock have this in common, that they give us three Gods. Mr. Cudworth has tried to reply to this objection. He rejects the answers of the Fathers, who had alleged a unity of will or consent among the three persons, or who had said that there was only one divine nature in the three persons, just as there is only one specific human nature in all men. Mr. Cudworth places unity in the fact that the other two persons depend on the father, who is the source of divinity, and if this subordination did not exist, he says that it would be necessary to recognize three gods. . . . According to the Scholastics there is only one divine essence in number, and according to Dr Cudworth there are three. But it also ensues that there are three Gods, for to say that there are three essences, all powerful, infinite, eternal, and necessary, is to say that there are three gods. . . . It seems that M. Cudworth, seeing this difficulty, wants there to be only one that is all-powerful, i.e. the father, as the head of the others, but in this way, he makes the other two persons impotent, and takes from them their divinity. Thus he seems in the end to fall back, despite himself, on the doctrine of the Unitarians. And his would seem to be a mild form of Arianism." Cf. Nye, *Considerations*, 13–19.

86. Richard Hooker was born around 1554, and died in 1600. The publishing history of the eight books that make up the *Lawes* is complex. The first four books were published for the first time in 1593, the fifth in 1597, and the last three posthumously (respectively, the sixth and the eighth in 1648, the seventh in 1662). See in this connection the very well documented introductions to the various books provided by the *Folger Library Edition of The Works of Richard Hooker*.

87. Hooker, *Of The Lawes of Ecclesiasticall Politie. The fift Booke*, 106. Cf. Nye, *Considerations*, 26; *Extrait*, 544.

88. See Nye, *Considerations*, 26; *Extrait*, 544.

89. See Nye, *Considerations*, 27; *Extrait*, 544.

90. See Nye, *Considerations*, 27; *Extrait*, 544.

91. See Nye, *Considerations*, 28; *Extrait*, 544.

92. Leibniz provides a summary as follows (*Extrait*, 544): "The generation of the son is the destruction of the father, for the divine substance, in becoming engendered, ceases to be unengendered, and the son will take the place of the Father." Cf. Nye, *Considerations*, 28–29. The concluding part of the *Considerations* also presents some interesting observations about the relation between faith and reason. "The last resort of the Trinitarians," notes Leibniz in his *Extrait* (p. 544), "is to say that the Trinity is an inexplicable mystery; after having persuaded people that it is found in the Holy Scripture, they say that after that it is useless to want to go further. But it is one thing to say that a mystery is inexplicable, and it is quite another to find it contradictory, in which case it is no longer a mystery but an error." Cf. Nye, *Considerations*, 29–30. It should be remarked that Nye does not contest the legitimacy of the notion of mystery as such; rather, he contests the fact that in the case of the Trinity we are dealing not with a truth that surpasses the limits of understanding of human reason but with a contradictory notion. Since a truth can never be self-contradictory, the dogma of the Trinity must be rejected as false (see ibid., 30). But this is precisely the line of demarcation between Nye and the authors he directly criticizes. Wallis, Sherlock, and even South would, in

the end, all agree that a contradictory notion must be false. The point is that, in their opinion, the Trinity has not been shown to be self-contradictory.

93. See Thomas Burnett to Leibniz, 4/14 June 1695 (A I, 11, 507) and 29 January (8 February) 1696 (A I, 12, 407). See also A I, 10, 654–655, and A I, 13, 715.

94. See Leibniz to Thomas Smith, 14/24 October 1694 (A I, 10, 602).

95. See Thomas Smith to Leibniz, 13 (23) December 1694 (A I, 10, 654).

96. See ibid.

97. See ibid. See also what Thomas Burnett writes for Princess Electress Sophie in December 1696 (extract by Leibniz from the letter; A I, 13, 715).

98. See LBr 132 Bl. 16 (text published in A I, 12, 367, in a note to the letter of Leibniz to Thomas Burnett of Kemney dating from the end of January 1696; A I, 12, N. 248). Leibniz, toward the end of January 1696, writes to Thomas Burnett (A I, 12, 367): "I have seen some of the leaflets that these Messieurs have written against the Doctors of received Theology, among which there is a piece entitled Questions on the Deity, which they have had the audacity to distribute among the members of the past parliament, which caused it to be publicly burned." This is the text published anonymously in 1693 by Freke *A Dialogue by Way of Question and Answer Concerning the Deity . . . A Brief, but Clear Confutation of the Doctrine of the Trinity* (see chapter 9). Leibniz continues to Burnett: "I had the curiosity to examine it with attention, as well as some others all apparently written by one author." The reference would seem to be to Nye's *Considerations*. On the involvement of the bishop of Salisbury, Gilbert Burnet, in the Trinitarian polemics, see Thomas Burnett of Kemney to Leibniz, 17 (27) November 1695 (A I, 12, 164); Leibniz to Thomas Burnett, 20/30 January 1699 (GP III, 250); *Sur Gilbert Burnet. An Exposition of the Thirty Nine Articles of the Church of England. London 1699*, 1701–1706 (GRUA, 455). See also the article by Greig, "The Reasonableness of Christianity?" 631–651. As Thomas Burnett relates, another illustrious prelate of the Church of England, the bishop of Canterbury J. Tillotson (the predecessor of Sherlock as dean of St. Paul's), was involved in the Trinitarian polemics, even to the point of being accused of Socinianism (see Thomas Burnett to Leibniz, 17 [27] November 1695; A I, 12, 164 and Thomas Burnett to Leibniz, 29 January [8 February] 1696; A I, 12, 407).

99. Sherlock, *A Defence of Dr. Sherlock's Notion of a Trinity in Unity.*

100. See South, *Tritheism*, 17–23.

101. See chapter 3, note 48. Though not denying it, Le Clerc never acknowledged directly that he was the author of the *Epistolae*. Twenty years after its publication, Johann Andreas Schmidt could still write to Leibniz (22 December 1696 [1 January 1697]; A I, 13, 442): "Finally, I also want to know this, who is hidden under the name of Liberius de S. Amore," receiving from Leibniz the reply (A I, 13, 536): "Liberius a S. Amore is believed to be none other than Jean Le Clerc."

102. See South, *Tritheism*, 82–83. The reference of South is to the first and third of the *Epistolae Theologicae* (dedicated, respectively, to the hypostatic union of the two natures of Christ and to the Trinity), as well as to the imprudent statement by Sherlock that "This is a very plain and intelligible account of this great and venerable Mystery, as plain and intelligible as the Notion of One God" (*Vindication*, 68). It was Le Clerc, with his juvenile faith in the explanatory power of Cartesian reason, who, according to South, opened up the way for such statements.

103. See South, *Tritheism*, 83–85.

104. See Liberius de Sancto Amore, *Epistolae Theologicae,* 103–104. Philippus van Limborch, presenting some objections about Le Clerc's doctrine of the Trinity to Le Clerc himself in a letter of 6 October 1682, writes: "You think the persons in the divine essence are nothing but different ways of thinking, or different series of thinking, which God simultaneously fashions." In Le Clerc, *Epistolario (1679–1689),* vol. I, 62.

105. See Liberius de Sancto Amore, *Epistolae Theologicae,* 5.

106. See ibid., 7.

107. See South, *Tritheism,* 84.

108. A I, 11, 687. Several times in his correspondence with Leibniz Thomas Burnett sings the praises of Le Clerc, complaining of the unjust suspicions of Socinianism and heterodoxy, from which stemmed the opposition to him shown by some influential circles in the English world of learning. See, for example, A I, 13, 385.

109. See, for example, Leibniz to Thomas Burnett, 22 November (2 December) 1695 (A I, 12, 175). See also the letters of 11/21 June 1695 (A I, 11, 515) and 17/27 July 1696 (A I, 12, 734), also addressed to Thomas Burnett.

110. Commenting briefly on the doctrines of the Trinity of Sherlock and Wallis in a letter sent to Thomas Burnett at the end of January 1696, Leibniz writes (A I, 12, 368): "You know the Author of Liberius a S. Amore better than I do, and you know how he explains things. But perhaps he also goes too far in the other direction." Leibniz seems to be saying that Le Clerc, like Sherlock, is too inclined to introduce new terms, instead "of contenting himself with the sacred expressions" (ibid.). About a year later, in another letter to Thomas Burnett (1/11 February 1697), Leibniz again expresses his opinion on the doctrine of the Trinity set forth in the *Epistolae Theologicae* (A I, 13, 549–550): "I am sorry that there is no way of accommodating *Mr. Le Clerc* in England. Liberius de S. Amore (for this book is attributed to him) has done him wrong. I have often to deal with people who raise objections drawn from that book. . . . As for Mons. Le Clerc, although I consider him highly for his erudition, I find that he is too quick in his opinions, and that he often runs after novelty without having sufficient grounds for it."

111. See Thomas Burnett of Kemney to Leibniz, 29 January (8 February) 1696 (A I, 12, 407). Leibniz, for his part, though not dissociating himself from it, does not endorse Thomas Burnett's favorable opinion.

112. See A I, 12, 406–407. Thomas Burnett refers to the sermon given at Oxford on 28 October 1695 by Joseph Bingham. The doctrine of the Trinity expounded in it on the basis of Sherlock's terminology was judged heretical and officially condemned by the University of Oxford with a decree of 25 November 1695 (Bodleian Library, G.A. Oxon b. 111 [25]). See also *An account of the decree of the University of Oxford against some heretical tenets* (London, 1695) (Bodleian Library, G.A. Oxon b. 137 [1]).

113. A I, 12, 407: "This arrest has already produced a piece by Doctor Sherlock who calls it an examination of the decree of the university of Oxford, etc. And another has also replied to him." See, respectively, Sherlock, *A Modest Examination of the Authority and Reasons Of the Late Decree of the Vice-Chancellor of Oxford,* and Wallis, *An Answer to Dr. Sherlock's Examination of the Oxford decree.*

114. See Thomas Burnett of Kemney to Leibniz, 14 (24) June 1696 (A I, 12, 644).

115. See also Leibniz to Gerhard Meier, 20 (30) October 1693 (A I, 9, 595), and Leibniz to Thomas Burnett of Kemney, 7/17 March 1696 (A I, 12, 477). At the time of writing his *Remarques,* Leibniz seems to be unaware of the identity of South, cited both in Nye's *Considerations* and in Leibniz's text as "S—th."

116. Leibniz first read the *System* during the spring of 1689, when he was in Rome, where he had occasion to see Cudworth's work at Adrien Auzout's. A series of extracts (A VI, 4, N. 351; VE, N. 406) in which, among other things, there is some mention of pagan presentiments of the Trinity, probably dates from this period. It was only at the end of 1703 and the beginning of 1704 that Leibniz managed to obtain a copy of the *System*, through the daughter of the Cambridge Platonist, Lady Damaris Masham, with whom he corresponded until 1705. In Leibniz's copy of the *System* there is a series of underlinings, two references to Hobbes (pp. 63 and 175), and a cross-reference from p. 146 to p. 178. A second series of extracts, still unpublished (LH I 1, 4 Bl. 49–53) and datable to around 1704, seems to come from the time of this new reading of Cudworth's work.

117. See *Remarques sur le livre d'un Antitrinitaire Anglois,* 546.

118. Ibid.: "Firstly I remain in agreement with the fact that the commandment of supreme worship of a single God is the most important of all, and must be considered the most inviolable. That is why I do not believe that one should admit three absolute substances, each of which is infinite, all-powerful, eternal, and sovereignly perfect." Later on (ibid., 548) Leibniz states: "I would even dare to say that having posited three infinite Spirits, as absolute substances, there would be three Gods."

119. Ibid., 546: "It would seem also that it is at least a very dangerous thing to conceive the Verb and the Holy Spirit as intellectual substances that are inferior to the great God, and yet worthy of divine worship; for such worship must be rendered only to a single absolute, sovereign, and infinite individual substance."

120. Leibniz, writing to Thomas Burnett in February 1697, joins the chorus of criticism (A I, 13, 549–550): "Provided that one never worships anything in a true divine worship except the sovereign substance, one cannot blame our practice. Instead, the Socinians confess that they worship a simple Creature, and have ideas of God unworthy of His greatness. So the well-understood Theory and Practice of the Universal Church are incomparably better; provided that care is taken not to attach sovereign worship to the humanity of Jesus Christ, as do some misinformed people, above all among the Roman Catholics." As we have seen, already in his early work *De Incarnatione Dei seu de Unione Hypostatica* Leibniz did not miss the opportunity to charge the Socinians with idolatry, a charge they normally brought against the Trinitarians (see chapter 3).

121. The charge appears in the following works: Basset, *An Answer to the Brief History of the Unitarians* (see particularly pp. 90–91); Fullwood, *A Parallel* (see particularly chapter I).

122. See Nye, *Considerations,* 32–33; *Extrait,* 544–545.

123. *Remarques sur le livre d'un Antitrinitaire Anglois,* 546: "However, the Sabellian opinion, which considers the Father, the son and the Holy Spirit only as three names, or as three aspects [regards] of one and the same being, could not be made to agree with the passages of the Holy scripture, except by forcing them in a strange manner."

124. Ibid.

125. In Wallis's opinion, the authentic starting point of the Socinians is not the proclaimed insufficiency of scriptural sources but rather the judgment of reason, according to which the dogma of the Trinity is impossible. It is on the basis of this judgment that the various scriptural passages in favor of the Trinity are given a different interpretation. The controversy will therefore be resolved (concludes Wallis) by tackling the issue of possibility, avoiding vain disputes on the interpretation of the biblical passages (cf. Wallis, *The Doctrine of the Blessed Trinity,* 5, 8–9).

126. *Remarques sur le livre d'un Antitrinitaire Anglois,* 547.

127. See *Notationes Generales* (A VI, 4, 552–53; VE, 185–186); *De Trinitate* (A VI, 4, 2346; VE, 274); *Circa Geometrica Generalia,* 147. For a discussion of these texts and a more detailed analysis of the meaning of the distinction proposed by Leibniz, see chapter 5. As we shall see later, this distinction returns in *Sceleton Demonstrationis* (A I, 11, 234); *Nouveaux Essais,* book IV, chap. 18 (A VI, 6, 498); *Vernünfftige Religion* (GRUA, 70); *Ad Christophori Stegmanni Metaphysicam Unitariorum,* 184; *Theodicy,* "Preliminary Discourse," § 22 (GP VI, 63–64).

128. *Remarques sur le livre d'un Antitrinitaire Anglois,* 547.

129. On this point see particularly chapter 5.

130. *Remarques sur le livre d'un Antitrinitaire Anglois,* 547: "I know that there are some scholastic authors who believe that this principle of Logic and Metaphysics *quae sunt eadem uni tertio, sunt eadem inter se* [things that are identical to a third thing are identical to each other] does not apply to the Trinity. But I am not at all of their opinion, and I believe that this would mean giving the victory to the Socinians, in overturning one of the first principles of human reasoning, without which one would no longer know how to reason about anything, nor be sure of anything. This is why I was very surprised to see that some learned people among the scholastic Theologians have stated that what one asserts of the Trinity would be a formal contradiction in the creatures, for I believe that what is a contradiction in terms, is a contradiction everywhere."

131. Ibid., 547–548: "No doubt one could be content to stop there, and to say only that one recognizes and worships only one single God who is all-powerful and one in number, a sole absolute individual, in which, however, there are three substantial, and individual but relative beings, which the Holy Scripture calls father, son or Word, and Holy Spirit, and which the Church calls persons; as actually a father and a son are called persons, and one must judge equally as regards the Holy Spirit. That these three persons have this relationship among them, that the father is the principle of the other two, that the eternal production of the son is called birth in the scripture, and that of the Holy Spirit is called procession. But that their exterior actions are undivided, except for the function of incarnation, together with all that depends on it, which is peculiar to the son, and that of sanctification, which is peculiar to the Holy Spirit."

132. Ibid., 548.

133. See the first part of this chapter and Antognazza, "Leibniz e il concetto di persona," 207–237.

134. See *Symbole et Antisymbole des Apostres,* 537–538: "One does not very well know what it is that person, nature and union are in these divine matters."

135. The parallel with jurisprudence is one of Leibniz's favorites. Cf., for example, the *Commentatiuncula de Judice Controversiarum.* In *De Arte Combinatoria* (A VI, 1, 168) and in the *Nova Methodus* (A VI, 1, 294) theology is defined as almost a kind of jurisprudence.

136. See in particular chapters 2 and 4.

137. *Remarques sur le livre d'un Antitrinitaire Anglois,* 548.

138. Leibniz to Thomas Burnett, 17/27 July 1696 (A I, 12, 730). The game of morra consists in guessing the total number of fingers held up by oneself and one's opponent. See also *Symbole et Antisymbole des Apostres,* 538: "The safest thing is to stick to the expressions of the Holy Scripture, without claiming to explain them."

139. In a letter to Thomas Burnett (end of January 1696) Leibniz comes back to the question of the term *person*, specifying (A I, 12, 368): "As regards this word person, although it is not entirely as one could desire, yet since one will hardly find anything better which is authorized by the Church, one would not be able to do without it without also getting rid at the same time and for the same reason of everything that one adds to the mysteries beyond the express words of scripture." To Basnage de Beauval, who in January 1697 complains (GP III, 131): "The disputes regarding the Trinity continue among the scholars even in the Anglican church. . . . from the moment in which one wants to explain this mystery, it is impossible not to give the heretics something to seize upon, and avoid falling either into Tritheism or Sabellianism. Reason finds here such great embarrassment, that it runs the risk of succumbing under the weight of the difficulties," Leibniz replies (3/13 February 1697; GP III, 134): "As for the *disputes of the Anglican Church regarding the Trinity*, I have seen something about them. I do not believe that it is possible to refrain from all explanation, unless one wants to grant victory to the adversaries, provided one explains cautiously and exactly."

140. A I, 12, 368. In this connection a letter to Thomas Burnett of 7/17 March 1696 is significant. After having written (A I, 12, 477): "As regards the controversies on the Trinity, it seems to me that it is very difficult to reason properly, when definitions of the terms are lacking: you gentlemen, too, will be hard put to conclude anything," Leibniz does not, however, hold back from giving a concise explanation of his own, while at once hastening to add (ibid.): "But it is always better not to make any innovations in the terms on such a delicate subject, and one so little known." See also Leibniz to Thomas Burnett of Kemney, end of January 1696 (A I, 12, 368). As for the advisability of keeping the term *person*, Leibniz writes on 10/20 February 1695 to Thomas Smith (A I, 11, 274): "Nevertheless, I would keep the name of 'persons,' which is replaced by a circumlocution by Wallis, and I see you are also inclined in this direction. For even if the word at first sight leads the minds to think of something more independent, nonetheless in its origin among the Latins it has a relative meaning and for some time has been, in a sense, consecrated by the Church. In explaining and considering the mysteries, it behoves us neither to be self-effacing, nor presumptuous."

141. *Theodicy*, "Preliminary Discourse," § 5 (GP VI, 52): "The Mysteries can be *explained* so much as is necessary to believe them; but one can not *comprehend* them."

142. See Gerhard Meier to Leibniz, 1 (11) October 1693 (A I, 9, 580).

143. Leibniz to Gerhard Meier, 20 (30) October 1693 (A I, 9, 595).

144. Regarding the conditions needed for legitimately believing to be in the presence of an authentic revelation, or, in other words, regarding the different levels of the motives of credibility, see in particular chapter 4. The analysis of Frémont, "La triple vérité," 43–55, in whose opinion proof, in the case of faith, would, for Leibniz, be "null," does not seem acceptable. On the other hand, the reasons given by Cave, "A Leibnizian Account of Why Belief in the Christian Mysteries Is Justified," 463–473, to justify faith in the Christian mysteries, do not seem to go to the heart of Leibniz's reasoning.

145. See *Remarques sur le livre d'un Antitrinitaire Anglois*, 548–549.

146. Ibid., 548: "I would even dare to say that if we posit three infinite Spirits as absolute substances, there would be three Gods, despite their perfect understanding, which would make them understand everything that goes on in one another. Something more is needed for a numeric unity, otherwise God, who understands our thoughts perfectly, would be essentially united with us, so as even to constitute one and the same

individual. Moreover, it would be a union of several natures, if each person has his own, i.e. if each person has his own infinitude, his own knowledge, his own all-mightiness; and this would not be at all the union of three persons who have one and the same individual nature, despite the fact that this should be the case [according to orthodoxy]." Sherlock, in his *Vindication*, tries to forestall the objection (raised here by Leibniz) that God, who perfectly understands our thoughts, would be essentially united to us. It is not enough, maintains Sherlock, in order for there to be an essential unity between two or more minds, that one of them knows and perfectly understands the other (or the others). For there to be numerical unity a mutual consciousness, i.e., a perfect mutual knowledge and understanding, is needed (see Sherlock, *Vindication*, 75).

147. *Remarques sur le livre d'un Antitrinitaire Anglois*, 549: "I dare say that a personality like the one Cicero meant to speak of when he said: tres personas unus sustineo [I, being one, sustain three persons], does not suffice." See also Leibniz to Thomas Burnett of Kemney, end of January 1696 (A I, 12, 367–368): "I see that some people have believed that Mons. Sherlock said too much in saying that there are three substances in the Trinity, each of whom has its own thought or *self conscientiousness* and whose unity is to understand each other perfectly, and that Monsieur Wallis has not said enough in maintaining that these are only three modalities or relations."

148. *Remarques sur le livre d'un Antitrinitaire Anglois*, 549: "It is not sufficient to say that the father, the son, and the holy spirit differ by relations similar to Modes such as postures, presences, or absences. These sorts of relations ascribed to one and the same substance would never make three different persons existing at the same time. Thus I imagine that Mr. S[ou]ht [sic], whoever he may be, cannot at all have been satisfied with that."

149. See Leibniz to Friedrich Simon Löffler, 2 January 1695 (A I, 11, 123): "When *Sherlock*, a famous Theologian among the English, lately wrote about the Trinity, establishing three substances conscious of each other, to some he seemed to incline towards Tritheism. On the contrary, *Wallis*, explaining the Trinity through three relations of the same substance [per tres ejusdem substantiae relationes], seemed to others to create a confusion of persons. And this is in any case charged by the Antitrinitarians in scattered books, but in truth these statements can be reconciled, if rightly understood"; Leibniz for Friedrich Simon Löffler (*Sceleton Demonstrationis*), 26 January (5 February) 1695 (A I, 11, 234): "Lately some disputes have arisen in England between famous Theologians of the Anglican Church itself, whom therefore our neo-Arian [William Freke] affronts. To be sure, Wallis distinguished persons by means of relations [personas distinxit relationibus], and thus the Arian imputed to him that he took away diversity, nor understood otherwise than when in human matters the same one upholds the two persons of Father and Son in a different respect. Sherlock, saying that in God there are three substances conscious of themselves, seemed to the same Arian to lean toward Tritheism, and indeed he incurred the reprehension of some of his party. But it is charitable [to think] that perhaps words are stronger than in the best part they may be interpreted [as saying]. And both doctrines receive a sound meaning"; Leibniz to Thomas Smith, 10/20 February 1695 (A I, 11, 274): "A very daring little book, with the title Questions about the Deity [Freke, *A Dialogue By Way of Question and Answer, Concerning the Deity* (London, 1693)] came into my hands, from which I saw that Wallis and Sherlock are insulted by some as inclining toward opposite extremes regarding the Trinity, but I do not doubt that both actually understood the height of the matter and the chief points of

the Catholic dogma. Wallis most of all, as his critical acumen is well known to me. Nor do I hope otherwise from Sherlock; when you too write, that he is bombarded more with insults than with arguments, and some of yours praised the Man's great erudition to me." See also the letters of Leibniz to Thomas Burnett of Kemney of, respectively, the end of January 1696 (A I, 12, 368) and 7/17 March 1696 (A I, 12, 477). Writing again to Thomas Burnett on 17/27 July 1696, though continuing to admit Sherlock's merits, Leibniz expresses some reservations about the accuracy of his doctrines: "To speak just between you and me, although Mons. Sherlock is a clever man, and an eloquent one, I have judged by a piece that you sent me on his behalf [Sherlock, *The Case of the Allegiance due to Sovereign Powers*], and about which I sent you some notes [see A I, 11, N. 349], when you had not yet left Germany, that he does not always take pains to form distinct notions."

150. *Ad Christophori Stegmanni Metaphysicam Unitariorum*, 188. On this text see chapter 12.

151. *Remarques sur le livre d'un Antitrinitaire Anglois*, 549. On this point see also chapter 12.

152. Leibniz to Thomas Burnett of Kemney, end of January 1696 (A I, 12, 368). See also the following texts. Leibniz to Thomas Burnett of Kemney, 7/17 March 1696 (A I, 12, 477): "One may say that the persons of the Trinity are three Relative Beings in a single absolute substance [trois Estres Relatifs dans une seule substance absolue]." Leibniz to Thomas Burnett, 1/11 February 1697 (A I, 13, 549): "When one explains the Trinity in a proper way, and one has made its basis to consist not in three absolute beings [trois estres absolus], but in three real relations [trois relations réelles], there is nothing unreasonable about it." Leibniz to Basnage de Beauval, 3/13 February 1697 (GP III, 134): "One can boldly say that there are three relative realities in a single absolute substance [trois realités relatives dans une seule substance absolue]."

153. *Remarques sur le livre d'un Antitrinitaire Anglois*, 549.

154. Ibid.: "One must admit that there is no example in nature that corresponds sufficiently to this notion of divine persons."

155. Ibid. See also Leibniz to Thomas Burnett of Kemney, August–September* 1697; A I, 12, N. 260.

156. Ibid., 550.

157. Ibid.

158. On this text see chapter 3.

159. See *De Scriptura, Ecclesia, Trinitate* (A VI, 4, 2289; VE, 433); *De Deo Trino* (A VI, 4, 2292; VE, 661). On these texts see chapter 7.

160. See *De Conatu et Motu, Sensu et Cogitatione* (A VI, 2, 282–283): "Thinking is nothing but the sense of comparison, or more succinctly, the sense of many things simultaneously or one in many. . . . When I think immediately I think myself and something else. That is: when I think immediately I perceive [sentio]. Indeed, when I think immediately I think many things, and one in many. Whatever it is that I think, that is what I perceive: certainly I perceive myself and something else [me sentire et aliud], or diversity."

161. Udo Thiel points out the presence of the notion of a "redoublement" of the spirit in the doctrine of consciousness advanced by Ralph Cudworth: "*Duplication* . . . is included in the Nature of . . . *Consciousness*, which makes a Being to be Present with it self, Attentive to its own Actions, or Animadversive of them, to perceive it self to Do or

Suffer, and to have a *Fruition* or *Enjoyment* of it self." (Cudworth, *The True Intellectual System*, 159; see also "The Contents"). Cf. Thiel, "Cudworth and Seventeenth-Century Theories of Consciousness," 79–99 (in particular 91–92); Thiel, "Leibniz and the Concept of Apperception," 195–209 (in particular 199). In the first series of Leibniz's extracts from the *System*, dating from 1689 (cf. note 116), there is, however, no trace of Cudworth's notion of duplication.

162. See *Origo Animarum et Mentium* (A VI, 4, 1461;VE, 292–293): "The person who understands and the person who is understood are, in a certain way, certainly two; although in a certain other way they are one and the same. They are in fact one and the same by hypothesis. It is in fact supposed that the mind understands itself. They are nevertheless two for the very fact that the two between which there is a certain relation are in a certain manner different." On this point see chapter 7.

163. *Remarques sur le livre d'un Antitrinitaire Anglois*, 550. In *De Deo Trino* (A VI, 4, 2292; VE, 661), after having presented the mind that thinks itself as the example that best illustrates the mystery of the Trinity, Leibniz immediately adds: "On the one hand, what happens in the created Mind in some way, in God occurs in the most perfect manner [in Deo locum habet perfectissima ratione]."

164. To Thomas Burnett, who reported the proposal, advanced by Le Clerc, of translating the term *logos* with *ratio* (reason) (see A I, 11, 504–505), Leibniz writes on 11/21 June 1695 (A I, 11, 516): "Mr. le Clerc is right in translating logos with *Ratio* rather than *Verbum*. Also the Theologians say that they mean mental word [*verbum mentis*][;] it is true that this means the idea rather than the act or faculty of reasoning, that is to say the immediate object of thought. There would be a lot to say about all these things."

165. *Remarques sur le livre d'un Antitrinitaire Anglois*, 550.

166. Cf. note 116.

167. LH I 1, 4 Bl. 49–53. Bl. 53 refers to the parts of the *System* that directly regard the Trinity (cf. in particular Cudworth, *The True Intellectual System*, 550–632).

168. See LH I 1, 4 Bl. 53: "Proclus in instit. Theol. [*Institutio Theologica*] n. 21. From the first one there are many *henades*, from the first mind many minds, from the first soul many souls"; Cudworth, *The True Intellectual System*, 555.

169. LH I 1, 4 Bl. 53.

170. Ibid.: "But in truth both minds and souls are Monads. The true Trinity is not composed of substances, but of principles; like the created Monad from active and passive. But the active principle itself comes from three corresponding to the Trinity, for in God there is nothing passive." See also Leibniz to Morell, 4/14 May 1698 (GRUA, 126): "As all spirits are unities, one can say that God is the primitive unity, expressed by all other unities according to their capacity. His goodness moved him to act, and there are in him three primacies [primautés], power, knowledge, and will; from this results the operation or the creature, which is varied according to the different combinations of unity with zero; that is of the positive with the privative, for the privative is nothing but limits, and there are limits everywhere in the creature, as there are points everywhere in a line."

Chapter 9. The Case of Freke: On the Mathematical Method in Theology

1. Hanover, Niedersächs. Hauptstaatsarchiv, Celle Br. 16 III England Nr 60 Bl. 413; Cal. Br. 24 England Nr 39 Bl. 358. Cf. A I, 10, 17; A I, 12, 367; LBr 132 Bl.16.

2. On the distribution of the second part of the pamphlet to the members of the English Parliament and the consequent vote of condemnation of the book as an "infamous and scandalous pamphlet," see Wallace, *Antitrinitarian biography*, vol. III, 389.

3. See GP III, 111.

4. See Leibniz to Princess Electress Sophie, early March 1694 (A I, 10, 17).

5. See ibid., 18. See also Leibniz to Friedrich Simon Löffler, 7 (17) March 1694 (A I, 10, 681–682), and Freke, *A Dialogue*, 3–5.

6. See A I, 10, 18, and Freke, *A Dialogue*, 3–5, 7–8.

7. See in particular chapter 7.

8. See A I, 10, 18, and Freke, *A Dialogue*, 1 and 6; *A Brief, but Clear Confutation of the Doctrine of the Trinity*, 9–10. See also GP III, 111, and A I, 10, 682.

9. Leibniz is referring to the first part of Freke's pamphlet (pp. 1–8), organized as a series of thirty-seven questions that are answered by quoting passages from the scriptures.

10. See the second part of the pamphlet (pp. 9–16).

11. A I, 10, 19. Leibniz expresses himself even more severely two years later in a letter to Thomas Burnett of Kemney (A I, 12, 367): "I have seen a part of the loose sheets that these Gentlemen have written against the Doctors of received Theology; among others, there is a piece entitled Questions on the Deity, which someone had the temerity to distribute among the members of the past parliament, which had as a consequence that it was publicly burned. I was curious enough to examine it carefully. . . . The only merit of this piece lay in its having been burned."

12. See Friedrich Simon Löffler to Leibniz, 4 (14) January 1694 (A I, 10, N. 469).

13. See Leibniz to Friedrich Simon Löffler, 7 (17) March 1694 (A I, 10, 681–682). Leibniz's extracts have not been found.

14. Cf. A I, 10, N. 476; N. 478; N. 479; N. 486. See also Joh. Friedrich Leibniz to Leibniz, 1 (11) May 1694 (A I, 10, N. 477).

15. See Friedrich Simon Löffler to Leibniz, 12 (22) December 1694 (A I, 10, N. 489).

16. See Leibniz to Friedrich Simon Löffler, 2 January 1695 (A I, 11, 122).

17. See A I, 11, 123.

18. See Friedrich Simon Löffler to Leibniz, 16 (26) January 1695 (A I, 11, 195).

19. See A I, 11, N. 142. This outline replaces a previous sketch of the dissertation, which Leibniz also received. The first sketch, to which Leibniz's remarks contained in A I, 11, N. 161 refer, has not been found.

20. A I, 11, N. 162. Leibniz opens his remarks by observing (A I, 11, 223): "There are many things that, in my opinion, need to be pointed out with regard to your demonstration." In the letter of accompaniment he repeats (26 January [5 February] 1695; A I, 11, 222): "I am actually forced to emend the outlines of your demonstration, sometimes erasing a passage, sometimes replacing it by another." Leibniz seems to be just as dissatisfied with the first sketch sent by Löffler (A I, 11, 223): "In the sketch of the other demonstration sent to me there are many things that require consideration."

21. Löffler writes in the letter that accompanies the outline (A I, 11, 195): "Axioms are reasons by which I prove propositions, hypotheses are statements that confirm both axioms and their application to propositions, and postulates contain those statements that serve to answer the objections of the Adversaries." Leibniz replies (A,

I, 11, 223–224): "The distinction that you make between Hypotheses and Axioms is not recognized; and what you call Hypotheses you could with equal justice include among the Axioms." There follow the definitions of axiom ("universal proposition which needs no demonstration"), hypothesis ("proposition which we use in demonstrations, which indeed also needs demonstration, though we refrain from this demonstration, being content to show that, having admitted it, the rest follows"), and postulate ("A *postulate* is, properly speaking, a petition that we be allowed to do something, and thus it constitutes, in respect to real problems or constructions, what Axioms or Hypotheses are in respect to speculative theorems or demonstrations."). Leibniz also points out to his nephew that hypotheses are valid only when they are conceded by the adversary. Similar criticisms are found also in Leibniz's observations on the first sketch of the dissertation (cf. A I, 11, N. 161).

22. See A I, 11, 224. Cf. A I, 11, 223. The same type of statement is found in a later letter by Leibniz to Löffler (24 February [6 March] 1695; A I, 11, 311).

23. See A I, 11, 224. Cf. A I, 11, 223.

24. See A I, 11, 224–225. Cf. A I, 11, N. 161.

25. See A I, 11, 225.

26. Ibid.

27. Ibid. Cf. A I, 11, N. 161.

28. See A I, 11, 225–227. Cf. A I, 11, N. 161.

29. See A I, 11, 227, and A I, 11, 223.

30. See A I, 11, 227.

31. Cf. in particular the first part of Freke's pamphlet, in which the Antitrinitarian theses are supported exclusively by reference to the scriptures.

32. See Leibniz to Friedrich Simon Löffler, 2 January 1695 (A I, 11, 122).

33. A I, 11, 228: "*Def. I. God* is the most perfect substance, i.e., having all perfections. *Def.2. Spirit* is intellective immaterial substance. *Def. 3. Angel* is a complete created Spirit. *Def. 4. Several persons* in the numerically same absolute substance means several essentially relative intelligent singular substances [plures substantias singulares intelligentes essentialiter relativas]. *Def. 5. Eternity* is the necessity of existing."

34. Ibid.

35. Ibid., 229.

36. Ibid.: "*Hyp. 2. To the Father belongs the highest divinity.* On this all the Antitrinitarians agree with us."

37. See the first hypothesis (ibid.): "*Hyp. I. The Holy Scripture, such as the Protestants admit, is the word of God.* It is known that this hypothesis is granted by the adversaries; for the same Scripture that the Protestants admit is admitted also by the Antitrinitarians, with the exception of a very few texts, which they call into question, such as [the text] by John concerning the three who bear witness [I John 5:7–8]. But this is not what we are concerned about at present."

38. See the first proposition (ibid., 231): "*Prop. I. The Holy Scripture ascribes to Christ the attributes of the only one true or most high God.* These are properties of the most high God: he is eternal (by *lem.* 4.); he is the creator of all other things (by *lem.* 2.); everything is done through him, [and] this is something which cannot be understood of the creature, as an instrument of creation (by L. 3.), etc. But the Holy Scripture ascribes these and other similar things to Christ, as the texts handed down teach." Lemmas 2, 3, and 4 demonstrate the following (ibid., 230): "*Lem. 2. Only God creates all other*

things from nothing, and indeed both at the beginning and by his continuous creation to *conserve them as long as they subsist. . . . Lem. 3. A creature cannot be an instrument* *of creation. . . . Lem. 4. Only God is eternal."*

39. Ibid., 231: "*Prop. II. The Holy Scripture ascribes to Christ attributes that more* *properly and aptly are applied to the most high God, than to a creature.* Such are: to be the son of God in an excellent way, to have the character of divine hypostasis, to have been generated before all centuries, to be opposed to the angels in general and to the Gods of the underworld, etc. These things are to be shown by passages of Scripture, and simultaneously demonstrated; they are passages that can be very aptly understood about the most high God, if they are not drawn by violence in another direction. In this connection, the beginning of the Gospel of John is pertinent. For the interpretation of the sacred antiquity is to be employed to illustrate these things."

40. See ibid., 232: "*Prop. V. The ancient tradition of the true catholic church ascribes* *the most high divinity to Christ.* This is to be shown from passages of the ancients even before the Council of Nicaea and the contrary statements are to be refuted."

41. See ibid.: "*Prop. IV. Christ is to be worshiped.* This is shown from Scripture and the true catholic ancient church."

42. Ibid., 231: "*Lem. 5. According to the proper meaning of the words, only the most* *high God is said to be religiously worshipped.* This is shown from passages of Scripture, and for further illustration from passages of the Church Fathers."

43. Ibid., 232: "*Prop. III. In the passages indicating the divinity of Christ, there is no* *need of drawing back from the proper meaning of the words.* Here a reply is to be made to the flights and objections of the adversaries, by which they try to show that, if the words are taken literally, absurdities follow, and the same work will counteract the new English Arian [William Freke]." The defense strategy is implicit here.

44. The conclusion regarding the divinity of the Son is reached by the demonstration of the sixth proposition (ibid., 232): "*Prop. VI. The most high divinity is to be ascribed* *to Christ.* For the Holy Scripture, which is the word of God (by *hypoth.* I.) ascribes to him the attributes of the one most high God (by *Prop.* I.), and also those things that more properly and aptly are applied to the most high God (by *prop.* 2.), and so does the ancient catholic tradition (by *prop.* 5.) and especially adoration is attributed to him (by *prop.* 4.), which properly is to be understood only of the most high God (by *lem.* 5.). Moreover, this is a matter in which we are dealing with a danger to salvation, since we are concerned with the worship of the supreme God. Therefore, unless there is a need to do so (and here there is none), (by *prop.* 3.) one should not draw back from the proper meaning of the words of God and the sense of the true catholic Church; (by *ax.* 2.) therefore supreme divinity is to be ascribed to Christ."

45. See ibid., 233: "Just as many propositions can be clearly formed in the same way regarding the Holy Spirit and so propositions VIII. IX. X. XI. XII. XIII. XIV will proceed merely by replacing 'Christ' with 'the Holy Spirit.'"

46. Ibid., 229: "*Lem. I. God is one. Demonstration:* If there were several Gods, either they would have the same perfections, and so there would be no difference among them, and thus they would be just one God, as is understood; or they would have different perfections, and so none of them would have all perfections, i.e., would be the most perfect, which is contrary to *Def. I.*" Ibid., 233: "*Prop. XV. The Father, the Son and the* *Holy Spirit are persons different from one another.* This is to be shown both against the Sabellians and, as regards the Father and the Holy Spirit, against the Socinians." Leibniz

is referring, on the one hand, to the modalist theory of the Sabellians, and on the other to the Socinian doctrine that the Holy Spirit is only one of God's virtues.

47. Ibid., 233.

48. See the fourth definition (ibid., 228): "*Several persons* in the numerically same absolute substance means several essentially relative intelligent singular substances." See also *Examen Religionis Christianae* (A VI, 4, 2365; VE, 2419).

49. A I, 11, 234: "They are in fact three substances, indeed different from one another, but only as regards their essential relations, not in truth as regards their absolute essential attributes. Thus the demonstration of the unity of God in *lem. I.* does not deny the plurality of persons. For even if there is only one substance, having all perfections—both absolute and relative—that is, God taken absolutely, there can nevertheless be in it several persons differing in their relative perfections."

50. See Friedrich Simon Löffler to Leibniz, 20 February (2 March) 1695; A I, 11, N. 204.

51. See A I, 11, 301. The reference is to the work by Calov, *Metaphysica Divina*, 761. On the meaning of 'incommunicable' with reference to the notion of person, see chapter 7.

52. See A I, 11, 301.

53. See ibid., 301–302: "Even if, in truth, relative substance implies the same as mode of subsisting, yet the term 'substance' could offend some people."

54. Leibniz to Friedrich Simon Löffler, 24 February (6 March) 1695 (A I, 11, N. 209).

55. A I, 11, 311: "The Theological Compendia say that a person is a subsisting *hyphistamenon*, indeed they are not used to calling it only a subsisting or mode of subsisting; personal relations are rather *tropoi hyparxeōs*, than persons themselves."

56. It should be pointed out that the "definitions" at the beginning of the *Sceleton Demonstrationis* (including, among others, that of "*Several persons* in the numerically same absolute substance") are understood as explanations of terms (see A I, 11, 228).

57. Cf. in particular §§ 21–22 of the *Commentatiuncula* (A VI, 1, 550–551) and § 5 of the "Preliminary Discourse" of the *Theodicy* (GP VI, 52).

58. A I, 11, 311: "But since in divine matters these things are distinguished better by our mode of understanding than the thing itself, perhaps you could abstain from both and say: several persons in the same absolute singular substance in number are understood by means of several relative incommunicable modes of subsisting in it [per plures in ea modos subsistendi relativos incommunicabiles]. I willingly add the mention of relative and absolute, on account of the reasons which are there manifest. Moreover, in my opinion it would be more cautious to say so, than if you say that the persons [of the Trinity] are modes, making of them modal or incomplete entities, and at the same time you will also avoid formulations which may seem too concrete and still obtain the thing itself, when you express all that through which [per quid] a person is constituted." One should note the stress laid by Leibniz on the distinction between "absolute" and "relative."

59. Ibid., 312: "Therefore I write these things, so that you may give less offense to others, who are often not very aware of the true use of terms, for otherwise it can be very rightly said that one and every person is a subsisting [being] or singular substance [unam quamque personam esse subsistentem seu substantiam singularem] [.]"

60. Ibid. Leibniz himself, in the copy of the outline in his possession, corrects the definition of person and the sixteenth proposition (cf. ibid., 228 and 234).

61. Cf. also ibid., 311: "Personal relations are rather *tropoi hyparxeōs*, than persons themselves."

62. On the conception of relations as individual properties of a subject, cf. Mugnai, *Leibniz' Theory of Relations* (in particular p. 133). On the Trinitarian relations, see also chapters 7 and 12.

63. See *Ad Christophori Stegmanni Metaphysicam Unitariorum*, 188. For a comment on this text see chapter 12.

64. Friedrich Simon Löffler to Leibniz, 6 (16) March 1695 (A I, 11, 326): "Regarding those things pertaining to my dissertation at another time."

65. See Friedrich Simon Löffler to Leibniz, 4 (14) August 1697 (A I, 14, N. 240).

66. Löffler's dissertation, entitled *De Divinitate Christi ex Rom. IX, v. 5*, was published in Carpzov, *Disputationes Academicae*, no. XXVIII. Löffler limits himself to copious quotations from the church fathers (ibid., 6–44) and a detailed exegesis of Romans 9:5 (ibid., 44–96).

67. See Johann Andreas Schmidt to Leibniz, 22 December 1696 (1 January 1697); A I, 13, 442: "I have often thought about teaching our theology with a mathematical method, but in the Academies I have such a quantity of work that no leisure is left to me for meditating on these things, let alone bringing them to fulfillment."

68. Leibniz to Johann Andreas Schmidt, 29 January (8 February) 1697 (A I, 13, 535). Leibniz states, a few days later, in a letter to Thomas Burnett of Kemney (1/11 February 1697; A I, 13, 551): "An able Theologian, who has taught mathematics, lately consulted me as to whether one could write Theology using a mathematical method. I replied to him that one assuredly could, and that I myself had made some attempts in that sense, but that such a work could not be achieved, without also previously giving some Elements of Philosophy at least in part, in a mathematical order, that is to say as much as is necessary for Theology."

69. See Leibniz to Johann Andreas Schmidt, 29 January (8 February) 1697 (A I, 13, 535).

70. Leibniz to Thomas Burnett of Kemney, 1/11 February 1697 (A I, 13, 554): "I make a distinction . . . between two types of propositions. The first type can be demonstrated absolutely by a metaphysical necessity, and in an irrefutable manner; the second type can be demonstrated morally, that is, in a way that gives what is called moral certitude. . . . So, therefore, the truths and consequences in Theology are of two types; one type has a Metaphysical certitude, and the other has a moral certitude. The first type presupposes the definitions, axioms and theorems, taken from true Philosophy, and from natural Theology; the second type presupposes in part History and facts, and in part the interpretation of the texts."

71. Leibniz discusses at length in his letter to Thomas Burnett of 1/11 February 1697, the lack of an "'art of estimating the degrees of proofs, which is still not found in the Logicians, but of which only the Jurists have given some specimens which are not to be despised, and can serve as a start for establishing the science of proofs, capable of verifying the historical facts, and of giving the meaning of texts." (A I, 13, 554–555). See in particular the following passage (ibid., 555): "One often says with justice, that reasons should not be counted, but weighed; however, no one has given us this scale that ought to serve to weigh the force of the reasons. This is one of the greatest defects of our Logic, the effects of which we feel even in the most important and most serious matters of life, regarding justice, the tranquillity and good of the state, the health of mankind,

and even religion. . . . If God grants me further life and health, I will make it my main concern." Cf. also Leibniz to Johann Andreas Schmidt, 29 January (8 February) 1697 (A I, 13, 535–536). In a later letter to Thomas Burnett, Leibniz confidently states (GP III, 259): "These very precepts of moral certitude, indeed even of simple probability" can "be demonstrated with geometrical or metaphysical accuracy." From the context in which this statement is found, however, it emerges that Leibniz does not think it is possible, at least for us, to apply the mathematical method also to this sphere. In fact, he continues to distinguish between the "mathematical certainty" (a priori) of necessary truths and the "moral certainty" (a posteriori) of truths of fact (including revealed truths) (see ibid.). However, it remains true that Leibniz here seems to let himself be led along by a confident hope in the resolutive powers of reason, extending also to the sphere of moral certainty a demonstrative rigor that he usually and more coherently reserves for the sphere of necessary truths.

72. Leibniz to Johann Andreas Schmidt, 29 January (8 February) 1697 (A I, 13, 535): "Indeed, Natural Theology is purely philosophical. Revealed theology is determined by a revelation, either immediate or mediated, so to speak; i.e., its truths are either received clearly by revelation, or are deduced from it by consequence and interpretation. Therefore immediate Revelation requires the demonstration of its authority; mediated [Revelation requires] the demonstration of the meaning, whenever this is not plainly manifest. Authority means that we show the revelation to be genuine, and divine, as Huet noted [Huet, *Demonstratio Evangelica*]. Each demonstration, both of the authority and of the meaning, cannot always proceed by necessary truths, but sometimes by arguments which, collected into one, give at least the certitude that we call moral."

73. See Leibniz to Thomas Burnett of Kemney, 1/11 February 1697 (A I, 13, 554): "in order to make good use of this History and these texts; and in order to establish the truth and antiquity of the facts, and the genuineness, and the divinity of our Sacred books, and even the antiquity of the Church, and finally the meaning of the texts, it is still necessary to have recourse to true Philosophy, and in part to natural Jurisprudence. So it seems that such a work requires not only History, and ordinary Theology, but also philosophy, mathematics, and jurisprudence."

74. A I, 13, 578. See also Johann Andreas Schmidt's reply, 22 February (4 March) 1697 (A I, 13, N. 363).

Chapter 10. Stillingfleet versus Locke and Toland:
On Clear and Distinct Ideas

1. London, 1697. Although the *Vindication* is issued with the date of 1697, Thomas Burnett of Kemney promptly informed Leibniz of its publication already in December 1696 (A I, 13, 383–384). See also Thomas Burnett of Kemney to Princess Electress Sophie, 16 December 1696 (A I, 13, 715); Leibniz to Thomas Burnett, 1/11 February 1697 (A I, 13, 548), and Basnage de Beauval to Leibniz, 14 (24) January 1697 (GP III, 131).

2. Leibniz possessed the first edition of Locke's *Essay* (London, 1690) and the French translation by Pierre Coste (Amsterdam, 1700), made from the fourth edition of the work. Cf. Leibn. Marg. 38 and Leibn. Marg. 39. Leibniz's underlinings and marginal notes are published, respectively, in A VI, 6, N. I/1* and in A VI, 6, N. I/3*. For quotations from the *Essay* I have used the critical edition by Nidditch (*The Clarendon Edition of the Works of John Locke*).

3. Between December 1696 and February 1700, the correspondence between Leibniz and Thomas Burnett deals on several occasions with the discussion between Locke and Stillingfleet. See in particular the following letters: Th. Burnett to Leibniz, 3 (13) May 1697 (A I, 14, N. 104); Leibniz to Th. Burnett, 8/18 May 1697 (A I, 14, N. 132); Th. Burnett to Leibniz, 23 July (2 August) 1697 (A I, 14, N. 223); Leibniz to Th. Burnett, 24 August (3 September) 1697 (A I, 14, N. 264); Th. Burnett to Leibniz, 28 January (7 February) 1698 (GP III, 218–219); Leibniz to Th. Burnett, probably April 1698 (GP III, 219–223); Th. Burnett to Leibniz, 26 July/5 August 1698 (GP III, 242–243); Leibniz to Th. Burnett, 20/30 January 1699 (GP III, 243–253); Th. Burnett to Leibniz, 18 February 1699 (GP III, 253–254); Leibniz to Th. Burnett, 1699 (GP III, 254–265); Leibniz to Th. Burnett, 2/13 February 1700 (GP III, 265–272). Cf. also "Extrait de la lettre de Monsieur Bournet à M. Jablonski," 29 January 1699 (LBr 132, Bl. 86–87), and "Extrait de la lettre de M. Burnet," January 1700 (LBr 132, Bl. 101).

4. To Stillingfleet's *Vindication*, Locke replies with *A Letter to the Right Reverend Edward Lord Bishop of Worcester* (London, 1697). In his letter of 3 (13) May 1697 (A I, 14, N. 104), Thomas Burnett announces to Leibniz that Locke has sent a copy of the book, and that the publication of Stillingfleet's reply is imminent (*The Bishop of Worcester's Answer to Mr. Locke's Letter* [London, 1697]). Already in June 1697 Thomas Burnett was able to send Leibniz a copy (see Thomas Burnett of Kemney to Leibniz, London, 23 July [2 August] 1697; A I, 14, N. 223). Locke's reply (*Reply to the Right Reverend the Lord Bishop of Worcester's Answer to his Letter* [London, 1697]), a copy of which Locke himself sent to Thomas Burnett for the illustrious thinker of Hanover, did not reach Leibniz (see Thomas Burnett to Leibniz, 28 January [7 February] 1698, GP III, 219; Leibniz to Thomas Burnett, 20/30 January 1699, GP III, 248; 2/13 February 1700, GP III, 269; *Nouveaux Essais*, A VI, 6, 64). Leibniz managed to obtain, respectively, Stillingfleet's second Answer (*The Bishop of Worcester's Answer to Mr. Locke's Second Letter* [London, 1698]) and Locke's second reply, concerning it (*Reply to the Right Reverend the Lord Bishop of Worcester's Answer to his Second Letter* [London, 1699]). With Locke's second *Reply* the series of polemical writings between Locke and the bishop of Worcester is concluded. In February 1700 Leibniz wrote to Thomas Burnett (GP III, 268–269): "I now have all the pieces of the dispute between the late Mons. de Worcester and Mons. Lock, except for Mons. Lock's second letter [Locke, *Reply*, 1697] which I still lack."

5. In the summer of 1698 Thomas Burnett informed Leibniz that Locke "would be very glad to know your opinion of this controversy between him and the Bishop of Worcester" (GP III, 242). Leibniz replied with a letter several pages long (Leibniz to Thomas Burnett, 20/30 January 1699; GP III, 243–253), a transcription of which Burnett sent to Locke (see Thomas Burnett to Locke, 17 [27] March 1669, in Locke, *The Correspondence*, vol. VI, 586–590; the transcription of Leibniz's letter is preserved in the Bodleian Library, MS. Locke c.13, ff. 169–170).

6. Besides the abovementioned transcription of Leibniz's letter of 20/30 January 1699, Thomas Burnett sent Locke a series of Leibniz's reflections on Locke's second reply to Stillingfleet (*Réflexions sur la seconde réplique de Locke*, probably written in late 1699 or early 1700; A VI, 6, N. I/4) together with Leibniz's letter to Burnett (2/13 February 1700; GP III, 265–272) to which the *Réflexions* were appended (see Thomas Burnett to Locke, 13 [23] April 1700, in Locke, *The Correspondence*, VII, 57–59). Among Leibniz's writings regarding the discussion between Locke and the bishop of

Worcester mention should also be made of the long report on Stillingfleet's *Vindication* and Locke's *Letter* in reply, dating from the end of 1698 (*Compte rendu de la Vindication de Stillingfleet et de la Lettre de Locke*, A VI, 6, N. I/3), and the pages of the "Préface" to the *Nouveaux Essais* that deal specifically with the polemic (A VI, 6, 60–65). In A VI, 6, there are also *Extrait de la seconde réplique de Locke* (late 1699–early 1700; A VI, 6, N. I/6) and the passages underlined by Leibniz, respectively, in the *Vindication* and in Stillingfleet's first *Answer* (1697) (A VI, 6, N. I/2*; A VI, 6, N. I/5).

7. A clear presentation of the terms of the polemic between Locke and Stillingfleet is given by Sina, *L'avvento della ragione*, 408–420. See also Sina's brief introduction and notes to the Italian translation of *Letter to the Right Reverend Edward Lord Bishop of Worcester* (in Locke, *Scritti filosofici e religiosi*, 477–617).

8. See *Compte rendu de la Vindication de Stillingfleet et de la Lettre de Locke*; A VI, 6, 16.

9. See Stillingfleet, *Vindication*, chaps. II, III, IV, VIII, IX.

10. See *Compte rendu* (A VI, 6, 16).

11. In 1696 John Toland published anonymously in London *Christianity not Mysterious: Or, a Treatise shewing, That there is Nothing in the Gospel Contrary to Reason, Nor Above it: And that no Christian Doctrine can be properly call'd a Mystery.*

12. Nye, *Considerations*, 30.

13. This specifically Socinian sense of the expression *supra rationem* is pointed out by Zbigniew Ogonowski. See in particular Ogonowski, "Le 'Christianisme sans Mystères,'" 205–223.

14. Cf. *Compte rendu* (A VI, 6, 22): "Finally, Mons. L'Eveque de Worcester agrees with the Unitarians (*Vindic.* p. 289), that we always need grounds or reasons for our faith, that we must understand the meaning of revelations, that we must reject contradictions and whatever is contrary to the principles of sense and reason; but he challenges them to show these contradictions and contrary points in our mysteries."

15. Cf. another of the basic texts of English Unitarianism, the abovementioned *Brief Notes on the Creed of St. Athanasius* (p. 16): "If *the Church* is to interpret Scripture for us, we must admit both [Trinity and transubstantiation]; but if *Reason*, we can admit neither." A clear denunciation of the priority given by the Socinians to reason is found, for example, in the book by the Lutheran theologian Kesler, *Logicae Photinianae Examen*, to which Leibniz himself refers in his *Compte rendu* (A VI, 6, 17).

16. See the third and last part of *Christianity not Mysterious*: "Sect. III. That there is nothing Mysterious, or above Reason in the Gospel." According to Toland the term "mystery" in the New Testament indicates things that are understandable but concealed behind symbolic and metaphorical expressions. Ogonowski, "Le 'Christianisme sans Mystères,'" 206, points out that "Toland's theses on the subject of the mysteries of religion were already implicitly contained in the doctrines of Faustus Socinus and were explicitly expressed by Joachim Stegmann senior in his treatise *De iudice et norma controversiarum fidei*, written in the 1630s and published in Amsterdam in 1644."

17. Stillingfleet, *Vindication*, 231: "I do not find that our Unitarians have explained the Nature and Bounds of Reason in such manner, as those ought to have done, who make it the Rule and Standard of what they are to believe." Leibniz underlines this passage in his copy of the *Vindication* (cf. A VI, 6, N. I/2*). See also *Compte rendu* (A VI, 6, 16).

18. See *Compte rendu* (A VI, 6, 17) and the first part ("Sect. I. Of Reason") of *Christianity not Mysterious*.

19. *Compte rendu* (A VI, 6, 17). See Stillingfleet, *Vindication*, 232, and A VI, 6, N. I/2*.

20. See *Compte rendu* (A VI, 6, 17); Stillingfleet, *Vindication*, 232 and A VI, 6, N. I/2*.

21. See Stillingfleet, *Vindication*, 233–234.

22. See ibid., 252.

23. Ibid., 252–253. See also *Compte rendu* (A VI, 6, 21).

24. See Stillingfleet, *Vindication*, 259–261. In the *Compte rendu*, Leibniz summarizes as follows the explanation of the notion of person given by Stillingfleet (A VI, 6, 21): "The notion of person (p. 259) comes from the distinction between individuals, which would occur, even if there were no external differences, and it is this individual and incommunicable subsistence of an intelligent being that constitutes personality. So a person is a complete intelligent substance with a manner of subsistence that is peculiar to it[.]" On the discussion between Locke and Stillingfleet regarding the idea of person in the framework of the Trinitarian polemics, see Antognazza, "Leibniz e il concetto di persona," esp. 209–218.

25. A VI, 6, 21. Cf. Stillingfleet, *Vindication*, 260–262.

26. Leibniz summarizes thus in his *Compte rendu* (A VI, 6, 17): "Now, according to the author of *Christianity not Mysterious*, ideas can enter the spirit only through the senses, or by the soul's reflection on its own operations, and since the idea of Substance (which is needed, especially in discussing the Trinity, as well as that of person), does not enter by way of the senses, and does not depend on the operations of the spirit, it follows, in M. de Worcester's opinion, that, according to these principles, substance cannot be the object of reason."

27. Ibid. Cf. Locke, *Essay*, I, IV, 18. Leibniz continues the *Compte rendu* by quoting the famous example of the turtle that carries the elephant that carries the earth (cf. Locke, *Essay*, II, XXIII, 2; Locke, *Letter*, p. 14; Stillingfleet, *Vindication*, 235).

28. See *Compte rendu* (A VI, 1, 18) and Leibniz to Thomas Burnett of Kemney, 20/30 January 1699 (GP III, 245).

29. See Stillingfleet, *Vindication*, 234–262; *Compte rendu* (A VI, 6, 17–21).

30. See *Compte rendu* (A VI, 6, 18).

31. Ibid.

32. See ibid., 22–29.

33. See ibid., 22, and Locke, *Letter*, 1–2.

34. *Compte rendu* (A VI, 6, 23–24) and GP III, 245.

35. See Locke, *Letter*, 32–33, and *Compte rendu* (A VI, 6, 24).

36. See Leibniz to Thomas Burnett, 20/30 January 1699 (GP III, 243–253). Leibniz's comment is based on Stillingfleet's *Vindication*, on Locke's *Letter*, and on the bishop's *Answer* to it (all published in 1697), as well as on Locke's *Essay* (see GP III, 245). Leibniz says he has not yet seen Locke's *Reply* (1697) (see GP III, 248), which in fact he never received. On this letter to Thomas Burnett see note 5.

37. See GP IV, 422–426; A VI, 4, N. 141. The *Meditationes de Cognitione, Veritate et Ideis* were published in the *Acta Eruditorum* of November 1684.

38. GP III, 247. See also Leibniz to Thomas Burnett, 2/13 February 1700 (GP III, 269); *Réflexions sur la seconde réplique de Locke* (A VI, 1, 29); Leibniz to Thomas Burnett, undated (GP III, 256–57).

39. GP III, 247.

40. Ibid.

41. Ibid., 246. My italics. Cf. Locke, *Letter*, 15–16.

42. See Thomas Burnett to Leibniz, 18 February 1699 (GP III, 254).

43. See Leibniz to Thomas Burnett, undated (GP III, 256–257). Leibniz seems never to have sent this letter, and instead sent to Thomas Burnett a new version (2/13 February 1700; GP III, 265–272), much more moderate in tone.

44. See Leibniz to Thomas Burnett, 2/13 February 1700 (GP III, 269).

45. In his letter to Thomas Burnett of 20/30 January 1699 Leibniz writes (GP III, 245): "I, in fact, consider the notion of substance as one of the keys of true philosophy."

46. See GP III, 245. *De Primae Philosophiae Emendatione, et de Notione Substantiae* can also be found in GP IV, 468–470.

47. See in particular ibid., 469.

48. *Compte rendu* (A VI, 6, 26).

49. Leibniz to Thomas Burnett, 20/30 January 1699 (GP III, 245).

50. Ibid., 246.

51. Ibid. In truth also Stillingfleet admits the difference between Locke's position and Toland's regarding the denial of the mysteries, as Leibniz points out (ibid.): "This is what M. de Worcester also recognized: if he had done it even more strongly from the very beginning, he would have removed from Mr. Lock any reason to fear that one could confuse him with this author."

52. *Réflexions sur la seconde Réplique de Locke* (A VI, 6, 29).

53. See ibid. See also GP III, 269.

54. See Leibniz to Thomas Burnett, undated (GP III, 256): "The notion that we have of green, which is a more composite color, is not only clear, but even distinct, since it is accompanied by a definition or analysis, by which this notion is resolved into certain requisites or ingredients. But the notion of blue is only clear and not distinct. It is clear, because we can recognize what is or is not blue, without fail; but it is not distinct, for we do not know more distinctly what this *I-know-not-what* that we perceive, without understanding it, consists of." According to Leibniz, this difference between clear and distinct, here exemplified by a case taken from sense experience, holds good also in the case of abstract notions such as that, discussed above, of substance (see for example GP III, 247).

55. See *Meditationes de Cognitione, Veritate et Ideis* (GP IV, 422–426).

56. See chapter 4.

57. The *Annotatiunculae*, dating from 8 August 1701 and published in 1726 in the *Appendix* to the *Collection of Several Pieces of John Toland* (60–76), can also be found in DUTENS V, 142–149, from which I quote. On the direct encounter between Leibniz and Toland, which took place on the occasion of Toland's visit to the court of Hanover in 1701, cf. Heinemann, "Toland and Leibniz," 437–457, and Jacob, *The Newtonians and the English Revolution*, esp. 230–232. In Sina, *L'avvento della ragione*, among the critical reactions to *Christianity not Mysterious* there is also a discussion of Leibniz's *Annotatiunculae* (see in particular pp. 463–468). Among those who have written about Leibniz and Toland see Tognon, "Leibniz et Toland," 784–793; Lamarra, "An Anonymous Criticism from Berlin to Leibniz's Philosophy," 89–102; Fichant, "Leibniz et Toland: Philosophie pour princesses?" 421–439; Woolhouse, "John Toland and 'Remarques critiques sur le système de Monsr. Leibnitz de l'harmonie préetablie,'" 80–87; Brown, "The Leibniz-Toland Debates on Materialism and the Soul," 147–154.

58. See *Annotatiunculae* (DUTENS V, 142): "When lately a book written in English, which I had often heard of, but not yet seen, about Christianity lacking mysteries, came into my hands, I could not help but read it through at once, and as is my custom I jotted down some notes on paper while reading, as I not seldom do when the Books happen to be noteworthy."

59. Ibid.: "And, so that my good will may not be suspect, I willingly persuade myself that the aim of the Author, a man endowed with uncommon learning and genius, and as I think well intentioned, was that he should call back men from theoretical Theology to practice, from disputes about the person of Christ to the study of imitating his life; and yet the way by which he pursued his aim does not seem to be always sufficiently correct and clear."

60. Ibid., 142–143: "The title of the Book seems to me to go farther than is warranted, for it reads: Christianity not Mysterious, that is, a Treatise showing that there is nothing in the Gospel that is contrary to reason, nothing above reason; and therefore no Christian doctrine can, properly speaking, be called by the name of mystery. Indeed, all confess that there must be nothing in Christian Theology which is contrary to reason, i.e., absurd; but I do not see by what probability it can be said that there is nothing in it which is above reason, i.e., which cannot be comprehended by our reason: since the divine nature itself, which is infinite, is necessarily incomprehensible: just as also in all substances there is something infinite, whence it is that only incomplete notions can be perfectly understood by us, such as those of numbers, figures, and other modes of this kind abstracted by our mind from things. . . . [W]e, who are endowed with a finite intellect, do not have a distinct consideration of infinite varieties, which nonetheless, especially in the comprehension of divine matters, would very often be needed." Cf. also ibid., 142: "Yet it must not therefore be denied, that the divine doctrines which reason cannot perceive were revealed to us by Christ."

61. See ibid., 143: "Therefore I am astonished, right at the beginning of the book, in the preliminary formation of the status of the dispute, that those are disapproved of who say: 'what cannot be comprehended is to be worshiped'; yet nothing seems to me to be more certain than this utterance: unless, perhaps, we interpret comprehension [comprehensionem], as elsewhere the famous Author does (*sect. 3, chap. 2*) as meaning nothing but cognition [cognitionem]; which, however, is not the usual meaning, nor then is it easily employed in popular usage."

62. See ibid., 147: "Furthermore, I call that *comprehension* not only when distinct ideas are involved, but also when they are adequate; that is, when one has not only a definition or resolution of the term proposed, but also the resolution of any term composing it back into its primitive elements, as we experience in numbers." Cf. the *Meditationes de Cognitione, Veritate et Ideis* (GP IV, 422–426), a text to which Leibniz constantly refers in the course of the Locke-Stillingfleet polemic and that is also the background for the *Annotatiunculae*.

63. See DUTENS V, 143.

64. See ibid., 145.

65. See ibid., 147.

66. See ibid., 148: "I only note what is said in § 54. [actually § 53: see Toland, *Christianity not Mysterious*, 134] *Faith comes from hearing, but if what we hear is not understood [non intelligantur] then our faith is vain, even null*; this is indeed very true: but yet the understanding of the words [intellectum verborum] is very different from the

comprehension of the thing [comprehensionem rei], as even appears in natural things. For often either the ideas that we have, or the method of reasoning from the ideas that we have, are not sufficient to understand the connection of subject and predicate even if they provide some information about the subject and predicate."

67. See ibid., 145: "Truly, what is said in this passage *no one can believe what he does not conceive of in his mind* [*nisi quod animo concipit*] is true, if it is not extended too far. It is necessary for the words to have some meaning, but the objects of experience show that it is not always necessary to reach distinct concepts, much less adequate ones. . . . [W]e give faith to them [quibus fidem adhibemus] although regarding many immediate objects of the senses (such as colors and odors) we do not have distinct concepts. Even in metaphysics our famous Author, together with very many others, speaks of *substance* as support, of *cause*, and many other things, albeit sufficiently distinct notions are probably commonly lacking"; ibid., 147: "And nothing prevents also some divinely revealed dogmas from being of this kind, since they cannot be explained satisfactorily by any force of reason, although somehow [utcunque] they are reached by the mind and can also be duly cleared of the charge of contradiction"; ibid., 148: "Also the Mysteries in theological matters are possible and intelligible [possibilia and intelligibilia sunt]. For who doubts that there is no contradiction and the words are understood [verba intelligantur], although the manner of explanation [modus explicandi] in both cases transcends the power of our reason."

68. See Toland, *Christianity not Mysterious*, 75.

69. Leibniz in the *Compte rendu* summarizes as follows Stillingfleet's argument (A VI, 6, 21–22): "The rest of this chapter by Mons. l'Eveque de Worcester [Stillingfleet, *Vindication*, chap. X] is taken up with a reply to the author of *Christianity not Mysterious*, and to some new Unitarians. This adversary of the mysteries says that one should not call a mystery all those things of which we do not have an adequate idea, nor a distinct vision of all their properties simultaneously; otherwise everything would be a mystery. Thus he seems to acknowledge that we never have adequate ideas. But M. de Worcester deduces from this (*Vindicat.* p. 267), that, following these principles, we can know nothing, and we must affirm nothing, since the author wishes us to give our approbation only to what we comprehend [comprend]; however, we can comprehend nothing without adequate ideas."

70. Cf. Sina, *L'avvento della ragione*, 444. Leibniz, moreover, in his *Annotatiunculae* repeats that a precise classification of ideas was eluded by Locke and Stillingfleet in the course of their polemic (see DUTENS V, 149).

71. DUTENS V, 147: "If by the term Mystery is meant anything that exceeds our present understanding [praesentem rationem nostram superat], then there are also innumerable physical mysteries to be observed. Thus if it is asked whether the inner knowledge of water is above our reason, I reply that it is beyond our present understanding . . . but nonetheless I do not despair that some day it may be possible to provide a satisfactory explanation of the phenomena."

72. Ibid.: "There are many things placed above human reason, and not only ours, but also of our posterity."

73. Ibid.

74. Ibid., 148: "For *Mystery* means something more than *a thing which was indeed previously unknown, but, when revealed, easy to understand.* For when it is said, *God was made manifest in the flesh, was seen by the Angels, and taken up in glory,* these

are things to be understood that transcend created nature and the force of reason." Cf. Toland, *Christianity not Mysterious*, 91 and 96–97.

75. DUTENS V, 147: "Yet he himself adduces the passage of *Paul* I. Cor. II. 9, 10. where it is said 'What no eye has seen, nor ear heard, nor the heart of man conceived, these things God has prepared for those who love him.' By which it appears that something is understood which is unknown to us, not only because it is not said to us, but also because though it may be said to us, it cannot be perceived unless our senses are exalted and we come into the presence of the thing by some higher experience: just as a blind man cannot judge about colors, even if the doctrine of colors is expounded to him, unless his eyes are opened."

76. Ibid., 147–148: "Moreover, what he says in § 30., *nothing great is performed if an incomprehensible truth is revealed*, I do not think this is always rightly said. So in the natural world also the detection of a magnetic needle is and will be a great thing, even if its operations remain perpetually unexplained to us. In the same way, in Theology a truth for which reason cannot be given [ratio reddi nequit] can nevertheless be of great moment for the economy of salvation."

77. Ibid., 149: "Distinguished philosophers of our time recognized many things in nature as being above the powers of our reason. Certain illustrious Cartesians hold that the union of soul and body is miraculous." Leibniz seems to be referring to the occasionalist doctrine.

78. See GP VI, 595–596. See also § 55 of the "Preliminary Discourse" of the *Theodicy* (GP VI, 81). For a discussion of these texts see chapter 3.

79. DUTENS V, 149: "And yet I may hope that some things admit of some explanation from what has been said, an example of which I also gave regarding the union of the soul and body; yet, otherwise I recognize the incomprehensible sublimity of the inner workings of nature arising from the influence of the infinite, which is the source of clear and yet confused ideas (which we have of any sensible qualities) of which no creature can be completely deprived, and which in the dispute between the illustrious men *Stillingfleet and Locke* I think were not sufficiently distinguished from others. And indeed all these things doubtless show that it is much less to be marveled at if things which far surpass the powers of reason occur in divine matters."

80. Ibid., 148: "In *Conclusion* the famous author hopes for an *intelligible explanation of the doctrine of the New Testament.* I also believe that such an explanation can be given, indeed (even if perhaps in scattered form), I think it already exists, if we are content with some inferior degree of intelligibility." Cf. Toland, *Christianity not Mysterious*, 174–175.

81. For example, Leibniz, having established that miracles are above reason (see DUTENS V, 146), adds: "Nevertheless, he rightly recognizes that [Miracles] are possible and intelligible. But in this way also the Mysteries in theological matters are possible and intelligible [possibilia and intelligibilia sunt]. For who doubts that there is no contradiction and the words are understood, although the manner of explanation transcends in both cases the power of our reason."

82. Cf. the well-known expression of the *Theodicy* (§ 61 of the "Preliminary Discourse") that human reason differs from divine reason (GP VI, 84) "as a drop of water differs from the Ocean, or rather as the finite from the infinite."

83. DUTENS V, 147: "Besides, there are many things placed above human reason, and not only ours, but also of our posterity, or indeed not only what now exists, but

also what will ever be in this life that we lead on earth, and which certainly will be intelligible to us once we are translated to a nobler state."

84. See ibid.

85. Ibid.: "Moreover, our Author notes well that many things were unknown to Philosophers and could not be arrived at by reason alone, not because they are incomprehensible, but because they depend on a matter of fact known only by divine Revelation. As an example he cites the doctrine of *Adam's fall*, which removes difficulties about the cause of sin, by which Philosophers were exasperated."

86. Ibid., 148: "The definition of *Miracle* that he exhibits agrees, unless I am mistaken, fairly satisfactorily with the usual doctrine of the Theologians, as being *above the laws and ordinary operations of nature*. . . . [M]iracles are, so to speak, transitory mysteries"; ibid., 146: "The famous Author concedes, as is appropriate, that *miracles were produced by Christ*; but by this very thing, in my judgment, he also concedes that there is something to be believed in the Christian Religion which is above our reason; for what else are miracles but operations which cannot be derived from the laws of created nature which even the most powerful created intellect can perceive."

87. See ibid., 148: "Mysteries are of doctrine, and miracles are of history."

88. See the first chapter of the second section of *Christianity not Mysterious*: "The Absurdities and Effects of admitting any real or seeming Contradiction in Religion." Leibniz comments (DUTENS V, 144–145): "As regards the *common notions* with which divine truths agree or do not agree, now for a long time prudent Theologians have distinguished between those which are of a metaphysical necessity, where the contrary implies a contradiction, with which no divine truth can be in conflict, and physical truths, which are drawn from experience, and, so to speak, from the custom of the world, and nothing prevents God from derogating from it, since even in natural things we often see such things happen. . . . But, having posited this, let us examine whether one thing can be reduced to the other, as the Author says, *whether the contradiction is real or apparent*. In truth, I cannot persuade myself of this."

89. DUTENS V, 145: "I understand here that an *apparent contradiction* is that which is given when the matter has not been sufficiently discussed." Cf. also ibid., 146: "This at any rate is very true, that there is nothing in the divine revelation that is not worthy of God, who is the highest reason: but we know nonetheless that even in the economy of nature many things seem absurd to us on account of our ignorance, because we are not placed at the true center, whence the beauty of things must be observed."

90. A VI, 1, 515. See in this connection chapter 4.

91. DUTENS V, 145: "Indeed I confess that we should regularly follow appearances, and hold them as truths; but since often many things appear contrary to one another, the rule necessarily is left aside, and one must try to discover which greater likelihood then is to be followed. In this we should not consider so much which opinion [sententia] is more probable, but also which is safer." Cf. *Theodicy*, "Preliminary Discourse," § 28 (GP VI, 67), and *Commentatiuncula*, § 33 (A VI, 1, 552–553).

92. See DUTENS V, 145.

93. See ibid.

94. Ibid.

95. See in this connection *Commentatiuncula*, §§ 34–35 (A VI, 1, 553–554), where a similar argument is found.

96. DUTENS V, 145–146: "It is said that 'Revelation is only a manner of information, not an argument extorting assent'; if the meaning of this utterance is that Revelation has no more authority than a teacher whom we believe only because he proves, or because he explains things by distinct concepts, it cannot stand. For the Revealer does not play only the role of a teacher or master, but also of a witness, nay an indefeasible judge." Leibniz, around 1685, writes in *De Ratione et Revelatione* (VE, 263): "The domestic principle of our faith remains that it is not human reason, but the authority of the revealing God." Cf. Toland, *Christianity not Mysterious*, 37–38.

97. DUTENS V, 146.

98. See Locke, *Essay*, IV, XVI, 14. On the relation between faith and reason in Locke's thought, see Sina, *L'avvento della ragione* (esp. chap. VI).

99. DUTENS V, 146.

100. See ibid.: "Therefore even in human affairs we do not always need *evidence in things* (as the famous Author requires), provided it exists *in persons*, so that it is made sure by trust in them"; ibid., 144: "I can admit that *the basis of persuasion is evidence*, provided there is no abuse of this doctrine. For even if that of which we are persuaded is not always evident, yet evidence must be involved in the manner of persuading. For instance, the authority of those by whom we believe that something has happened must be evident to us, even though we do not always perceive how it is attained. . . . And this *Evidence* is present in the matters of divine faith by those arguments which commonly many Theologians (less elegantly indeed) call *motives of credibility*." In his *Réflexions sur la seconde Réplique de Locke*, referring to Locke's distinction between "certainty of knowledge" and "assurance of faith," Leibniz comments (A VI, 6, 31): "I will say only that it seems that the assurance that faith requires still must depend on a knowledge of the circumstances that assure us of the fact."

101. These are the concluding words of Locke's "Postscript" to the *Letter* of reply to Stillingfleet (see Locke, *Letter*, 227).

102. See in this connection chapter 4.

103. Rumors about Locke's troubles in this regard reach Leibniz by way of the unfailing Thomas Burnett. Cf. "Extrait de la lettre de Monsieur Locke à M. Jablonski," 29 January 1699 (LBr 132, Bl. 87); Thomas Burnett to Leibniz, 25 January 1704 (LBr 132, Bl. 137) (transcriptions in Jolley, *Leibniz and Locke*, 43–44). Among the many contributions regarding the relations between Locke and Socinianism, see the very well documented (and yet profoundly different in their conclusions) studies by Sina, *L'avvento della ragione* (esp. 395–420); Firpo, "John Locke e il Socinianesimo," 35–124; Ogonowski, "Wiara i rozum w doktrynach religijnych socynian i Locke'a [Faith and Reason in the Religious Doctrines of the Socinians and Locke]," 425–450. Particular attention to Leibniz's position regarding the charge of Socinianism brought against Locke is found in Jolley, *Leibniz and Locke* (esp. chaps. II and III; a previous version of chap. II appeared in *Journal of the History of Ideas* with the title "Leibniz on Locke and Socinianism").

104. See *Compte rendu* (A VI, 6, 22–23): "Monsieur Locke . . . seems to lament that he has been mixed up in this dispute with the Unitarians and with the author of *Christianity not mysterious*, although his whole work of the *Essay on Human Understanding* does not contain anything that can in the least resemble an objection against the Trinity. I do not want to enter this discussion, and I do not doubt that people will give this solid and judicious author the justice that is due to him, as M. de Worcester has already done in his reply."

105. See Leibniz to Thomas Burnett, 20/30 January 1699 (GP III, 245–246).

106. See Edwards, *Some Thoughts concerning the several causes and occasions of Atheism.*

107. This is the French translation by Pierre Coste, the future translator of the *Essay.*

108. Basnage de Beauval to Leibniz, 21 June 1696 (GP III, 126): "The translation of Mr. Locke's *The Reasonableness of Christianity* has been printed here. To prove that Christianity is reasonable, he deprives it of everything that is mysterious and incomprehensible, and reduces faith to a simple belief that J[esus] C[hrist] is the Messiah, without going further. He maintains that the Apostles proposed only this for our belief, and that this is sufficient for salvation."

109. See Thomas Burnett of Kemney to Leibniz, 6 (16) December 1696 (A I, 13, 382). Basnage de Beauval too (14 January 1697; GP III, 131) takes care to inform Leibniz that "Mr. Locke's book *The Reasonableness of Christianity* has been attacked, and he has replied." Locke's reply, to which Burnett and Basnage refer, is Locke, *A Vindication of the "Reasonableness of Christianity etc."* Edwards repeats his charges in *Socinianism Unmask'd.* The new attack is followed by Locke's second *Vindication* (*A Second Vindication of the "Reasonableness of Christianity"*).

110. This is the hypothesis of Jolley, *Leibniz and Locke,* 48–49, referring to a letter of 4 (14) May 1697, in which Thomas Burnett, informing Leibniz about the publication of Locke's second *Vindication,* states (A I, 14, 182): "He has not sent you a copy, because he is not putting his name to this matter *The reasonablenesse of the christian religion,* for the novelty of his manner therein could scandalize the clergy, etc. etc. You must not name him on this matter." Burnett's caution, however, seems to have come too late: both the letters by Basnage cited and the information given by Burnett himself show that the authorship of *Reasonableness* and of the two (also anonymous) *Vindications* was far from being a secret.

111. Locke died on 8 November 1704 (28 October, old style), assisted by Lady Masham.

112. See Lady Masham to Leibniz, 24 November 1704 (old style; GP III, 366).

113. GP III, 367.

114. Cf., for example, the rule for interpreting the scriptures proposed in the second axiom of *Sceleton Demonstrationis* (A I, 11, 229).

115. In *Sceleton Demonstrationis* Leibniz states, as regards the attribution of divinity to Jesus Christ that "this is a matter in which we are dealing with a danger to salvation" (ibid., 232). Similar considerations hold true for the Holy Spirit (see ibid., 233). See also chapter 6.

116. Cf. Jolley, "Leibniz on Locke and Socinianism." Jolley's article starts from the following statement by Leibniz in a letter of 1709 to Friedrich Wilhelm Bierling (GP VII, 488–489): "Many other things can be disapproved of in Locke, since he covertly undermines even the immaterial nature of the soul. He inclined toward the Socinians (just like his friend le Clerc) whose philosophy of God and the mind was always poor."

117. Leibniz to Malebranche; GP I, 361. The letter, undated, must be later than 14 December 1711, the date on which Malebranche writes to Leibniz to give him his remarks on the *Theodicy.* See Jolley, "Leibniz on Locke and Socinianism," 244. The animosity toward Le Clerc (apparent also in the letter to Bierling cited in the previous note) may have been caused by an extremely cutting judgment on Leibniz's philosophy expressed by the professor of Amsterdam around 1705 (Hanover, Niedersächs.

Hauptstaatarchiv, Dep. 84 Cal. 13 z. 63 Nr. 31 Bl. 551; the text is also given in Le Clerc, *Epistolario*, vol. II, 612–613).

118. See *GG. Leibnitii Cogitationes Miscellaneae in Nonnulla Loca Nov. Liter. Anni 1715. Ex Novis Literar. Anni 1716* (DUTENS V, 191). Cf. Jolley, *Leibniz and Locke*, 49.

Chapter 11. *Islam, Kabbalah, and the Trinity:* *The Polemic Regarding the* Historical Dissertations *by M. V. de La Croze*

1. M. V. de La Croze, an erudite French orientalist, was born in Nantes in 1661 and died in Berlin in 1739.

2. La Croze, *Dissertations historiques*, "Preface," fol. *9v.

3. Cf. ibid., 1–163. See in particular pp. 41–47.

4. Cf. ibid., 182–256: *Examen abregé du Nouveau systeme du Pere Hardouin, sur sa Critique des anciens Auteurs.* J. Hardouin (1646–1729) maintains that all the writings of classical antiquity, with the exception of Homer, Herodotus, Cicero, Pliny the Elder, and some works by Virgil and Horace, were in reality composed by monks in the thirteenth century under the direction of Severus Archontius. La Croze believes that Father Hardouin's theory is the result of a plot organized by the Jesuits in order to discredit completely the prestige of ancient literature. He attacks Hardouin again in *Vindiciae Veterum Scriptorum*.

5. Cf. La Croze, *Dissertations historiques*, 257–328: *Recherches historiques sur l'état ancien et moderne de la religion chrestienne dans les Indes.*

6. See La Croze, *Reflexions historiques et critiques sur le Mahometisme, et sur le Socinianisme*, in *Dissertations historiques*, 21ff.

7. See ibid., 47–54.

8. See ibid., 42–43.

9. See ibid., 61–62. La Croze is referring to Bull's *Defensio Fidei Nicaenae* (Oxford, 1685). A revised edition was published in Oxford in 1688. Bull's aim is to show, on the basis of statements made by the church fathers before the Council of Nicaea, that the Christians of the first three centuries also believed in the divinity of Christ and the Holy Spirit. Cf. also the following works: Bull, *Judicium Ecclesiae Catholicae Trium Primorum Seculorum*; Bull, *Primitiva et Apostolica Traditio*. As we shall see below, it is the reference to Bull that aggravates La Croze's troubles, involving Leibniz in them as well.

10. Besides pointing out Michael Servetus's relations with exponents of Islam, La Croze, for example, dwells at length on the case of Adam Neuser (a Palatine minister) and Iohannes Sylvanus, both of them supporters, in the second half of the seventeenth century, of a sort of sincretism between Islam and the "new Photinianism" (cf. La Croze, *Dissertations historiques*, 101ff.) Cf. Burchill, *The Heidelberg Antitrinitarians*.

11. See La Croze, *Dissertations historiques*, 133–134. On the opposition between F. Socinus and F. David regarding the adoration of Jesus Christ, see in particular ibid., 142–145.

12. Cf. ibid., 152ff. La Croze admits, however, that Seidel and the semi-Judaizers were attacked by Socinus.

13. See ibid., 158.

14. See ibid., 147–151. After having stated that (ibid., 147) "all Christians posit the Existence of God as the basis of their Theology, and they demonstrate this existence by

natural reasons," La Croze quotes a passage from the *Praelectiones Theologicae* by F. Socinus (in Socinus et al., *Bibliotheca Fratrum Polonorum,* vol. I, chap. 2, 537) to show that he denies "that there are any reasons that prove the existence of God" and scandalously tortures the scriptural texts that "prove that one can know God by contemplation of his Works" (La Croze, *Dissertations historiques,* 148).

15. See ibid., 164–181: *Lettre de Monsieur de Leibniz à l'Auteur des Reflexions sur l'Origine du Mahometisme.* The letter can be seen in DUTENS V, 479–485, from which I quote. On the publication of the *Dissertations historiques,* Leibniz extends his approval also to the continuation of La Croze's work. See Leibniz to La Croze, 14 October 1707 (DUTENS V, 486) and 5 November 1707 (DUTENS V, 487–488).

16. La Croze himself calls Muhammed an impostor and a blasphemous fanatical prophet (see La Croze, *Dissertations historiques,* 42–43).

17. Leibniz might have been thinking of Moses saying, "Would that all the Lord's people were prophets" (Numbers 11:29). See Leibniz to Thomas Burnett of Kemney, 17/27 July 1696 (A I, 12, 730): "As regards deism, which the Clergy of England is accused of in the book of an anonymous author, may it please God that everyone were at least deist, that is to say, perfectly convinced that everything is governed by a sovereign wisdom." Leibniz is referring to the book by Stephens, *An Account of the Growth of deism in England,* to which Willis replies in *Reflexions upon a Pamphlet.* Cf. Thomas Burnett of Kemney to Leibniz, 14/24 June 1696 (A I, 12, 644), and Leibniz to Thomas Burnett of Kemney, August–September* 1697 (A I, 14, 434–435).

18. See DUTENS V, 479. See also ibid., 481.

19. In his early *Justa Dissertatio* (A IV, 1, N. 15) Leibniz complains that Islam and Socinianism reduce religion to natural religion (A IV, 1, 372–373): "The Turks have no revealed dogmas, their whole religion is natural. . . . It is nearly in the same spirit as the Socinian religion, which is almost reduced to the purely natural, all revelations or mysteries having been either openly rejected or eluded by interpretation." Daniel Cook notes that Leibniz's appreciation of Islam and Judaism has, as its main aim, the conversion of the other two great monotheistic religions to Christianity (Cook, "Leibniz's Use and Abuse of Judaism and Islam," 283–297. See in particular p. 292).

20. The thesis that Leibniz's program was Deist in nature is strenuously upheld by Hoffman, *Die Leibniz'sche Religionsphilosophie* (see in particular p. 103).

21. DUTENS V, 481: "But the main thing is to remove from them the opinion that they have of us, that we multiply the Divinity."

22. See ibid., 481. Aside from the abovementioned English Trinitarian polemics (cf. chapter 8), Leibniz is referring to the work by Faydit, *Alteration du dogme théologique,* vol. I, *Traité de la Trinité.*

23. See DUTENS V, 481. The thesis of the close relation between Socinianism and Islam had already been maintained by Leibniz in his *Justa Dissertatio* (winter 1671–1672; A IV, 1, N. 15) and in the *Breviarium* (autumn 1672; A IV, 1, N. 16). According to Leibniz, the affinity between Arminianism (widespread in Holland), Socinianism, and Islam, would facilitate an alliance of the Dutch with the Turks, in the case of an invasion of Holland by the France of Louis XIV (see in particular *Justa Dissertatio,* A IV, 1, 372–373, and *Breviarium,* A IV, 1, 396).

24. See DUTENS V, 481.

25. Ibid.

26. See in particular chapter 7.

27. DUTENS V, 481.

28. Ibid., 481–482.

29. Ibid., 482: "It seems that the Council of Nicaea did nothing but establish, with its decisions, a doctrine that was already dominant in the Church. It is true that there are some older passages where the expressions were not very correct, but that is only because there were not yet fixed formulations, and they were often misinterpreted."

30. See ibid. A brief exposition by Leibniz of the main traits of Arianism can be found in A I, 10, 18 (cf. chapter 9).

31. See La Croze, *Dissertations historiques*, 61–62. See also the notes regarding Cudworth's *System*, dating from around 1704, in which Leibniz dwells on the pages dedicated to the theology of the Trinity of the church fathers contemporaneous with Arius (LH I 1, 4 Bl. 53). Cf. Cudworth, *The True Intellectual System*, 604–614.

32. Leibniz's remarks, dating from around 1709, were published by A. Foucher de Careil under the title of *Réfutation inédite de Spinoza par Leibniz*. A critical edition has been published by Philip Beeley in the *Leibniz Review* 12 (2002): 1–14. As is rightly pointed out by Friedmann, *Leibniz et Spinoza*, the title chosen by Foucher de Careil in reality does not reflect the content of the text (see ibid., 176–177: "The 'Animadversiones,' taken as a whole, are not especially dedicated to Spinoza, but constitute a critical extract that Leibniz made, as was his wont, about a work [the *Elucidarius Cabalisticus*] which particularly interested him"). The main marginal notes found in Leibniz's copy of the *Elucidarius Cabalisticus* (Ms. IV, 398a) are published in GRUA, 556–557.

33. Tatian, a pre-Nicene church father born in Siria around 120, was converted to Christianity by his study of the scriptures, in which he found an answer to his intellectual search for truth. The term *barbarian* was opposed to that of *Greek*, in the sense of "cultivated." In the *Oratio ad Graecos*, Tatian lays claim to the superiority of a non-Greek, and hence "barbarian," religion such as Christianity.

34. *Réfutation*, 16; *Leibniz Review* 12 (2002): 4. Cf. Tatianus, *Oratio ad Graecos*, (Cologne, 1686), 145. The *Oratio ad Graecos* can be found also in Migne, ed., *Patrologiae Cursus Completus: Series Graeca*, vol. VI, 803–888.

35. Cf. the long and authoritative entry on the Kabbalah by G. Scholem for the *Encyclopaedia Judaica*. See also Scholem's entry on Adam Kadmon. A concise presentation of some of the key concepts of the Lurianic Kabbalah is provided by Orio de Miguel, "Adam Kadmon," 267–282 (esp. pp. 267–269), and by Coudert, *Leibniz and the Kabbalah*, ix-xi. In Leibniz's *Réfutation*, 14; *Leibniz Review* 12 (2002): 4, the figure of Adam Kadmon is briefly characterized as follows: "Below Ensoph is Adam Cadmon, i.e., the whole set of Sephiras, lights, numerations and Aeons, he is not the only-begotten, but the first-born."

36. *Réfutation*, 16; *Leibniz Review* 12 (2002): 4: "Nor therefore is Tatian a predecessor of Arius."

37. LH IV 3, 3d, Bl. 1v: "Arius became a heretic (by denying the only-begotten [unigenitum] or) confusing the first-born with the only-begotten." The reading proposed by Foucher de Careil and by Beeley for this passage of Leibniz's *Animadversiones* is not correct; see *Réfutation*, 16; *Leibniz Review* 12 (2002): 4: "Arius became a heretic (by denying the first-born [primogenitum], or) confusing the first-born with the only-begotten."

38. See *Réfutation*, 16–18; *Leibniz Review* 12 (2002): 4; Bull, *Defensio Fidei Nicaenae*, chaps. V–IX (see in particular pp. 337 and 377).

39. See *Réfutation*, 18–20; *Leibniz Review* 12 (2002): 4–5.

40. See *Réfutation*, 20; *Leibniz Review* 12 (2002): 5.

41. In talking about the attempts to reconcile the Kabbalah and Christianity, Leibniz on 10/20 January 1688 writes to Landgraf Ernst von Hessen-Rheinfels (A I, 5, 43): "Many still mock such undertakings, but I am of another opinion. I consider all things for what is good in them, and am very glad of this difference of spirits and designs, which causes nothing to be neglected, and advances the honor of God and the good of man in various ways." Leibniz even sees a symbolic reference to the Trinity in the so-called Fuxi order of the ancient Chinese hexagrams of *Yi Jing* (the "book of changes") (see Leibniz to Joachim Bouvet, 18 May 1703, in Widmaier, ed., *Leibniz korrespondiert mit China*, 187).

42. I shall focus here only on this aspect of the relation between the Kabbalah and Leibniz's thought, without going into a discussion of the possible influence exerted by the Kabbalistic doctrine on Leibniz's monadology.

43. Leibniz met van Helmont for the first time in 1671. It was van Helmont who introduced him to von Rosenroth. In January 1688 Leibniz spent several days with von Rosenroth at Sulzbach, discussing the Kabbalah. On the relations between Leibniz, van Helmont, and von Rosenroth cf. Coudert, *Leibniz and the Kabbalah*. See also ibid., chapter 1, for information and comments on the critical literature regarding Leibniz and the Kabbalah. As Coudert wrote in a previous article: "Like their Christian-Kabbalist predecessors, Helmont and Rosenroth thought they could use the Kabbala to verify Christian doctrine and thereby hasten the conversion of pagans and Jews." (Coudert, "A Cambridge Platonist's Kabbalist Nightmare," 636). One of the aims of their research, Coudert points out, was to show that the Kabbalah contained a recognition of the doctrine of the Trinity (see ibid., 637). See also Edel, "Leibniz und die Kabbala," 212.

44. Knorr von Rosenroth, *Kabbala Denudata*; Knorr von Rosenroth, *Kabbalae Denudatae Tomus Secundus*.

45. Leibniz to Simon de La Loubère, 4 February 1692 (A I, 7, 554).

46. See *Réfutation*, 7; *Leibniz Review* 12 (2002): 2.

47. In the first series of Leibniz's notes on Cudworth's *System*, dating from around 1689, Leibniz annotates the thesis that in the Kabbalah a doctrine of the Trinity can be found (see A VI, 4, 1945; VE, 1883). This thesis is to be understood as part of Cudworth's general plan to show that if triads similar to the Trinity are found in non-Christian philosophies and religions, this strengthens the Trinitarian conception of God advanced by Christianity. On the relations between Leibniz and the Kabbalistic circle formed around the other famous Cambridge Platonist, Henry More, see Brown, "Leibniz and More's Cabbalistic Circle," 77–95.

48. Anne, Viscountess Conway, daughter of Sir Henry Finch and wife of Edward Conway, died in 1679. On Conway see Hutton, *Anne Conway: A Woman Philosopher*.

49. See Leibniz to Thomas Burnett, 24 August 1697 (GP III, 217); *Nouveaux Essais*, book I, chap. 1 (A VI, 6, 72); Leibniz to Lady Masham, December 1703 (GP III, 336–337). Orio de Miguel, "Adam Kadmon," insists on the similarities between Lady Conway's philosophy and Leibniz's thought. Regarding the influence of Anne Conway on Leibniz's thought see also the following works: Merchant, "The Vitalism of Anne Conway," 255–269; Duran, "Anne Viscountess Conway," 64–79 (esp. 65–68); Conway, *The Conway Letters*, esp. XXVI–XXIX, 452–457.

50. See chapter III, 7–26.

51. See Leibniz's notes from his conversations with von Rosenroth published in Foucher de Careil, *Leibniz, la philosophie juive et la Cabale*, esp. p. 58: "I have perused with him [von Rosenroth] the *Kabbala denudata.*"

52. Leibniz to Ernst von Hessen-Rheinfels, 10/20 January 1688; A I, 5, 43.

53. Although in the letter to La Croze Leibniz speaks explicitly only of the first two filiations, it is clear that the following passage implicitly refers also to the third, represented by the Incarnation (DUTENS V, 482): "It seems that some Fathers . . . conceived of two filiations in the Messiah before he was born of the holy virgin *Mary.*"

54. In Foucher de Careil, *Leibniz, la philosophie juive et la Cabale*, 58–59.

55. See *Réfutation*, 16, 20–22. The function of mediator in the production of the world assigned to the Word that proceeds immediately from God is underlined in pp. 38–40 of the *Réfutation*.

56. See GRUA, 557, and Wachter, *Elucidarius Cabalisticus*, chap. V, § 4: "What is it that is farther from the faith of the faithful than to confess . . . that the son of God was not born twice but thrice."

57. Referring to the second generation of the Son as the firstborn of the creatures, Leibniz comments (DUTENS V, 482): "That which seems in agreement with the doctrine of the pre-existence of souls, taught by *Origen* and some other Fathers, wherein that of the Messiah must hold first place: as it would also seem that this was the idea that the ancient Kabbalistic Jews had of their *Adam Kadmon.*" Leibniz returns to the Kabbalistic doctrine of the preexistence of souls in one of the marginal notes to the *Elucidarius Cabalisticus* (see GRUA, 557).

58. See Leibniz to Lorenz Hertel, 8 (18) January 1695 (A I, 11, N. 14). *Seder Olam*, Leibniz's copy of which is conserved in Hanover (Niedersächsische Landesbibliothek, T-A 6193), was published in 1693. Leibniz devoted two essays to it: *Sur un petit livre intitulé Seder Olam, Publié environ 1693 ou 1694* (LH I 5, 2 Bl. 22; published in Foucher de Careil, *Leibniz, la philosophie juive et la Cabale*, 49–54); *Seder Olam seu Ordo Seculorum 1693. 12°* (LH I 5, 2 Bl. 24). The general judgment expressed in the letter to Hertel is severe (A I, 11, 20): "I read this book some time ago, and I found in it some good thoughts, but mixed up with a quantity of fancies, which are not supported by any foundation of reason or the Holy Writ." See also A I, 11, 18 and 22.

59. See A I, 11, 18–19.

60. See ibid., 19: "The supreme infinite, that is to say, the absolute being, is incapable of proportion with regard to the rest of things, and there is no medium between this sovereign being and the creatures. True philosophy does not allow that there is a being inferior to God, yet superior to all the other possible beings." In a different version of the same letter to Hertel, Leibniz writes (A I, 11, 21): "The author speaks in various ways of the Messiah, sometimes he says that he is the true God, equal to the father, and of the same nature, sometimes he makes him a medium between God and the creatures, which is hardly a tenable position. There cannot be any middle between the absolute Being, and limited being."

61. See A I, 11, 19: "One cannot see why God needed an instrument in order to create things, since such an instrument would also have to be created, and so one would have to have an infinity of instruments, or it is clearly necessary to admit that God can create without any instrument."

62. See ibid., 19–20. Orio De Miguel points out that this thesis is present also in the *Principia Philosophiae* by Anne Conway (cf. "Adam Kadmon," 271 and 280).

63. See *Réfutation*, 12–14; *Leibniz Review* 12 (2002): 3: "Our [Wachter] established that the World or Worlds are a necessary and immanent effect of the divine nature; now, moreover, [what is] immanent to this thing and emanating, is very singularly one with that thing, in the way in which all conceive that the thing and the mode of the thing are not distinguished on the part of the thing. These [doctrines] are wrong." According to Edel, *Leibniz und die Kabbala*, 215 and 217, in the *Réfutation* Leibniz rejects Spinoza's pantheism, using a nonpantheistic interpretation of the Kabbalah (and in particular of the *Sefirot*). Scholem underlines that the question of Kabbalistic emanationism is subject to controversial interpretations. For a concise discussion of the problem by Scholem cf. "Kabbalah," 563–570.

64. The reason why the Trinity cannot be seen in the first three Sefirot (*Keter, Hokhmah,* and *Binah*) is that the Sefirot are inferior to God or *Ein-Sof*. See *Réfutation*, 14–16. Leibniz's notes regarding his conversations with von Rosenroth in 1688 deal briefly with a comparison between the Kabbalistic doctrine and the doctrine of the Trinity (in Foucher de Careil, *Leibniz, la philosophie juive et la Cabale*, 59): "There are different interpretations of the divine persons. The Son corresponds to the class of Messiah, and the Holy Spirit to that of souls." It should be noted that on the title page of the first volume of *Kabbala Denudata* there is a symbolic representation of the Trinity through the ten Sefirot.

65. The letter by Henry Hedworth (1626–1705) published at the end of Nye's *Brief History* is typical. An outstanding exponent of English Socinianism, Hedworth justifies Antitrinitarianism in the light of the Protestant Reformation, considering the Unitarian position to be perfectly authorized by the Protestant principle concerning the exclusive authority of the scriptures in matters of faith and the doctrine of fundamental and nonfundamental articles of faith approved by the Church of England. A consequence of these two theses, argues Hedworth, is that issues subject to different interpretations, since they are not clearly expressed in the scriptures, are to be considered not the object of faith but matters of opinion, which everyone is free to share or not share.

66. DUTENS V, 483: "The history of the modern Antitrinitarians is rather curious. It seems that some Italians and some Spaniards, who are the founders of this sect, wished to refine the reformation begun by the Germans and the French, but they have nearly destroyed our religion instead of purifying it." When speaking of "Italians" and "Spaniards," Leibniz is mainly referring to Lelius and Faustus Socinus and to Michael Servetus.

67. This is clear in the comment on the matter of Adam Neuser (see note 10). Leibniz denies that the introduction of the Reformation in the Palatinate was, in itself, the cause of Neuser's attempt to make an alliance with the Turks based on their shared Antitrinitarianism. Neuser, though coming from the ranks of the Reformed, was a renegade, and his errors should therefore not be attributed to the latter (see DUTENS V, 483).

68. Ibid.: "It is true that the severity exerted against them, and particularly against *Servetus*, is inexcusable, since it is only the bad will, and not the error, in him that can be punished. *The penalty of error is to be taught.* One has some right to take measures to prevent the propagation of a pernicious error, but also that is all one has a right to do, and these measures must be the mildest possible." The following remark, regarding Servetus, highlights Leibniz's enlightened attitude (ibid.): "I have, moreover, more compassion for the misfortune of *Servetus*, as his worth must have been extraordinary, since we have recently discovered that he had a knowledge of the circulation of the blood,

which surpasses everything that one finds before him." Previously, in a letter to Thomas Burnett of Kemney dating from 22 November (2 December) 1695 (A I, 12, N. 136), Leibniz had denied that Servetus had discovered the circulation of the blood. In the same letter he thanks Burnett for having shown him Servetus's book against the Trinity (*De Trinitatis Erroribus Libri Septem*). It is from this copy that Leibniz must have taken, around January 1695, the long, still unpublished extract conserved at the Niedersächsische Landesbibliothek (*Relatio ex Opere Serveti de Trinitatis Erroribus Lib. VII*, Ms I 36, Bl. 1–4). Leibniz returns to the question of the discovery of the circulation of the blood in a letter to Thomas Burnett dating from 1699, taking an attitude similar to that shown in the letter to La Croze (GP III, 255): "I see there is a passage of the famous Servetus, which actually says something in this connection. Even merely for this reason, he ought not to have been burnt." Cf. also GP III, 267. A mention of Servetus's work *De Trinitatis Erroribus Libri Septem* is contained in a letter of 25 October (4 November) 1695, addressed by Thomas Burnett to Princess Sophie; an extract from this letter made by Leibniz is conserved in Hanover (Niedersächsische Landesbibliothek, Ms XXIII 387a Bl. 243–244). For further bibliographical information, a very useful source is Kinder, *Michael Servetus*.

69. DUTENS V, 483: "I would not wish to attribute the unhappy end of some Antitrinitarians to their error of understanding, but rather to the disorder of their heart, or even to some judgments of God, of which we do not know the reasons. Good people are often unhappy. Moreover, a difficult death, accompanied by raving and ranting, being an effect of illness and constitution, can be the lot of the best Christian in the world." Cf. La Croze, *Dissertations historiques*, 125–126. Leibniz returns to the matter in his correspondence with the Socinian Samuel Crell (see chapter 12). Writing to Leibniz on 7 June 1708, Crell is glad to see Leibniz's criticisms of some theses of the *Dissertations historiques*, expressed in the letter to La Croze. In particular Crell protests vigorously against the interpretation of an unhappy death as a sure sign of divine disapproval, giving in this connection a series of counterexamples (see LBr 182, Bl. 3). Leibniz replies on 12 July 1708 (LBr 182, Bl. 4–5): "I agree with you, as also I did not hide in a letter published by a friend, that arguments which are drawn from the happiness or unhappiness of the adversaries are of no force. Therefore neither does a calm death prove the truth, nor does a difficult death prove error. . . . For there is no promise of God about temporal happiness, whether in living or in dying[.]" Leibniz demonstrates his intellectual honesty, showing that he is also willing to acknowledge the merits of his adversaries' arguments (see, for example, the second draft of Leibniz's letter to Crell, LBr 182, Bl. 6: "The things that you tell about the peaceful passing away of so great a part of the forefathers of the Unitarians are rightly presented as a counterargument").

70. DUTENS V, 484: "As there have been, and as there still are among the Antitrinitarians, people who live a very moral life, just as there are among the Turks, it is necessary to have pity on them, and implore for them God's clemency and mercy."

71. Ibid.: "I find it very bad, Monsieur, as do you, that *Socinus* seems to want to deny the natural knowledge of God, and that he applies himself to eluding the passages of the holy Scripture that teach it in formal terms." Cf. La Croze, *Dissertations historiques*, 147–151. DUTENS V, 482: "The Socinians are more audacious than the Muslims on points of doctrine: for, not content with combatting this mystery, and eluding some very strong passages, they weaken even natural Theology, when they deny that God has foreknowledge of contingent things, and when they combat the

immortality of man's soul. And in their desire of distancing themselves from the Scholastic Theologians, they upturn all that Theology has of great and sublime, even making God limited. Instead, as one knows, there are some Muslim Doctors, who have of God ideas worthy of his grandeur. *Conrad Vorstius,* carried away by his aversion for everything that comes from the School, arrives at some extreme positions that are incompatible with the supreme and immense perfection of God: but the Socinians showed him the way." Cf. Vorstius, *De Deo* (see also *De Scriptura, Ecclesia, Trinitate;* A VI, 4, 2290; VE, 434, and Leibniz to Ernst von Hessen-Rheinfels; A I, 6, 159). As we saw in chapter 10, the suspicion of Socinianism advanced by Leibniz against Locke rests precisely on matters that, according to Leibniz, belong to the sphere of natural theology, such as the immortality of the soul.

72. DUTENS V, 484.

73. LBr 517, Bl. 17v.

74. "Sentiments d'un Docteur de Sorbonne," 332–347.

75. See ibid., 335–346. On this polemic see note 4.

76. See "Sentiments d'un Docteur de Sorbonne," 332–333.

77. Ibid., 333: "But to combat Socinianism, he is no less Unitarian. And can all the Unitarians today have any other idea of Jesus Christ, than what the Socinians have?"

78. See ibid. In reality La Croze, in the passage of the *Dissertations historiques* referred to, does not even hint at Bull's doctrine of the Trinity, merely noting that the Anglican bishop has "with much erudition justified the Council of Nicaea, against the accusations of the Socinians" (see La Croze, *Dissertations historiques,* 61–62).

79. "Sentiments d'un Docteur de Sorbonne," 333.

80. LBr 517, Bl. 20v.

81. DUTENS V, 490.

82. DUTENS V, 491: "I doubt that the author of the memoir that Mr. le Clerc has published is a Jesuit. It would perhaps be appropriate to despise him whoever he is; indeed I would almost be of the opinion, Monsieur, that one should not reply to him, neither you, nor me. But this is what seems most advisable to me, if you agree; that you write to Mr. le Clerc, that instead of replying to this Doctor, or supposed Doctor, you believe that it is sufficient to give a little review of your work, and that you ask him to insert it in his journal; in making this review you can say, that you cannot vouch for all the opinions that Mr. Bull may have, but you only applaud the justification of the Council of Nicaea. As for me, the best thing would be perhaps to say nothing at all in this review, since I am not at all concerned about what this author says."

83. LBr 517, Bl. 22r.

84. See La Croze, "Réponse à un Écrit qui a pour titre: Sentiments d'un Docteur de Sorbonne," 166–183.

85. See, for example, the opening remarks of the reply (ibid., 167): "It is easy to see that the Author of these Opinions is not a Doctor of the Sorbonne. . . . He who speaks is an angry Jesuit, who has truly in his heart the interests of his order."

86. See ibid., 169–170.

87. LH I 20 Bl. 132–134: *von Leibniz eine Entgegnung auf einen Angriff "dans une pièce inserée au 14. tome de la Biblioth. choisie, intitulée: Sentimens d'un docteur de Sorbonne sur les dissertations historiques publiées depuis peu en Hollande à l'occasion d'une lettre jointe à cet ouvrage, que j'avois écrite au sauvant auteur de ces dissertations, sur les Sociniens"* etc. The text probably dates from the beginning of 1708. The

two versions, LH I 20 Bl. 132 and 134 and LH I 20 Bl. 133, respectively, are both unpublished. Although it has been hypothesized that they are drafts of a letter to Le Clerc, there is, at present, insufficient evidence to substantiate this hypothesis. Cf. Le Clerc, *Epistolario*, vol. IV, xxi.

88. LH I 20 Bl. 133. See also the first version of the text (LH I 20 Bl. 132): "Having learned that I was attacked in the 14th Volume of the Bibliothèque choisie, I have read this piece entitled Opinions of a doctor of the Sorbonne on the dissertations Historiques published a while ago in Holland, on the occasion of a letter added to this work that I wrote to the learned author of these dissertations, on the subject of the first of them regarding the Socinians, which he had given to me to read in Manuscript. I am a little astonished that one speaks with such scorn of these dissertations without going into almost any detail. There are, in my modest opinion, some good things, which can be of benefit . . . although I admit that I am not entirely in agreement with the author, especially as regards the Jesuits and the oriental Missionaries, of whom he speaks in the two other dissertations, which I read only after they were printed. He makes some good remarks, but I have a better opinion of the order of Jesuits, than to believe that they tend to overturn the authority of the ancient Manuscripts and titles, although some particulars among them go too far on this score." Leibniz is referring to the theories of Father Hardouin, which according to La Croze were part of a Jesuit plot to discredit the authority of ancient literature.

89. LH I 20, Bl. 133. On pp. 61–62 of the *Dissertations historiques,* La Croze in effect limits himself to praising Bull's defense of the Council of Nicaea (cf. note 78).

90. See LH I 20 Bl. 132r: "I am convinced of the good intentions of many missionaries, judging that what they have done should not be despised, and that often it is not their fault if they have not been more successful. . . . If the Reverend Father Hardouin disavows the system ascribed to him, so much the better: one must congratulate him, for this system is without doubt untenable. . . . Despite everything, I feel that it is not a bad thing that this father has thrown this apple among the scholars. For this is justly the way to force them to establish the philology of ancient Manuscripts on solid foundations, as I have often urged."

91. LH I 20 Bl. 132v and 134r.

92. LH I 20 Bl. 132r and 132v.

93. LBr 517, Bl. 25v. La Croze is referring to the review of the *Dissertations historiques* published by Basnage de Beauval in *Histoire des Ouvrages des Savans,* January–February and March 1708, 53–66.

94. LBr 517, Bl. 25v.

95. Ibid. In reality, Le Clerc, at the end of La Croze's reply, states that he is equally distant both from the author of the *Dissertations historiques* and from Father Hardouin and the Jesuits (see *Bibliothèque choisie* 15 (1708), 183). Nevertheless, he does not hide the lack of enthusiasm with which he agreed to insert the reply (see ibid., 183–184: "I have done what was urged of me only out of pure civility, although I had reasons not to be involved in all this").

96. Leibniz to La Croze, 1 May 1708 (DUTENS V, 493).

97. La Croze to Leibniz, 15 May 1708 (LBr 517, Bl. 27r): "I have not much cause to complain of Mr le Clerc: he inserted my reply in his 15th Volume, and although he said something against me, that does not hurt me much. As for Mr de Beauval, he has not even read my work: he made his extract from a letter that Mr Ancillon sent him. This

is a constant fact, and of which I have the proofs in my hands." La Croze is probably referring to Charles Ancillon (1659–1715).

98. See Leibniz to La Croze, 19 May 1708 (Berlin AK d. W. Hschr. 3, 2a Bl. 57–58).

99. On the contrary, the opinion expressed by Basnage de Beauval regarding Leibniz's letter printed in the *Dissertations historiques* is totally positive: "Mr. Leibnitz's Letter on the *Reflexions etc.* of Mr. de la Croze is wise and judicious. He praises his erudition and his zeal; and he makes some observations." In *Histoire des Ouvrages des Savans,* January–February and March 1708, 62.

100. Berlin AK d. W. Hschr. 3, 2a Bl. 57–58: "I have read with attention what Mr de Beauval says of your dissertations; I find that, in actual fact, he does not render you all the justice due to you: however, I have not noticed a clear design to put a wrong construction on everything, or in a bad part." In the collection of the *Histoire des Ouvrages des Savans* conserved in the Leibniz-Archiv (Aa–A 202), the passages of the review discussed in the rest of this letter are underlined or marked in the margin, most probably by Leibniz.

101. See *Histoire des Ouvrages des Savans,* January–February and March 1708, 53: "The Author's Preface is all full of lamentations on the corruption and perversity that reign in all Religions." Leibniz underlines "lamentations."

102. Berlin AK d. W. Hschr. 3, 2a Bl. 57–58: "The word Lamentations right at the beginning seems a bit sharp pag. 53."

103. See *Histoire des Ouvrages des Savans,* January–February and March 1708, 66: "As he has the reputation of a Scholar, he also assumes the authority of one." The passage is marked in the margin.

104. Berlin AK d. W. Hschr. 3, 2a Bl. 58: "When he said that you have the reputation of a scholar he says at least something avowed by all those who are sincere and who have the honor of knowing you at least by reputation, but those who have the advantage of knowing you personally will add that this reputation is very true."

105. Ibid.: "What goes up to pag. 61 can pass. But it seems to me that on pag. 61 he attributes to you an opinion that I have not observed in your dissertations, as if you approve of the torture of heretics. He seems to want to scoff on p. 64, where he says that there would seem to be more eccentricity than danger in the design of P. Hardouin, if you have not discovered any profound mysteries in it." See *Histoire des Ouvrages des Savans,* January–February and March 1708, 61: "But for the purposes of the Author, one should not forget that he gladly approves of the torture of those *Apostates* and those *unfortunates* who fall into the hands of the Christian Princes"; ibid., 64: "Thus there would seem to be more eccentricity than danger in the design [of Father Hardouin], if Mr. de la Croze has not discovered any profound mysteries in it." Both passages are marked in the margin in Leibniz's copy.

106. Berlin AK d. W. Hschr. 3,2a Bl. 58: "For the rest, I find that he speaks passably well of your work."

107. See La Croze to Leibniz, 7 June 1708 (LBr 517, Bl. 31r): "Mr. de Beauval's extract is full of false charges against me. I could not refrain from making a modest complaint about this"; La Croze to Leibniz, 28 September 1708 (LBr 517, Bl. 38r–39r): "I no longer wish to be available to receive all the insults of the Polish Brethren, who will never forgive me for what I have said against the Socinians. . . . I am having a second Tome of French Dissertations printed in Holland. In the Preface I will mention

the Polish Brethren, and the attack that they have launched against me. I will speak of it only to say why I do not speak of it."

Chapter 12. The Socinians Again

1. For the youthful polemic against Wissowatius, see chapter 2.

2. The indication of Amsterdam as the place of publication (given on the title page of the book) does not deceive Leibniz, who, on the basis of the quality of the paper and typographical characters, divines the region in which the book was printed; see GRUA, 70: "Seems printed in Saxony (judging from the paper and characters)." For the quotations from *Vernünfftige Religion*, I used the critical edition by Tadeusz Namowicz in Wissowatius, *Religio Rationalis: Editio Trilinguis*, 123–167.

3. *Religio Rationalis Seu De Rationis Judicio, in Controversis Etiam Theologicis, ac Religiosis, Adhibendo, Tractatus*. Wissowatius, whose name appears on the title page of the Latin edition, composed the *Religio Rationalis* between 1676 and 1678, the year of his death. The extant copies of the first Amsterdam edition are dated 1685. However, the fact that Pierre Bayle reviews the work in his *Nouvelles de la République des Lettres* in September 1684, indicating that year as the date of publication, suggests that at least some copies, now lost, had on the title page the date of 1684 (see Ogonowski, "Andrzej Wiszowaty," 15). Besides the German version of the *Religio Rationalis* there was also a French translation by Charles Le Cène (1647–1743), published for the first time in 1982 in the *Editio Trilinguis* mentioned above.

4. Leibniz's notes, dating from around 1706, are partially published in GRUA, 69–72. Leibniz's text (LH IV, 3, 10, Bl. 10–14) was drawn up on three occasions. On Zeidler and the German version of the *Religio Rationalis* cf. Namowicz, "Zur deutschen Übersetzung," 113–120.

5. LH IV, 3, 10, Bl. 14r (cf. GRUA, 69): "The author of the book has much that is good"; LH IV, 3, 10, Bl. 12v (cf. GRUA 70): "Sophianus' vernunfftige Religion is, in most parts, well written"; LH IV, 3, 10, Bl. 13r (cf. GRUA, 72): "Our Author seems to be a learned man, and one who has read good books"; LH IV, 3, 12r (cf. GRUA, 70): "The Author of the little book is a [Socinian] Unitarian."

6. GRUA, 70: "The author of the Preface [is] somewhat, as they say, pietistic."

7. Synesius Philadelphus [J. G. Zeidler], "Vorrede," in Sophianus [Wissowatius], *Die Vernünfftige Religion*, 123.

8. GRUA, 71: "Synesius indeed imagines that reason after the fall is no longer sound, but I uphold the opposite, with Sophianus. Reason is and remains good, it is only that we are distracted from sufficient attention by emotions or passions." Cf. *Theodicy*, "Preliminary Discourse," § 61: "Since this portion of Reason that we possess is a gift of God, and consists in the natural light we retain in the midst of corruption, this portion is in conformity with the whole, and it differs from the reason that is in God only as a drop of water differs from the Ocean, or rather as the finite differs from the infinite."

9. See GRUA, 70, and Synesius [pseud.], "Vorrede," in Sophianus [pseud.], *Die Vernünfftige Religion*, 126.

10. GRUA, 70: "It is too much to say that through the help of these sciences not one letter in the Bible can be correctly explained." See Synesius [pseud.], "Vorrede," in Sophianus [pseud.], *Die Vernünfftige Religion*, 126.

11. See Synesius [pseud.], "Vorrede," in Sophianus [pseud.], *Die Vernünfftige Religion,* 126: "[One still has to consider] that divine secrets necessarily have to be understood in a different way by one person / from another / and therefore one is orthodox, and another is not pseudo-orthodox."

12. GRUA, 70.

13. Cf. chapter 2.

14. Cf. J. Stegmann Sr., *De Iudice et Norma Controversiarum Fidei Libri Duo,* composed before 1633 (the year Stegmann died) and published posthumously in Amsterdam in 1644; Toland, *Christianity not Mysterious.* For Joachim Stegmann and Toland see the study by Ogonowski, "Le 'Christianisme sans Mystères,'" cited in chapter 10.

15. See Sophianus [pseud.], *Die Vernünfftige Religion,* 129–130. Ogonowski emphasizes the fact that in Socinian thought the categories of "mystery" and "superrationality" still appear. They take on, however, a peculiar meaning that is distinctive of Socinian rationalism: those truths of faith that cannot be discovered by human reason without divine revelation are superior to reason, but once they have been revealed they are immediately understood, thus losing in effect their character of "superrationality" (see Ogonowski, "Le 'Christianisme sans Mystères,'" and Ogonowski, "Leibniz und die Sozinianer," esp. 391–393).

16. See Sophianus [pseud.], *Die Vernünfftige Religion,* 144. See also ibid., 135.

17. Cf. *Commentatiuncula de Judice Controversiarum* (A VI, 1, 550–551): "Faith is believing. Believing is to hold as true. Truth is not of words but of things; for whoever holds something to be true, thinks he grasps the thing according to what the words signify, but no one can do this, unless he knows what the words mean or at least thinks about their meaning. . . . [I]t is necessary that the intellect should not fall nakedly over the words, like a parrot, but that some sense should appear before it, albeit a general and confused one, and almost disjunctive, as the country fellow, or other common man, has of nearly all theoretical things." For commentary on this text see chapter 4.

18. See Sophianus [pseud.], *Die Vernünfftige Religion,* 132–134: "Whoever says / he believes what he does not at all understand / knows not what Belief is / knows also not what he believes; and therefore he believes in fact nothing / but it only seems to him [he believes]. . . . Certainly nobody can believe something / other than what he considers true. . . . If reason is not necessary to grasp the articles of faith / then consequently it follows / that the articles of faith should be presented to irrational animals . . . / especially those which can imitate the human voice / like parrots."

19. See ibid., 132. On p. 133 Wissowatius backs himself up with the authority of Thomas Aquinas: "For that reason Thomas Aquinas writes very well in the [*Summa Theologica*] second part of the second part Quest. I. art. 5. that matters of faith cannot be demonstrated / yet it is entirely possible to prove / that they are not impossible."

20. See ibid., 132: "A blind agreement cannot be considered a real agreement [according to the Latin version of *Die Vernünfftige Religion:* 'assensus caecus non est vere ac proprie assensus']." Ibid., 133: "The Christian faith revolves around the truth / that God has revealed about divine things. . . . Then where one is not certain / that something is true / or at least not contrary to the manifest truth [according to the Latin version: 'vel saltem non adversum veritati manifestae'] / and therefore credible and not impossible; so he could not take it to heart / that he believes it."

21. GRUA, 72. Leibniz in particular appreciates the quotations from White, *Villicationis Suae de Medio Animarum Statu Ratio Episcopo Chalcedonensi Reddita,* and

Magni, *Iudicium de Acatholicorum et Catholicorum Regula Credendi;* see GRUA, 72 and Sophianus [pseud.], *Die Vernünfftige Religion,* 150–151.

22. Ogonowski, in his concise presentation of the contents of *Religio Rationalis* ("Andrzej Wiszowaty," 16), goes so far as to state that the role of reason in religion developed by Joachim Stegmann Sr. "is, in principle, identical to that which we find in Wiszowaty." However, Ogonowski, in his more analytical studies on the relation between faith and reason in Socinian thought, is the first to call attention to the differences between the initial, more moderate, Socinian positions and the final, crystalline rationalism represented by *De Iudice et Norma Controversiarum Fidei Libri Duo* by Joachim Stegmann (cf. the cited articles of Ogonowski, "Le 'Christianisme sans Mystères,'" and "Leibniz und die Sozinianer").

23. Regarding Meyer's work and the polemics it caused, see chapter 4.

24. See GRUA, 71–72.

25. LH IV, 3, 10, Bl. 13r (cf. GRUA, 71): "Sophianus has very good examples p. 22ff. that the holy scripture has to be clarified with reason, and pag. 37ff. that the holy scripture itself often adds a proof of its doctrines." LH IV, 3, 10, Bl. 14r (cf. GRUA, 69): "The author of the book has much that is good. It would be possible to extract from it, p. 22 to 25, the examples where the holy scripture has to be explained by means of reason and not literally . . . and from p. 35 to 38 the examples where the holy scripture itself brings forth proof of its own words." Leibniz is referring respectively to the following types of examples given by Wissowatius: (*Die Vernünfftige Religion,* 136–137) "When all of the words of the scripture are taken literally / and one does not use the judgment of healthy reason / to understand them correctly / how many other foolish contradictions and unbelievable things would someone be expected to believe? For example: If it is stated / that God is the sun. Ps. 84. Item / a shield . . . Item that God has limbs / such as eyes / ears / mouth / nose/ hands and feet that are again and again attributed to him in the scripture. From those passages / that one has read / and not understood by means of reason / the opinion of the Anthropomorphists usually arises" (a series of examples of this type follows); (*Die Vernünfftige Religion,* 142–143) "It is true that even in the holy scriptures some sentences are not bluntly set forth as commandments [according to the Latin version: 'non per solam authoritatem'] / but are proposed also with reasonable grounds / that can be grasped through human intelligence and reason / made stronger and proved. Therefore Christ warns us against worrying about food and clothing not bluntly as a commandment / but also through different reasons / Matth. VI. 21 / 22 / 23 / 24 / 25 / 26 and following. That God will give his children all good things / when they ask him / he also supports through an argument from small things to big things. Matth. VII. 11" (a series of examples of this type follows). Unlike what might seem to be the case from a first reading of Leibniz's remarks, it is therefore clear from the examples Leibniz refers to that he is very far from wanting to advance a rationalistic exegesis of the biblical text like that championed, for example, by Lodewijk Meyer. On the clear necessity of abandoning the literal meaning of the scriptures in cases of anthropomorphism, cf. *Nouveaux Essais,* book IV, chap. 18, § 9 (A VI, 6, 499–500).

26. See Sophianus [pseud.], *Die Vernünfftige Religion,* 138.

27. See LH IV, 3, 10, Bl. 10. The list, interrupted—as was Leibniz's habit—by brief observations, is omitted by GRUA.

28. GRUA, 70.

29. Ibid. See Sophianus [pseud.], *Die Vernünfftige Religion,* 138: "Three times one is three, not actually one. And three times a single one is three / not actually a single one."

30. For a detailed discussion, see chapter 7. Cf. also chapters 8 and 13.

31. See Sophianus [pseud.], *Die Vernünfftige Religion,* 139: "Something infinite can only be one in its category / or in its kind / or in its class. That is why there cannot be several infinite [beings] in one class."

32. GRUA, 70–71. The same type of reply can be found immediately after the transcription of the twentieth rule in LH IV, 3, 10 Bl. 10r: "Indeed in space they are more than one, even countless infinite straight lines."

33. GRUA, 71.

34. Cf. for example *Examen Religionis Christianae* (A VI, 4, 2365; VE, 2419). See chapter 7.

35. Sophianus [pseud.], *Die Vernünfftige Religion,* 139.

36. Wissowatius, *Religio Rationalis: Editio Trilinguis,* 38.

37. Cf. in particular the discussion that took place between Leibniz and his nephew Friedrich Simon Löffler following Leibniz's definition of the persons of the Trinity as "essentially relative intelligent singular substances" (*Sceleton Demonstrationis;* A I, 11, 228, 233). See in this connection chapter 9.

38. See *Ad Christophori Stegmanni Metaphysicam Unitariorum,* 121. The second part of this chapter is devoted to this text.

39. *Symbole et Antisymbole des Apostres,* 538. See also *Il n'y a qu'un seul Dieu* (A VI, 4, 2211; VE, 435).

40. Sophianus [pseud.], *Die Vernünfftige Religion,* 139.

41. See LH IV, 3, 10, Bl. 10r.

42. See Leibniz's reply in the *Defensio Trinitatis* (A VI, 1, 528) to a similar objection raised by Wissowatius.

43. See Sophianus [pseud.], *Die Vernünfftige Religion,* 139: "Each one who generates is prior to the generated / and everything that is generated / is only after that which generates."

44. GRUA, 71: "That (p. 29) what generates is prior to the generated is not true, however. If the sun were eternal, its light or rays would also be eternal."

45. See Sophianus [pseud.], *Die Vernünfftige Religion,* 140: "Disparata cannot really be predicated at the same time of a thing / much less of one another. God the Most High / and the human being are Disparata." The same objection had already been raised by Wissowatius in his letter to Barone Boineburg, to whom Leibniz opposes his *Defensio Trinitatis* (A VI, 1, 523).

46. See GRUA, 71: "And what (p. 30) is said of disparate things, can be answered by noting that the Soul and body are also disparate things, and yet are united. Thus also the Godhead can dwell in a special way in a creature." This strategy is very clear in A VI, 3, 371 (*Epistolae Tres D. B. de Spinoza ad Oldenburgium*). See in this connection chapter 7.

47. See GRUA, 71.

48. Ibid., 70.

49. Ibid., 72.

50. See chapter 1, note 75.

51. Cf. Leibniz to Ernst von Hessen-Rheinfels, 10* January 1691 (A I, 6, 159–160): "As regards the Socinians of whom V. A. S. speaks, I do not approve of their ideas. . . .

[T]hey also have very badly founded opinions of God and the soul . . . according to the Metaphysics of a certain Stegmann that I have seen in Manuscript at the late Mons. Le Baron de Boinebourg's residence." In the *Compte Rendu de la Vindication de Stilling-fleet et de la Lettre de Locke,* dating from the end of 1698, Leibniz reiterates his negative judgment (A VI, 6, 17): "I also remember to have seen other times a Manuscript Metaphysics by an author of theirs [Leibniz is referring to the Socinians], called Stegmann, who, however, gave me no satisfaction at all."

52. In § 16 of the "Preliminary Discourse" of the *Theodicy,* referring to the metaphysics of the Socinians, Leibniz writes (GP VI, 59): "As for their Metaphysics, one could learn about it by reading that of the Socinian Christoph Stegmann, which has not yet been printed; I saw it in my youth, and lately it was given to me." In general, his judgment on Socinian philosophy is critical (§ 18 of the "Preliminary Discourse"; GP VI, 60): "The two Protestant factions quite agree, when it is a matter of making war on the Socinians: and since the philosophy of these sectarians is not very exact, it has very often been possible to beat it into ruins." Cf. also *Nouveaux Essais* (A VI, 6, 497). The copy of the manuscript treatise *Christophori Stegmani Rupinensis Marchici Metaphysica Repurgata.* Lögnitzii Ipsis kalend. Januar. MDCXXXV, with various corrections in Leibniz's own hand, is conserved at the Niedersächsische Landesbibliothek (LH IV I, 9, Bl. 1–56).

53. Samuel Crell, nephew on his father's side of the famous Socinian theologian Johannes Crell (1590–1633), was born at Kreuzburg (Silesia) in 1660 and died in Amsterdam in 1747. Educated in Socinian and Remonstrant environments, his theological positions differ in several ways from those of traditional Socinianism, as can be seen in the summary of the main points of difference between his theology and that of Faustus Socinus, conserved among Leibniz's papers (*Praecipua Capita Christianae Theologiae, in Quibus Samuel Crellius à Socino Dissentit.* LBr 182, Bl. 7; we shall return to this text shortly). Leibniz had a brief exchange of letters with Samuel Crell in 1707 and 1708. Two letters from Samuel Crell to Leibniz, dated, respectively, 1 December 1707 (LBr 182, Bl. 1) and 7 June 1708 (LBr 182, Bl. 2–3) are extant, as well as Leibniz's reply (12 July 1708), in two different versions (LBr 182, Bl. 4–5, and LBr 182, Bl. 6). The correspondence between Leibniz and Samuel Crell (to which Nicholas Jolley refers in "An Unpublished Leibniz MS on Metaphysics," 162, 165) can be found in Ogonowski, "W sprawie korespondencji Leibniza z Samuelem Crellem," 333–350 (see ibid., 337–342, the two letters from Crell to Leibniz; 343–349, the two versions of Leibniz's reply; 350, *Praecipua Capita Christianae Theologiae, in Quibus Samuel Crellius à Socino Dissentit*).

54. LBr 182, Bl. 1.

55. See LBr 182, Bl. 2: "I am sending Ostorodt's Animadversiones in Philosophiam, similar to Stegmann's Metaphysics." Among the manuscripts left by Christophorus Ostorodt, who died in 1611, the *Bibliotheca Anti-Trinitariorum,* p. 91, lists the "Animadversiones in Philosophiam."

56. LBr 182, Bl. 4. See also LBr 182, Bl. 6.

57. Cf. here note 51.

58. See Samuel Crell to Leibniz, 1 December 1707; LBr 182, Bl. 1: "Moreover, this Metaphysics does not satisfy me in every respect."

59. *Ad Christophori Stegmanni Metaphysicam Unitariorum,* in Jolley, "An Unpublished Leibniz MS on Metaphysics," 176–189. On the dating of the text see ibid., 162–163.

60. For a discussion of these problems, see Jolley, "An Unpublished Leibniz MS on Metaphysics." Jolley calls attention in particular to the relation between the principle of noncontradiction and the principle of sufficient reason established by Leibniz in his remarks.

61. See *Ad Christophori Stegmanni Metaphysicam Unitariorum*, 176: "It is known that those who approve the Theology of Faustus Socinus and such, and attack many mysteries of the Christian faith, but most of all the Trinity in the divine Unity, and the incarnation of the divine nature in Christ, have established a Philosophy of their own."

62. See Stegmann, *Metaphysica Repurgata*, "Third chapter. About the universal, divisible, communicable, and abstract essence. And about the singular, indivisible, incommunicable, concrete essence" (LH IV I, 9, Bl. 22): "A singular essence is one that is not common to many things, and hence is not said of many things; hence a singular Being [Ens] is defined as what has an essence not shared by others, and so it has an essence which is not appropriately said of others. Therefore those who claim that a singular essence is common to many things involve themselves in a very foul contradiction."

63. *Ad Christophori Stegmanni Metaphysicam Unitariorum*, 183–184.

64. See in particular chapter 5.

65. Cf. in particular *De Trinitate* (A VI, 4, 2346; VE, 274): "Can it be said that *The father is that only God [pater est unicus ille Deus]?* I do not think so."

66. *Notationes Generales* (A VI, 4, 552–53; VE, 185–186).

67. *Ad Christophori Stegmanni Metaphysicam Unitariorum*, 188.

68. Cf. Thomas Aquinas, *Summa Theologica*, part I, quest. XXIX, art. IV: "Therefore a divine person signifies a relation as subsisting."

69. See Stegmann, *Metaphysica Repurgata* (LH IV I, 9, Bl. 51): "Before I leave the subject, I shall briefly discuss the heart of the matter, whether, beyond this accidental relation there is another subsistent one, as maintain those who do not blush to say that the divine person is a relation, and this is subsisting [subsistentem]. Against them we firmly say: I. that every relation, by whatever name it may even come to be called, is an accident, since every relation inheres or adheres to the subject or substance, either immediately, as is the case between subsisting things, or by mediation, as is the case among Accidents (for no one who is of a sound mind has easily denied that there are Accidents of Accidents): indeed, the terms Inhere and Adhere, as regards the issue of Relations, are equivalent. II. We say that no person, and therefore not even the divine person, is a relation. For a relation is nothing but the mutual respect between the related and the correlated. But this respect is not a person. For a person is Substance, whereas the respect is an accident, as what does not subsist through itself [non per se subsistit], but inheres or adheres to a related and correlated thing. Moreover, we have shown elsewhere that a person is a Substance and chiefly an intelligent one."

70. *Ad Christophori Stegmanni Metaphysicam Unitariorum*, 188.

71. See Mugnai, *Leibniz' Theory of Relation*, 116–117.

72. See Stegmann, *Metaphysica Repurgata* (LH IV I, 9, Bl. 51): "We come to the accident, which is either a quantity or a quality: and the quantity is either discrete, from which comes Arithmetic, or continuous, from which comes Geometry. Quality is either absolute, or relative. Absolute quality is what is prōtos and is not per se referred to something else [per se ad aliud non refertur]. The nature of a relative quality is that of being referred to something else. . . . What is referred [Quod refertur] is called a related

[relatum], foundation [fundamentum], likewise a *terminus a quo;* that to which it is referred, it is called a correlated [correlatum], *terminus ad quem,* likewise *terminus* in an absolute sense." Leibniz summarizes (*Ad Christophori Stegmanni Metaphysicam Unitariorum,* 188): "He divides the Accident into quantity and quality. Quantity into discrete, from which comes Arithmetic, and continuous, from which comes Geometry. Quality into absolute and relative [respectivam], which is Relation."

73. *Ad Christophori Stegmanni Metaphysicam Unitariorum,* 188.

74. Cf. *Nouveaux Essais,* book II, chap. XII, § 3 (A VI, 6, 145): "This division of the objects of our thought into substances, modes, and relations is rather agreeable to me. I believe that qualities are nothing else than modifications of substances and the understanding adds relations to them." Attention is called to this passage by Mugnai, *Leibniz' Theory of Relations,* 112–113. On relations as "results" see also ibid., 117.

75. *Ad Christophori Stegmanni Metaphysicam Unitariorum,* 188.

76. See also ibid.: "Then the author discusses Relations in divine matters, which are plainly of a different kind, and by our way of thinking constitute the persons."

77. Cf. in particular *Origo Animarum et Mentium* (A VI, 4, 1461; VE, 292–293): "The person who understands and the person who is understood are, in a certain way, certainly two; although in a certain other way they are one and the same. They are in fact one and the same by hypothesis. It is in fact supposed that the mind understands itself. They are nevertheless two for the very fact that the two between which there is a certain relation are in a certain manner different." For a more detailed comment on this text see chapter 7.

78. Stegmann, *Metaphysica Repurgata* (LH IV I, 9, Bl. 51). Stegmann then exemplifies (LH IV I, 9, Bl. 51–52): "[God] qua Father is referred to the Son; qua Creator, to the Creatures; qua Preserver, to the things preserved; qua justifier to those justified; qua glorifier to those to be glorified; qua condemner to those to be condemned; qua punisher to those to be punished, etc." Cf. *Ad Christophori Stegmanni Metaphysicam Unitariorum,* 188: "He objects that more persons would come forth, since there are more relations in God."

79. *Ad Christophori Stegmanni Metaphysicam Unitariorum,* 188.

80. Of course, given Leibniz's superessentialism and his doctrine of the complete concept, one might well wonder whether in his metaphysics there are the resources for sufficiently grounding the distinction between essential and nonessential properties.

81. Stegmann, *Metaphysica Repurgata* (LH IV I, 9, Bl. 52): "We say that no subsistent Relation exists, since every Subsistent is a Substance; moreover, no Relation, as we said above, is a Substance, but every one is an accident."

82. See *Ad Christophori Stegmanni Metaphysicam Unitariorum,* 188: "He also objects that every subsistent is a substance."

83. Cf. A VI, 1, 508: "*Substance* is a being subsisting through itself [per se subsistens]."

84. *Ad Christophori Stegmanni Metaphysicam Unitariorum,* 188: "But one thing is to be what subsists absolutely, which properly we call substance; another thing is to be what subsists relatively, as the persons in divine affairs."

85. See A VI, 4, 2289; VE, 433, and A VI, 4, 2365; VE, 2419.

86. See *Ad Christophori Stegmanni Metaphysicam Unitariorum,* 188.

87. The *Notationes Quaedam ad Aloysii Temmik Philosophiam* were edited and published by Mugnai both in VE, 1082–1088, and in *Leibniz' Theory of Relations,*

155–160. I quote from this latter edition. Temmik's identity remains uncertain (see Mugnai, *Leibniz' Theory of Relations*, 154).

88. *Notationes Quaedam ad Aloysii Temmik Philosophiam*, 156.

89. Ibid., 159.

90. A VI, 4, 2292; VE, 661.

91. *Remarques sur le livre d'un Antitrinitaire Anglois*, 549–550.

92. Cf. Mugnai, *Leibniz' Theory of Relations*, 116–117.

93. *Notationes Quaedam ad Aloysii Temmik Philosophiam*, 159.

94. See Temmik, *Philosophia Vera Theologiae et Medicinae Ministra*, 89–94 ("What is a Being totally existing, or subsisting?") of the first *opusculum* (*Lamuelis Soliloquium Metaphysicum, sive Scientia Entium et Entitatum ex Universalissimis Dictaminibus Intellectûs Deducta, ad Firmamentum Dogmatum Theologicorum, Coordinata à R. D. Aloysio Temmik, Theologo*).

95. Ibid., 89. Leibniz underlines this passage and writes in the margin: "NB: this would favor the Monothelites." (See *Leibniz's Marginal Notes and Remarks to Temmik's Text*, in Mugnai, *Leibniz' Theory of Relations*, 163.) To make operations depend on subsistence would favor the erroneous opinion that, as in Christ there is only one subsistence or personality, so too there would be only one will. If it is not human nature that underlies the characteristics or *notiones*, one falls into Monothelitism (see *Notationes Quaedam ad Aloysii Temmik Philosophiam*, 159: "P. Temmik p. 89 says that only faith shows the difference between substance and subsistence, and that indeed substance underlies [substare] the accidents, but subsistence underlies the operations. But if human nature does not underlie [non substat] the *notiones*, we shall fall into the Monothelite doctrine"). On Leibniz's aversion to Monothelitism, seen as a form of undue confusion between the operations of the human and divine natures in Christ, see in particular chapter 7.

96. See Temmik, *Philosophia Vera Theologiae et Medicinae Ministra*, 90: "The personality or hypostasis, and created subsistence formally consists in the negative, and such a being does not subsist, unless it is a being which is not hypostatically tied to any other; it is limited by no one's law in its exercise; it owes its operations to no other, etc. Therefore, indeed, by virtue of the subject the created suppositum is an existing substance: however, by virtue of the form, it is the negation of the said limitation and obligation to another person, and it is subject to no such superior person."

97. See ibid.: "Faith does not allow it to be obscure that in truth the uncreated personality lies in a positive perfection, superadded to nature. For if there were only the Deity, saying the negation of subjection to another person, as the Deity is individually one, so there would be only one person." Leibniz underlines the words "the uncreated personality lies in a positive perfection, superadded to nature."

98. LBr 182, Bl. 7. For this text cf. here note 53.

99. Samuel Crell to Leibniz, 7 June 1708 (LBr 182, Bl. 2r and 2v): "Regarding the Divinity of Christ Jesus . . . as I may nearly use your own words, very Illustrious Sir, in the letter written to the recent Author of the historical Dissertations, I recognize that the union of the Divinity with human nature is as close as possible." The reference is to Leibniz's letter of 2 December 1706, published by M. V. de La Croze in the *Dissertations historiques*. The passage in question can be found in DUTENS V, 481. On this text by Leibniz see chapter 11.

100. LBr 182, Bl. 2v.

101. In the first draft of his reply, after treating at some length the divine knowledge of contingent futures, Leibniz does not dwell on the question of the divinity of Christ, considering the subject too complex to be dealt with on this occasion (LBr 182, Bl. 4v): "Other sections of your letter, in which there are very many things of considerable importance, I shall not deal with now, lest my letter should become too long; it is better for the aim of seeking the truth not to distract the mind's attention, but more diligently to dwell on one thing at the time, and then proceed by degrees." A brief comment on Crell's position is to be found, however, in the second draft of the letter (see the quotation in the following note).

102. Leibniz to Samuel Crell, 12 July 1708 (LBr 182, Bl. 6r and 6v): "Wise men conceive the Trinity and the incarnation in such a way that every [trace of] tritheism is excluded; therefore they maintain that the highest divinity dwells in Christ's human nature. . . . [Y]ou, too, do not seem to me to be very far from this way of thinking."

Chapter 13. The Curtain Call

1. The "Preliminary Discourse" opens with the following words (§ 1; GP VI, 49): "I begin with the preliminary Issue *regarding the conformity of Faith with Reason*, and the usage of Philosophy within Theology, because it has considerable influence on the principal matter that will be discussed, and first of all because *Mr. Bayle* has brought it up everywhere."

2. GP VI, 59. Leibniz goes on to quote the treatises of the Lutheran theologian A. Kesler against the Socinian philosophy and the *Metaphysica Repurgata* of Stegmann (see chapter 12). Cf. also *Nouveaux Essais*, book IV, chap. 18, § 9 (A VI, 6, 497–498).

3. Cf. the article "Manichéens" in the *Dictionaire historique et critique* by Pierre Bayle. The edition to which Leibniz generally refers is the second, published in Rotterdam in 1702.

4. A brief summary of Bayle's position was made by Leibniz in the summer of 1706 from an article by Le Clerc published in tome X of the *Bibliothèque choisie* of 1706 ("Remarques sur la Réponse pour Mr. Bayle au suject du III et X. Article de la Bibliothèque Choisie [9 (1706)]," *Bibliothèque choisie* 10 (1706): 364–426; see in particular 394–401); GRUA, 62–63: "In the Reply for Mr. Bayle to Mr. Le Clerc we find what follows on p. 18: 'The doctrine of Mr. Bayle (discussed here) comes down to these three propositions: I. The natural light and Revelation let us know clearly that there is only one Principle of all things and that this Principle is infinitely perfect. II. The way of reconciling the moral evil and the physical evil of mankind with all the attributes of this one infinitely perfect Principle of all things surpasses the light of philosophy, so that the objections of the Manicheans leave difficulties that human reasoning cannot resolve. III. Notwithstanding this, one must firmly believe what the natural light and revelation teach us about the unity and the infinite perfection of God; as we believe, by faith and by our submission to the divine authority, the mystery of the Trinity, that of the incarnation, etc."

5. See in particular "Preliminary Discourse," §§ 1, 29, 39, 61.

6. See in particular ibid., §§ 7 and 11.

7. See ibid., § 13. Leibniz refers to the controversy aroused by the theses of the Lutheran theologian Daniel Hofmann, who maintained the separation and opposition of philosophy and theology. Leibniz had already dwelt on the matter in his early years (see chapter 1). For a more detailed discussion see Antognazza, "Hofmann-Streit."

8. See "Preliminary Discourse," §§ 22, 25, 26, 39. A very similar position is found in a text dating from the years immediately prior to the publication of the *Theodicy*, the so-called *Réfutation Inédite de Spinoza par Leibniz* (see chapter 11). Criticizing the book by Wachter, *Elucidarius Cabalisticus*, Leibniz writes (*Réfutation*, 74; *Leibniz Review* 12 [2002]: 14): "The author thinks that theology neither seeks help from philosophy nor suffers harm from it p. 77. He is wrong: Philosophy and Theology are two truths that agree with one another, nor can one truth be in conflict with another truth, and thus if Theology were in conflict with true philosophy, it would be false. He says that philosophy rests on a foundation of scepticism, viz. relative reason by which men conceive of things by hypothesis: as if, indeed, true philosophy were based on hypotheses. He says that the more Theology and philosophy are in disagreement, the less Theology can be contaminated by grave suspicion: but on the contrary, since one truth agrees with another truth, Theology will be suspect if it is in conflict with reason. Not long ago the Averroist philosophers of the fifteenth and sixteenth centuries who upheld the doctrine of double truth were rebutted. Against them, the Christian philosophers have come on the scene to show that philosophy and Theology co-operate." That it is always possible to reply to objections against the truth is maintained by Leibniz in opposition to Bayle also in the brief *Note sur Bayle, Réponse pour M. Bayle à M. Leclerc* (GRUA, 63; cf. note 4).

9. In the *Nouveaux Essais* (book IV, chap. 18, § 9; A VI, 6, 498), Leibniz describes the two opposing positions as follows: "One can generally say, that the Socinians are too quick at rejecting everything that does not conform to the order of nature, even when they cannot prove its absolute impossibility. But also their adversaries sometimes go too far, and push the mystery to the borders of contradiction; and by so doing they offend the truth which they are trying to defend."

10. See "Preliminary Discourse," § 17 (GP VI, 60): "Calovius and Scherzer, authors expert in Scholastic philosophy, and many other able Theological authors replied at some length to the Socinians, and often with success; since they were not satisfied with the general and a bit offhand answers that were commonly used against them, and which simply stated that their Maxims were good in philosophy but not in theology[.]" Cf. Calov, *Socinismus Profligatus*; Calov, *Scripta Anti-Sociniana*; Scherzer, *Collegium Anti-Socinianum*. In the *Réfutation inédite de Spinoza*, 72, Leibniz insists on the fact that the conformity of faith to reason does not imply the subjection of faith to reason.

11. GP VI, 63–64. The way to reject the charge of contradiction is once again the distinction between God taken absolutely and God taken relatively (see in particular chapter 5) (ibid.): "Thus when one says that the Father is God, that the Son is God, and that the Holy Spirit is God, and that at the same time there is only one God, although these three Persons are different from one another, one must consider that this term *God* does not have the same meaning at the beginning and at the end of this expression. In fact, here it means the Divine Substance, there it means a Person of the Divinity." Cf. also *Nouveaux Essais*, book IV, chap. 18, § 9 (A VI, 6, 498): "I was surprised to see one day in the *Summa of Theology* by Father Honoré Fabry [Fabri, *Summula Theologica*, treatise I, chap. 8, 2], who by the way was one of the most learned men of his order, that he denied (as some other Theologians still tend to do) the applicability in divine matters of this great principle: *that things that are the same as a third thing are the same as each other*. This is to give victory to the adversaries without realising it and to take away all certainty from reasoning. One should rather

say that this principle is misapplied in divine matters. . . . It is therefore necessary that two propositions which are both true at the same time be not contradictory; and that if A and C are not the same thing, then B, which is the same as A, must be taken differently from B which is the same as C."

12. The judgment expressed by Watson, "Leibnitz, Locke and the English Deists," in *The Interpretation of Religious Experience*, part 1, 208, whereby "Leibnitz' attempts to base the old distinction between what transcends reason and what contradicts reason on the distinction between conditional and absolute necessity, is . . . futile and inept," seems, in the last analysis, to beg the question insofar as this claim is based on the prior conviction that transcending reason must coincide with being contrary to it (see ibid., 209: "When Leibnitz draws this futile distinction, one cannot but suspect that it was only in accommodation to the so-called 'mysteries' of faith, which, taken literally, no doubt transcend reason, but only because they contradict it").

13. See "Preliminary Discourse," §§ 17, 23, 63; *Nouveaux Essais*, book IV, chap. 18, § 9 (A VI, 6, 498–499).

14. "Preliminary Discourse," § 23 (GP VI, 64): "The distinction that one commonly makes between what is *above reason*, and what is *against reason*, agrees quite well with the distinction that we just made between the two types of necessity. For what is against reason is against the absolutely certain and indispensable truths; and what is above reason, is only against what one commonly experiences or comprehends. That is why I am amazed to see that there are people of spirit who fight against this distinction, and that Mr. Bayle is among these. This distinction is certainly well founded. A truth is above reason, when our spirit (or even every created spirit) cannot comprehend it: and such is, in my opinion, the Holy Trinity; such are the miracles reserved to God alone, as, for example, the Creation; such is the choice of the order of the Universe, which depends on the Universal Harmony, and on the distinct knowledge of an infinite number of things at once. But a truth will never be against reason, and very far from a dogma fought and refuted by reason being incomprehensible, one can say that nothing is easier to comprehend or more manifest than its absurdity." On the 'mystery' of universal harmony and its analogy with the perichōrēsis of the Trinity, cf. Introduction. Leibniz's insistence on the parallel between incomprehensibility in the supernatural sphere and incomprehensibility in the natural sphere is particularly evident in the *Annotatiunculae Subitaneae ad Tolandi Librum De Christianismo Mysteriis Carente* (8 August 1701; see chapter 10).

15. See "Preliminary Discourse," §§ 28, 32, and 79.

16. *Nouveaux Essais*, book IV, chap. 18, § 9 (A VI, 6, 499–500): "But it seems to me that there is still a matter that the authors I am talking about have not sufficiently examined, and that is: Suppose that on the one hand one has the literal meaning of a text of the *Holy Scripture*, and that on the other hand one has a great appearance of a *Logical impossibility*, or at least a recognized *physical impossibility*; then is it more reasonable to give up the literal meaning or to give up a philosophical principle? Certainly there are some passages where one would have no difficulty in abandoning the literal meaning, as when the *Scriptures* give hands to God, and attribute to him such things as anger, penitence, and other human affections. Otherwise it would be necessary to side with Anthropomorphism, or certain fanatics of England, who believe that Herod was actually metamorphosed into a fox, when Jesus Christ calls him by that name. It is here that the rules of interpretation are invoked, and if they offer nothing that goes against the

literal meaning in favor of the philosophical maxim, and if moreover the literal meaning contains nothing that ascribes some imperfection to God, or entails some danger in the practice of piety, it is more certain and even more reasonable to follow it."

17. GP VI, 91–92. See Bayle, *Dictionaire historique et critique*, 2nd ed., 3140.

18. See chapter 2.

19. Leyser, *Apparatus Literarius Singularia Nova Anecdota*, 210–211.

20. Leibniz writes, in § 33 of the "Preliminary Discourse" (GP VI, 69): "Among the Jurists one calls *presumption* that which has to pass for truth provisionally, if the contrary is not proved, and it says more than *conjecture*." See also *Defensio Trinitatis* (A VI, 1, 522); *Elementa Juris Naturalis* (A VI, 2, 567); *Nouveaux Essais*, book IV, chap. 14, § 4 (A VI, 6, 457). On the concept of presumption, see chapter 2.

21. *Nouveaux Essais*, book IV, chap. 18, § 9; A VI, 6, 499. The context is that of the discussions on the Trinity and the Eucharist (ibid.): "Sometimes one argues about certain principles, as to whether they are logically necessary, or whether they are only physically necessary. Such is the dispute with the Socinians, as to whether subsistence can be multiplied when the singular essence is not; and the dispute with the Zwinglians, as to whether a body can be only in one place." Cf. also, slightly before, the already mentioned reference to the Socinians (A VI, 6, 498): "One can say generally that the Socinians are too quick to reject everything that does not conform to the order of nature, even when they cannot prove its absolute impossibility."

22. See in particular "Preliminary Discourse": § 73 (GP VI, 92–93); § 75 (GP VI, 93–94); § 77 (GP VI, 96); § 78 (GP VI, 96). In the Latin translation of the *Theodicy* by Des Bosses, revised by Leibniz, in an addition to § 58—the first time that, in the "Preliminary Discourse," the 'strategy of defense' is explicitly expounded—the authority of Thomas Aquinas is invoked (*Summa Theologica*, part I, quest. I, art. VIII) as the source of this procedure (see *Tentamina Theodicaeae*, 1719).

23. See "Preliminary Discourse," § 72 (GP VI, 91–92).

24. Ibid., § 5 (GP VI, 52): "There is often a bit of confusion in the expressions of those who put together Philosophy and Theology, or Faith and Reason: they confuse *explain, comprehend, prove* and *support* [*expliquer, comprendre, prouver, soutenir*]. And I find that Mr. Bayle, penetrating though he may be, is not always exempt from this confusion. The Mysteries can be *explained* so much as is necessary to believe them; but one can not *comprehend* them, nor show *how* they arise; even in physics we explain several sensible qualities up to a certain point, but in an imperfect manner, for we do not comprehend them. Nor is it possible for us, either, to *prove* the Mysteries by reason: for everything that can be proved *a priori*, or by pure reason, can be comprehended. All that remains for us to do, therefore, after having given faith to the Mysteries on the basis of the proofs of the truth of Religion (what one calls the *motives of credibility*), is to be able to *support* them against objections; without which we would have no grounds for believing them; since everything that can be refuted in a solid and demonstrative way cannot but be false; and the proofs of the truth of religion, which can give only a *moral certitude*, would be counterbalanced and even outweighed by the objections which would give an *absolute certitude*, if they were convincing and entirely conclusive. This little can suffice us to remove the difficulties regarding the use of Reason and Philosophy with regard to religion."

25. See ibid., §§ 56, 57, 59, 63, 73, 77, 85, 86.

26. Ibid., § 5 (GP VI, 52).

27. See ibid., § 73 (GP VI, 92): "To *comprehend* something, it is not enough to have some ideas of it, but it is necessary to have all the ideas of everything that goes into its makeup, and all these ideas must be clear, distinct and *adequate.*"

28. See, respectively, "Preliminary Discourse," § 5 (GP VI, 52) and § 77 (GP VI, 96).

29. Ibid., § 59 (GP VI, 83): "Whoever proves a thing *a priori*, explains it by the efficient cause; and whoever can give such reasons in an exact and sufficient manner, is also able to comprehend the thing." Cf. also the *Meditationes de Cognitione, Veritate et Ideis*, dating from 1684 (A VI, 4, 589; GP IV, 425). Leibniz continues, in § 59 of the "Preliminary Discourse," criticizing R. Lulle (1235–1316) and B. Keckermann (1571–1609) for having tried to "comprehend" (i.e., demonstrate) the Trinity, instead of being content to defend it from objections (GP VI, 83): "This is why the Scholastic Theologians have already blamed Ramon Lull for having undertaken to demonstrate the Trinity by Philosophy. This supposed demonstration can be found in his Works [Lull, *Disputatio Fidei et Intellectus,* part II], and Bartholomäus Keckermann, a celebrated author among the Reformed, having made a very similar attempt regarding the same Mystery [Keckermann, *Systema SS. Theologiae Tribus Libris Adornatum,* book I, ch. 3], has been equally censured by some modern Theologians. Therefore, those who would like to account for this mystery and make it comprehensible are to be censured, but those who work to support it against the objections of the adversaries are to be applauded."

30. See "Preliminary Discourse," § 5 (GP VI, 52).

31. See ibid.

32. See ibid., § 2 (GP VI, 50).

33. See chapter 4.

34. See "Preliminary Discourse," § 1 (GP VI, 49–50): "One can compare Faith with Experience, since Faith (as for the reasons that verify it) depends on the experience of those who have seen the miracles, on which the revelation is based, and on the trustworthy Tradition which has handed them down to us, both by the Scriptures, and by the account of those who have preserved them. It is a bit like when we base ourselves on the *experience* of those who have seen China, and on the *credibility* of their account, when we give faith to the marvels that they tell us of regarding this distant country."

35. Ibid., §§ 54 and 55 (GP VI, 80–81): "It is not always necessary to require what I call *adequate notions*, involving nothing which is not explained, since we are unable to provide such notions even for sensible qualities, such as heat, light, and sweetness. So we agree that the mysteries receive an explanation, but this explanation is imperfect. It is enough that we have some analogical understanding of a mystery such as the Trinity or the Incarnation, so that in receiving them we do not utter words entirely devoid of meaning: but it is not at all necessary that the explanation should go as far as one would wish, that is to say, to the extent of comprehension and to the *how.* . . . [W]hen we speak of the union of the Word of God with human nature, we must be contented with an analogical knowledge, such as the comparison of the union of the Soul with the body can give us; and for the rest we must be content to say that the incarnation is the closest union that can exist betwen the Creator and the creature, without there being any need to go further." See also the following sections: § 66 (GP VI, 88): "The mysteries receive a necessary *explanation* of the words, so that they are not mere *sine mente soni*, words that signify nothing: and I have also shown that it is necessary for one to be able to *reply to objections*, and that otherwise one would need to reject the thesis"; § 74 (GP VI,

93): "When I am so obliging as to explain myself by some distinction, it is enough for the terms I use to have some meaning, as in the mystery itself; so one will comprehend something in my response; but it is not at all necessary that one should comprehend everything that it involves; otherwise one would comprehend the mystery"; § 76 (GP VI, 95): "It is permitted to them who support the truth of a mystery to concede that the mystery is incomprehensible; and if this confession were sufficient to declare them vanquished, there would be no need of objections. A truth can be incomprehensible, but never so far so that it can be said that one comprehends nothing at all of it. In that case it would be what the ancient Schools called *Scindapsus* or *Blityri* (Clem. Alex. Strom. 8 [Clement of Alexandria, *Stromata*, 8]), that is to say, words devoid of meaning."

36. Besides the sections cited in the previous note, see also: § 5 (GP VI, 52): "Furthermore, even in physics we explain several sensible qualities up to a certain point, but in an imperfect manner, for we do not comprehend them"; § 73 (GP VI, 92): "There are a thousand objects in Nature, in which we understand something, but which we do not therefore comprehend."

37. "Preliminary Discourse," § 29 (GP VI, 67): "This is a thing that presents no problem for Theologians who know what they are doing, viz. that the *motives of credibility* justify, once and for all, the authority of the Holy Scripture before the Tribunal of Reason, so that afterward Reason surrenders to it, as to a new light, and sacrifices to it all its likelihoods. It is a bit like a new Head sent by the Prince, who must show his Letters Patent in the Assembly where he will later have to preside. . . . [F]or it must be that the Christian religion has some characteristics that the false religions do not have; otherwise Zoroaster, Brahma, Somonacodom and Muhammed would be just as credible as Moses and Jesus Christ."

38. *Theodicy*, §§ 149–150 (GP VI, 198–199).

39. *Examen Religionis Christianae (Systema Theologicum)*; A VI, 4, 2365; VE, 2419.

40. GP VI, 615. See also the "Preface" to the *Theodicy* (GP VI, 27): "The perfections of God are those of our souls, but he possesses them without limits: he is an Ocean, of which we have received only drops: there is in us some power, some knowledge, some goodness, but they are all entire in God."

41. Bisterfeld, *Philosophiae Primae Seminarium*, 86.

42. See A VI, 1, 156. Similar considerations hold good also for some remarks by Leibniz contained in an exchange of letters of the summer of 1698 with A. Morell. Replying to Morell, who in a letter of 14 August expounds the theory whereby in every creature there is the Paracelsian trinity of sulfur, mercury, and salt (see GRUA, 134: "The Creature is a virtue emanated from the divinity, which has wished to be made manifest; that is why the progression of existence is made in and by everything in Trinity, and all beings possess this character, and it is what philosophers call Sulfur, Mercury and Salt, and these three make up and are all things"), Leibniz writes (29 September 1698; GRUA, 139): "I would side rather with those who recognize in God as in every other spirit three properties [formalités]: force, knowledge, and will [force, connoissance, et volonté]. For every action of a spirit requires *posse, scire, velle*. The primitive essence of every substance is constituted by *force*; it is this force in God that accounts for the fact that God exists necessarily, and everything that exists emanates from him. Then comes *light* or wisdom, which comprehends all the possible ideas and all the eternal truths. The last factor is *love* or will, which chooses from among all possible things that which is best, and this is the origin of the contingent truths, or of the actual world. Thus the will

is born when the force is determined by the light. This Trinity is, in my opinion, more distinct and more solid than that of salt, sulfur and mercury, which derives only from a badly understood chemistry." A striking combination of the traditional *analogia Trinitatis* with the symbolism of the binary calculus is found in a previous letter to Morell (4–14 May 1698; GRUA, 126): "As all spirits are unities, one can say that God is the primitive unity, expressed by all other unities according to their capacity. His goodness moved him to act, and there are in him three primacies [primautés], power, knowledge, and will; from this results the operation or the creature, which is varied according to the different combinations of unity with zero; that is of the positive with the privative, for the privative is nothing but limits, and there are limits everywhere in the creature, as there are points everywhere in a line. However, the creature is something more than limits, for it has received some perfection or virtue from God."

43. See Introduction.

Bibliography

Leibniz

In this section only those texts by Leibniz actually cited in this book are listed. For information regarding the main editions used, the reader is referred to the Abbreviations. The works are listed chronologically; the date accompanied by an asterisk indicates the period from which the text probably dates; a double date indicates the difference between the Julian calendar (old style) and the Gregorian calendar (new style).

Notae ad Joh. Henricum Bisterfeldium, 1663–1666*, A VI, 1, N. 7.

Dissertatio de Arte Combinatoria, 1666, A VI, 1, N. 18.

Nova Methodus Discendae Docendaeque Jurisprudentiae, 1667, A VI, 1, N. 10.

De Transsubstantiatione, 1668*, A VI, 1, N. 15/2.

Demonstrationum Catholicarum Conspectus, 1668–1669*, A VI, 1, N. 14.

Confessio Naturae contra Atheistas, spring 1668*, A VI, 1, N. 13.

Johannis Bodini Colloquium Heptaplomeres, autumn 1668–spring 1669*, A VI, 2, N. 32.

Specimen Demonstrationum Politicarum pro Eligendo Rege Polonorum Novo Scribendi Genere Exactum, spring 1669, A IV, 1, N. 1.

Defensio Trinitatis contra Wissowatium, spring 1669*, A VI, 1, N. 16.

Leibniz to Jakob Thomasius, 20/30 April 1669, A II, 1, N. 11; 6/16 April 1670, A II, 1, N. 17.

De Rationibus Motus, August–September 1669*, A VI, 2, N. 38/1.

Leibniz to Joh. Andreas Bose, 25 September (5 October) 1669, A I, 1, N. 36.

Leibniz to Daniel Wülfer, 19 December 1669, A I, 1, N. 37.

Leibniz to Gottlieb Spitzel, 12/22 December 1669 and 7 April 1671, A I, 1, N. 28 and N. 76.

Refutatio Objectionum Dan. Zwickeri contra Trinitatem et Incarnationem Dei, 1669–1670*, A VI, 1, N. 17.

De Incarnatione Dei seu de Unione Hypostatica, 1669–1670*, A VI, 1, N. 18.

Commentatiuncula de Judice Controversiarum, 1669–1670*, A VI, 1, N. 22.

De Ratione Perficiendi et Emendandi Encyclopaediam Alstedii, autumn 1669–beginning 1671*, A VI, 2, N. 53.

De Unitate Ecclesiae Romanae, autumn 1669–1671*, A VI, 1, N. 21.

Excerpta ex Literis Io. Fabricii, Ioannis Filii, ad Boineburgium de Itinere Suo Belgico, 1670*, in I. D. Gruber, *Commercii Epistolici Leibnitiani . . . per partes publicandi, tomi podromi pars altera,* 1314–1320. Hanover and Göttingen: I. W. Schmidius, 1745.

Leibniz to Phil. Jakob Spener, 11/21 December 1670, A I, 1, N. 60.

Elementa Juris Naturalis, 1670–1671*, A VI, 1, N. 12.

Hypothesis Physica Nova, winter 1670–1671*, A VI, 2, N. 40.

Theoria motus abstracti, winter 1670–1671*, A VI, 2, N. 41.

De Materia Prima, 1670–1671*, A VI, 2, N. 42/3.

Grundriss eines Bedenkens von Aufrichtung einer Societät, 1671*, A IV, 1, N. 43.

Leibniz to Heinrich Oldenburg, 11 March and 29 April (9 May) 1671; A II, 1, N. 46 and N. 57.

Leibniz to Lambert van Velthuysen, early May 1671, A II, 1, N. 51.

Leibniz to Duke Johann Friedrich, 21 May 1671, A II, 1, N. 58; second half of October 1671*, A II, 1, N. 84; autumn 1679*, A II, 1, N. 213, N. 214; A I, 2, N. 186, N. 187.

Leibniz for Duke Johann Friedrich, *De Usu et Necessitate Demonstrationum Immortalitatis Animae,* enclosed with the letter of 21 May 1671, A II, 1, N. 59.

De Conatu et Motu, Sensu et Cogitatione, spring–autumn 1671*, A VI, 2, N. 42/4.

Trinitas. Mens, spring–autumn 1671*, A VI, 2, N. 42/5.

Specimen Demonstrationum de Natura Rerum Corporearum ex Phaenomenis, second half of 1671*, A VI, 2, N. 45.

De Demonstratione Possibilitatis Mysteriorum Eucharistiae, autumn 1671*, A VI, 1, N. 15/4.

Leibniz to Antoine Arnauld, early November 1671, A II, 1, N. 87; 9 October 1687, GP II, 111–129.

Justa Dissertatio, winter 1671–1672, A IV, 1, N. 15.

Breviarium, autumn 1672, A IV, 1, N. 16.

Confessio philosophi, autumn 1672–winter 1672–1673*, A VI, 3, N. 7.

Aus und zu einem Briefwechsel Kuhlmann-Kircher, winter 1674–1675*, A VI, 3, N. 14.

Auszüge aus Schriften Boyles. Aus the Excellency of Theology, December 1675–first half of February 1676*, A VI, 3, N. 16/1.

De Origine Rerum ex Formis, April 1676*, A VI, 3, N. 74.

De Mente, October 1676, GRUA, 266.

Epistolae Tres D. B. de Spinoza ad D. Oldenburgium, second half of October 1676*, A VI, 3, N. 26.

Excerpta ex Walenburgiorum Libris, first half of 1677*, A VI, 4, N. 422; VE, N. 7.

Persona. Paraphrase zu Valla, autumn 1677–summer 1680*, A VI, 4, N. 433; VE, N. 149.

Metaphysica S. Augustini, 1677–1716*, A VI, 4, N. 332/2; VE, N. 372/2.

Symbole et Antisymbole des Apostres, 1678*, in M. R. Antognazza, "Inediti leibniziani sulle polemiche trinitarie." *Rivista di filosofia neo-scolastica* 83, no. 4 (1991): 535–538.

Leibniz for (unidentified person), extract from the *Conversations chrétiennes* by Malebranche, with remarks by Leibniz, 1678*, A II, 1, N. 196.

Dialogus inter Theologum et Misosophum, second half of 1678–first half of 1679*, A VI, 4, N. 397; VE, N. 1.

Circa Geometrica Generalia, 1678–1680*, in M. Mugnai, *Leibniz' Theory of Relations,* 139–147. Stuttgart: Steiner, 1992.

Il n'y a qu'un seul Dieu, 1678–1686*, A VI, 4, N. 396; VE, N. 113.

Dialogue entre Theophile et Polidore, summer–autumn 1679*, A VI, 4, N. 399; VE, N. 9.

Leibniz to François de La Chaise, May 1680*, A II, 1, N. 227.

De Scriptura, Ecclesia, Trinitate, 1680–1684*, A VI, 4, N. 403; VE, N. 112.

De Deo Trino, 1680–1684*, A VI, 4, N. 404; VE, N. 148.

De Persona Christi, 1680–1684*, A VI, 4, N. 405; VE, N. 147.

Origo Animarum et Mentium, March–June 1681*; A VI, 4, N. 275, VE, N. 81.

Leibniz to Landgraf Ernst von Hessen-Rheinfels, especially the correspondence of the period 1681–1691, A I, 3; A I, 4; A I, 5; A I, 6; A II, 1.

Universum Corpus Pansophicum, first half of 1683*, A VI, 4, N. 237/4; VE, N. 320/4.

De Unitate Ecclesiae, second half of 1683, A IV, 3, N. 16.

De Schismate, second half of 1683, A IV, 3, N. 18.

Reunion der Kirchen, end 1683, A IV, 3, N. 19.

Notationes Generales, summer 1683–beginning 1685*, A VI, 4, N. 131; VE, N. 58.

Meditationes de Cognitione, Veritate et Ideis, 1684, GP IV, 422–426; A VI, 4, N. 141; VE, N. 241.

Leibniz to Joh. Friedrich Leibniz, 16 (26) December 1684, A I, 4, N. 570.

De Mundo Praesenti, spring 1684–winter 1685–1686*, A VI, 4, N. 301; VE, N. 107.

Annotatiunculae Praeparatoriae ad Opuscula Apologetica, 1685*, A VI, 4, N. 406; VE, N. 371.

Specimen Demonstrationum Catholicarum seu Apologia Fidei ex Ratione, 1685*, A VI, 4, N. 410; VE, N. 250.

De Ratione et Revelatione, 1685*, VE, N. 72.

De Romanae Ecclesiae Dogmatibus, 1685*, VE, N. 114.

De non Violando Principio Contradictionis in Divinis contra Honoratum Fabri, February–October 1685*, A VI, 4, N. 414; VE, N. 387.

Conferentia ad Apologiam Catholicae Veritatis, autumn 1685*, A VI, 4, N. 415; VE, N. 4.

De Trinitate, autumn 1685*; A VI, 4, N. 416, VE, N. 75.

Positiones, autumn 1685–February 1686*, A VI, 4, N. 418; VE, N. 388.

Principium Scientiae Humanae, winter 1685–1686*, A VI, 4, N. 157; VE, N. 231.

Discours de Métaphysique, beginning 1686*, GP IV, 427–463; A VI, 4, N. 306; VE, N. 370.

Specimina Calculi Rationalis, April–October 1686*, A VI, 4, N. 171; VE, N. 420.

Examen Religionis Christianae (Systema Theologicum), April–October 1686*, A VI, 4, N. 420; VE, N. 512.

De Religione Magnorum Virorum, spring 1686–end 1687*, GRUA, 35–44; A VI, 4, N. 421; VE, N. 524.

De Lingua Philosophica, end 1687–end 1688*, A VI, 4, N. 186; VE, N. 97.

Notes from the conversations with Knorr von Rosenroth, 1688, in A. Foucher de Careil, *Leibniz, la philosophie juive et la Cabal.* Paris: Auguste Durand, 1861.

Excerpta ex Cudworthii Systema Intellectuale, spring–summer 1689*, A VI, 4, N. 351; VE, N. 406.

De Rerum Creatione Sententiae, 1689–1690, A VI, 4, N. 332/3; VE, N. 372/3.

Extraits de D. Petau, 1691–1695*, GRUA, 332–338.

Extraits des Arminiens, 1691–1695*, GRUA, 338–346.

Leibniz to Gerhard Meier, especially the correspondence of the period 1692–1694, A I, 8; A I, 9; A I, 10.

Leibniz to Simon de La Loubère, 4 February 1692, A I, 7, N. 312.

Leibniz to Jacques-Bénigne Bossuet, 1/11 October 1692, A I, 8, N. 102.

Extrait from the book by Stephen Nye *Considerations on the Explications of the Doctrine of the Trinity, By Dr. Wallis, Dr. Sherlock, Dr. S[ou]th, Dr. Cudworth and Mr. Hooker, published anonymously in London in 1693*, 1693*, in Antognazza, "Inediti leibniziani sulle polemiche trinitarie," 539–545.

Remarques sur le livre d'un Antitrinitaire Anglois, 1693*, in Antognazza, "Inediti leibniziani sulle polemiche trinitarie," 546–550.

Sur un petit livre intitulé Seder Olam, Publié environ 1693 ou 1694, after 1693, in Foucher de Careil, *Leibniz, la philosophie juive et la Cabale*, 49–54.

Seder Olam seu Ordo Seculorum 1693. 12°, after 1693, LH I 5, 2 Bl. 24.

De Primae Philosophiae Emendatione, et de Notione Substantiae, 1694, GP IV, 468–470.

Leibniz to Princess Electress Sophie, especially the correspondence of March 1694, A I, 10.

Leibniz to Friedrich Simon Löffler, especially the correspondence of the period 1694–1695, A I, 10; A I, 11.

Leibniz to Thomas Smith, of particular importance some letters written between 1694 and 1697, A I, 10; A I, 11; A I, 13.

Leibniz to Basnage de Beauval, especially the correspondence of the period 1694–1697, GP III.

Système nouveau de la nature et de la communication des substances, 1695; GP IV, 477–487.

Leibniz to Lorenz Hertel, 8 (18) January 1695, A I, 11, N. 14; May 1716, in J. Burckhard, *Historiae Bibliothecae Augustae Quae Wolffenbutteli Est pars III*, 347. Leipzig: I. C. Meisner, 1746.

Sceleton Demonstrationis (Leibniz for Friedrich Simon Löffler), 26 January (5 February) 1695, A I, 11, N. 163.

Relatio ex Opere Serveti, January 1695*, Niedersächsische Landesbibliothek, Ms I 36 Bl. 1–4.

Extraits de Twisse, 1695*, GRUA, 347–359.

Extract made by Leibniz from a letter of 25 October (4 November) 1695 (Thomas Burnett to Princess Electress Sophie), November 1695*, Niedersächsische Landesbibliothek, Ms XXIII 387a Bl. 243–244.

French translation, made by Leibniz, of a letter by Thomas Burnett to Princess Electress Sophie, November 1695, LBr 132, Bl. 16, cf. A I, 12, 367.

Tabula Juris, 1695–1696*, GRUA, 791–797.

Leibniz to Thomas Burnett of Kemney, especially the correspondence of the period 1695–1700, A I, 11; A I, 13; A, I, 14; GP III; LBr 132.

Leibniz to Johann Andreas Schmidt, 29 January (8 February) 1697 and 16 (26) February 1697, A I, 13, N. 327 and N. 346.

Passages soulignés par Leibniz dans son exemplaire de la Vindication de Stillingfleet, 1697–1700*, A VI, 6, N. I/2*.

Über die menschliche Natur Christi. Auszüge aus Kirchenvätern, 1698, LH I 9, 12 Bl. 377 and 395.

Unvorgreiffliches Bedencken über eine Schrift genandt "Kurze Vorstellung," early 1698–early 1699*, LH I 9, 2, Bl. 106–167; LH I 9, 4, 174–315 (final draft with many corrections in Leibniz's hand); LH I 7, 5, Bl. 95–99.

Leibniz to Andreas Morell, 4–14 May 1698 and 29 September 1698, GRUA, 125–128 and 136–140.

Tentamen Expositionis Irenicae Trium Potissimarum inter Protestantes Controversiarum, September 1698, LH I 9, 7 Bl. 355–356.

Defense of the *Tentamen Expositionis Irenicae* (1699*), in P. Schrecker, "G.-W. Leibniz. Lettres et fragments inédits." *Revue philosophique de la France et de l'Étranger* 118 (1934): 86–89.

Passages soulignés par Leibniz dans l'ouvrage de Stillingfleet, 1698–1700*, A VI, 6, N. I/5.

Compte rendu de la Vindication de Stillingfleet et de la Lettre de Locke, end 1698*, A VI, 6, N. I/3.

Extrait de la lettre de Monsieur Bournet à M. Jablonski, 29 January 1699, LBr 132, Bl. 86–87.

Réflexions sur la seconde réplique de Locke, end 1699–beginning 1700*, A VI, 6, N. I/4.

Extrait de la seconde réplique de John Locke, end 1699–beginning 1700*, A VI, 6, N. I/6.

Extrait de la lettre de M. Burnet, January 1700, LBr 132, Bl. 101.

Annotatiunculae Subitaneae ad Tolandi Librum De Christianismo Mysteriis Carente, 8 August 1701, DUTENS V, 142–149.

Sur Gilbert Burnet. An Exposition of the Thirty-Nine Articles of the Church of England. London 1699, 1701–1706, GRUA, 453–477.

Leibniz to Sophie, 18 November 1702, in *Die Werke von Leibniz,* edited by Onno Klopp, vol. 8, 397. Hanover: Klindworth, 1873. Reprint, Hildesheim: Olms, 1973.

Note referring to the Incarnation, 1702*, GP VI, 521.

Raisons que M. Jaquelot m'a envoyées pour justifier l'Argument contesté de des-Cartes qui doit prouver l'existence de Dieu, avec mes reponses, 20 November 1702, GP III, 442–447.

Tractatio de Deo et Homine, 1702*, GP III, 28–38.

Leibniz to Joachim Bouvet, 18 May 1703, in R. Widmaier, ed., *Leibniz korrespondiert mit China. Der Briefwechsel mit den Jesuitenmissionaren (1689–1714),* 179–196. Frankfurt a. M.: Klostermann, 1990.

Leibniz to Lady Damaris Masham, 1703–1705; GP III.

Nouveaux Essais sur l'Entendement Humain, summer 1703–spring 1705, A VI, 6, N. 2.

Auszüge aus R. Cudworth, The True Intellectual System of the Universe, 1704*, LH I 1, 4 Bl. 49–53.

Parallele entre la raison originale ou la loy de la nature, le paganisme ou la corruption de la loy de la nature, la loy de Moyse ou le paganisme réformé, et le Christianisme ou la loy de la nature rétablie, after 1704*, GRUA, 46–61.

Synopsis, 1705*, GRUA, 473–477.

Note sur Bayle, Réponse pour M. Bayle à M. Leclerc, summer 1706, GRUA, 62–64.

Sophianus, Vernünfftige Religion, 1706*, LH IV 3, 10 Bl. 10–14, partially published in GRUA, 69–72.

Leibniz to Mathurin Veyssières de La Croze, especially the correspondence of the period 1706–1708, LBr 517 and Berlin Akademie der Wissenschaften Handschriften 3, 2a Bl. 57–58; partially published in DUTENS V.

Lettre de Monsieur de Leibniz à l'Auteur des Reflexions sur l'Origine du Mahometisme, 2 December 1706, DUTENS V, 479–484.

Leibniz to Bartholomew Des Bosses, especially the correspondence of the period 1706–1712, GP II.

Leibniz's marginal notes and remarks to Temmik's text, after 1706*, in Mugnai, *Leibniz' Theory of Relations,* 160–164.

Notes sur J. G. Wachter, Elucidarius Cabalisticus, Romae 1706, after 1706, Niedersächsische Landesbibliothek, Ms IV, 398a, partially published in GRUA, 556–557.

Remarque de l'Auteur du Systeme de l'Harmonie préetablie sur un endroit des Memoires de Trevoux du Mars 1704, 1708, GP VI, 595–596.

Von Leibniz eine Entgegnung auf einen Angriff "dans une pièce inserée au 14. tome de la Biblioth. choisie, intitulée: Sentimens d'un docteur de Sorbonne sur les dissertations historiques publiées depuis peu en Hollande à l'occasion d'une lettre jointe à cet ouvrage, que j'avois écrite au sauvant auteur de ces dissertations, sur les Sociniens" etc., early 1708*, LH I 20 Bl. 132–134.

Animadversiones circa Assertiones Aliquas Theoriae Medicae Verae Clar. Stahlii; Cum Ejusdem Leibnitii ad Stahlianas Observationes Responsionibus, 1708*, DUTENS II, part ii, 131–161.

Praecipua Capita Christianae Theologiae, in Quibus Samuel Crellius à Socino Dissentit, 1708*, LBr 182, Bl. 7, also in Z. Ogonowski, "W sprawie korespondencji Leibniza z Samuelem Crellem." *Archiwum Historii Filozofii i Myśli Spolecznej* 27 (1981): 333–350 (cf. 350).

Leibniz to Samuel Crell, 12 July 1708, LBr 182 Bl. 4–6, also in Ogonowski, "W sprawie korespondencji Leibniza z Samuelem Crellem," 343–349.

Ad Christophori Stegmanni Metaphysicam Unitariorum, after mid-1708, in N. Jolley, "An Unpublished Leibniz MS on Metaphysics," *Studia Leibnitiana* 7, no. 2 (1975): 176–189.

Leibniz to Friedrich Wilhelm Bierling, 1709, GP VII, 487–489.

Animadversiones, 1709*, LH IV 3, 3d, in A. Foucher de Careil, ed., *Réfutation inédite de Spinoza par Leibniz*. Paris, 1854.

Essais de Théodicée sur la bonté de Dieu, la liberté de l'homme et l'origine du mal, 1710, GP VI (cf. also the Latin translation by Des Bosses: *Tentamina Theodicaeae de Bonitate Dei, Libertate Hominis et Origine Mali*, Frankfurt: C. J. Bencard, 1719).

Fragment referring to the Incarnation, 1710*, in A. Robinet, *Malebranche et Leibniz. Relations personelles*, 413–414. Paris: Vrin, 1955.

Leibniz to Nicolas Malebranche, end 1711*, GP I, 360–361.

Principes de la Nature et de la Grace, fondés en raison, 1714, GP VI, 598–606.

Monadologie, 1714, GP VI, 607–623.

G.G. Leibnitii Cogitationes Miscellaneae In Nonnulla Loca Nov. Liter. Anni 1715. Ex Novis Literar. Anni 1716, 1715, DUTENS V, 191.

Notationes Quaedam ad Aloysii Temmik Philosophiam, end 1715–1716, in Mugnai, *Leibniz' Theory of Relations*, 155–160; VE, N. 242.

Leibniz to Sebastian Korthold, 21 January and 19 March 1716, DUTENS V, 337–338.

Leibniz to Polycarp Leyser, 5 May 1716, LBr 559, Bl. 12–13.

In the following sections (fifteenth to eighteenth centuries; nineteenth to twenty-first centuries) are listed the works directly consulted in the preparation of this book.

Fifteenth to Eighteenth Centuries

An account of the decree of the University of Oxford against some heretical tenets. London, 1695.

Allix, P. *A Defence of the Brief History of the Unitarians, Against Dr. Sherlock's Answer in his Vindication of the Holy Trinity*. London, 1691.

Alsted, J. H. *Definitiones Theologicae Secundum Ordinem Locorum Communium Traditae*. Frankfurt: C. Eifrid, 1626.

———. *Distinctiones per Universam Theologiam Sumptae*. Frankfurt: C. Eifrid, 1626.

———. *Quaestiones Theologicae Breviter Propositae et Expositae*. Frankfurt: C. Eifrid, 1627.

———. *Encyclopaedia, Septem Tomis Distincta*. Herborn, 1630.

Basnage de Beauval, H. "Article IV. Reflexions Historiques sur divers Sujects." *Histoire des Ouvrages des Savans* (January–February and March 1708): 53–66.

Basset, W. *An Answer to the Brief History of the Unitarians, Called also Socinians*. London: John Everingham, 1693.

Baumgarten, S. J., ed. *Nachrichten von einer hallischen Bibliothek*. Halle: Joh. Justinus Gebauer, 1749.

Bayle, P. *Dictionaire historique et critique*. 2nd ed. 3 vols. Rotterdam: Reinier Leers, 1702.

Bayle, P. *Réponse aux Questions d'un Provincial*. 1704–1707. In *Oeuvres Diverses*. The Hague: P. Husson, 1727–1731.

Bellarmino, R. *Disputationes de Controversiis Christianae Fidei adversus Huius Temporis Haereticos, Tribus Tomis Comprehensae.* Ingolstadt: D. Sartorius, 1586–1593.

Biel, G. *Epitome et Collectorium ex Occamo super Quatuor Libros Sententiarum.* Tübingen, 1501.

Bisterfeld, J. H. *De Uno Deo Patre, Filio ac Spiritu Sancto Mysterium Pietatis . . . Breviter Defensum.* Leiden: Elzevier, 1639.

———. *Philosophiae Primae Seminarium.* Leiden: Daniel and Abraham Gaasbeck, 1657.

———. *Elementorum Logicorum Libri Tres. . . . Accedit, Ejusdem Authoris, Phosphorus Catholicus, seu Artis Meditandi Epitome. Cui Subjunctum Est, Consilium de Studiis Feliciter Instituendis.* Leiden: H. Verbiest, 1657.

Bock, F. S. *Historia Antitrinitariorum, Maxime Socinianismi et Socinianorum.* Vol. 1. Königsberg and Leipzig: G. L. Hartungius, 1774–1784.

Bodin, J. *Colloquium Heptaplomeres de Rerum Sublimium Arcanis Abditis.* 1593. Critical edition by G. Günter and F. Niewöhner. Wiesbaden: Harrassowitz, 1996.

Boyle, R. *Chymista Scepticus vel Dubia et Paradoxa Chymico-Physica. . . . Ex Anglico in Latinum Sermonem Traducta.* Rotterdam: A. Leers, 1662.

———. *The Excellency of Theology compar'd with natural philosophy.* London: Henry Herringman, 1674.

Brief Notes on the Creed of St. Athanasius. In *The Acts of Great Athanasius. With Notes, By way of Illustration, On his Creed; And Observations on the Learned Vindication of the Trinity and Incarnation, by Dr. William Sherlock.* London, 1690.

Buddeus, J. F. *Observationes Selectae ad Rem Litterarium Spectantes.* Halle, 1701.

Bull, G. *Defensio Fidei Nicaenae.* Oxford: Sheldonian Theatre, 1685.

———. *Judicium Ecclesiae Catholicae Trium Primorum Seculorum, de Necessitate Credendi Quod Dominus Noster Jesus Christus Sit Verus Deus.* Amsterdam: G. Gallet, 1696.

———. *Primitiva et Apostolica Traditio Dogmatis in Ecclesia Catholica Recepti, De Iesu Christi Servatoris Nostri Divinitate.* London: R. Smith, 1703.

Burckhard, J. *Historiae Bibliothecae Augustae Quae Wolffenbutteli Est Pars III.* Leipzig: I. C. Meisner, 1746.

Burmann, C. *Trajectum Eruditum.* Utrecht: Jurianus of Paddenburg, 1738.

Calov, A. *Metaphysica Divina Pars Generalis.* Rostock, 1640.

———. *Socinismus Profligatus, Hoc Est, Errorum Socinianorum Luculenta Confutatio.* Wittenberg: Michael Wendt, 1652.

———. *Scripta Anti-Sociniana in Unum Corpus Redacta.* 3 vols. Ulm: G. W. Kühnen, 1677–1684.

———. *Revelatum Sacro-Sanctae Trinitatis Mysterium Methodo Demonstrativa Propositum.* Jena: I. A. Melchior, 1735.

Carpzov, J. B. *Disputationes Academicae, Philologicae, Polemicae, Diversis Temporibus Habitae.* Leipzig, 1699.

Comenius, J. A. *De Christianorum Uno Deo, Patre, Filio, Spiritu Sancto. Fides Antiqua, contra Novatores.* Amsterdam: J. Janssonius, 1659.

Conway, A. *Principia Philosophiae Antiquissimae et Recentissimae de Deo, Christo et Creatura; Id Est, de Spiritu et Materia in Genere.* Amsterdam, 1690.

————. *The Conway Letters: The Correspondence of Anne, Viscountess Conway, Henry More, and Their Friends, 1642–1684.* Edited by Majorie Hope Nicolson. Rev. ed. with an introduction and new material ed. by Sarah Hutton. Oxford: Clarendon Press, 1992.

Crell, J. *De Uno Deo Patre Libri Duo.* Rakow: S. Sternacius, 1631.

Cudworth, R. *The True Intellectual System of the Universe.* London: Richard Royston, 1678.

Descartes, R. *Meditationes de Prima Philosophia.* 1641. Vol. 7 of *Oeuvres de Descartes.* Edited by C. Adam and P. Tannery. Paris: Vrin, 1964.

————. *Principia Philosophiae.* 1644. Vol. 8 in *Oeuvres de Descartes.* Edited by C. Adam and P. Tannery. Paris: Vrin, 1964.

Edwards, J. *Some Thoughts concerning the several causes and occasions of Atheism.* London: J. Robinson and J. Wyat, 1695.

————. *Socinianism Unmask'd.* London: J. Robinson, 1696.

Fabri, H. *Summula Theologica.* Lyon: L. Anisson, 1669.

Faydit, P. *Alteration du dogme théologique par la philosophie d'Aristote: ou fausses idées des scholastiques sur toutes les matières de la religion.* Vol. 1. *Traité de la Trinité.* N.p., 1696.

Fontenelle, B. Le Bovier de. "Éloge de M. Leibnitz." In *Histoire de l'Académie des sciences. Année 1716.* Paris: Impr. Royale, 1718, 94–128.

Feller, J. F. *Otium Hanoveranum sive Miscellanea ex Ore et Schedis Illustris Viri Piae Memoriae, Godofr. Guilielmi Leibnitii.* Leipzig: J. C. Martinus, 1718.

Freher, P. *Theatrum Virorum Eruditione Clarorum.* Nuremberg: J. Hofmann, 1688.

Freke, W. *A Vindication of the Unitarian, Against a Late Reverend Author On the Trinity.* London, 1690.

————. *The Arrian's Vindication of Himself, against Dr. Wallis's Fourth Letter on the Trinity.* N.p., 1691.

————. *A Dialogue By Way of Question and Answer, Concerning the Deity. All the Responses being taken verbatim out of the Scriptures. A Brief, but Clear Confutation of the Doctrine of the Trinity.* London, 1693.

Fullwood, F. *A Parallel: Wherein it appears, that the Socinian Agrees with the Papist, If not exceeds him in Idolatry, Antiscripturism and Fanaticism.* London: A. and J. Churchill, 1693.

————. *The Socinian Controversie touching The Son of God.* London: A. and J. Churchill, 1693.

Grawer, A. *Libellus de Unica Veritate.* Weimar: Typis Weidnerianis, 1618.

Hedworth, H. *Controversy Ended.* London: Francis Smith, 1673.

Hobbes, T. *Elementorum Philosophiae Sectio Prima de Corpore.* 1655. Vol. 1 of T. Hobbes, *Opera Philosophica Quae Latina Scripsit Omnia in Unum Corpus Nunc Primum Collecta.* Edited by W. Molesworth. Aalen: Scientia, 1961 (reprint of the edition of 1839–1845).

Hofmann, D. *Propositiones de Deo, et Christi Tum Persona Tum Officio.* Helmstedt: I. Lucius, 1598.

————. *Pro Duplici Veritate Lutheri, a Philosophis Impugnata, et ad Pudendorum Locum Ablegata. Disputatio.* Magdeburg: Andreas Dunckerus, 1600.

————. *Aurea et Vere Theologica Commentatio super Quaestione Num Syllogismus Rationis Locum Habeat in Regno Fidei.* Magdeburg: Andreas Dunckerus, 1600.

————. *Declaratio.* In Grawer, *Libellus de Unica Veritate.*

Hooker, R. *Of the Lawes of Ecclesiasticall Politie.* 1593–1662. Vols. 1–3 of *Folger Library Edition of The Works of Richard Hooker.* Cambridge, Mass.: Harvard University Press, 1977–1981.

————. *Of The Lawes of Ecclesiasticall Politie. The fift Booke.* London: John Windet, 1597.

Howe, J. *A Calm and Sober Enquiry Concerning The Possibility of a Trinity in the Godhead.* London: Tho. Parkhurst, 1694.

Huet, P. D. *Demonstratio Evangelica ad Serenissimum Delphinum.* Paris, 1679.

Jaucourt, L. de [L. de Neufville, pseud.]. *Vie de Mr. de Leibnitz.* In G. W. Leibniz, *Essais de Théodicée sur la Bonté de Dieu, la Liberté de l'Homme et l'Origine du Mal.* Vol. 1, 1–120. Amsterdam: François Changnion, 1734.

Jöcher, C. G. *Allgemeines Gelehrten-Lexicon.* Leipzig: J. F. Gleditsch, 1750–1751.

Keckermann, B. *Systema SS. Theologiae Tribus Libris Adornatum.* Hanau: Guilielmus Antonius, 1602.

Kesler, A. *Logicae Photinianae Examen.* Wittenberg: Typis and Sumptibus Christiani Tham, 1624.

————. *Physicae Photinianae Examen.* Erfurt: Sumptibus J. Birckneri, 1631.

————. *Metaphysicae Photinianae Partis Generalis [et Specialis] Examen.* 4th ed. Wittenberg: A. Hartmann, 1666.

Knorr von Rosenroth, C. *Kabbala Denudata, seu Doctrina Hebraeorum Transcendentalis et Metaphysica atque Theologica.* Sulzbach: Abraham Lichtenthaler, 1677.

————. *Kabbalae Denudatae Tomus Secundus: Id Est Liber Sohar Restitutus Cui Adjecta Adumbratio Cabbalae Christianae ad Captum Judaeorum.* Frankfurt: David Zunner, 1684.

König, J. F. *Theologia Positiva Acroamatica.* Greifswald: J. Wildius, 1669.

Labadie, J. de. *Extrait de quelques propositions erronées et scandaleuses couchées dans le livre du Sr. Louys Wolzogen . . . intitulé, "l'Interprête des Ecritures."* N.p., n.d.

————. *Quatorze remarques importantes, sur le jugement prononcé . . . contre le Sr. de Labadie,* N.p., n.d.

La Croze, M. V. De. *Dissertations historiques sur divers sujets.* Rotterdam: Reinier Leers, 1707.

————. *Vindiciae Veterum Scriptorum.* Rotterdam: Reinier Leers, 1708.

————. "Réponse à un Ecrit qui a pour titre: Sentiments d'un Docteur de Sorbonne sur un libelle intitulé, Dissertations Historiques sur divers sujets." *Bibliothèque choisie, pour servir de suite à la Bibliothèque universelle* 15 (1708): 166–183.

[Le Clerc, J.] *Liberii de Sancto Amore Epistolae Theologicae, in Quibus Varii Scholasticorum Errores Castigantur.* Irenopoli [Saumur]: Typis Philalethianis [i.e., Isaac Desbordes], 1679.

Le Clerc, J. "*Remarques sur la Réponse pour Mr. Bayle au suject du III. et X. Article de la Bibliothèque Choisie [9 (1706)].*" *Bibliothèque choisie, pour servir de suite à la Bibliothèque universelle* 10 (1706): 364–426.

————. *Epistolario.* 4 vols. Edited by Maria Grazia and Mario Sina. Florence: Olschki, 1987–1997.

Le Long, J. *Bibliotheca Sacra in Binos Syllabos Distincta.* Paris: F. Montalant, 1723.

Lessing, G. E., ed. *Des Andreas Wissowatius Einwürfe wider die Dreieinigkeit.* In G. E. Lessing, *Zur Geschichte und Litteratur. Aus den Schätzen der Herzogl. Bibliothek zu Wolfenbüttel.* 2nd contribution, XII, 371–418. Braunschweig: Waysenhaus-Buchh., 1773.

Letter to the Reverend Doctor South. Upon Occasion of a late Book Entituled, Animadversions upon Dr. Sherlock's Book, In Vindication of the Trinity. London: John Newton, 1693.

Leyser, P. *Apparatus Literarius Singularia Nova Anecdota Rariora ex Omnis Generis Eruditione Depromens Studio Societatis Colligentium.* 1st collection. Wittenberg: Samuel Hannaver, 1717.

————. *Amoenitatum Literarium Reliquiae.* Leipzig, 1729.

Lipenius, M. *Bibliotheca Realis Philosophica Omnium Materiarum, Rerum, et Titolorum, in Universo Totius Philosophiae Ambitu Occurrentium.* Frankfurt a. M.: J. Fridericus, 1682.

————. *Bibliotheca Realis Universalis Omnium Materiarum, Rerum et Titolorum, in Theologia, Jurisprudentia, Medicina et Philosophia Occurrentium.* Frankfurt a. M.: J. Fridericus, 1685.

Locke, J. *An Essay concerning Humane Understanding: in Four Books.* London: Th. Basset, 1690 (see also the critical edition of the *Essay* by P. H. Nidditch in *The Clarendon Edition of the Works of John Locke.* Oxford: Clarendon Press, 1975).

————. *The Reasonableness of Christianity, as delivered in the Scriptures.* London: A. and J. Churchill, 1695.

————. *A Vindication of the "Reasonableness of Christianity etc." From Mr. Edwards's Reflections.* London: A. and J. Churchill, 1695.

————. *A Second Vindication of the "Reasonableness of Christianity" By the Author of the "Reasonableness of Christianity."* London: A. and J. Churchill, 1697.

————. *A Letter to the Right Reverend Edward Lord Bishop of Worcester, concerning some Passages relating to Mr. Locke's "Essay of Humane Understanding": in a late Discourse of his Lordship, in Vindication of the Trinity.* London: A. and J. Churchill, 1697.

————. *Reply to the Right Reverend the Lord Bishop of Worcester's Answer to his Letter.* London: A. and J. Churchill, 1697.

————. *Reply to the Right Reverend the Lord Bishop of Worcester's Answer to his Second Letter,* London: A. and J. Churchill, 1699.

————. *Essai philosophique concernant l'entendement humain.* Translated by P. Coste. Amsterdam: Schelte, 1700.

————. *The Correspondence.* Edited by E. S. de Beer. 8 vols. Oxford: Clarendon Press, 1976–1989.

————. *Scritti filosofici e religiosi.* Edited by M. Sina. Milan: Rusconi, 1979.

Löffler, F. S. *De Divinitate Christi ex Rom. IX, v. 5.* No. XXVIII in J. B. Carpzov, *Disputationes Academicae, Philologicae, Polemicae, Diversis Temporibus Habitae.* Leipzig, 1699.

Lull, R. *Disputatio Fidei et Intellectus.* Part II of R. Lulle, *Tractatus Parvus de Logica et de Disputatione Fidei et Intellectus Valde Utilis.* Barcelona, 1512.

Magni, V. *Iudicium de Acatholicorum et Catholicorum Regula Credendi.* Vienna: M. Cosmerovius, 1641.

Malebranche, N. *Conversations chrétiennes dans lesquelles on justifie la vérité de la religion et de la morale de Jésus-Christ.* Mons: G. Migeot, 1677 (revised edition, Brussels: J. Fricx, 1677).

Meisner, B. *Philosophia Sobria.* Wittenberg, 1614.

Meyer, L. *Philosophia S. Scripturae Interpres; Exercitatio Paradoxa, in Qua, Veram Philosophiam Infallibilem S. Literas Interpretandi Normam Esse, Apodictice Demonstratur, et Discrepantes ad Hac Sententiae Expenduntur, ac Refelluntur.* Amsterdam, 1666.

Milbourne, L. *Mysteries in Religion Vindicated.* London: Walter Kettilby, 1692.

Nye, S. *A Brief History of the Unitarians, Called also Socinians.* London, 1687.

———. *Doctor Wallis's Letter Touching the Doctrine of the Blessed Trinity.* N.p., 1690.

———. *Some Thoughts upon Dr. Sherlock's Vindication of the Doctrine of the Holy Trinity.* London, 1690 (second, enlarged edition, 1691).

———. *Answer to Dr. Wallis's Three Letters Concerning the Doctrine of the Trinity.* London, 1691.

———. *Observations on the Four Letters of Dr. John Wallis, Concerning the Trinity and the Creed of Athanasius.* London, 1691.

———. *An Accurate Examination of the Principal Texts Usually alledged for The Divinity of our Saviour.* London, 1692.

———. *Considerations on the Explications of the Doctrine of the Trinity, By Dr. Wallis, Dr. Sherlock, Dr. S—th, Dr. Cudworth, and Mr. Hooker; as also on the Account given by those that say, the Trinity is an Unconceivable and Inexplicable Mystery.* London, 1693.

———. *Considerations on the Explications of the Doctrine of the Trinity. Occasioned by four Sermons.* London, 1694.

Observations on the Learned Vindication of the Trinity and Incarnation, by Dr. William Sherlock. In *The Acts of Great Athanasius,* London, 1690.

Paquot, J. N. *Memoires pour servir à l'histoire litteraires des dix-sept provinces des Pays-Bas, de la Principauté de Liège, et de quelques contrées voisines.* Vol. 1. Louvain: Impr. Académique, 1765.

Petau, D. *Theologicorum Dogmatum Tomus Ius [–IVtus].* Paris: S. Cramoisy, 1644–1650.

Quenstedt, J. A. *Theologia Didactico-Polemica.* Leipzig: T. Fritsch, 1715 (1st ed., 1685).

Raey, J. De. *Clavis Philosophiae Naturalis, seu Introductio ad Naturae Contemplationem Aristotelico-Cartesiana.* Leiden: J. and D. Elsevier, 1654.

Raue, J. *Subita et Necessaria Defensio adversus Sex Primas Lectiones V. Cl. Joh. Scharfii . . . Idque Conatus Est, ut Novissimam Logicam pro Salute Juventutis Accrescentem, in Herbis, Quod Ajunt, Extingueret.* Rostock, 1636.

———. *Invitatio ad Sacrae Eloquentiae Studium.* Rostock, 1636.

————. *Tractatus de Propositionibus Modalibus contra Scharfium.* Rostock, 1636.

————. *Obtestatio Publica ad D. Georgium Kruquium de Rationibus, Quas Habeat adversus Logicam Novissimam.* Rostock, 1637.

————. *Prior Fundamentalis Controversia pro Logica Novissima. Addita Sunt et Labyrinthus Logicorum circa Hanc Praecipue Materiam, et Filum Ariadnaeum.* Rostock, 1638.

Sand, C. *Bibliotheca Anti-Trinitariorum.* Freistadt: J. Aconius, 1684.

Scharfius, J. *Manuale Logicum,* Wittenberg, 1652.

Scherzer, J. A. *Collegium Anti-Socinianum.* Leipzig: F. Lanckisius, 1672.

"Sentiments d'un Docteur de Sorbonne, sur un Libelle intitulé, Dissertations Historiques sur Divers Sujets." *Bibliothèque choisie, pour servir de suite à la Bibliothèque universelle* 14 (1708): 332–347.

Servetus, M. *De Trinitatis Erroribus Libri Septem.* Hagenau: Iohann Setzer, 1531.

Sherlock, W. *A Vindication of the Doctrine of the Holy and Ever Blessed Trinity, and the Incarnation of The Son of God.* London: W. Rogers, 1690.

————. *The Case of the Allegiance due to Sovereign Powers.* London: W. Rogers, 1691.

————. *An Apology for Writing against Socinians, in Defence of the Doctrines of the Holy Trinity and Incarnation.* London: Will. Rogers, 1693.

————. *A Defence of Dr. Sherlock's Notion of a Trinity in Unity.* London: W. Rogers, 1694.

————. *A Modest Examination of the Authority and Reasons Of the Late Decree of the Vice-Chancellor of Oxford, and Some Heads of Colleges and Halls.* London: W. Rogers, 1696.

Slevogt, P. *Pervigilium de Dissidio Theologi et Philosophi in Utriusque Principiis Fundato.* Jena: Gansanius, 1623.

Socinus, F., et al. *Bibliotheca Fratrum Polonorum Quos Unitarios Vocant.* 8 vols. Amsterdam, after 1656 (the ninth and last volume, collecting the works of S. Przypkowski, was added in 1692: *Cogitationes Sacrae ad Initium Evangelii Matthaei et Omnes Epistolas Apostolicas.* Amsterdam, 1692).

South, R. *Animadversions upon Dr. Sherlock's Book, entituled A Vindication of the Holy and Ever-Blessed Trinity.* 2nd ed. London: Randal Taylor, 1693 (first ed. Oxford: Worcester College, 1693).

————. *Tritheism Charged upon Dr Sherlock's New Notion of the Trinity.* London: John Whitlock, 1695.

Spinoza, B. *Tractatus Theologico-Politicus.* 1970. In C. Gebhardt, ed., *Spinoza Opera.* Vol. 3. Heidelberg: Carl Winters Universitätsbuchhandlung, 1924.

Spizelius, T. *De Atheismo Eradicando ad Virum Praeclarissimum Dn. Antonium Reiserum Augustanum etc. Epistola.* Augsburg: G. Goebelius, 1669.

Stegmann, C. *Metaphysica Repurgata.* Lögnitzii, 1635 (manuscript copy with several corrections in Leibniz's hand: Niedersächsische Landesbibliothek, LH IV I, 9, Bl. 1–56).

Stegmann, J. *De Judice et Norma Controversiarum Fidei Libri II.* Amsterdam: Godfridus Philadelphus, 1644. Critical edition by J. Domański and Z. Ogonowski. Warsaw: Państwowe Wydawnictwo Naukowe, 1963.

Stephens, W. *An Account of the Growth of deism in England*. London: For the Author, 1696.

Stillingfleet, E. *A Discourse in Vindication of the Doctrine of the Trinity*. London: Henry Mortlock, 1697.

——. *The Bishop of Worcester's Answer to Mr. Locke's Letter*. London: Henry Mortlock, 1697.

——. *The Bishop of Worcester's Answer to Mr. Locke's Second Letter*. London: Henry Mortlock, 1698.

Suarez, F. *Metaphysicarum Disputationum . . . Tomi Duo*. Salamanca, 1597.

Temmik, A. *Philosophia Vera Theologiae et Medicinae Ministra*. Cologne [actually Würzburg]: W. Michahelles and J. Adolph, 1706.

Thummius, T. *Tapeinōsigraphia Sacra, Hoc Est, Repetitio Sanae et Orthodoxae Doctrinae de Humiliatione Christi Theanthrōpou*. Tübingen: Theodoricus Werlin, 1623.

Toland, J. *Christianity not Mysterious: Or, a Treatise shewing, That there is Nothing in the Gospel Contrary to Reason, Nor Above it: And that no Christian Doctrine can be properly call'd a Mystery*. London, 1696.

Tournemine, R. J. "Conjectures sur l'union de l'âme et du corps." *Memoires pour l'Histoires des Sciences et des beaux Arts* 7 (1704): 231–237.

Twisse, W. *Dissertatio de Scientia Media*. Arnheim: Jacobus à Biesium, 1639.

Valla, L. *De Elegantia Linguae Latinae Libri Sex*. Rome: J. P. de Lignamine, 1471.

van Helmont, F. M. *Seder Olam sive Ordo Seculorum, Historica Enarratio Doctrinae*. N.p., 1693.

van Walenburch, A. and P. *Tractatus Generales de Controversiis Fidei*. Cologne: I. W. Friess Jr., 1670.

——. *Tractatus Speciales, de Controversiis Fidei*. Cologne: I. W. Friess Jr., 1670.

van Wolzogen, L. *De Scripturarum Interprete adversus Exercitatorem Paradoxum Libri Duo*. Utrecht: J. Ribbius, 1668.

van Wolzogen, L., ed. *Jugemens de plusieurs professeurs et docteurs en théologie . . . qui prononcent unanimement orthodoxe le livre de Louys de Wolzogue, "De L'Interprète de l'Ecriture."* Utrecht: J. Ribbius, 1669.

Vorstius, C. *De Deo, seu Disp. X de Natura et Attributis Dei*. Burgsteinfurt, 1610.

Wachter, J. G. *Elucidarius Cabalisticus sive Reconditae Hebraeorum Philosophiae Brevis et Succincta Recensio*. Rome, 1706.

Wallis, J. *The Doctrine of the Blessed Trinity Briefly Explained, In a Letter to a Friend*. London: Tho. Parkhurst, 1690.

——. *A Second Letter Concerning the Holy Trinity*. London: Tho. Parkhurst, 1691.

——. *An Explication and Vindication of the Athanasian Creed. In a Third Letter*. London: Tho. Parkhurst, 1691.

——. *A Fourth Letter, Concerning the Sacred Trinity*. London: Tho. Parkhurst, 1691.

——. *Fifth Letter, Concerning the Sacred Trinity*. London: Tho. Parkhurst, 1691.

——. *Sixth Letter, Concerning the Sacred Trinity*. London: Tho. Parkhurst, 1691.

——. *A Seventh Letter, Concerning the Sacred Trinity*. London: Tho. Parkhurst, 1691.

——. *An Eighth Letter Concerning the Sacred Trinity*. London: Tho. Parkhurst, 1692.

——. *Three Sermons Concerning the Sacred Trinity*. London: Tho. Parkhurst, 1691.

———. *Theological Discourses; containing VIII Letters and III Sermons Concerning the Blessed Trinity.* London: Tho. Parkhurst, 1692.

———. *An Answer to Dr. Sherlock's Examination of the Oxford decree.* London: M. Whitlock, 1696.

Weigel, E. *Universi Corporis Pansophici Caput Summum . . . Exhibens Reale Non Imaginarium Artis Magnae Sciendi Specimen Trinuno-Combinatorium.* Jena: Bauhöfer, 1673.

White [Albius, Anglus], T. *Villicationis Suae de Medio Animarum Statu Ratio Episcopo Chalcedonensi Reddita.* Paris, 1653.

Willis, R. *Reflexions upon a Pamphlet, intituled, An Account of the Growth of Deism in England.* London: John Newton, 1696.

Wissowatius, A. *Wissowatius ad Baronem Boineburgium.* Mannheim, 1665 (in A VI, 1, N. 16/2).

———. *Religio Rationalis seu De Rationis Judicio, in Controversiis Etiam Theologicis, ac Religiosis, Adhibendo, Tractatus.* Amsterdam, 1685. German translation: A. Wissowatius [A. Sophianus, pseud.], *Die Vernünfftige Religion / Das ist Gründlicher Beweiß / daß man das Urtheil gesunder Vernunfft auch in der Theologie, und in Erörterung der Religions-Fragen gebrauchen müsse.* Amsterdam [actually Halle], 1703. Both the original Latin text and the German translation are published in A. Wissowatius, *Religio Rationalis. Editio Trilinguis.* Braunschweig: Waisenhaus-Buchdruckerei und Verlag, 1982.

Wissowatius, B. *Anonymi Epistola Exhibens Vitae ac Mortis Andreae Wissowatii.* In Sand, *Bibliotheca Anti-Trinitariorum.*

Wolff, C. "Elogium Godofredi Guilielmi Leibnitii." *Acta Eruditorum* (July 1717): 322–336.

Zedler, J. H. *Grosses Vollständiges Universal-Lexicon aller Wissenschafften und Künste.* Leipzig and Halle: J. H. Zedler, 1732–1750.

Zwicker, D. *Irenicum Irenicorum, Seu Reconciliatoris Christianorum Hodiernorum Norma Triplex, Sana Omnium Hominum Ratio, Scriptura Sacra, et Traditiones.* N.p., 1658.

———. *Compelle Intrare Seu Tractatus Tractatuum de Contradictione. Qua Fere Sola, Probe Cognita, Pleraeque Hodiernae Ecclesiae, Misere (Proh Dolor!) Collapsae, Nominatim Vero Romana, Graeca, Lutherana, et Calviniana, si Velint, Instaurari, et ad Pacem Mutuo Colendam Adduci Facillimo Negocio Possunt.* N.p., 1666.

Nineteenth to Twenty-first Centuries

Aarsleff, H. "Bisterfeld." In *Dictionary of Scientific Biography.* New York: Charles Scribner's Sons, 1970.

Adams, R. M. *Leibniz: Determinist, Theist, Idealist.* New York and Oxford: Oxford University Press, 1994.

———. "Leibniz's Examination of the Christian Religion." *Faith and Philosophy* 11, no. 4 (1994): 517–546.

Aiton, E. J. *Leibniz: A Biography.* Bristol and Boston: Hilger, 1985.

Angelelli, I. "On Identity and Interchangeability in Leibniz and Frege." *Notre Dame Journal of Formal Logic* 8 (1967): 94–100.

———. "The Techniques of Disputation in the History of Logic." *Journal of Philosophy* 67 (1970): 800–815.

———. "On Johannes Raue's Logic." In *Leibniz' Auseinandersetzung mit Vorgängern und Zeitgenossen*, edited by I. Marchlewitz and A. Heinekamp, 184–190. Stuttgart: Steiner, 1990.

Antognazza, M. R. "Inediti leibniziani sulle polemiche trinitarie." *Rivista di filosofia neo-scolastica* 83, no. 4 (1991): 525–550.

———. "Die Polemik des jungen Leibniz gegen die Sozinianer." In *Leibniz und Europa: VI Internationaler Leibniz-Kongress*. Vol. 1, 17–24. Hanover: G. W. Leibniz-Gesellschaft, 1994.

———. "Die Rolle der Trinitäts-und Menschwerdungsdiskussionen für die Entstehung von Leibniz' Denken." *Studia Leibnitiana* 26, no. 1 (1994): 56–75.

———. "Leibniz e il concetto di persona nelle polemiche trinitarie inglesi." In *L'idea di persona*, edited by V. Melchiorre, 207–237. Milan: Vita e Pensiero, 1996.

———. "Hofmann-Streit: Il dibattito sul rapporto tra filosofia e teologia all'Università di Helmstedt." *Rivista di filosofia neo-scolastica* 88, no. 3 (1996): 390–420.

———. "Immeatio and Emperichoresis: The Theological Roots of Harmony in Bisterfeld and Leibniz." In *The Young Leibniz and His Philosophy. 1646–1676*, edited by S. Brown, 41–64. Dordrecht: Kluwer, 1999.

———. "The Defence of the Mysteries of the Trinity and the Incarnation: An Example of Leibniz's 'Other' Reason." *British Journal for the History of Philosophy* 9, no. 2 (2001): 283–309.

———. "Debilissimae Entitates? Bisterfeld and Leibniz's Ontology of Relations." *Leibniz Review* 11 (2001): 1–22.

———. "Leibniz and the Post-Copernican Universe: Koyré Revisited." *Studies in History and Philosophy of Science* 34 (2003): 309–327.

———. "Bisterfeld and Immeatio: Origins of a Key Concept in the Early Modern Doctrine of Universal Harmony." In *Spätrenaissance-Philosophie in Deutschland. 1570–1650*, edited by M. Mulsow. Tübingen: Niemeyer, forthcoming.

Antognazza, M. R., and H. Hotson. *Alsted and Leibniz on God, the Magistrate and the Millennium*. Wolfenbütteler Arbeiten zur Barockforschung, vol. 34. Wiesbaden: Harrassowitz, 1999.

Baruzi, J. "Trois Dialogues Mystiques Inédits de Leibniz." *Revue de Metaphysique et de Morale* 13 (1905): 1–38.

———. *Leibniz et l'organisation religieuse de la Terre d'après des documents inédits.* Paris: Alcan, 1907.

———. *Leibniz: Avec de nombreux textes inédits.* Paris: Bloud, 1909.

Baur, F. C. *Die christliche Lehre von der Dreieinigkeit und Menschwerdung Gottes in ihrer geschichtlichen Entwicklung.* Vol. 3. Tübingen: Osiander, 1841–1843.

Beeley, P. *Kontinuität und Mechanismus: Zur Philosophie des jungen Leibniz in ihrem ideengeschichtlichen Kontext.* Stuttgard: Steiner, 1996.

Belaval, Y. "L'harmonie." In Y. Belaval, *Études leibniziennes: De Leibniz à Hegel.* Paris: Gallimard, 1976.

Bianchi, D. "Some Sources for a History of English Socinianism: A Bibliography of 17th Century English Writings." *Topoi: An International Review of Philosophy* 4 (1985): 91–120.

Bianchi, M. L. *Signatura rerum: Segni, magia e conoscenza da Paracelso a Leibniz.* Rome: Edizioni dell'Ateneo, 1987.

Bietenholz, P. G. *Daniel Zwicker, 1612–1678: Peace, Tolerance, and God the One and Only.* Florence: Olschki, 1997.

Boeckh, A. "Leibnitz in seinem Verhältniß zur positiven Theologie." *Historisches Taschenbuch*, n.s., 5 (1844): 481–514.

Bordoli, R. *Ragione e scrittura tra Descartes e Spinoza: Saggio sulla 'Philosophia S. Scripturae interpres' di Lodewijk Meyer e sulla sua recezione.* Milan: F. Angeli, 1997.

Brown, S. "Leibniz and More's Cabbalistic Circle." In *Henry More (1614–1687): Tercentenary Studies*, edited by S. Hutton, 77–95. Dordrecht: Kluwer, 1990.

———. "The Leibniz-Toland Debates on Materialism and the Soul at the Court of the Queen of Prussia." In *Nihil sine Ratione: Mensch, Natur und Technik im Wirken von G. W. Leibniz, VII. Internationaler Leibniz-Kongress.* Vol. 1, 147–154. Berlin: G. W. Leibniz-Gesellschaft, 2001.

Burchill, C. J. *The Heidelberg Antitrinitarians: Johann Sylvan, Adam Neuser, Matthias Vehe, Jacob Suter, Johann Hasler.* Baden-Baden-Bouxwiller: Valentin Koerner, 1989.

Burgelin, P. "Théologie naturelle et théologie révélée chez Leibniz." In *Akten des [I.] Internationalen Leibniz-Kongresses Hannover, 14.–19. November 1966.* Vol. 4, 1–20. Wiesbaden: Steiner, 1969.

Burkhardt, H. *Logik und Semiotik in der Philosophie von Leibniz.* Munich: Philosophia Verlag, 1980.

Buzon, F. de. "L'harmonie: Métaphysique et phénoménalité." *Revue de Métaphysique et de Morale* 100 (1995): 95–120.

Caccamo, D. "Ricerche sul socinianesimo in Europa." *Bibliothèque d'Humanisme et Renaissance* 26 (1964): 573–607.

Cassirer, E. *Leibniz' System in seinen wissenschaftlichen Grundlagen.* Marburg an der Lahn: Elwert, 1902.

Cave, E. "A Leibnizian Account of Why Belief in the Christian Mysteries Is Justified." *Religious Studies* 31, no. 4 (1995): 463–473.

Chmaj, L. *Andrzej Wiszowaty jako działacz i myśliciel relijny.* Krakow: Krakowska Spółka Wydawnicza, 1922.

Colligan, J. H. *The Arian Movement in England.* Manchester: At the University Press, 1913.

Cook, D. J. "Leibniz's Use and Abuse of Judaism and Islam." In *Leibniz and Adam*, edited by M. Dascal and E. Yakira, 283–297. Tel Aviv: University Publishing Projects, 1993.

Coudert, A. P. "A Cambridge Platonist's Kabbalist Nightmare." *Journal of the History of Ideas* 36 (1975): 633–652.

———. *Leibniz and the Kabbalah.* Dordrecht: Kluwer, 1995.

———. "Leibniz, Knorr von Rosenroth, and the Kabbalah Denudata." In *Im Spiegel des Verstandes. Studien zu Leibniz*, edited by K. D. Dutz and S. Gensini, 9–28. Münster: Nodus Publikationen, 1996.

Couturat, L. *La logique de Leibniz d'après des documents inédits*. Paris: Alcan, 1901.

Dascal, M. "La Razon y los misterios de la fe segun Leibniz." *Revista Latino-americana de filosofia* 1, no. 3 (1975): 193–226. English translation: "Reason and the Mysteries of Faith: Leibniz on the Meaning of Religious Discourse." In M. Dascal, *Leibniz: Language, Signs and Thought*, 93–124. Amsterdam and Philadelphia: Benjamins, 1987.

———. "Strategies of Dispute and Ethics: Du tort and La place d'autruy." In *Leibniz und Europa: VI Internationaler Leibniz-Kongress*. Vol. 2, 108–115. Hanover: G. W. Leibniz-Gesellschaft, 1995.

———. "La balanza de la razón." In *La racionalidad: Su poder y sus límites*, edited by O. Nudler, 363–381. Buenos Aires: Paidós, 1996.

———. "Nihil sine Ratione: Blandior Ratio." *Nihil sine Ratione: Mensch, Natur und Technik im Wirken von G.W. Leibniz, VII Internationaler Leibniz-Kongress*. Vol. 1, 276–280. Hanover: G. W. Leibniz-Gesellschaft, 2001.

Dibon, P. *La Philosophie Néerlandaise au siècle d'Or*. Vol. 1: *L'enseignement philosophique dans les Universités à l'époque précartésienne (1575–1650)*. Paris: Elsevier, 1954.

———. *Regards sur la Hollande du siècle d'or*. Naples: Vivarium, 1990.

Dijksterhuis, E. J., et al. *Descartes et le cartésianisme hollandais*. Paris and Amsterdam: PUF–Editions Françaises d'Amsterdam, 1950.

Duproix, J. *Raison et foi d'après Leibnitz*. Lausanne: Bridel, 1901.

Duran, J. "Anne Viscountess Conway: A Seventeenth-Century Rationalist." *Hypatia* 4, no. 1 (1989): 64–79.

Edel, S. "Leibniz und die Kabbala-eine europäische Korrespondenz." In *Leibniz und Europa: VI. Internationaler Leibniz-Kongress*. Vol. 1, 211–219. Hanover: G. W. Leibniz-Gesellschaft, 1994.

Eisenkopf, P. *Leibniz und die Einigung der Christenheit: Überlegungen zur Reunion der evangelischen und katholischen Kirche*. Munich: Schöningh, 1975.

Fichant, M. "Leibniz et Toland: Philosophie pour princesses?" *Revue de synthèse*, 4th ser., 116 nos. 2–3 (1995): 421–439.

Firpo, M. "John Locke e il Socinianesimo." *Rivista storica italiana* 92, no. 1 (1980): 35–124.

Foucher de Careil, A., *Leibniz, la philosophie juive et la Cabale*. Paris: Auguste Durand, 1861.

———, ed. *Réfutation inédite de Spinoza par Leibniz*. Paris, 1854.

Fouke, D. C. "Metaphysics and the Eucharist in the Early Leibniz." *Studia Leibnitiana* 24, no. 2 (1992): 145–159.

Frémont, C. "La triple vérité." *Revue des Sciences philosophiques et théologiques* 76, no. 1 (1992): 43–55.

Friedmann, G. *Leibniz et Spinoza*. Revised and enlarged edition. Paris: Gallimard, 1962.

Garber, D. "Motion and Metaphysics in the Young Leibniz." In *Leibniz: Critical and Interpretative Essays*, edited by M. Hooker, 160–184. Manchester: Manchester University Press, 1982.

Gil, F. "Du droit à la Théodicée: Leibniz et la charge de la preuve dans les controverses." *Revue de synthèse*, 3d ser., 118–119 (1985): 157–173.

Goldenbaum, U. "Leibniz as a Lutheran." In *Leibniz, Mysticism and Religion*, edited by A. P. Coudert et al., 169–192. Dordrecht: Kluwer, 1998.

———. "Transubstantiation, Physics and Philosophy at the Time of the Catholic Demonstrations." In *The Young Leibniz and His Philosophy, 1646–1676*, edited by S. Brown, 79–102. Dordrecht: Kluwer, 1999.

———. "Die Commentatiuncula de judice als Leibnizens erste philosophische Auseinandersetzung mit Spinoza nebst der Mitteilung über ein neuaufgefundenes Leibnizstück." In *Labora Diligenter*, edited by M. Fontius et al., 61–107. Stuttgart: Steiner, 1999.

Greig, M. "The Reasonableness of Christianity? Gilbert Burnet and the Trinitarian Controversy of the 1690s." *Journal of Ecclesiastical History* 44, no. 4 (1993): 631–651.

Guhrauer, G. E. *Gottfried Wilhelm Freiherr von Leibnitz: Eine Biographie*. Breslau: Hirt, 1842.

Heinekamp, A. *Das Problem des Guten bei Leibniz*. Bonn: H. Bouvier, 1969.

———. "Das Glück als höchstes Gut in Leibniz' Philosophie." In *The Leibniz Renaissance: International Workshop (Florence 1986)*, 99–125. Florence: Olschki, 1989.

Heinemann, F. H. "Toland and Leibniz." *Philosophical Review* 54 (1945): 437–457.

Hoffman, H. *Die Leibniz'sche Religionsphilosophie in ihrer geschichtlichen Stellung*. Tübingen and Leipzig: J. C. B. Mohr (Paul Siebeck), 1903.

Holze, E. *Gott als Grund der Welt im Denken des Gottfried Wilhelm Leibniz*. Stuttgard: Steiner, 1991.

Hotson, H. "Alsted and Leibniz: A Preliminary Survey of a Neglected Relationship." In *Leibniz und Europa: VI Internationaler Leibniz-Kongress*. Vol. 1, 356–363. Hanover: G. W. Leibniz-Gesellschaft, 1994.

———. *Johann Heinrich Alsted, 1588–1638: Between Renaissance, Reformation, and Universal Reform*. Oxford: Clarendon Press, 2000.

Hutton, S. *Anne Conway: A Woman Philosopher*. Cambridge: Cambridge University Press, 2004.

Jacob, M. C. *The Newtonians and the English Revolution*. Ithaca: Cornell University Press, 1976.

Jalabert, J. *Le Dieu de Leibniz*. Paris: Presses Universitaires de France, 1960.

Jolley, N. "An Unpublished Leibniz MS on Metaphysics." *Studia Leibnitiana* 7, no. 2 (1975): 161–189.

———. "Leibniz on Locke and Socinianism." *Journal of the History of Ideas* 39, no. 2 (1978): 233–250.

———. *Leibniz and Locke: A Study of the New Essays on Human Understanding*. Oxford: Clarendon Press, 1984.

Jürgensmeier, F. *Johann Philipp von Schönborn (1605–1673) und die römische Kurie*. Mainz: Selbstverlag der Gesellschaft für mittelrheinische Kirchengeschichte, 1977.

Kabitz, W. *Die Philosophie des jungen Leibniz: Untersuchungen zur Entwicklungsgeschichte seines Systems*. Heidelberg: Carl Winter's Universitätsbuchhandlung, 1909.

Kinder, A. G. *Michael Servetus*. Baden-Baden-Bouxwiller: Editions Valentin Koerner, 1989.

Kolakowski, L. *Chrétiens sans Église: La conscience religeuse et le lien confessionnel au XVIIe siècle*. Translated from the Polish by Anna Posner. Paris: Gallimard, 1969.

Korcik, A. "La Defensio Trinitatis contra Wissowatium de Leibniz en rapport avec la polémique de Scharff avec Rauen." *Organon* 4 (1967): 181–186.

Kot, S. *Socinianism in Poland: The Social and Political Ideas of the Polish Antitrinitarians in the Sixteenth and Seventeenth Centuries.* Translated from the Polish by Earl Morse Wilbur. Beacon Hill Boston: Starr King Press, 1957.

Kvacsala, J. "Johann Heinrich Bisterfeld." *Ungarische Revue* 13 (1893): 40–59 and 171–197.

Lagrée, J., and P.-F. Moreau. "Louis Meyer et Spinoza." In L. Meyer, *La Philosophie Interprète de l'Ecriture Sainte,* translation from the Latin, annotations, and introduction by J. Lagrée and P.-F. Moreau. Paris: Intertextes Éditeur, 1988.

Lamarra, A. "Leibniz e la perichōrēsis." *Lexicon philosophicum: Quaderni di terminologia filosofica e storia delle idee* 1 (1985): 67–94.

Lamarra, A. "An Anonymous Criticism from Berlin to Leibniz's Philosophy: John Toland against Mathematical Abstractions." In *Leibniz in Berlin,* edited by H. Poser and A. Heinekamp, 89–102. Stuttgart: Steiner, 1990.

———. "Théologie, métaphysique, science générale: Une lettre inédite de Leibniz à A. L. Königsmann (1712)." *Studia Leibnitiana* 24, no. 2 (1992): 133–144.

Leinkauf, T. "'Diversitas identitate compensata' Ein Grundtheorem in Leibniz' Denken und seine Voraussetzungen in der frühen Neuzeit." Parts 1–2. *Studia Leibnitiana* 28 (1996): 58–83; 29 (1997): 81–102.

Leinsle, U. G. *Reformversuche protestantischer Metaphysik im Zeitalter des Rationalismus.* Augsburg: Maro, 1988.

Loemker, L. E. "Leibniz and the Herborn Encyclopedists." *Journal of the History of Ideas* 22 (1961): 323–338.

———. *Struggle for Synthesis: The Seventeenth-Century Background of Leibniz's Synthesis of Order and Freedom.* Cambridge, Mass.: Harvard University Press, 1972.

Look, B. *Leibniz and the "vinculum substantiale."* Stuttgart: Steiner, 1999.

McLachlan, H. J. *Socinianism in Seventeenth-Century England.* Oxford: Oxford University Press, 1951.

Mahnke, D. *Leibnizens Synthese von Universalmathematik und Individualmetaphysik.* Halle: Max Niemeyer, 1925.

Mansi, J. D., ed. *Sacrorum Conciliorum Nova et Amplissima Collectio.* 53 vols. Paris: H. Welter, 1901–1927.

Mathieu, V. *Leibniz e Des Bosses (1706–1716).* Turin: Giapichelli, 1960.

———. *Introduzione a Leibniz.* 2nd ed. Bari: Laterza, 1986.

Meinsma, K. O. *Spinoza et son cercle: Étude critique historique sur les hétérodoxes hollandais.* Paris: Vrin, 1983 (enlarged French edition of K. O. Meinsma, *Spinoza en zijn Kring.* The Hague, 1896).

Mercer, C. *Leibniz's Metaphysics: Its Origins and Development.* New York and Cambridge: Cambridge University Press, 2001.

Merchant, C. "The Vitalism of Anne Conway: Its Impact on Leibniz's Concept of the Monad." *Journal of the History of Philosophy* 17, no. 3 (1979): 255–269.

Migne, J. P., ed. *Patrologiae Cursus Completus: Series Graeca.* 161 vols. Paris: J. P. Migne and Garnier Fratres, 1857–1866.

Molitor, E. "Leibniz in Mainz." *Jahrb. für das Bistum Mainz* 5 (1950): 457–472.

Moll, K. *Der junge Leibniz.* 3 vols. Stuttgart and Bad Cannstatt: Fromman-Holzboog, 1978–1996.

———. "Die erste Monadenkonzeption des jungen Leibniz und ihre Verbindung zur mechanistischen Wahrnemungstheorie von Thomas Hobbes." In *Leibniz' Auseinandersetzung mit Vorgängern und Zeitgenossen,* edited by I. Marchlewitz and A. Heinekamp, 53–62. Stuttgart: Steiner, 1990.

Muff, M. *Leibnizens Kritik der Religionsphilosophie von John Toland.* Affoltern am Albis: J. Weiss, 1940 (Phil. diss., Zürich).

Mugnai, M. "Der Begriff der Harmonie als metaphysische Grundlage der Logik und Kombinatorik bei Johann Heinrich Bisterfeld und Leibniz." *Studia Leibnitiana* 5, no. 1 (1973): 43–73.

———. *Astrazione e realtà: Saggio su Leibniz.* Milan: Feltrinelli, 1976.

———. *Leibniz' Theory of Relations.* Stuttgart: Steiner, 1992.

———. *Introduzione alla filosofia di Leibniz.* Turin: Einaudi, 2001.

Müller, K., and G. Kröner. *Leben und Werk von G. W. Leibniz: Eine Chronik.* Frankfurt a. M.: Klostermann, 1969.

Muller, R. A. *Dictionary of Latin and Greek Theological Terms: Drawn Principally from Protestant Scholastic Theology.* Carlisle: Paternoster Press, 1985.

Namowicz, T. "Zur deutschen Übersetzung." In A. Wissowatius, *Religio Rationalis: Editio Trilinguis,* 113–120. Braunschweig: Waisenhaus-Buchdruckerei und Verlag, 1982.

Narbutt, O. "Sylogizmy Wiszowatego w świetle krityki Leibniza." *Ruch filozoficzny* 21, no. 4 (1962): 413–416.

Ogonowski, Z. "Wiara i rozum w doktrynach religijnych socynian i Locke'a." In *Studia nad arianizmem,* edited by L. Chmaj, 425–450. Warsaw: PWN, 1959.

———. "Le 'Christianisme sans Mystères' selon John Toland et les Sociniens." *Archiwum historii filozofii i myśli spolecznej* 12 (1966): 205–223.

———. "W sprawie korespondencji Leibniza z Samuelem Crellem." *Archiwum historii filozofii i myśli spolecznej* 27 (1981): 333–350.

———. "Andrzej Wiszowaty." In A. Wissowatius, *Religio Rationalis: Editio Trilinguis,* 9–23. Braunschweig: Waisenhaus-Buchdruckerei und Verlag, 1982.

———. "Leibniz und die Sozinianer." In *Theatrum Europaeum,* edited by R. Brinkmann et al., 385–408. Munich: Fink, 1982.

Olaso, E. de. "Leibniz y el arte de disputar." *Diálogos* 9 no. 24, (1973): 7–31. French version: "Leibniz et l'art de disputer." In *Akten des II. Internationalen Leibniz-Kongresses, Hannover, 17.–22. Juli 1972.* Vol. 4, 207–228. Wiesbaden: Steiner, 1975.

Orio de Miguel, B. "Adam Kadmon: Conway, Leibniz and the Lurianic Kabbalah." In *Leibniz and Adam,* edited by M. Dascal and E. Yakira, 267–282. Tel Aviv: University Publishing Projects, 1993.

Petersen, P. *Geschichte der aristotelischen Philosophie im protestantischen Deutschland.* Leipzig: Verlag Felix Meiner, 1921.

Pichler, A. *Die Theologie des Leibniz aus sämmtlichen gedruckten und vielen noch ungedruckten Quellen.* Munich: Cotta, 1869–1870.

Pintacuda de Michelis, F. *Socinianesimo e tolleranza nell'età del razionalismo.* Florence: La Nuova Italia, 1975.

Piro, F. "Leibniz e il progetto degli 'Elementa de mente et corpore.'" *Il Centauro: Rivista di filosofia e teoria politica* 11–12 (1984): 106–116.

Piro, F., *Varietas identitate compensata. Studio sulla formazione della metafisica di Leibniz.* Naples: Bibliopolis, 1990.

Piro, F., ed. "G. W. Leibniz. Harmonia e Conatus. Scritti e frammenti sullo spazio, il movimento, il pensiero e le passioni (1671)." *Il Centauro: Rivista di filosofia e teoria politica* 11–12 (1984): 204–220.

Ratschow, C. H. *Lutherische Dogmatik zwischen Reformation und Aufklärung.* Part II. Gütersloh: Gütersloher Verlagshaus Gerd Mohn, 1966.

Rhode, G. "Mainz und der europäische Osten." In *Miscellanea Moguntina*, 41–77. Wiesbaden: Steiner, 1964.

Riley, P. "'New' Political Writings of Leibniz." *Journal of the History of Ideas* 55, no. 1 (1994): 147–158.

Roncaglia, G. *Palaestra Rationis: Discussioni su natura della copula e modalità nella filosofia 'scolastica' tedesca del XVII secolo.* Florence: Olschki, 1996.

Rossi, P. *Clavis Universalis: Arti mnemoniche e logica combinatoria da Lullo a Leibniz.* Milan and Naples: Riccardo Ricciardi, 1960.

Rutherford, D. *Leibniz and the Rational Order of Nature.* New York and Cambridge: Cambridge University Press, 1995.

Schadel, E. "Epilog: Trinität und Philosophie." In *Bibliotheca Trinitariorum*, edited by E. Schadel. Munich: K. G. Saur, 1988.

———. "Zu Leibniz 'Defensio Trinitatis': Historische und systematische Perspektiven, insbesondere zur Theodizee-Problematik." In *Leibniz. Tradition und Aktualität: V. Internationaler Leibniz-Kongress. Vorträge*, 856–865. Hanover: G. W. Leibniz-Gesellschaft, 1988.

———. *Zu 'Defensio Trinitatis': Historische und systematische Perspektiven, insbesondere zur Theodizee-Problematik.* In *Actualitas Omnium Actuum*, edited by E. Schadel, 235–305. Frankfurt a. M.: Peter Lang, 1989.

———. "Monad as Triadic Structure: Leibniz's Contribution to Post-Nihilistic Search for Identity." In *G. W. Leibniz: Analogía y expresión*, edited by Q. Racionero and C. Roldán, 521–536. Madrid: Editorial Complutense, 1994.

Schmaus, M. *Katholische Dogmatik.* Munich: Verlag Max Hueber, 1938–1941.

Schneiders, W. "Harmonia Universalis." *Studia Leibnitiana* 16, no. 1 (1984): 27–44.

Scholem, G. "Adam Kadmon." In *Encyclopaedia Judaica.* Jerusalem: Keter, 1972.

———. "Kabbalah." In *Encyclopaedia Judaica.* Jerusalem: Keter, 1972.

Schrohe, H. *Johann Christian von Boineburg, Kurmainzer Oberhofmarschall.* Mainz: Falk, 1926.

Scribano, M. E. *Da Descartes a Spinoza: Percorsi di teologia razionale nel Seicento.* Milan: Angeli, 1988.

Secretan, P. "A propos du Dieu de Leibniz." *Freiburger Zeitschrift für Philosophie und Theologie* 27, nos. 1–2 (1980): 24–35.

Sina, M. *L'avvento della ragione: 'Reason' e 'Above Reason' dal razionalismo teologico inglese al deismo.* Milan: Vita e Pensiero, 1976.

Skelly, B. D. *Leibniz's Revelation-Inspired Metaphysics: An Exercise in Reconciling Faith and Reason.* Ann Arbor, Michigan: U.M.I., 1991 (Phil. diss., University of Massachussetts).

Sparn, W. "Das Bekenntnis des Philosophen: Gottfried Wilhelm Leibniz als Philosoph und Theologe." *Neue Zeitschrift für systematische Theologie und Religionsphilosophie* 28, no. 2 (1986): 139–178.

Stemmer, P. "Perichorese: Zur Geschichte eines Begriffs." *Archiv für Begriffsgeschichte* 27 (1983): 9–55.

Tarabocchia Canavero, A., ed. *L'infinita via. Ragione, natura e Trinità da Anselmo a Tommaso.* Bergamo: Pierluigi Lubrina Editore, 1990.

Thiel, U. "Cudworth and Seventeenth-Century Theories of Consciousness." In *The Uses of Antiquity*, edited by S. Gaukroger, 79–99. Dordrecht: Kluwer, 1991.

———. "Leibniz and the Concept of Apperception." *Archiv für Geschichte der Philosophie* 76 (1994): 195–209.

Tognon, G. "Leibniz et Toland: Une lettre inédite à propos de Lettres to Serena." In *Leibniz: Werk und Wirkung, IV. Internationaler Leibniz-Kongress*, 784–793. Hanover: G. W. Leibniz-Gesellschaft, 1983.

Totok, W., and C. Haase, eds. *Leibniz: Sein Leben—sein Wirken—seine Zeit.* Hanover: Verlag für Literatur und Zeitgeschehen, 1966.

Trapnell, W. H. *The Treatment of Christian Doctrine by Philosophers of the Natural Light from Descartes to Berkeley.* Oxford: The Voltaire Foundation at the Taylor Inst., 1988.

Tulloch, J. *Rational Theology and Christian Philosophy in England in the Seventeenth Century.* 2 vols. Edinburgh and London: William Blackwood and Sons, 1872.

Ultsch, E. *Johann Christian von Boineburg, ein Beitrag zur Geistesgeschichte des 17. Jahrhunderts.* Würzburg: C. J. Becker Universitätsdruckerei, 1936.

Utermöhlen, G. "Vereinigung der Konfessionen." In *Leibniz und Europa*, edited by A. Heinekamp and I. Hein, 95–114. Hanover: Schlütersche Verlag, 1993.

van der Linde, A. *Benedictus Spinoza Bibliographie.* The Hague: M. Nijhoff, 1871.

van der Tak, W. G. "De Ludovico Meyer." *Chronicon Spinozanum* 1 (1921): 91–100.

Varani, G. *Leibniz e la "Topica Aristotelica."* Milan: IPL, 1995.

Vercruysse, J. "Bibliotheca Fratrum Polonorum: Histoire et bibliographie." *Odrodzenie i Reformacja w Polsce* 21 (1975): 197–212.

Wallace, R. *Antitrinitarian Biography: Or Sketches of the Lives and Writings of Distinguished Antitrinitarians.* 3 vols. London: E. T. Whitfield, 1850.

Watson, J. *The Interpretation of Religious Experience.* Parts 1 and 2. Glasgow: Maclehouse, 1912.

Wiedeburg, P. *Der Junge Leibniz: Das Reich und Europa.* Wiesbaden: Steiner, 1962–1970.

Wiehart-Howaldt, A. *Essenz, Perfektion, Existenz. Zur Rationalität und dem systematischen Ort der Leibnizschen Theologia Naturalis.* Stuttgart: Steiner, 1996.

Wilbur, E. M. *A History of Unitarianism: Socinianism and Its Antecedents.* Cambridge, Mass.: Harvard University Press, 1946.

————. *A Bibliography of the Pioneers of the Socinian-Unitarian Movement in Modern Christianity in Italy, Switzerland, Germany, Holland.* Rome: Edizioni di Storia e Letteratura, 1950.

————. *A History of Unitarianism: In Transylvania, England, and America.* Cambridge, Mass.: Harvard University Press, 1952.

Wilson, C. *Leibniz's Metaphysics: A Historical and Comparative Study.* Princeton and Manchester: Princeton University Press and Manchester University Press, 1989.

————. "Nostalgia and Counterrevolution: The Case of Cudworth and Leibniz." In *Leibniz' Auseinandersetzung mit Vorgängern und Zeitgenossen,* edited by I. Marchlewitz and A. Heinekamp, 138–146. Stuttgart: Steiner, 1990.

Woolhouse, R. S. "John Toland and 'Remarques critiques sur le système de Monsr. Leibnitz de l'harmonie préetablie.'" *Leibniz Society Review* 8 (1998): 80–87.

Wundt, M. *Die deutsche Schulmetaphysik des 17. Jahrhunderts.* Tübingen: J. C. B. Mohr (Paul Siebeck), 1939.

Zingari, G. "Leibniz, San Tommaso e la scolastica." *Aquinas* 36, no. 2 (1993): 265–298.

Index

Abelard, Peter, 232n72

absolute substance, xxiii, 73, 79, 103, 106–109, 115–116, 154, 159, 201n117, 208n75, 215n41, 237n118, 239n146, 241n152, 244n33, 246n48, 246n56

accident, definition of, 193n155, 196n44

action, principle of, 32. *See also* motion

Adam, 84

Adam Kadmon, 140–43

adumbratio. See shadowing

Adumbratio Kabbalae Christianae (Van Helmont), 142

Alsted, Johann Heinrich, 35, 177n50, 214n39

Anabaptists, 76

analogia entis, 69–70

analogia Trinitatis: binary calculus and, 283n42; in Bisterfeld's thought, 10–11; classic doctrine of, xx; mind

and Trinity, 8, 29–30, 41–47, 80–83, 108–9, 159, 192n123, 221n26; monads and, 110, 167–68; universal harmony and, xx-xxiii

analogy, reasoning by, xviii

Andreas Wissowatius Einwürfe wider die Dreieinigkeit, Des (Lessing), 21

Angelelli, Ignacio, 17

Animadversiones in Philosophiam (Ostorodt), 156

Animadversions upon Dr. Sherlock's Book (South), 96–98

Annotatiunculae Subitaneae ad Tolandi Librum (Leibniz), xxv, 126–29, 131–32, 252n57

Anselm, Saint, 13, 181n99

anthropolatry, 88

Antitrinitarianism, xvii, 19, 54, 76, 137–38, 144, 264n65, 264n66. *See also* English Trinitarian polemics; Socinianism

Aphthartodocetes, 14, 182n109